FILMS IN AMERICA 1929–1969

FILMS IN AMERICA 1929-1969

MARTIN QUIGLEY, JR.
RICHARD GERTNER

GOLDEN PRESS NEW YORK

"The only conspicuous trouble with the motion picture industry is the human race. It is from this race that the movies have to draw both their personnel and their patronage."

Terry Ramsaye

ACKNOWLEDGMENTS

The authors and publishers wish to express their appreciation to all those who gave so generously of their time and help in the preparation of this volume, and particularly to the following: DeWitt Bodeen, screenwriter and film historian, for his careful reading of the text, and John E. Allen, who supplied most of the movie stills used in the book.

We are also indebted to the many other individuals and organizations who helped in providing the hundreds of movie stills appearing on these pages. Without their patience and assistance, many of the pictures could not have been obtained. Our special thanks to: Bettmann Archive, The Memory Shop, Metro-Goldwyn-Mayer Inc., Warner Bros. Pictures, Inc., Paramount Pictures, Sigma III, Jay Remer of 20th Century-Fox, Martin Michel of National Screen Service, Lee Schwartz of Columbia Pictures, and Marion Billings.

We also wish to thank Terry Hearn for her great patience and skill in typing the manuscript.

Cover and Book Design by Remo Cosentino

 Printed in the U.S.A. Published by Golden Press, New York, N.Y., a division of Western Publishing Company, Inc.

Library of Congress Catalog Card Number: 78-125278

TABLE OF CONTENTS

Note: Films are arranged according to the year they were released in America. Within each year, the order is random. For an alphabetical listing, the index should be consulted.

FOREWORD

The aim of this book is twofold: (1) to furnish concise but comprehensive information and analysis of a representative number of motion pictures (nearly 400) significant in the development of screen entertainment in the United States since the advent of sound, and (2) to outline briefly the historical evolution and impact of the American film industry.

Up to now access to reviews and other data covering any large number of films has been limited. Most existing books of an historical character have focused primarily on individuals and institutions. This one places the emphasis on the films themselves.

Films have been selected for their effect in one or more of the following ways: on the public, as measured by box-office response; on film makers, for artistic or technological merit; on an individual, through significant advancement of his screen career, be it as a performer, director, producer or some other creative capacity; and, finally, on censorship, as landmarks on the road to freedom of the screen.

Most readers should find included the great majority of the films in which they are interested. It is inevitable some will find pictures missing that they would like covered. Any selection process demands a degree of arbitrariness. Some pictures are not included simply because they are similar to others which are. Some pictures are included which have few merits as films but are important as mirrors of public taste in their time.

The authors, who have seen thousands of films and read tens of thousands of film reviews and millions of words of film news and comment, have tried to apply the standards of selection as objectively as possible. The films included are not personal lists of favorites. Many good films are omitted simply because they were judged not to be as historically significant as others.

No attempt has been made to pick a uniform number of films each year. There are long lists and short ones —vintage screen years and poor ones—just as it happened. With all pictures listed year by year in order of their exhibition in the United States, many myths about screen history will be dispelled. For example, any critics who assert that Hollywood's product—or the product of the world's studios—had a uniform sameness in any year or period will have their opinions refuted. The variety of the films' appeal is a hallmark all through the years.

Martin Quigley, Jr.

Richard Gertner

New York, N.Y.
May 1, 1970

May McAvoy and Al Jolson in *The Jazz Singer*—recipient of a special Academy Award at the first Academy ceremony on May 16, 1929.

THE BIRTH OF SOUND

The birth of sound in films was a slow, fitful and painful process which took three years. In 1926 came feature pictures synchronized with music and movie shorts with some singing and talking. Later there were films with singing, a few lines of dialogue and other sound effects. Finally there appeared "100% All-Talking" features, as some advertisements read.

At first, most of the studios turned a deaf ear to Western Electric, to inventors Lee De Forest and Theodore Case and others who urged that sound be added to pictures. Of the larger studios, only the huge Fox Film Corporation, headed by William Fox, encouraged sound research. Warner Bros., a small and struggling studio, turned to sound in desperation but with high enthusiasm.

Landmarks of the years 1926–28 were *Don Juan,* Warner Bros.' first Vitaphone-synchronized picture; *The Jazz Singer,* the first film with singing and a little dialogue, also from Warners; and Movietone and Movietone News, Fox Films' sound-on-film system which eventually prevailed as the sound method over the Vitaphone sound-on-disks.

The sound-on-film system was a product of the electronic age, made practical by the photoelectric cell. The sound-on-disk system was essentially a child of the phonograph. In the early months of the sound revolution hundreds of theatres had to install both systems to play the productions coming on the market. Dozens of companies (most of which quickly disappeared) rushed to supply equipment. Some equipment was of good quality with some sound-on-film installations giving many years of service. Other equipment never operated properly and had to be junked immediately.

Silence Versus Sound

For the millions of people who have never seen a silent movie, or have seen only excerpts shown for comic effect, it is difficult to understand the mystique of silent pictures. Silence itself was rationalized as a positive factor in creating screen entertainment. In the silent era it was thought that silence supplemented the actors' pantomime effects and made a definite contribution to the psychological power of the screen.

In addition to this reasoning, there were practical considerations that initially discouraged trade interest in sound. The silent system had been successful; sound introduced technical problems at every step—in the studio, with prints and in the theatres; and it constituted a threat to Hollywood's foreign market. The silent screen had become an international language, with the stars of Hollywood known and appreciated throughout the world. It was easy to translate silent titles into any number of languages. The practice of dubbing dialogue was not yet even a dream.

As late as the middle of 1928, trade opinion still regarded all dialogue pictures as experiments. (Even in 1932 a prominent author in Hollywood, Welford Beaton, wrote a book predicting that "the sound madness" would soon be over. Cecil B. DeMille wrote a foreword, noting that he did not agree with all of the writer's opinions.) But the public was the arbiter. Audiences liked synchronized pictures. They liked films with songs, sound effects and a few spoken words. And they liked all-talking pictures most of all, even when the dramatic qualities and production values were far inferior to the better silent films.

Don Juan with Estelle Taylor, Warner Oland, John Barrymore and Montagu Love.

The Voice of Vitaphone

The Vitaphone system of Warner Bros. was first demonstrated to the press on August 2, 1926, at the Warner Theatre, New York City, and to the public at a gala premiere four days later. The showing was hailed by Professor Michael I. Pupin, president of the American Institute of Electrical Engineers, in these words: "No closer approach to resurrection has ever been made by science." Critics were almost as ecstatic, a typical one writing, "Absolute synchronization, natural reproduction of voices and perfect tonal quality demonstrated . . . the newest and probably most wonderful invention connected with motion pictures since the invention of motion pictures themselves."

Synchronized pictures were appreciated within the trade not so much as a step to all-talking films but as something to replace or substitute for the stage prologue and presentation acts and orchestras then common in the larger theatres known as deluxe houses. These stages and orchestra luxuries were beyond the means of smaller theatres and those in towns and villages. These theatres had to be content with a "wheezing organ or thumping piano" for the musical accompaniment to the pictures. They could not afford any stage prologue or presentation acts.

The historic first presentation of Vitaphone began with Will H. Hays, president of the Motion Picture Producers & Distributors of America, Inc., speaking from the screen. Hays congratulated Warner Bros., Western Electric, Bell Telephone Laboratories and Walter J. Rich for the remarkable achievement. An observer commented: "The timing of Mr. Hays' voice with the movement of his lips and his gestures was so perfected that it was as if he himself were speaking from the stage. The voice, too, was perfectly that of Mr. Hays and would have been readily recognized as such to anyone hearing and not seeing the screening."

The first Vitaphone numbers included the overture from *Tannhäuser* by the New York Philharmonic Orchestra under the direction of Henry Hadley; violinist Mischa Elman playing Dvořák's "Humoresque," accompanied by Josef Bonime at the piano; Roy Smeck in "His Pastimes" and "The Song of the Volga Boatman"; Marion Talley in the Caro Nome aria from Verdi's *Rigoletto;* Harold Bauer playing the Chopin Polonaise in A Flat and then "An Evening on the Don." Next came Efrem Zimbalist, with Bauer at the piano, in variations of Beethoven's "Kreutzer Sonata"; Giovanni Martinelli sang "Vesti la Giubbia" from *I Pagliacci.* The finale had Anna Case in "La Fiesta" with dancers and the Metropolitan Opera chorus, accompanied by the Vitaphone Symphony Orchestra under the direction of Herman Heller. This was followed by several reels of a prologue to the feature film, *Don Juan,* featuring the 107-piece Philharmonic Orchestra playing a special score composed by Major Edward Bowes, David Mendoza and Dr. William Axt. At the intermission the overture from *Mignon* was played over the Vitaphone sound system.

The film, starring John Barrymore, supported by Mary Astor, Estelle Taylor and others, was directed by Alan Crosland from a story by Bess Meredyth. It had only a musical accompaniment—no singing, speaking or special sound effects.

An editorial in *Exhibitors Herald,* an industry weekly, commented, "Vitaphone justifies the high expectations. The musical accompaniment of *Don Juan* is wonderfully well done and is a great contribution to the effectiveness of the picture. Lack of adequate musical facilities has been the one chief thing which has made a picture presentation in a leading theatre appear as a different subject than the same picture when shown in a small theatre to the accompaniment of a wheezy organ or a carelessly thumped piano. The Vitaphone solves this difficulty and solves it effectively."

At the time *Don Juan* opened there was only one theatre equipped for it. By the end of 1926 about three dozen other openings were made in key cities with each piece of Vitaphone equipment virtually hand-crafted. Everywhere the public responded in great numbers but the trade generally regarded these special Vitaphone road-show engagements as curiosities. The basic business for most theatres continued to be silent films for two more years and, for some, even three and four years.

Other Headlines of 1926

In 1926, shortly after *Don Juan* opened in New York, a prominent leader of the industry held a trade luncheon in Boston to launch the first film of his administration as president of Film Booking Offices of America (F.B.O.). The man was Joseph P. Kennedy and the film was *Bigger Than Barnum's*. Kennedy's next attraction was *Her Honor the Governor*. Another early F.B.O. film was Red Grange in his first film, *One Minute to Play*. As might be expected, the Boston newspapers carried lengthy articles saluting Kennedy as a favorite son and former Harvard baseball star who was now making such an auspicious start in the motion picture industry (where he found the great financial success and zest for public recognition that would shape his family's later life). Jimmie Walker, Mayor of New York, and Francis Ouimet, the golf champion, were among those charmed by the Kennedy approach into issuing enthusiastic endorsements of F.B.O. films.

Also significant in 1926 in the long campaign for freedom of the screen were the remarks made by Governor Al Smith at the dedication of the Fox Film Exchange in Albany. Smith said, "Censors obstruct the film art." New York censorship then and for some years in the future had effects throughout the whole country because few distributors bothered to restore cuts made by N.Y. censors when prints were shipped to other centers. Films banned in New York, the largest market, often were not considered worth distributing elsewhere.

However, the event of the year which made the maximum effect on the public was not *Don Juan* or Kennedy's new films or Al Smith looking to screen freedom: It was the death of Rudolph Valentino on August 23, 1926. It was this occurrence that made, for example, the *New York Herald Tribune* wake up and acknowledge for the first time that the movies constitute one of the greatest forces of modern times.

If it can be written that *Don Juan* was to cause a storm in the motion picture world, it must be said that Valentino's death was a hurricane of record proportions. Not until the death of President John F. Kennedy in 1963 was the American public so involved in the passing of a public figure. When Valentino lost his fight for life, millions felt that a dear friend, even a lover, had been cruelly taken away.

It was perhaps fitting that the greatest star of the silent screen, so far as public mass appeal was concerned, should die at the very pinnacle of his career in silent films, for Valentino could never have successfully made the transition to the talkies. His voice, like that of some other stars, did not match the character of his dashing screen image.

A New Year–A New Voice

Equally significant, technologically speaking, with the opening of *Don Juan* were the first demonstrations of the Movietone sound-on-film system at the Sam Harris Theatre in New York City, on January 21, 1927. The program included four songs by Raquel Meller, which preceded the showing of a silent film of major importance, *What Price Glory?* The second Movietone demonstration, featuring the new Movietone News, was at the same theatre on May 25. Included was the takeoff of Col. Charles A. Lindbergh on his solo flight to Paris. Everyone, public and trade alike, realized immediately that sound and talking added greatly to the impact of newsreels. No one argued for the value of silence in news films.

Vilma Banky and Rudolph Valentino in *Son of the Sheik*.

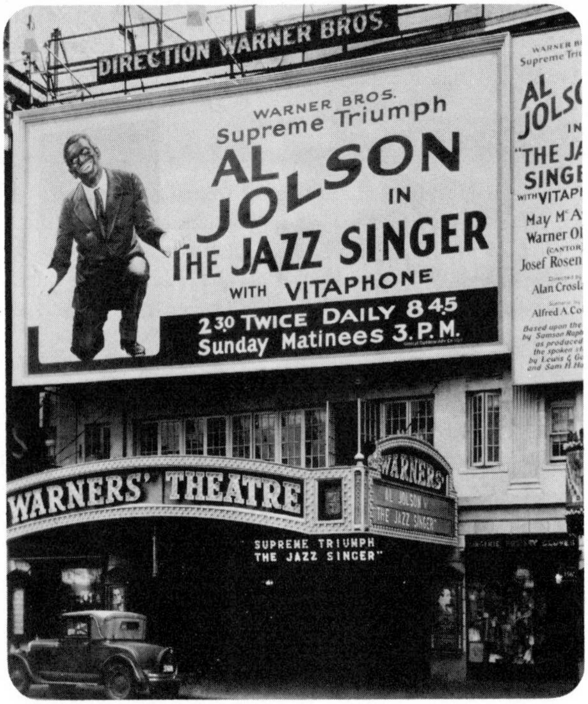

Poster for *The Jazz Singer,* the first Vitaphone feature with singing and spoken lines.

It was also realized that sound would be excellent for short subjects. Vitaphone subjects of one- and two-reel length were produced by Warner Bros. shortly after the opening of *Don Juan.* Also, during the summer of 1927, Vitaphone made the first religious short subject with sound, featuring two Baptist ministers of Jamestown, Virginia, in a reel made for the Jamestown Anniversary. Later the reel was made available gratis to theatres equipped for Vitaphone.

Considerable attention was generated by Warner Bros. with the announcement that George Jessel, star of the successful stage attraction, had been signed to play the same role in the film of *The Jazz Singer,* planned as the first Vitaphone feature with singing and spoken lines. However, by late May of 1927, Al Jolson, who had never previously made a picture, was engaged to replace Jessel at a salary of $150,000. A contemporary trade story said, "Jessel refused to go on with making the picture unless Warner Bros. agreed to pay him for the singing parts in addition to the amount as an actor."

On its opening October 6, 1927, in New York *The Jazz Singer* received poor reviews, but the public's response was tremendous. One writer commented, "Vitaphone songs get great applause but picture receives little." Observing that the Broadway premiere audience had frequently broken out in applause, a journalist noted, "It was for Al Jolson and his songs. The picture itself didn't cause a ripple." Another remarked, "It would be sad to think of what would happen to the picture without the Vitaphone and Jolson's songs."

The songs of *The Jazz Singer* were "Dirty Hands, Dirty Face," "Toot, Toot, Tootsie, Goodbye," "Blue Skies," "Mother of Mine, I Still Love You" and "Mammy." Jolson also sang the Kol Nidre. The film was directed by Alan Crosland "whose many successes will not be enhanced by this production." The script was by Al Cohn, a pioneer screen writer.

It was tragic that Sam Warner, the one of the four Warners who had pushed most actively for the Vitaphone, died in Hollywood just one day before *The Jazz Singer* was so enthusiastically hailed by moviegoers in New York. At his funeral the Kol Nidre recording by Al Jolson and the Vitaphone Choir was played.

Despite the loss of Sam Warner, the studio went ahead with plans for more features and shorts using the Vitaphone. One series of shorts was named Vitaphone Vaudeville. Byran Foy was made director of Vitaphone sound shorts.

But Silence Is Still Golden

However, despite the interest in Movietone demonstrations, further engagements of *Don Juan,* the Synchronized Picture, and the opening of *The Jazz Singer,* 1927 was still basically a year of the silent screen. Hit attractions were *Rookies* (MGM), *Tell It to the Marines* (MGM), *The Kid Brother* (Paramount), *Slide Kelly Slide* (MGM), *The King of Kings* (Pathé), *Flesh and the Devil* (MGM), *Seventh Heaven* (Fox), *Wings* (Paramount) and *It* (Paramount).

In other respects 1927 was like the years immediately preceding. Censorship was a big issue, and William Randolph Hearst called for Federal film censorship in an editorial in all his newspapers. For this he was chided for being inconsistent, since he was an aggressive advocate of freedom of the press. Trade opinion was that some films might well "be cleaned up" but that the job should be done voluntarily in Hollywood and not by the government.

Wings with Richard Arlen and Charles "Buddy" Rogers.

Harold Lloyd in *The Kid Brother.*

Flesh and the Devil with Greta Garbo and John Gilbert.

Senator Smith W. Brookhart of Iowa campaigned against block booking of films and introduced legislation to bar the practice. He also advocated a jail sentence for any film distributor who would not sell to independent theatre owners.

Joseph P. Kennedy sponsored a series of lectures by outstanding leaders of the motion picture business at Harvard University. Participants included many of the most influential film men: Will H. Hays; Adolph Zukor, head of Paramount; A. H. Giannini, of the Bank of America; Jesse L. Lasky; Earle W. Hammons of Educational Pictures; Milton Sills; Sidney R. Kent; Robert H. Cochrane; Sam Katz; William Fox; and Harry M. Warner.

On May 11, 1927, the Academy of Motion Picture Arts and Sciences was founded in Hollywood. This organization later became famous around the world for the Academy Awards, the highest honors of the American film industry.

Also, in May of 1927, G. B. Shaw spoke to the United States and to the world through Movietone News. Critics were impressed with the potential of sound films when they saw the impact such a distinguished and colorful author could make on the screen. President Calvin Coolidge said, "The progress that has been made in both education and entertainment in this tremendous enterprise [the U.S. motion picture industry] is an outstanding achievement of the opening years of this century."

About this time there was renewed attack by bankers on the high cost of production. They asserted that a "program picture" should cost no more than $150,000. Meanwhile, in New York, Lee De Forest filed a suit charging that Movietone and Fox infringed on his Phonofilm patents. Theodore Case who, with Earl Sponable, developed Movietone, had formerly been associated with De Forest. Significant also was the opening of the Roxy Theatre in New York City, named after its managing director, Samuel L. "Roxy" Rothafel. The Roxy became a showcase for Fox films and in 1953 was again the center of industry attention during the introduction of CinemaScope.

The year 1927 marked the passing of Marcus Loew, one of the legitimate pioneers who had risen from a humble beginning to the position as the most influential man in the film business as founder of Loew's Theatres which controlled MGM pictures. When Loew married, he and his bride lived in a New York slum room without a window. At his death his home overlooking Hempstead

Jean Arthur and Richard Dix in *Warming Up.*

Harbor on Long Island was a mansion complete with fifty servants, three Mack trucks and a huge express cruiser on which he commuted during the summer to a dock in the East River owned by the New York Yacht Club. Not acceptable under the club's membership restrictions, he was allowed to use the dock in exchange for purchasing 1,000 gallons of gas weekly, an amount he doubted his yacht ever consumed.

The Price of Progress

1928 was the third year of the transition from silents to talkies. It was the year when synchronized pictures, *The Jazz Singer* with its songs by Al Jolson, a number of Vitaphone sound shorts, and also a few issues of Movietone News, appeared in key theatres in all major cities and a number of towns throughout the country. It was a year that was climaxed by the first all-talking film—the Vitaphone *The Lights of New York* from Warner Bros. It was not notable as film entertainment but it made another landmark on the road to a living screen.

For the movie moguls of the times, in production as well as distribution and exhibition, 1928 was the year of great anxiety that control of the industry would pass to others, that is, the great electrical companies. Western Electric had pioneered with Vitaphone, which the Warners embraced when they were in desperate economic plight. Western Electric and Electrical Research Products, Inc. (ERPI), both affiliates of the Bell Telephone System, were important factors in both recording and equipment for theatres. The other major supplier was RCA with its Photophone.

Since prices for the equipment were high—and theatres *had* to have sound to play the new films that were so attractive to the public—the electrical companies had a strong interest in exhibition. They were the only major sources of studio recording equipment and facilities for duplicating the disks and processing the sound-on-film. Their potential grip on production was very real, too. By July of 1928, Western Electric had installed its equipment in four hundred theatres, 95 percent of which were equipped to handle both sound-on-disk and sound-on-film features. Costs ranged from $5,000 to $15,000 for a fifteen-year rental. RCA's charges for Photophone were on a sliding scale according to the number of theatre seats and were for a ten-year rental: up to 750 seats, $7,500; to 1,500, $9,000; to 3,000, $12,500; and over 3,000 seats, $16,000. There quickly came on the market a number of other sound systems, some cheap, some inferior; most of the names soon faded away.

Not all attempts to add sound to films were successful. Many features were completed as silents, and then some sound effects and a few lines of dialogue were added to take advantage of the public's infatuation with synchronized pictures. One example was Paramount's *The Patriot,* starring Emil Jannings and Lewis Stone. A critic commented, "The mob voices destroy the feeling and impressiveness of the mob scenes and a few words linked with Jennings' pantomime render rather less effective than more effective these scenes."

Sound Marches On

In August of 1928, the first sound trailer, or preview, appeared. It was made by National Screen Service for *Warming Up* with Richard Dix. There was also a silent version of both trailer and feature.

The whole field of acoustics began to receive attention. Experts wrote about the design requirements for making theatres suitable for reproduction of music and speaking. F. H. Richardson began his classic study, *The Fundamental Principles of Sound Pictures.* A trade paper launched a weekly department called "Synchronized Pictures." Studios rushed to build sound stages. Voice tests became common. MGM retained the services of a distinguished scientist, Professor Rufus B. von Kleinsmid, to help evaluate the voices of its actors.

Censorship in this period of transition remained an acute problem. An interesting case concerned *Dawn,* a British picture about Edith Cavell, an army nurse executed as a spy by the Germans in World War I. Otto H. Kahn, prominent New York banker, resigned from the sponsoring committee over plans to exhibit the film. Kahn and others were outraged at the "indecency" of showing the execution of a woman. The affair attracted so much attention that a screening had to be arranged for Mayor Jimmy Walker to rule on whether the film was fit for public showing. The movie was released.

As 1928 ended, worry was still being expressed about developing sound in motion pictures "without affecting an imitation of realism, instead of an illusion of realism, as is the case of the silent picture. . . . A great question which the future will decide is just how fully a motion picture may be audible vocally without destroying instead of helping psychological interest which has been an essential characteristic of the silent drama."

While critics and producers worried, audiences spoke loudly at the box office: They wanted talking pictures. All the studios made plans for many releases in 1929, not knowing and really not caring whether sound would be a permanent change or passing cycle. In the meantime more and more theatres were converting to sound. By Christmas, 1928, about 10 percent of the theatres of the United States were equipped for talkies, and thousands more planned to put in equipment in 1929.

The silent screen was finished. A new art form had been born. From 1929 on, it was—and is—the sound screen, with its own mystique.

Anita Page, Charles King and Bessie Love in *The Broadway Melody* (1929), the first talking picture to win an Academy Award.

1929

Talking Pictures, as movies with music, sound effects and dialogue were then called, largely supplanted silent pictures in the year famous in American history for its continuing great stock boom—followed by the monumental crash which came in October. By the year's end, nearly ten thousand theatres were "wired for sound." Yet most films were also issued in silent versions, mainly in the interest of sales abroad.

The year was also notable in that Martin Quigley, writer and editor-publisher of *Exhibitors Herald,* began drafting a Production Code. He recognized that the impact of sound could intensify trends in production which had been fanning the fires of censorship. Also, the complexities of sound film-making demanded productions which would not be at the mercy of scissors-wielding censors. Quigley proposed a written guide to be voluntarily adhered to by the industry. His collaborators in drafting the document were two Jesuits, Rev. Daniel A. Lord, who had been technical adviser for the production of *The King of Kings* (1927) and Rev. F. J. Dinneen, a member of Chicago's Motion Picture Commission.

Theatre business was excellent, stimulated by the public's interest in sound films and a better overall quality of attractions. There was a substantial weekly increase in attendance over 1928. Installation of sound equipment in studios and theatres increased capital investment in the industry to a huge $500,000,000. Not surprisingly, production costs soared, with an average feature now budgeted at $150,000, an increase of over 20 percent from the year before. About 75,000 people were employed in film making in Hollywood. A fifth of this number were extras and only one extra earned as much as $3,500 during the entire year. The extra's average daily fee was ten dollars, though many received as little as three or four dollars a day.

The corporate merger activity continued at a high pitch. The biggest deal was made by William Fox, head of Fox Films, to acquire control of Loew's, Inc., at the lofty price of $125 per share. Ultimately the deal collapsed under anti-trust and economic pressures. During the year, Warner Bros. bought Fox's holdings in First National, and Columbia Pictures completed the establishment of its own national distribution system. Sometimes the corporate maneuvering took attention away from essential business. Terry Ramsaye, a film historian, commented at the time, "Movies made millions for their makers and the millions made the makers into magnates who have since been so busy magneting that the movies have been largely forgotten."

Ben Hur, a silent film directed by Fred Niblo and released as a road show attraction in 1926, was still setting box-office records. Jack Alicoate, editor and publisher of the *Film Daily,* wrote: *"Ben Hur,* called Metro's folly before release. Now holds the gross record for all time. Over eight million dollars already in with about half from abroad. Some gross. Some picture. Some business. Sez We."

In October, Judge T. J. Thatcher ruled the industry's arbitration system illegal but upheld the exhibition contract with its credit system. The following year the Supreme Court banned the credit system on the grounds that it was used to coerce independent exhibitors. Then independents formed Allied States Association.

Stars of the year: Clara Bow, Lon Chaney, William Haines, Hoot Gibson, Colleen Moore, Buddy Rogers, Richard Barthelmess, Ken Maynard, Tom Mix and Nancy Carroll.

Rio Rita with Georges Renavent, Bebe Daniels and John Boles.

Jeanette MacDonald and Maurice Chevalier in *The Love Parade.*

RIO RITA

Musicals were more and more the rage, and Hollywood producers turned them out one after the other, going to the Broadway stage to secure many properties. Such a one was the Guy Bolton-Fred Thompson operetta *Rio Rita,* which Florenz Ziegfeld had produced in New York.

For RKO it was the first major sound film, and they made it on a lavish scale. The first half was shot in black-and-white and the second in Technicolor (then a two-color process), and critics remarked it would have been better had the entire film been tinted. But both critics and audiences were pleased to see a film musical which did not have a backstage plot for a change.

Rita was played by Bebe Daniels, who at age thirteen had been Harold Lloyd's leading lady in the "Lonesome Luke" comedies. *Rio Rita* was her first sound film, and she received excellent notices, one New York critic declaring she was a "revelation—the best of the silent stars yet made audible." Captain Stewart was acted by John Boles, a stage-trained singer who had appeared with Geraldine Farrar in her only venture into light opera. He was already on the way to becoming a film matinee idol (he had debuted in Gloria Swanson's *The Love of Sunya* three years before), and *Rio Rita* increased his popularity.

The picture also served to introduce the stage comedian team of Bert Wheeler and Robert Woolsey to the screen, repeating their stage roles. They had a fair success in films but nothing to compare with that of Abbott and Costello, who starred in a remake of *Rio Rita* produced by MGM in 1942. The later version had little relationship to the original, being fitted out with Nazi spies, saboteurs, and trick radio instruments. Kathryn Grayson was Rita, and John Carroll sang opposite her.

Producer: William Le Baron. **Director:** Luther Reed. **Scriptwriter:** Reed. **Principal Players:** Bert Wheeler, Robert Woolsey, Bebe Daniels, John Boles and Dorothy Lee. **Running time:** 135 minutes. **Released:** RKO.

THE LOVE PARADE

The director of *The Love Parade,* Ernst Lubitsch, first wanted to be an actor, and he trained under Max Reinhardt in Berlin before the First World War. Later he turned producer of films and finally director, coming to Hollywood to direct Mary Pickford in *Rosita* (1923). It is in the last capacity that he was to find his niche and to become famous for the "Lubitsch touch"—a subtle style in which gestures and glances take on meanings that are not on the surface. It lent itself best of all to comedy (from *Design for Living* to *Ninotchka,* to pick two).

The Love Parade starred Maurice Chevalier and Jeanette MacDonald. As usual the plot was slight: an advertisement summed it up aptly as the story of "a handsome high-born pair who become man and wife by decree of the state and lovers by instinct." Nonetheless, it had the "touch"—and had it set to music. Chevalier, who was already the idol of France, captivated Ameri-

In Old Arizona with Warner Baxter (as the Cisco Kid), Dorothy Burgess and Edmund Lowe.

cans in this picture (his second sound film) with his charm and singing voice, which, though it wasn't all that strong, he at least used expertly.

This was the screen debut of Miss MacDonald, whom Lubitsch had seen in a musical on Broadway where he had gone to search for a heroine for his film. Movie audiences liked her from the start, but her golden years were to commence when she co-starred in *Naughty Marietta* with Nelson Eddy in 1935.

Miss MacDonald appeared with Chevalier in three other films: *One Hour With You* (1931), *Love Me Tonight* (1932) and *The Merry Widow* (1934). Then along came Eddy, and Chevalier returned to France and the music halls—for a while.

The Love Parade is based on a play called *The Prince Consort* by Leon Xanrof and Jules Chanel, which was adapted by Ernest Vajda. Guy Bolton (of *Sally* fame) did the script.

Producer: Paramount. **Director:** Ernst Lubitsch. **Scriptwriter:** Guy Bolton. **Principal Players:** Maurice Chevalier and Jeanette MacDonald. **Running time:** 118 minutes. **Released:** Paramount.

IN OLD ARIZONA

"The first all-talking feature filmed outdoors" was the way they billed *In Old Arizona,* a western celebrating the adventures of that quixotic bandit of the gay nineties, the Cisco Kid. Released just seven months before *Hallelujah,* it was indeed an advance over the usual indoor set-bound "talkies" that had preceded it.

As one impressed observer put it in the pages of *Exhibitors Herald-World:* "The dialogue is crisp, characteristic, genuine, and it occurs as speech occurred in the open spaces on such occasions as the one pictured. So do the noises of horse, wagon, creaking harness and rumbling wheel and all the noises of outdoors and indoors."

Louella O. Parsons, movie columnist for the Hearst papers, concurred. She wrote that it was the first talkie "to make me forget the mechanical sound device" and she thought the outdoor scenery "gorgeous and magnificent." (It was filmed in Utah and California—not Arizona.)

Warner Baxter starred as the Cisco Kid; a romantic lead of the silent days, he had a rich speaking voice that enabled him to make the transition to sound with ease. His performance won him the 1928–29 Academy Award as best actor of the year.

His co-stars were Edmund Lowe as a hard-boiled sergeant not unlike the one he had played in *What Price Glory?* (1926) and Dorothy Burgess (in her film debut) as a siren with the unlikely name of Tonia Maria. Stage experience helped all the principals in handling their roles.

Two men are credited with the "direction in dialogue" (as ads at the time put it): Raoul Walsh and Irving Cummings.

Producer: Fox. **Directors:** Raoul Walsh and Irving Cummings. **Scriptwriter:** Tom Barry. **Principal Players:** Edmund Lowe, Dorothy Burgess and Warner Baxter. **Running time:** 95 minutes. **Released:** Fox.

The Broadway Melody with Mary Doran, Charles King, Anita Page and Bessie Love.

Mary Pickford in *Coquette.*

THE BROADWAY MELODY

The first talking picture to win an Academy Award was, appropriately, a musical. It was a big MGM production, and a forerunner in the genre with which that studio was to lead the world (runners-up: 20th Century-Fox, Warner's and Paramount).

The plot was new neither to the films nor the stage—a story of two small town girls who come to the Big City to try to crack Broadway. But the production numbers were lavish, and critics who liked it (many did not) thought it the first really successful talking picture—that is, one in which the images and the sounds really blended and didn't seem to be working against each other.

The public liked it, too, and for some of them it was the first "talkie" they saw. This was because many theatres just wired for sound chose it as their opening attraction. (There was a silent print, incidentally, for those houses that were slow to convert.)

The Broadway Melody is also notable as the first musical for which the lyrics were written by Arthur Freed, who was to become in later years the prime producer of musicals at MGM as well as song-writer. The big hit of *The Broadway Melody* was "You Were Meant for Me."

Another important name involved was Edmund Goulding, who supplied the story of *The Broadway Melody.* He had been at MGM since 1925 as both writer and director (*Sally, Irene and Mary, Women Love Diamonds,* etc.). It was as director that he would gain his greatest fame with such films as *Grand Hotel, Dark Victory, The Old Maid, Claudia, The Razor's Edge* and *Nightmare Alley.*

The stars of *The Broadway Melody* were Charles King, the former Ziegfeld song and dance man; and Anita Page and Bessie Love, who had been popular silent film stars.

Producer: MGM. **Director:** Harry Beaumont. **Scriptwriters:** Norman Houston and James Gleason. **Principal Players:** Charles King, Anita Page and Bessie Love. **Running time:** 102 minutes. **Released:** MGM.

COQUETTE

Mary Pickford, America's Sweetheart, the Queen of the Silent Screen, spoke for the first time in a movie in *Coquette.* She had been absent from films for a year and a half, apparently biding her time until the right property came along.

What she chose was a cornball melodrama, that had been written for the stage as a vehicle for Helen Hayes by George Abbott and Ann Preston, concerning a flapper in Dixie who falls in love with a man her father disapproves of. Dad is so upset he shoots the fellow dead and then kills himself, leaving the unfortunate heroine to face life alone. In the play, it had been the heroine who committed suicide.

Critics commented that Miss Pickford had a pleasing voice and noted that the role was quite a departure from those sweet little things that had made her famous. It

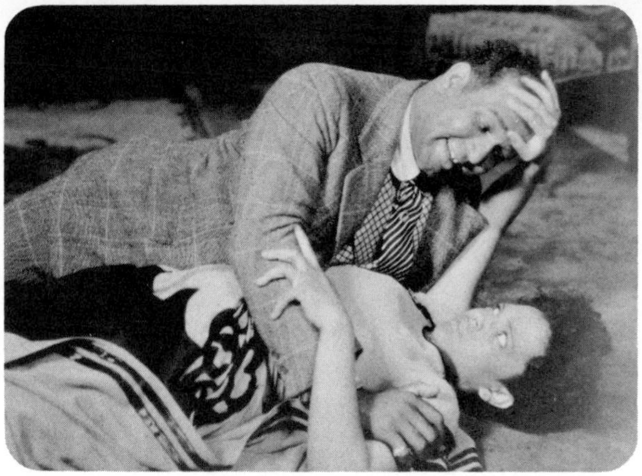

William Fountaine and Nina Mae McKinney in *Hallelujah*.

was a "modern" role and the character was not entirely sympathetic.

The Academy chose her best actress of the year (over Jeanne Eagels in *The Letter*) and *Coquette* was a popular success. Later in 1929 Miss Pickford appeared with her husband Douglas Fairbanks for the first and only time in a "talkie" version of Shakespeare's *The Taming of the Shrew*. In the next few years she made two films—*Kiki* in 1931 and *Secrets* in 1933. After that she turned to radio acting and then film production, handling such properties as *One Rainy Afternoon* and *The Gay Desperado*. Her great days as a major film actress were behind her.

Producer: United Artists. **Director:** Sam Taylor. **Scriptwriters:** John Grey and Allen McNeil. **Principal Players:** Mary Pickford, John Mack Brown, Matt Moore and John Sainpolis. **Running time:** 68 minutes. **Released:** United Artists.

HALLELUJAH

It was a time for firsts in the American film industry, and *Hallelujah* was the first all-talking, all-Negro musical. MGM was the pioneering company this time, and *Hallelujah* demonstrated the willingness of Irving Thalberg and his associates to take a gamble on a project that was admittedly a commercial risk.

It had long been a pet project of director King Vidor, whose interest in social issues was keen (war in *The Big Parade* of 1925 and unemployment in *The Crowd* of '28). It was evidently his desire to expose the plight of the black man in the South and the effects of discrimination upon him in this first sound film.

Unfortunately the characters he chose were hardly typical—a farmhand forced by circumstances into murder who reforms and becomes an evangelist, and the vamp who is his initial ruination, to name two. The lurid melodrama of the film tended to vitiate any ennobling intentions.

Still, *Hallelujah* is important and interesting for Vidor's direction. He was a pioneer this early in the era of sound in using the camera fluidly and employing the sound track with imagination. In a departure from customary practice, Vidor shot the film on location in Tennessee and dubbed in the sound effects later so that he could magnify them for dramatic effects. The night noises of the swamp in the climactic chase are particularly vivid. And the singing sequences in church are lively and colorful, as well as melodious.

Hallelujah was praised by many critics, but the public did not respond. Bookings of the picture were sparse, especially in the South.

Producer-Director: King Vidor. **Screenplay:** Wanda Tuchock and Ransom Rideout. **Principal Players:** Daniel L. Haynes, Nina Mae McKinney, William Fountaine, Harry Gray and Fannie Belle de Knight. **Running time:** 109 minutes. **Released:** MGM.

George Arliss and Joan Bennett in *Disraeli,* a typical "prestige" picture of the day—a stage success starring an important Broadway star. Arliss won an Oscar.

1930

The year's slogan was "Away from the ticker tape and back to hard work." While theatre business was only down moderately from the excellent results of 1929, film stocks ended the year down 60 percent from the pre-crash levels.

Warner Bros., which had played such an important role in the introduction of sound starting with the Vitaphone synchronization for *Don Juan* in 1926, finally gave up on its separate sound system requiring disks to be run in conjunction with the film projector. The sound-on-film system with the sound track printed on the same strip of film with the picture was found more satisfactory as well as simpler, both in studios and theatres. The sound-on-film had been pioneered by Fox with Movietone beginning in 1927.

At the time when the sound system he had gambled on was being accepted universally, William Fox lost his battle to keep control of Fox Films, and was forced to retire. Fox was always a schemer, and by arranging corporate mergers and acquiring sound patents, he came close to dominating the whole American film business. But he was forced into bankruptcy, and was later indicted for attempting to bribe a judge, eventually serving six months in prison.

In January, 1930, Will H. Hays, president of the Motion Picture Producers and Distributors of America, presided over a series of four meetings in Hollywood at which Martin Quigley explained the draft of the proposed Production Code. Rev. Daniel A. Lord, S.J. participated in the last of the meetings. On February 17 the producers formally approved the Code document and the board of directors of the MPPDA, meeting in New York on March 31, made the approval official, ushering in an era of voluntary self-regulation of the film industry which endured for over three decades.

It was an exciting year for products: *All Quiet on the Western Front,* directed by Lewis Milestone and starring Lew Ayres, Louis Wolheim and Arnold Lacey, was as much a sensation as the best-selling book had been. Harold Lloyd's first talking picture, *Welcome Danger,* was released to a world looking for a chance to laugh. Lawrence Tibbett, of the Metropolitan Opera, was in the first operetta in an early Technicolor process, *The Rogue Song.* Educational Film Exchanges distributed a large number of short subjects, including "talking comedies," with Jack White, Lupino Lane and Lloyd Hamilton. There were also Mack Sennett comedies.

Wide films had a brief vogue. In contrast to the standard width of 35mm (which dates from the time of Edison and continues to the present), 55mm film was used for *The Big Trail* in the Fox-Grandeur process. Even wider film, 70mm, was used for *Danger Lights,* an RKO Spoor-Berggren picture. These films required special studio cameras and over-sized projectors. The screen impact of the big pictures was impressive, but the industry, beset by the transition to sound and the economic slump, was in no mood for another technological change. Wide screen pictures did become common, primarily through the use of special lenses, later on (1952–53).

Hollywood in transition had the new and the old, the silent stars and those who would make their names in sound. Studios maintained silent production departments, for half the theatres at home and a greater percentage abroad could still play only silents.

Stars of the year: Joan Crawford, Clara Bow, William Haines, Janet Gaynor, Colleen Moore, Greta Garbo, Al Jolson, Richard Barthelmess, Rin Tin Tin and Tom Mix.

Ben Lyon and Jean Harlow in *Hell's Angels.*

All Quiet on the Western Front with William Bakewell and Lew Ayres.

HELL'S ANGELS

Four decades after its initial release, when it was something of a *cause célèbre,* Howard Hughes' *Hell's Angels* does not hold up well, except for its aerial sequences. It is one of those pictures of which the behind-the-scenes stories are more intriguing than what actually got on film.

Hughes was the scion of a rich Texas oil-drilling equipment family. He became interested in show business and went to Hollywood to invest a portion of his capital and his abilities at business in making movies. He formed the Caddo Company for that purpose, and had made three pictures (*Two Arabian Knights, The Racket* and *The Mating Call*) before he turned his attention to the air epic.

Sound came in as an important force after shooting was well underway; in a typical gesture, Hughes scrapped the footage finished and began again. Then there were problems with leading lady Greta Nissen, so she was replaced at great expense by Jean Harlow.

Finally, after three years in production, the film was released. It ran into trouble with numerous censors over some bawdy dialogue, sex sequences, and Miss Harlow's decolletage. Hughes fought the censors tooth and nail, winning sometimes and sometimes losing.

The aerial scenes were something to see, especially the Zeppelin raid over London, which looked more like the real thing than anything audiences had seen before.

Miss Harlow went on to become a big star—but not right away and not for Hughes. After several mediocre pictures at Universal, Columbia and Warners, she went to MGM, the company with "more stars than there are in the heavens." Miss Harlow never developed into much of an actress, but she had her moments, particularly as a natural comedienne. The film titles reflect her image: *Red-Headed Woman, Bombshell* and *Reckless.*

Hughes battled with the censors again, over *Scarface* in 1932, the brutal gangster picture in which the hero is obviously incestuously inclined to his sister, and then in 1943 with *The Outlaw* in which he introduced Jane Russell to the world. Her costumes were too brief for the censors, and they also took offense at her sexy love scene with Jack Beutel, who played Billy the Kid.

Producer-Director: Howard Hughes. **Scriptwriters:** Howard Estabrook and Harry Behn. **Principal Players:** Ben Lyon, James Hall, Jean Harlow. **Running time:** 135 minutes. **Released:** United Artists.

ALL QUIET ON THE WESTERN FRONT

Controversy is good for the box office (if it doesn't backfire) and few films since *The Birth of a Nation* had stirred up so much of it as this film version of the Erich Maria Remarque novel of World War I told from the viewpoint of the Germans.

In retrospect the tempest is amusing. On the one hand it was denounced as "brazen propaganda" designed to "undermine belief in the Army and in authority." The spokesman for this theory was Major Frank Pease, head

The Big Trail with John Wayne, David Rollins, Marguerite Churchill and Helen Parrish.

of the Hollywood Technical Directors Institute and a trouble-maker who also had decried the cordial reception given the great Russian director Sergei Eisenstein in California. Pease and his associates were actually able to get the Remarque film barred from a few Army posts.

Meanwhile, in Germany, the Nazis, led by Joseph Goebbels, picketed the movie and denounced it as pacifistic. The censor board banned the film as "damning the reputation of Germany." As for the Poles, they banned it as "pro-Teutonic"!

Carl Laemmle, Jr., who produced the picture, defended it as being anti-war rather than anti-German, and said it had done more to establish good will toward the German people than any factor since the Armistice. So much for the propaganda issue. Is the movie art?

The Academy of Motion Picture Arts and Sciences thought so; they named it best picture of the year. Most critics of the day concurred. Four decades later it is still highly regarded for its passionate and humanistic outlook and is ranked as one of the great anti-war films of all time.

The film was the first major triumph of director Lewis Milestone, and it made a star of Lew Ayres (as Paul Baumer) whose previous claim to fame was his appearance as the youthful lover of Greta Garbo in *The Kiss.* (He was later to become even more famous as Dr. Kildare in the medical series turned out by MGM.)

The battle sequences staged by Milestone hold up best of all, but some of the sentimental moments remain impressive today, too—especially the death of Paul as he reaches out to touch a butterfly. Milestone, by the way, had staged a nude sequence: The three young soldiers strip completely to swim a river and call on three French girls across the way. The men were photographed from the rear only, but this was considered daring back in 1930.

Producer: Carl Laemmle, Jr. **Director:** Lewis Milestone. **Dialogue Director:** George Cukor. **Scriptwriters:** Maxwell Anderson and George Abbott. **Principal Players:** Louis Wolheim, Lew Ayres and John Wray. **Running time:** 138 minutes. **Released:** Universal.

THE BIG TRAIL

Scarcely had the film industry begun to adapt to sound when along came another development (which was not all that new either): wide-gauge film. *The Big Trail* was one of the first pictures to be made in Grandeur, a 55mm color wide-screen process. It was a big-scale western, which was also notable for supplying John Wayne with his first important role.

It is a story of pioneers and it follows them in their prairie schooners from Missouri through the plains, across the deserts, into the mountains, and through the wilderness of Nebraska and Wyoming. There was naturally a fight between the settlers and the Indians which was exciting, but the spectacular highlight of the film was a terrific rain storm that almost drowned the large cast.

Audiences who saw *The Big Trail* in Grandeur were particularly impressed by this latter sequence; the first-

Check and Double Check with Freeman F. Gosden and Charles V. Correll.

Wallace Beery and Marie Dressler in *Min and Bill.*

night audience in Hollywood was so awed it rose to its feet and applauded. Most Americans, however, saw the film in a 35mm print on a standard screen.

The director of this epic was Raoul Walsh, an actor who played John Wilkes Booth in Griffith's *The Birth of a Nation* and who found that his real talents lay behind the camera. He made all types of pictures in a long career, but his forte was the "action" movie (*They Died With Their Boots On, Objective Burma, The Tall Men,* etc.).

Producer: Fox Films. **Director:** Raoul Walsh. **Scriptwriters:** Walsh and Hal G. Evarts. **Principal Players:** John Wayne, Marguerite Churchill, El Brendel and David Rollins. **Running time:** 122 minutes. **Released:** Fox.

CHECK AND DOUBLE CHECK

Amos 'n Andy, the famous black characters of radio played by white actors Freeman F. Gosden and Charles V. Correll, were brought to the screen with advertising to match the occasion: "The mightiest stars of all creation join the pageant of the titans," modestly proclaimed RKO Radio. The hyperbole continued: "The breathless magic of radio and the God-given genius of man have wrought in Amos 'n Andy the grandest phenomenon in the sweep of all show ages . . . unexampled . . . fantastic . . . one of the most superb and amazing manifestations of this roaring, rocking century!"

Their first film, *Check and Double Check,* almost lived up to the billing as far as the box office was concerned: It was one of the 15 top grossing pictures of the 1930–31 season.

Amos 'n Andy did not make another film until 1935 (*The Big Broadcast of 1936*), but their radio programs continued through the thirties. By the 1950's they were considered deplorable stereotypes of subservience to be banished into oblivion along with Mammy in *Gone With the Wind* and the indolent figure of Stepin Fetchit.

Producer: RKO Radio. **Director:** Melville Brown. **Scriptwriter:** J. Walter Ruben. **Principal Players:** Freeman F. Gosden, Charles V. Correll, Sue Carol and Charles Morton. **Running time:** 71 minutes. **Released:** RKO.

MIN AND BILL

Marie Dressler had been a top star of the early silent screen, but slid into obscurity until her "comeback" in *Anna Christie* in 1930. This film heralded her golden years: She became one of the two or three top drawing stars of the early thirties. When the *Motion Picture Herald* poll of exhibitors began in 1932, she placed at the head of the list for that year and for the one following.

In *Min and Bill* she had a typical role. She plays a good-hearted woman who agrees to rear the child of a friend—a woman of loose morals who wants nothing to do with her offspring. Min is a tough old bird; she finally kills the friend to prevent her foster daughter from discovering her true mother. At the end Min tries to

Whoopee with Eleanor Hunt and Eddie Cantor.

escape, but is arrested and charged with murder just as the daughter is starting on her honeymoon.

The opportunity for pathos supplied by this situation was milked by Miss Dressler for all it was worth, and it helped win her an Oscar. There were laughs in the picture, too, most of the comic scenes taking place between her and Wallace Beery, as Bill. They made a popular team but were co-starred only once again, in *Tugboat Annie* (1933). (Both were also in *Dinner at Eight* the same year, but not as related characters.)

The wicked mother was acted to the hilt by Marjorie Rambeau, who later was to play Miss Dressler's Tugboat Annie character in a sequel called *Tugboat Annie Sails Again* (1940).

Producer: MGM. **Director:** George Hill. **Scriptwriters:** Frances Marion and Marion Jackson. **Principal Players:** Marie Dressler, Wallace Beery, Dorothy Jordan and Marjorie Rambeau. **Running time:** 69 minutes. **Released:** MGM.

WHOOPEE

Despite a swing by the public away from the musicals that had abounded in the first years of sound, Florenz Ziegfeld and Sam Goldwyn starred the stage comedian Eddie Cantor in an elaborate production in Technicolor (then a two-color process). It was called *Whoopee,* which was also the title of a song featured in the film that has become a standard over the decades. *Whoopee* was a musical comedy by William Anthony McGuire based on Owen Davis' stage play *The Nervous Wreck.*

Cantor had appeared in silent films, notably a version of his stage hit *Kid Boots.* It took the talkies to make him a major film star, however, and *Whoopee* provided the breakthrough. Cantor sang the title number in one of the longest song sequences on record, but audiences liked it, and him.

He was the hero but also a comic in the role of a hypochondriac who brings ridiculous situations upon himself because of his imaginary ill health. The biggest laugh is produced when he explains how he could die from any one of his six ailments in no time at all.

Cantor is an acquired taste, but he made several other film musicals that enjoyed success: *Palmy Days, The Kid From Spain, Roman Scandals* and *Kid Millions,* among the most notable.

The dance numbers were arranged by Busby Berkeley, brought to Hollywood from Broadway by the producers. He was later to go to Warner Bros. where his revolutionary methods of direction were given full rein.

Producers: Florenz Ziegfeld and Samuel Goldwym. **Director:** Thornton Freeland. **Scriptwriter:** William Conselman. **Principal Players:** Eddie Cantor, Eleanor Hunt, Paul Gregory and John Rutherford. **Running time:** 94 minutes. **Released:** United Artists.

DISRAELI

When sound forced Hollywood to drop many of their top silent-movie stars (whose voices were unsuitable or didn't respond to training as quickly as the moguls wished), the film makers turned to the New York stage

Disraeli with Florence and George Arliss.

Edward G. Robinson in *Little Caesar.*

for talent. One of the first actors snagged by Warner Bros. was George Arliss, a distinguished gentleman who had made his reputation in such stage classics of the day as *The Second Mrs. Tanqueray* and *Hedda Gabler,* working with such luminaries as Mrs. Fiske and Jeanne Eagels.

His greatest stage success was in *Disraeli* (of which he had made a silent film version in 1921), and that is the property with which he was launched on the sound screen. He won an Oscar. It was the first of a series of "prestige" pictures in which he was starred, the most popular of which was *The Man Who Played God.* Arliss had great influence in the making of his films, choosing the casts for the most part himself and selecting almost invariably players with stage training. For the ingenue in the last named picture, he chose a new actress with three years' stage experience before she came to Hollywood. Her name was Bette Davis.

Disraeli was highly regarded by critics of the day, one of them remarking that the Arliss performance, "like the Magna Carta, the Declaration of Independence and documents in kind, is a thing to be put under glass and preserved for your children and mine and their children's children and so on, so long as the English language is spoken and English history is considered important." It hasn't worked out quite that way; only three decades later, the Arliss acting style was regarded as fustian.

Producer: Warner Bros. **Director:** Alfred E. Green. **Scriptwriter:** Julien Josephson. **Principal Players:** George Arliss, Joan Bennett, Anthony Bushnell and Doris Lloyd. **Running time:** 89 minutes. **Released:** Warner Bros.

LITTLE CAESAR

A tide of prison pictures (*The Last Mile, Numbered Men, The Big House,* among others) had run into difficulties with state censorship boards in 1930, but that did not deter Warner Bros. from starting a new trend late in the year—the gangster movie with sound. This generally showed the criminal outside the prison walls, and while he was punished at the end, the unfortunate effect was nearly always to glamorize him in the process. It marked the beginning of the "anti-hero."

Sound meant dialogue, and a new patois was created with *Little Caesar.* Expressions like "being taken for a ride" and "dishing it out" became part of the everyday language of Americans.

Little Caesar had the perfect actor to introduce the new style in Edward G. Robinson as the small-time crook with big-time ambitions which he realizes temporarily only to be shot down by his own kind. (The film ends with one of the most famous tag lines in screen history: "Mother of God, is this the end of Rico?") Robinson set up an image in this film which became so popular he was forced to repeat it to the point of parody: the tough-talking, thumb-gesturing, short and stocky hood. Everybody else in the cast was overshadowed—especially Douglas Fairbanks, Jr., who seemed out of place as the gangster friend of Robinson who tries to go straight.

The mastermind behind *Little Caesar* was Mervyn LeRoy, who had directed fourteen pictures (*Harold Teen, Naughty Baby* and others) before this gangster

Rear Admiral Byrd (center) and two of his assistants in a poster for the documentary *With Byrd at the South Pole.*

Marlene Dietrich in *The Blue Angel.*

film brought him to major prominence. It was he who saw the potential in the W. R. Burnett novel and persuaded Warners to let him make it.

Producer: Warner Bros.–First National. **Director:** Mervyn LeRoy. **Scriptwriter:** Francis Edward Faragoh. **Principal Players:** Edward G. Robinson, Douglas Fairbanks, Jr., Glenda Farrell and Sidney Blackmer. **Running time:** 81 minutes. **Released:** First National.

WITH BYRD AT THE SOUTH POLE

When Rear Admiral Byrd made his famous expedition to the Antarctic, Paramount sent along two cameramen to record it. The footage was edited to a feature eighty-two minutes long and, while the results have never been ranked by critics with the documentary work of Robert J. Flaherty, it drew large audiences in the summer of 1930, attracting many of those moviegoers who will turn out only for something off the beaten track.

Willard VanderVeer and Joseph T. Rucker were the cameramen who photographed everything from the departure of the expedition from New York to the activities on the high seas and the landing and exploration of the South Pole. Narration was by Floyd Gibbons, war correspondent and radio announcer.

There were cute touches that foreshadowed techniques of Walt Disney's nature films in shots of the penguins, seals and sharks. The picture won an Oscar for its cinematography.

THE BLUE ANGEL

Joseph von Sternberg had already made seven silent films in Hollywood (*Underworld, Docks of New York* and *The Last Command* among them) when he went to Germany in 1929 to direct Emil Jannings in this picture at the request of Jannings himself. Ironically, *The Blue Angel* is most remembered today as the film that catapulted Marlene Dietrich to worldwide fame for her vivid portrayal of the sultry cabaret singer who destroys the naive, sexually obsessed professor. But Jannings came in for his share of praise, and deservedly so: The actor made the degradation of the hero one of the most harrowing of such studies in screen history.

Perceptive critics of the time also lauded von Sternberg for directing a film rich in pictorial images and not at all static, as were most of the early sound pictures. He shot two versions of the film, one in German and one in English.

Having made Miss Dietrich a star, von Sternberg brought her to Hollywood, where he cast her in a series of films (*Morocco, Dishonored,* etc.) that were chiefly empty vehicles to show off her beauty. The scene of Miss Dietrich singing "Falling in Love Again" in the smoke-filled dive in Berlin in *The Blue Angel* remains the most vivid and enduring image the public has of her today.

Producer: Erich Pommer. **Director:** Joseph von Sternberg. **Scriptwriters:** von Sternberg, Carl Zuckmayer, Karl Vollmoller and Robert Liebman. **Principal Players:** Emil Jannings, Marlene Dietrich, Hans Alber and Kurt Gerron. **Running time:** 90 minutes. **Released:** Paramount.

Boris Karloff (left) in *Frankenstein,* the most famous horror film in the history of the screen.

1931

As a result of the Depression, box-office receipts were off from 10 percent to 35 percent. Admission prices were very low. How could they be otherwise, wondered a film trade paper columnist, when "Eggs are selling at 10¢ a dozen here in Omaha today"? A National Motion Picture Week was held in November with six million free tickets distributed. Theatres ran trailers featuring Eddie Cantor appealing for funds to aid the nation's unemployed.

Exhibitors also fought various local taxes on admission, asserting that such levies paved the way to "dark houses and Bolshevism." Sixteen theatres in Chicago were bombed in a bitter struggle over the union demand for "two men in the booth"; i.e., two projectionists on duty. Property damage was estimated in the millions, and at least one man died. But neither low grosses, taxes, nor union troubles ruffled Will Hays' optimism: "The motion picture industry has met successfully the business emergencies of the last eighteen months and the road ahead promises solid achievement but there are no bonanzas on the horizon."

Large circuits planned construction programs, and low costs—except for the most opulent theatres—encouraged the development. Average construction costs, exclusive of the architect's fee, were: for an 800-seat theatre in a small town, $65,000; for 1,500 seats in a medium-size city, $200,000 and for a deluxe theatre seating 3,500 in a major city, $3,000,000.

The larger first-run theatres in major cities still had live "prologues" presented before the feature. Many other theatres still employed organists. But Joseph M. Schenck, a producer, predicted a trend to smaller and more intimate theatres. "Prologues in these new theatres will be a thing of the past," he asserted. Yet 3,135 theatres were living in the past, able to show only silent films. An equal number of silent theatres had gone dark, financially unable to convert to sound.

In Hollywood, Joe Brandt of Columbia made a call, one frequently echoed over the years, for fewer and better pictures. The status of the writer began to receive greater recognition because improvisation on the set, practical and commonplace in silent films, was both dramatically unsatisfactory and costly in talking production. But few films were yet made in the newly developed color processes, because costs were so high. The average production dollar was spent as follows: players, 25¢; overhead, 20¢; sets, 19¢; director, 10¢; script, 10¢; locations, 8¢; film stock, 5¢; and costumes, 3¢.

Public outcries about objectionable titles was a concern to the trade. Samuel L. "Roxy" Rothafel changed the name of the Christmas week attraction at the Roxy in New York from *Part Time Wife* to *The Shepper-Newfounder*. He argued that the original title would keep children and their parents away. His business judgment was vindicated by the fact the picture grossed $140,000 in ten days, the best box-office performance in New York that year.

Stars of the year: Janet Gaynor, Charles Farrell, Joan Crawford, Norma Shearer, Marie Dressler, Wallace Beery, Clara Bow, Al Jolson, Colleen Moore and Greta Garbo.

Duncan Renaldo, Edwina Booth and Harry Carey in *Trader Horn*.

Frankenstein with Colin Clive and Boris Karloff.

TRADER HORN

Stories of the making of *Trader Horn* are just as intriguing—maybe more so—than the picture itself. This was the first expedition made by a Hollywood company to Africa (a place for which California had often substituted in previous films).

The press duly recorded the journey step by step, from the sailing from New York on March 29, 1929, to the arrival in Le Havre on April 4 and the trips to Genoa, Port Said, Suez and Mombasa, until the company reached Nairobi, where the base was established. The log of director W. S. Van Dyke, "an adventure-drama in itself," was published weekly in no less august a chronicle than *The New York Times*. The picture was two years in the making and cost almost a million and a half dollars—a gigantic sum in those days.

Then there was the legend which grew up around the female star of the film—Edwina Booth. She contracted a jungle fever while making the picture and later died—ostensibly from that disease. Or so the legend said. Actually, Miss Booth is still alive, though long retired from films.

As for the picture itself, it was, as had been anticipated, a huge success—a kind of *Bring 'Em Back Alive* with a plot. There were genuine crocodile-infested rivers; there was a battle between a leopard and a hyena; a rhinoceros stampede; and, naturally, the fierce-looking African natives who danced for the camera.

The plot was silly even for its day. It was the story of a sixteen-year-old white girl (Miss Booth) who rules cannibals with a lash in her hands. As one wit of the time put it: "She really is a wonder, blonde skin, snow white, not the slightest sign of tan although she has lived under Africa's tropical sun since she was a baby, walking in her bare feet, wearing nothing but her own golden hair and a little girdle of monkey fur around her waist." She falls in love with a white adventurer and gives up her kingdom for him.

Producer: MGM. **Director:** W. S. Van Dyke. **Scriptwriter:** Richard Schayer. **Principal Players:** Harry Carey, Edwina Booth and Duncan Renaldo. **Running time:** 120 minutes. **Released:** MGM.

FRANKENSTEIN

To advertise their second big horror film, *Frankenstein,* Universal took a more direct approach than they had with *Dracula*. They gave the public a "friendly warning," which went as follows: "If you have a weak heart and cannot stand intense excitement or even shock, we advise you NOT to see this production. If, on the contrary, you like an unusual thrill you will find it in *Frankenstein.*"

It was an effective approach and one that proved durable. They were still using it to sell horror movies in the 1960's.

The public has always tended to confuse Frankenstein, the doctor, with the monster he created, and Boris Karloff has ever since been "Frankenstein" in their minds instead of the machine-made man. Karloff was

The Champ with Wallace Beery (center) and the young Jackie Cooper.

a competent actor who had been mostly restricted to minor roles in movies. To gain fame he had to disguise his pleasant features behind grotesque makeup and portray a weird creature instead of a human being. Despite an occasional straight role on the stage in years thereafter, he was mostly known as the actor no horror film could afford to be without.

Karloff gave a much better performance as the monster than he is sometimes credited with. It was more than a matter of makeup; he used gesture, carriage and voice as well to make the beast come alive.

Like *Dracula, Frankenstein* had previously been a book (Mary Wollstonecraft Shelley) and a play (Peggy Webling). In directing *Frankenstein* James Whale used the camera more inventively than Tod Browning had in *Dracula.*

Producer: Carl Laemmle, Jr. **Director:** James Whale. **Scriptwriters:** Garrett Fort and Francis Edward Faragoh. **Principal Players:** Colin Clive, Mae Clarke, John Boles and Boris Karloff. **Running time:** 71 minutes. **Released:** Universal.

THE CHAMP

Wallace Beery had carved out a career for himself as a "heavy" in films made at Paramount, but it was not until he went to MGM and developed into a "good-bad man" that he became a major star. *The Champ* is typical of the picture with which MGM transformed his image.

Beery is cast as a prize fighter whose career has been ruined by drink. But his young son, played by Jackie Cooper, has such faith in him that the old man finally pulls himself together for a comeback—with fatal results. He wins, but the terrible beating taken in the process causes him to collapse and die in the dressing room, in the arms of his child.

Plainly, this is the stuff of which tear-jerkers are made, and audiences of the day dutifully wept and enjoyed themselves. Beery so endeared himself to them that by 1933 he had joined the ranks of the ten top money-making stars. He was in that select group again in 1934, his pictures over the period also including *Tugboat Annie, Dinner at Eight, The Bowery, Viva Villa* and *Treasure Island.*

Jackie Cooper was a popular juvenile of the day who sprang to attention in *Skippy* in 1931. He and Beery made two other pictures together: *The Bowery* and *Treasure Island.*

The Champ was directed by King Vidor, who had made the fabulous silent hit *The Big Parade.*

The Champ won screenwriter Frances Marion her second Oscar; she had won her first with *The Big House.*

Producer: MGM. **Director:** King Vidor. **Scriptwriter:** Frances Marion. **Principal Players:** Wallace Beery, Jackie Cooper and Irene Rich. **Running time:** 86 minutes. **Released:** MGM.

CIMARRON

In 1931 *Cimarron* was generally considered to be the finest western to reach the screen since *The Covered Wagon* in 1923. A few decades later it was not regarded

Cimarron with Richard Dix, Douglas Scott and Irene Dunne.

Virginia Cherrill and Charles Chaplin in *City Lights.*

so highly; it had been eclipsed many times, notably by *Red River, Shane* and *High Noon,* among others.

Actually *Cimarron* was more soap opera than western. The source was a novel of the same title by Edna Ferber, who did here for Oklahoma and its pioneers what she was to do many years later for Texas in *Giant.*

In typical Ferber fashion, the founding of Oklahoma is merely background to the rocky romance of a young married couple, Yancey and Sabra Cravat. There are subplots galore, and the action spans a period of forty years.

When the picture was remade in 1960 moviegoers were baffled as to why the hero kept deserting his family for long periods of time—to go off to a couple of wars, and to work in the oil fields. Back in 1931 moviegoers were more gullible and the question didn't arise.

The highlight of both versions comes early in the film—the staging of the land rush as the pioneers furiously drive their wagons to set up claims on the open land. Director Wesley Ruggles made it a much more exciting scene than Anthony Mann did twenty-eight years later.

The original *Cimarron* was a commercial hit; the second was not. A major reason the first did so well was the robust performance of dashing Richard Dix as Yancey. Irene Dunne played Sabra, in her first important screen role.

Producer: RKO. **Director:** Wesley Ruggles. **Scriptwriter:** Howard Estabrook. **Principal Players:** Richard Dix, Irene Dunne, Estelle Taylor, George E. Stone and Edna May Oliver. **Running time:** 124 minutes. **Released:** RKO.

CITY LIGHTS

By this time everybody in the industry had fully converted to sound—except for Charlie Chaplin. He made *City Lights* with himself starred again as the Little Tramp. It was one of his best movies ever, and it outgrossed most of the other films of the day, even though it had no spoken dialogue.

The beginning is endearing as Chaplin mocks the talkies: A statue is in process of being unveiled in a town square with the words of the pompous speakers unintelligible. Then the veil is lifted, and Chaplin is seen cuddled in the arms of the statue.

From that point on Chaplin mixes humor and pathos in his inimitable way as the tramp befriends a blind flower girl who thinks him a man of wealth. He manages to get money for an operation which restores her sight. The sentimental ending is irresistible: Now able to see, she presses a coin into the hand of a forlorn beggar and recognizes her old benefactor by his touch.

The humor is characteristically inventive: A prize fight episode is hilarious pantomime and farce, and the running gag of the millionaire who adores Charlie when drunk, but doesn't even recognize him when sober, is one to treasure.

It was to be five years before Chaplin would be seen in his next film—*Modern Times,* in which he also eschewed spoken dialogue.

Producer-Writer-Director: Charles Chaplin. **Principal Players:** Charles Chaplin, Virginia Cherrill, Florence Lee and Harry Myers. **Running time:** 87 minutes. **Released:** United Artists.

Adolphe Menjou, Pat O'Brien and Maurice Black in *The Front Page.*

Dracula with Bela Lugosi.

THE FRONT PAGE

Pat O'Brien made his motion picture debut in this version of the Broadway hit play by Ben Hecht and Charles MacArthur about the Chicago newspaper world. But it was Adolphe Menjou who ran away with the film in a casting switch from the worldly, sophisticated men he usually played. As the hardboiled city editor who schemes and connives to keep his star reporter (O'Brien) on the job, he snarled the slangy and biting dialogue with impressive verve.

Directed by Lewis Milestone, the picture was so successful it set a trend. Later in 1931, Warner Bros. released *Five Star Final,* which purported to be an indictment of tabloid journalism (and was hailed as such by some members of the press, while others tried to get it banned). Two years after that, Warners released *Hi, Nellie,* in which Paul Muni played a managing editor demoted to lovelorn columnist who redeems himself by playing detective and clearing the name of a dead man believed to be a criminal. Most newspaper men thought this film sheer hokum.

In 1940 Columbia remade *The Front Page* with the O'Brien character transformed into a woman played by Rosalind Russell, and the title changed to *His Girl Friday.* Cary Grant was cast as the managing editor whom she has divorced but remarries when he convinces her that reporting is in her blood. Again dialogue was predominant, but Howard Hawks kept things moving with even more zest than Milestone had managed.

Attesting even further to the durability of the Hecht-MacArthur work was an extremely successful revival of *The Front Page* on Broadway in 1969.

Producer: Caddo. **Director:** Lewis Milestone. **Scriptwriter:** Bartlett Cormack. **Principal Players:** Adolphe Menjou, Pat O'Brien, Mary Brian, Edward Everett Horton and Walter Catlett. **Running time:** 90 minutes. **Released:** United Artists.

DRACULA

Moviegoers unfamiliar with the Bram Stoker novel and the stage play adapted from it by Hamilton Deane and John L. Balderston must have been mystified by the advertisements for the picture as to what it was all about. These proclaimed it as the "story of the strangest passion the world has ever known"—a slogan that has seldom been matched for euphemism. Dracula's passion for women, of course, was restricted to biting them in the throat with his fangs, so he could then drain the blood from their bodies.

Anyhow, word soon got around and the public discovered for itself the difference between a vamp like Theda Bara and a vampire. Universal had an enormous hit on its hands—so big it put them in the horror film business on a large scale. *Dracula* went to theatres at the beginning of 1931, and at the end of that year Universal released *Frankenstein.* Decades later they retained their status as the two most famous horror pictures ever made.

Tod Browning, a specialist in the bizarre, directed *Dracula,* and created an eerie atmosphere that fit the

The Public Enemy with Mae Clarke and James Cagney.

plot perfectly. Unfortunately, the action tended to be choppy rather than fluid, and the film has a stagy look. What holds it together is the performance of Bela Lugosi in the leading role. He had played it on the boards (in New York and on tour) for three years, and had made it his alone. No other actor who played the role in subsequent film remakes and imitations ever approached him for the chilling and ominous feelings his mere presence aroused in the audience.

In 1969 a British company announced it planned to make the "definitive" version of *Dracula*. With Lugosi dead, how could they?

Producer: Carl Laemmle, Jr. **Director:** Tod Browning. **Scriptwriter:** Garrett Fort. **Principal Players:** Bela Lugosi, Helen Chandler, David Manners, Dwight Frye and Edward Van Sloan. **Running time:** 75 minutes. **Released:** Universal.

THE PUBLIC ENEMY

When James Cagney, playing a young hoodlum, smashed half a grapefruit into the face of Mae Clarke, his moll, history was made on two counts. First, the screen acquired an important new male star. Second, female characters were in for much rougher treatment from males on the screen than they had ever had before. Equality for women was now recognized in more than one sense!

The gangster cycle had been started by Warner Bros. the year before with *Little Caesar*. Now *The Public Enemy* pushed it even further in several directions, especially in the depiction of violence. Nothing in the previous picture had quite the same shattering (some said nauseating) impact as the final scene in *The Public Enemy* in which Cagney, kidnapped from a hospital bed, is delivered dead, plaster cast and all, to his family with the corpse toppling into the camera lens.

A postscript to *The Public Enemy* said the producers wanted to "depict honestly an environment that exists today in certain strata of American life, rather than glorify the hoodlum or the criminal." The film had a different effect: Cagney was playful and dynamic, and so much more appealing than the characters opposed to him that audiences rooted for him in spite of themselves.

A few years later Cagney was to reform on screen in *G-Men* (1935), and become one of the top box-office stars in the country. From 1939 to 1943 he placed among the top ten in the *Motion Picture Herald* poll of exhibitors, his greatest triumph being *Yankee Doodle Dandy* in 1942.

Producer: Warner Bros. **Director:** William A. Wellman. **Scriptwriter:** Harvey Thew. **Principal Players:** James Cagney, Jean Harlow, Edward Wood, Joan Blondell, Donald Cook and Mae Clarke. **Running time:** 83 minutes. **Released:** Warner Bros.

DADDY LONG LEGS

Feminine virtues of goodness, sweetness and wholesomeness had been epitomized on the silent screen by Mary Pickford. The image was still popular in the

Daddy Long Legs with Warner Baxter, Janet Gaynor and Edwin Maxwell.

early years of sound and the mantle was passed to Janet Gaynor.

Miss Gaynor began her career in silent films, first coming to major attention in *The Johnstown Flood* (1926). The following year fame was assured with her performance of the forlorn waif in *Seventh Heaven,* in which she co-starred with Charles Farrell. They became an extremely popular romantic team, appearing in musicals together as well as in love stories (*Sunny Side Up, Lucky Star, Delicious,* etc.).

Typical of the pictures in which the Gaynor charm was exploited is *Daddy Long Legs,* a Cinderella tale (from a novel by Jean Webster) about an orphan adopted by a millionaire who doesn't let her know who is responsible for her good fortune until curtain time—when, of course, both are beautifully in love. Ruth Chatterton played the part on the stage, and Mary Pickford did it on the silent screen.

Farrell apparently being too close to Miss Gaynor's own age to be convincing in this May-September romance, Warner Baxter was selected as her co-star. They, too, made a congenial team.

Miss Gaynor rode the crest of public favor for several years, appearing high on the *Motion Picture Herald* top star list from 1932 through 1934. In 1937 she was in *A Star Is Born,* and her performance as the small-town girl who realizes her dream of making it big in Hollywood is generally regarded as her best.

In 1955, 20th Century-Fox set *Daddy Long Legs* to music with considerable success. Leslie Caron took the updated Gaynor role, and Fred Astaire replaced Baxter.

Producer: Fox. **Director:** Alfred Santell. **Scriptwriter:** Sonya Levien. **Principal Players:** Janet Gaynor, Warner Baxter, Una Merkel and John Arledge. **Running time:** 80 minutes. **Released:** 20th Century-Fox.

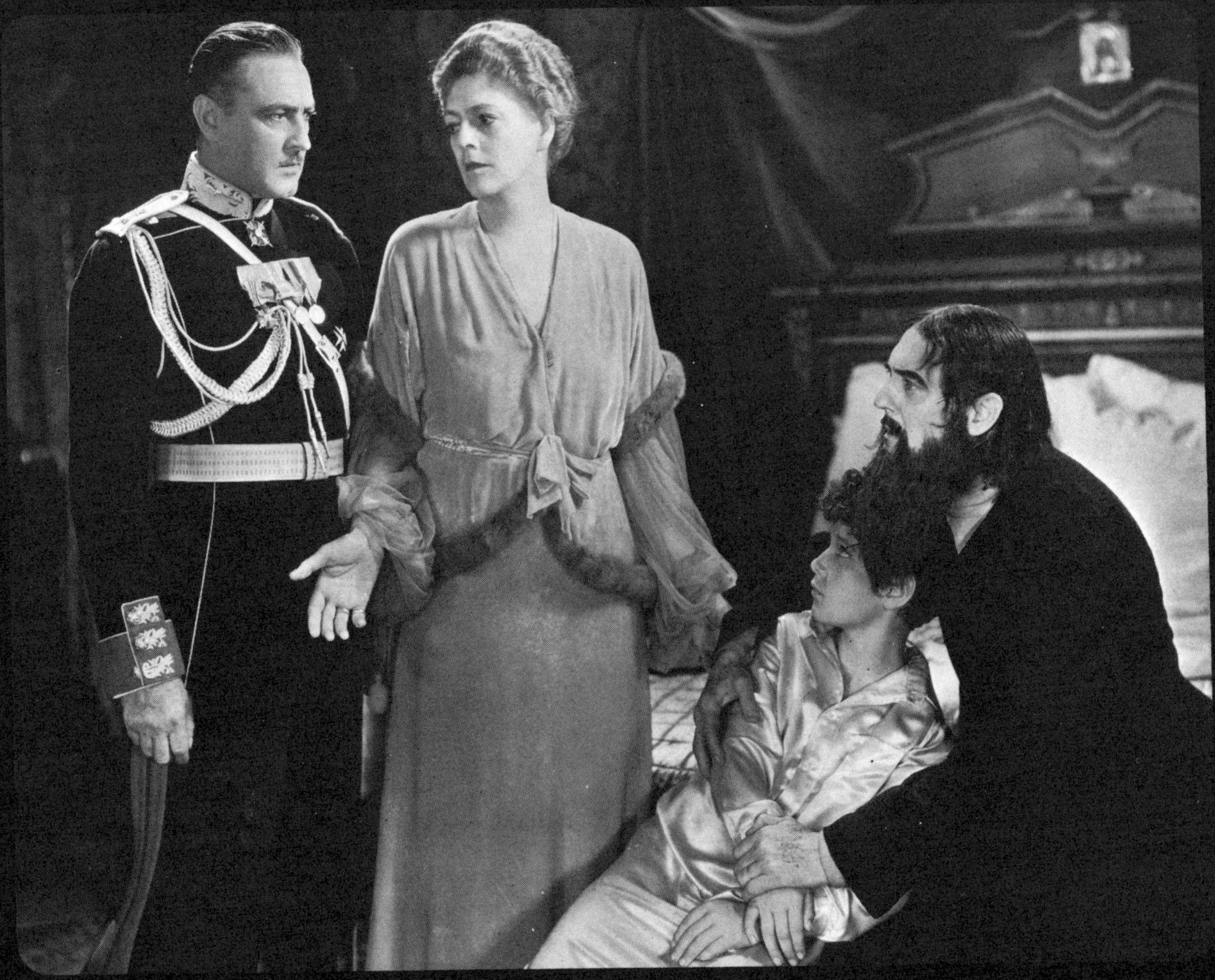

John Barrymore, Ethel Barrymore, Tad Alexander and Lionel Barrymore in *Rasputin and the Empress*, the only feature the three famous Barrymores ever made together.

1932

Movies did much to maintain flagging morale as the country and the world sank deeper and deeper into the Depression. With apples being sold at a nickel each by the unemployed on many street corners, discouraged job hunters often went to a theatre just to keep warm. Often they also found their spirits were somewhat revived by spending two hours in the world of fantasy in the company of stars they knew and loved. Nevertheless, attendance fell sharply, and many communities developed plans to provide free tickets to the jobless. In some places, vaudeville acts were used to bolster falling attendance, but live acts never regained the appeal they had in the pre-sound era. Some fifteen hundred theatres still operating were too poor even to offer sound movies, let alone vaudeville or any other "extra" attraction.

Partially as a result of the economic squeeze in Hollywood, the number of imported films rose sharply, up to 150 from 120 in 1931. But the average distributor's gross film rental for a foreign film for the entire United States was between ten and twenty thousand dollars. The most successful import was the English-made *The Dreyfus Case,* which took in a record $200,000 in distributor's gross. The foreign language sensation was *Zwei Herzen in 3/4 Takt* (*Two Hearts in 3/4 Time*), which grossed $80,000.

In Christmas-holiday week two magnificent modern theatres opened in Rockefeller Center. One was the 6,200 seat Radio City Music Hall, which was built for stage "presentation" shows only. Films were not part of the original program planned by Samuel L. "Roxy" Rothafel. The other theatre was of 3,700 seats and called the RKO Roxy. Later it was named the Center Theatre and was a model of what a large movie theatre should be like, from its opening with *The Animal Kingdom* until after World War II, when it was clawed out of its site on the lower floors of a building to make more office space.

It seems ironic that at first no one knew what to do with the Radio City Music Hall, though it was destined to become the world's prime theatre showing feature films. Of the original stage acts only the melodic Tuskegee Choir had the presence to fill the gigantic stage; most vaudeville acts were simply lost there. All kinds of suggestions were made to the owners, the Rockefellers. Some urged it to be made into a parking garage. But within a few weeks the feature was moved from the RKO Roxy down Sixth Avenue to the Music Hall, and ever since the Showplace of the Nation has had a program of a feature film and a one-hour stage show.

This was also the year of William Fox's attempted comeback. Had things gone as planned he would have had the film world in his palm, for he threatened to sue more than a hundred companies for infringement of his Tri-Ergon patents. The patents covered a flywheel device used in recording and reproduction, and a method of combining picture and sound on the final release print. There was some cause for alarm because Fox was proceeding on the basis of patents issued to him by the U.S. Patent Office at the order of Judge Jesse Adkins late in 1931.

More Washington trouble came in the form of a vicious attack by Senator Smith W. Brookhart of Iowa who accused the movie industry of immorality and unfair trade practices and called for corrective action by Congress.

Stars of the year: Marie Dressler, Janet Gaynor, Joan Crawford, Charles Farrell, Greta Garbo, Norma Shearer, Wallace Beery, Clark Gable, Will Rogers and Joe E. Brown.

Helen Vinson and Paul Muni in *I Am a Fugitive From a Chain Gang.*

Shooting Frank Buck's *Bring 'Em Back Alive.*

I AM A FUGITIVE FROM A CHAIN GANG

Mervyn LeRoy had started a trend to gangster movies with *Little Caesar* two years before; now he started another: films indicting social injustices. If *I Am a Fugitive From a Chain Gang* had not been so successful, it is doubtful whether he could have made *They Won't Forget* (an attack on lynching) or that MGM would have backed *Fury* (a study of mob rule) or even that 20th Century-Fox would have made *The Grapes of Wrath* eight years later.

The exposé of inhuman conditions on the chain gangs in Southern prison camps was inspired by a book by one Robert E. Burns (a pseudonym) that purported to be his own story written after he had escaped from such a jail. He was said to still be sought as a fugitive by the authorities at the time the picture was released—a timely element that no doubt had much to do with the popularity of the film.

LeRoy has contended that the picture was responsible for chain gangs being taken off the road in Georgia. That may be an exaggeration, but there is no question that it aroused public concern over the brutal practices depicted, and that newspapers published editorials calling attention to the film and its subject matter.

A strong share for the impact of the picture must be credited to the performance of Paul Muni as the man who is committed to prison for a crime he did not commit (which admittedly stacked the cards a bit), endures barbaric treatment at the hands of sadistic guards, makes a desperate escape and then lives in constant fear of being captured and returned to that hell. Many feel this is Muni's top screen performance, far superior to his characterizations of Pasteur and Zola.

Producer: Warner Bros. **Director:** Mervyn LeRoy. **Scriptwriters:** Sheridan Gibney and Robert Holmes. **Principal Players:** Paul Muni, Glenda Farrell, Helen Vinson and Preston Foster. **Running time:** 90 minutes. **Released:** Warner Bros.

BRING 'EM BACK ALIVE

Famed explorer Frank Buck wrote about his adventures with wild animals in the Malayan jungles in a book (co-authored by Edward Anthony) called *Bring 'Em Back Alive*. It became a best seller. Promotion of the film led the public to believe it had been photographed not only on the spot but at the time it happened. ("Every frame of this picture actually made in the jungle," proclaimed the ads.)

Actually, the events were all re-staged—not in Malaya, but in a compound adjacent to the city of Singapore where trappers brought their wares for sale to circus agents and buyers. Sequences from the book were performed for the camera under conditions described as "reasonably safe."

Before this became common knowledge in the film trade there had been skeptics, some of whom pointed out that Mr. Buck's makeup was suspiciously unruffled throughout. Terry Ramsaye commented: "The artificialities of the radio announcer's word and voice, which

Dr. Jekyll and Mr. Hyde with Fredric March and Miriam Hopkins.

purports to be Mr. Buck's, represent endeavors at theatricalism which have no bearing on the animal components of the picture, which constitute its chief claim to attention."

The public couldn't have cared less; it found the picture exciting, particularly a fight between a thirty-foot python and a Royal Bengal tiger. Other highlights included invasions of villages by "man-eating cats"; elephants on the rampage; and a giant crocodile devouring a black panther.

Producer: Van Beuren Corp. **Director:** Clyde E. Elliott. **Running time:** 70 minutes. **Released:** RKO.

DR. JEKYLL AND MR. HYDE

The horror film cycle, started the previous year with *Dracula* and *Frankenstein,* got another push forward with this remake of the old Robert Louis Stevenson thriller which had been filmed several times during the silent era. (John Barrymore starred in a 1920 version.) This first sound version was praised at the time, and when MGM did it again in 1941 with Spencer Tracy, critics compared the two, giving the nod on almost all counts to the 1932 version.

Fredric March starred on this occasion in the dual role, and his much-admired performance won him an Oscar (in a tie with Wallace Beery in *The Champ*). The performance, however, owed more than a little to the makeup men and to the ingenious method by which director Rouben Mamoulian worked out the transformation of Dr. Jekyll into Mr. Hyde. As late as 1967 Mamoulian refused to divulge exactly how he achieved the effects whereby the actor's face gradually changed in such a realistic fashion "right before the eyes of the audience," as it were. Experts have speculated that it was a matter of special makeup, and colored lights and filters.

Mamoulian was one of the first directors to use sound imaginatively; here he produced a chilling effect during the transformation scenes by magnifying the sound of a heart beat several times. He also employed a screen divided diagonally to show two simultaneous actions.

This popular film made a full-fledged motion picture star of March and also aided the career of Miriam Hopkins, who played the hapless Ivy murdered by Mr. Hyde.

Producer: Paramount. **Director:** Rouben Mamoulian. **Scriptwriters:** Samuel Hoffenstein and Percy Heath. **Principal Players:** Fredric March, Miriam Hopkins and Rose Hobart. **Running time:** 85 minutes. **Released:** Paramount.

A FAREWELL TO ARMS

Ernest Hemingway's novel of a love affair in World War I between a lieutenant and a nurse was considerably expurgated for the screen and then turned into a rather conventional romance. It was helped at the box office by the casting of Helen Hayes as Catherine Barkley. Miss Hayes, a popular stage actress who rose to fame in the twenties, had resisted overtures made by

A Farewell to Arms with Helen Hayes and Gary Cooper.

Henry Victor, Harry Earles and Olga Baclanova in *Freaks.*

Hollywood until 1931 when she agreed to appear in *The Sin of Madelon Claudet.* She won an Oscar the very first time out. After *A Farewell to Arms* she alternated films with stage work for several years, but she never became the big commercial draw in movies that she was on Broadway. She said in 1956 that her final film performance would be in *Anastasia,* but in 1969 she changed her mind and accepted a character role in *Airport.*

The story is quite different for her co-star in the Hemingway picture. Lt. Frederick Henry was portrayed by Gary Cooper, who was to become one of Hollywood's top box-office stars of all time. He placed in the *Motion Picture Herald* poll of exhibitors for eighteen years, making his first appearance in 1936 and his last in 1958. This is a record that has been surpassed by only two other actors—John Wayne and Bing Crosby—and equalled by no actress.

Farewell to Arms was directed by Frank Borzage, a specialist in love stories (*Seventh Heaven, A Man's Castle, Little Man, What Now?, Three Comrades, I've Always Loved You,* etc.).

In 1958 Charles Vidor directed an elaborate new production of *A Farewell to Arms* in which David O. Selznick cast his wife Jennifer Jones in the Catherine role. The actress received some of the worst reviews of her career, as did her co-star, Rock Hudson. The film was not well received by the public, either.

Producer: Paramount. **Director:** Frank Borzage. **Scriptwriters:** Benjamin Glazer and Oliver H. P. Garrett. **Principal Players:** Helen Hayes, Gary Cooper and Adolphe Menjou. **Running time:** 78 minutes. **Released:** Paramount.

FREAKS

American moviegoers (or those of the 1930's at least) liked to be aware that the monsters in films were actually fake. They apparently took comfort in the knowledge that underneath the grotesque makeup of Mr. Hyde lurked the handsome features of Fredric March and that the monster of Frankenstein was merely kindly Boris Karloff under the greasepaint.

Confronted with actual deformed people in *Freaks,* audiences were repelled. To make the picture, Tod Browning scoured circuses the country over and came up with Siamese twins, a bearded lady, an "armless wonder," and assorted midgets and dwarfs. There weren't enough strong stomachs in the audience to make the picture a profitable entry in the horror field for MGM.

One suspects the audience distaste went further than mere revulsion at the spectacle of these unfortunates. Everything that happens in *Freaks* takes place in the real world; it does not venture into the realm of fantasy. It is the story of the terrible revenge a community of circus freaks takes upon a beautiful trapeze performer who marries one of their members for his money and then tries to poison him. The vengeful crew cuts up her face, deforming her so that she becomes, as it were, one of them.

Powerfully told on the screen, the film builds in continual fascination to the horrifying ending which no one who sees it will ever forget. A commercial failure in its day, *Freaks* has become a favorite of film buffs and has

Grand Hotel with Joan Crawford, John Barrymore, Lionel Barrymore and Lewis Stone.

often been revived in New York by Times Square theatres specializing in horror pictures. It is one of those films of obviously dubious commercial potential that make one wonder how they ever got made in Hollywood (*Citizen Kane, The Night of the Hunter, All That Money Can Buy,* etc.).

Producer: MGM. **Director:** Tod Browning. **Scriptwriter:** Willis Goldbeck. **Principal Players:** Wallace Ford, Leila Hyams, Olga Baclanova and Roscoe Ates. **Running time:** 64 minutes. **Released:** MGM.

GRAND HOTEL

The slogan "all-star cast" has been applied over the years to films that really could not justify it, but it was certainly appropriate for MGM's *Grand Hotel,* which was, in fact, the first picture in the sound era to bring together so many major personalities at one time. It was a profitable device and often imitated thereafter by other studios.

The Vicki Baum play is not a work of high art, but it supplies a tremendous showcase for actors. The roles were cast with imagination and played with distinction by seven stars: Greta Garbo, John Barrymore, Joan Crawford, Wallace Beery, Lionel Barrymore, Lewis Stone and Jean Hersholt.

The highest praise went to Garbo for her poignant portrayal of the dancer, near suicide because of her fading career, who is rejuvenated by the hotel burglar known as the Baron. John Barrymore played that role, and their love scenes together were in the grand manner.

The other Barrymore put on quite a show, too, as the ailing provincial type come to the big city for a last fling before he dies. Lionel pulled out all the stops—he was alternately drunk, hostile and cringing, and he made love to Miss Crawford, cast as the stenographer and mistress of businessman Beery.

Miss Baum used the hotel as a kind of microcosm of the world, and the device was often employed again in films, including MGM's *Weekend at the Waldorf* in 1945 and Warner Bros.' *Hotel Berlin* in that same year. *Grand Hotel* deservedly won the Academy Award as best picture of its year.

Producer: MGM. **Director:** Edmund Goulding. **Scriptwriter:** William A. Drake. **Principal Players:** Greta Garbo, John Barrymore, Joan Crawford, Wallace Beery and Lionel Barrymore. **Running time:** 115 minutes. **Released:** MGM.

RASPUTIN AND THE EMPRESS

The title has only two names, but there were three plum roles in the script, and Irving Thalberg pulled a coup: He got the three Barrymores, Ethel, John and Lionel, to play them and appear on the screen together for the first and only time. Ethel was the Czarina; Lionel was Rasputin, the mad monk; and John acted "Prince Chegodieff," a fictional character taking the place of the real slayer of Rasputin.

It was a prestige picture for MGM and a commercial success as well, although not so much as Thalberg had

Rasputin and the Empress with Lionel, John and Ethel Barrymore.

hoped. It is recorded as one of the thirteen top-grossing pictures of 1933 (first released in December, 1932), but it did not make a profit on its investment. The film later became involved in extensive litigation, which was eventually lost by MGM.

Charles MacArthur wrote the screenplay, which treated the Romanoffs sympathetically—an aspect to which the new Russian government of the day and its admirers did not take kindly.

As for the acting, it may have thrilled audiences of the time, but more than three decades later it looks like ham fit for slicing.

Ethel Barrymore rolls her eyes so often, especially when she discovers the true nature of the villainous Rasputin, that it begins to appear she has given the empress an historically inaccurate affliction. Lionel was made up with such florid whiskers he evokes laughter from his first entrance, and John, while more restrained than usual, seems to be spoofing both the role and the audience. The scene in which he murders Rasputin, though accurate, is unintentionally funny: First he poisons him, then he beats him over the head with an iron bar, and then he throws him bodily into the river Neva!

John and Lionel had previously appeared in two pictures together: *Arsene Lupin* (1931) and *Grand Hotel* (1932).

Producer: MGM. **Director:** Richard Boleslawski. **Scriptwriter:** Charles MacArthur. **Principal Players:** John, Ethel and Lionel Barrymore, Ralph Morgan and Diana Wynyard. **Running time:** 127 minutes. **Released:** MGM.

Maureen O'Sullivan and Johnny Weissmuller in *Tarzan, the Ape Man.*

TARZAN, THE APE MAN

No fictional character has been as durable in films as that created by Edgar Rice Burroughs: the English baby lost in the jungle and reared to manhood by apes. They started making movies about him in the days of silent films (Elmo Lincoln was the first, and an outstanding Tarzan), and they were still coming out in the 1960's with an updated hero speaking perfect English instead of the broken dialect that Johnny Weissmuller mastered so well.

Weissmuller was a champion swimmer who made his motion picture debut in *Tarzan, the Ape Man.* It turned out to be ideal casting; experts on the genre still felt in the sixties that he had been the best.

MGM, which had more than its share of troubles when it went to Africa for *Trader Horn,* nonetheless sent cameramen to the dark continent for location work on this picture.

Maureen O'Sullivan made an attractive Jane in the first Weissmuller film and also played in some of the sequels, starting with *Tarzan and His Mate* in 1934 and continuing through *Tarzan's New York Adventure* in 1942.

When Weissmuller abdicated from the role, others took over: Lex Barker, Gordon Scott and Jock Mahoney being among the more notable.

Producer: MGM. **Director:** W. S. Van Dyke. **Scriptwriters:** Cyril Hume and Ivor Novello. **Principal Players:** Johnny Weissmuller, Neil Hamilton, Maureen O'Sullivan and C. Aubrey Smith. **Running time:** 101 minutes. **Released:** MGM.

Maedchen in Uniform with Emilia Unda as the head mistress.

MAEDCHEN IN UNIFORM

It is a long way from the restrained treatment of a lesbian theme in this classic German picture to the explicit love-making scenes of *Therese and Isabelle* in 1968. The older picture achieves a powerful emotional effect through indirection; the other is unabashedly directed to the prurient.

Maedchen in Uniform had been a stage play before it was made into a film in 1931. (It was released in the U.S. a year later.) It was much admired for its indictment of an educational system which sought to dehumanize girls in a boarding school through insistence on strict obedience to authority, and personal self-denial. A sensitive girl starved for affection turns for it to one of the teachers, a woman inclined to be sympathetic to the pupils in defiance of the wishes of the iron-willed head mistress. The girl's feelings for the teacher become so intense that they are interpreted as lesbianism, and rising pressures drive the student to attempt suicide.

The film was shown in large American theatres with subtitles—the first German picture with sound to receive such treatment. The titles were deliberately sparse, so exhibitors took to passing out printed synopses of the story to patrons who might otherwise miss some of the action.

A remake of the picture, also in German, was released here in 1965, starring Lilli Palmer as the teacher (the role Dorothea Wieck had played so memorably the first time) and Romy Schneider as the student (first acted by Hertha Thiele).

Producer: Carl Froelich Studios. **Director:** Leontine Sagan. **Scriptwriters:** Christa Winsloe and F. D. Andam. **Principal Players:** Dorothea Wieck, Hertha Thiele and Emilia Unda. **Running time:** 110 minutes. **Released:** John Krimsky and Gifford Froelich.

King Kong, the most famous of all science fiction movies and never matched for its special effects.

1933

The entertainment world, like every facet of life in the United States, was shaken by the Great Depression and the beginnings of the New Deal which marked 1933. The inauguration of Franklin D. Roosevelt brought into the White House two men from films: Mervin Hunter McIntyre, for years the representative of Pathé News in Washington; and Stephen T. Early, Paramount's representative there. Also, an exhibitor, Frank C. Walker, became executive secretary of the Recovery Council, and later Postmaster General and a power in the Democratic Party.

Roosevelt's dictum, "All we have to fear is fear itself," was as true for the motion picture business as for any other aspect of the economy. When the "bank holiday" was called, some theatres used scrip instead of money. All during the year there were feverish conferences to hammer out a "Blue Eagle" Code for industry trade practices. General Hugh S. Johnson, Recovery Administrator, appointed Sol A. Rosenblatt, a New York lawyer, to preside over the formation of all codes affecting practices in the amusement industries. It was predicted, in hopeful words, that 25,000 new jobs would be created. Before the end of the year President Roosevelt signed the code, and Eddie Cantor, among others, was appointed to the administration of the Fair Practices Code.

High salaries were attacked as "grotesque." At one time the major companies instituted cuts of 50 percent for everyone earning over $50 a week and 25 percent for those under $50. The outcries were great because the contrast between cutting the salary of a clerk making $60 a week in a film exchange, and that of a studio executive earning $3,000 or more, was incredible. But several of the larger companies were in receivership. Theatre admission prices fell, in some cases as much as 50 percent. Major theatre executives pleaded for a floor of twenty cents when some circuits cut to a fifteen-cent top, even in their first-run houses.

In addition to general economic problems, films were hit by the great strength of radio. These were the days of great popularity for Amos 'n Andy. Some theatres had to stop the movie and pick up that show on their loudspeakers.

The repeal of Prohibition caused more competition. Carl Laemmle, head of Universal Pictures, commented: "It is not legalizing of beer and booze which makes me fear a resultant harm to the picture business, but rather the return of the open saloon, whether called a saloon, a drug store or some other kind of store. And don't fool yourself about the competition of beer and pretzels. It's mighty strong competition!"

In Hollywood Sam Goldwyn called for cuts in the cost of production, saying some features cost $600,000 when they should be made for $300,000. However, Hollywood's financial rewards did not filter very far down: Half of all actors got less than $3,000 a year. There were 63 persons in the star category making over $50,000, and 196 featured players with annual incomes ranging from $10,000 to $50,000. Guild and union members received modest compensation. The Motion Picture Laboratory Association, after hard bargaining sessions, finally signed a contract for a forty-hour week at a $15 weekly minimum.

The big names in Hollywood were talking about *Cavalcade,* made by Winfield Sheehan, head of Fox production, at the incredible cost of one million dollars—how could a picture ever get back that sum? Irving Thalberg signed another contract as MGM production executive.

A few in Hollywood, New York and elsewhere were somewhat concerned about whether the recognition of Soviet Russia by the United States would result in the country being flooded by propaganda films.

A preview of stereophonic sound, which was to be a factor in theatres with Cinemascope in twenty years, came in a Washington demonstration by the Bell Telephone Laboratories. Directional sound picked up by microphones in Philadelphia was heard at the Capitol as living sound by those wearing special earphones.

Stars of the year: Marie Dressler, Will Rogers, Janet Gaynor, Eddie Cantor, Wallace Beery, Jean Harlow, Clark Gable, Mae West, Norma Shearer and Joan Crawford.

Norman Foster, Janet Gaynor, Louise Dresser and Will Rogers in *State Fair.*

Cavalcade with Diana Wynyard and Clive Brook.

STATE FAIR

Phil Stong's novel is a minor piece of Americana revolving around the members of a rural family in Iowa: a father whose pride and joy is a pig he has groomed personally to compete for a blue ribbon at the state fair; a mother whose specialty is mincemeat and pickles which she also enters for a prize; a daughter bored with farm life and not responsive to the neighbor who pursues; and a son equally disenchanted who also hopes to find some excitement and romance at the fair.

Who better to play the head of the household than Will Rogers, the much-beloved actor who in his later years came to epitomize the all-American small-town dad? He had started out in vaudeville with an act in which he sat on a pony on the stage, chewed gum, spun a rope and cracked jokes. Later he graduated to the Ziegfeld Follies where, minus the pony, he drawled his amusing comments on topics of the day. He made a silent film for Samuel Goldwyn in 1918—*Laughing Bill Hyde*—which was so successful that the producer signed him to an exclusive film contract, under which he made twelve other features. Other silents followed, and he made his first talkie in 1930 for Fox: *So This Is London.* Thereafter he turned out a string of successes before he died in a plane crash in 1935.

His role in *State Fair* was type casting, and so was the selection of the rest of the cast: sweet Janet Gaynor as the daughter; handsome Norman Foster as the son; and motherly Louise Dresser as the fourth member. Both offspring found romance at the fair in the persons of Lew Ayres and Sally Eilers. It was a high-powered cast, and the box office boomed.

The plot was so slight it seemed ideal for a musical, and it was turned into an engaging one in 1945 with a score by Richard Rodgers and Oscar Hammerstein II, out of which came two perennial songs: "It's a Grand Night for Singing" and "It Might as Well Be Spring." A third remake in 1962 was again a musical, but one less well performed, for which Rodgers wrote five new songs, none of which became hits or improved the show. In the 1945 version the family members were played by Charles Winninger, Fay Bainter, Jeanne Crain and Dick Haymes, with Dana Andrews and Vivian Blaine. In 1962 there were Tom Ewell, Alice Faye, Pamela Tiffin and Pat Boone, with Bobby Darin and Ann-Margret.

Producer-Director: Henry King. **Screenplay:** Sonya Levien and Paul Green. **Principal Players:** Janet Gaynor, Will Rogers, Louise Dresser, Norman Foster, Lew Ayres and Sally Eilers. **Running time:** 100 minutes. **Released:** Fox.

CAVALCADE

Cavalcade shows the procession of history and its effects upon the London household of the Marryot family. It starts with the Boer War (during the siege of Mafeking) and proceeds to record such epochal events as the death of Queen Victoria, World War I, the sinking of the Titanic and the birth of jazz—through all of which the hero and heroine keep a stiff upper lip.

This discursive tribute to the legend of British tenac-

42nd Street with Warner Baxter, Ruby Keeler, Bebe Daniels and Dick Powell.

ity was written as a stage play by Noel Coward, who is much better known for his light comedies of manners: *Private Lives, Design for Living,* and *Fallen Angels.* (He was to turn to more serious drama again during World War II with the film *In Which We Serve.*)

Cavalcade was made in Hollywood at the Fox West Coast Studios, with, however, a cast almost exclusively English, headed by Diana Wynyard and Clive Brook.

Though little shown or remembered today, *Cavalcade* was considered something of a sensation at the time. It opened at the Gaiety Theatre on Broadway, and the press was respectful. The Academy of Motion Picture Arts and Sciences went even further; it named *Cavalcade* best picture of the year.

The British were naturally even more responsive to this patriotic pageant. The play had run in London for four hundred performances (in eleven months) and the film did comparably well when it appeared.

Producer: Fox Films. **Director:** Frank Lloyd. **Scriptwriter:** Reginald Berkeley. **Principal Players:** Diana Wynyard, Clive Brook, Ursula Jeans, Herbert Mundin and Una O'Connor. **Running time:** 110 minutes. **Released:** Fox.

42ND STREET

Sound brought a flood of musicals in its wake, and one of the first film "originals"—as distinguished from a hit show transplanted from the stage—was *42nd Street.* Its plot came from a novel by Bradford Ropes which recounted the trials and tribulations of producing a musical comedy on Broadway. The format and characters have been imitated ever since.

Warner Baxter played the harried stage manager who, though his health is failing, is determined to do one more show before he retires; Bebe Daniels was the big star who breaks an ankle at the last minute; Ruby Keeler was the unknown who steps into the leading role; Guy Kibbee, the nervous "angel"; Dick Powell, the singing juvenile; and Una Merkel and Ginger Rogers, the tough chorus girls with hearts of gold. And so on.

Three decades later, audiences who saw *42nd Street* in revival could only laugh at the naiveté of the story and the overly elaborate production numbers, oblivious to the enthusiasm with which it was received in its day. In the 1960's the genre was ridiculed in an off-Broadway show called *Dames at Sea,* with Miss Keeler, as the sweet ingenue, coming in for the strongest kidding.

In addition to establishing Miss Keeler and Powell as a musical comedy team, *42nd Street* marked the debut at Warner Bros. of Busby Berkeley, the dance director, whose imaginative way with the camera (shooting numbers from angles no one had even dreamed of using before) set a new style in spectacular production numbers. He had previously worked for other studios which had not permitted him to let his imagination run as wild as Jack Warner did.

Producer: Warner Bros. **Director:** Lloyd Bacon. **Scriptwriters:** Rian James and James Seymour. **Principal Players:** Warner Baxter, Bebe Daniels, George Brent, Una Merkel, Ruby Keeler, Guy Kibbee, Dick Powell and Ginger Rogers. **Running time:** 89 minutes. **Released:** Warner Bros.

Frances Dee, Mabel Colcord, Joan Bennett, Jean Parker and Katharine Hepburn in *Little Women*.

LITTLE WOMEN

Katharine Hepburn, who came to Hollywood from a brief stage career, had made her mark as a "modern" woman in her debut film, *A Bill of Divorcement* (1932). In 1933 she made three pictures, in two of which her parts were women of the same type: *Christopher Strong* and *Morning Glory*. (Her performance as the aspiring actress in the second won her an Academy Award.)

Her third film of the year was *Little Women*, a costume drama, but she made of the tomboy, Jo, the same kind of headstrong, independent female she had previously played so well.

In fact it was Miss Hepburn's presence in that key role, as much as anything else, that put the picture in the top-grossing category. She helped take the edge off the sentimentality. The film was, in addition, a tasteful and reasonably restrained production of the Louisa May Alcott tale of four contrasting daughters and their beloved "Marmee." It is another of those films that are very much a part of their era; a remake in 1949 with June Allyson cast as Jo was dated and too sticky for latter-day tastes.

But moviegoers of the thirties, as one reviewer put it, "saw that the hearts of little women of yesterday were no different from the hearts of little women today."

Producer: Merian C. Cooper. **Director:** George Cukor. **Scriptwriters:** Sarah Y. Mason and Victor Heerman. **Principal Players:** Katharine Hepburn, Joan Bennett, Paul Lukas, Frances Dee, Jean Parker and Edna May Oliver. **Running time:** 107 minutes. **Released:** RKO.

Fay Wray and Bruce Cabot in *King Kong*.

KING KONG

The critics who have deplored both the paucity of ideas and the phoniness of the sentiments in many of Hollywood's pictures have had to stop their sniping when it comes to technical expertise. And none of Hollywood's special effects have been so universally admired as those achieved by Willis O'Brien in *King Kong*—not, at least, until Stanley Kubrick's *2001: A Space Odyssey* appeared in 1968.

Using stop-action model animation, O'Brien made King Kong and other denizens of the jungle come alive as many live actors in other fictional films had failed to do. In fact, King Kong seemed so real he became beloved; when he wept at the end, so did many in the audience. (Who could ever warm up to Dracula or to Frankenstein's creation—except to feel a vague pity for the latter?)

The idea for this most popular of all science fiction stories of the thirties (and even later) came from novelist Edgar Wallace and producer Merian C. Cooper (the latter known for the classic documentary *Grass*). A gigantic ape is brought back from Africa but escapes and nearly destroys New York City, ending up on top of the Empire State Building with Fay Wray in his massive paws while a squadron of airplanes shoot him down with machine guns. No one who has thrilled to those climactic moments will ever forget them.

Some critics like to read deeper meanings into the film, seeing it on the one hand as a parable of Beauty and the Beast in which the latter is destroyed rather than

I'm No Angel with Mae West.

The Private Life of Henry VIII with Charles Laughton.

transformed by his love. Others, like Bosley Crowther, have suggested audiences took King Kong to their hearts because they, too, felt oppressed by the Depression days which were still upon them. In other words, they empathized.

Ordinary moviegoers have had the best idea: Sit back and enjoy one of the most entertaining fantasies the medium has ever had to offer.

Producer-Director: Merian C. Cooper and Ernest Schoedsack. **Scriptwriters:** James Creelman and Ruth Rose. **Principal Players:** Fay Wray, Robert Armstrong and Bruce Cabot. **Running time:** 100 minutes. **Released:** RKO.

I'M NO ANGEL

Mae West burst upon the Hollywood scene in 1932 in a small role in *Night After Night,* with a line that has become a classic and sums up her ribald approach to life. An admiring female character comments on Miss West's attire: "Goodness, what beautiful diamonds!" Replies that volatile lady: "Goodness had nothing to do with it."

Miss West rolled her eyes and swayed her hips, and a new movie star was born. In *Night After Night* she was billed fourth, under George Raft, Constance Cummings and Wynne Gibson. The next year came *She Done Him Wrong* (an adaptation of her play *Diamond Lil*) and *I'm No Angel*—and she was second to none on the marquee. (In the former she spoke those other immortal words: "Come up and see me sometime.")

Miss West wrote the script of *I'm No Angel,* taking credit for the dialogue, which was her specialty. It was really a one-woman show, for she saw to it that she was on screen for 99 percent of the running time.

The part she wrote for herself was tailor-made—a gold digger, the role she played in variations throughout her career. Here she is the star attraction in a small-time traveling circus who zooms to the big time. At one point, as "queen of the iron cage," she sticks her head into the mouth of a ferocious lion!

Typical, too, is the courtroom scene in which she is on trial for breach of promise. She acts as her own lawyer with hilarious results.

Romantic interest was supplied by Cary Grant, who also had been in *She Done Him Wrong.*

Producer: Paramount. **Director:** Wesley Ruggles. **Scriptwriter:** Mae West. **Principal Players:** Mae West, Cary Grant and Edward Arnold. **Running time:** 87 minutes. **Released:** Paramount.

THE PRIVATE LIFE OF HENRY VIII

Charles Laughton strutted and bellowed his way into screen legend as the sixteenth-century monarch known as the "Bluebeard of Kings" in this elaborate Alexander Korda production. The depiction of Henry was dubious as history, but it was quite a show—thanks to this scene-stealer who had the advantage of speech over the flamboyant players who had preceded him in films about the King.

Dinner at Eight with Louise Closser Hale, Jean Harlow, Wallace Beery, Edmund Lowe, Karen Morley and Billie Burke.

Laughton was already known to American audiences through portrayals in Hollywood films like *If I Had a Million* and *The Sign of the Cross.* In the latter his unrestrained histrionics as Nero won him many admirers. He went back to England to play Henry and gave the British film industry its first big commercial hit in the United States since the emergence of sound.

Laughton dominated the film; his eating manners were as boisterous as his laughter; his drinking as lascivious as his loving; and his rages were monumental. He even got to go for pathos in the scene in which he discovers that the one wife out of six he thought was really true to him and whom he deeply loved had committed adultery with his own personal aide.

Englishmen hoped that the success of this picture would pave the way for other breakthroughs in the American market. There were no comparable successes, however, until the forties.

Producer: London Films–United Artists. **Director:** Alexander Korda. **Screenplay:** Arthur Wimperis and Lajos Biro. **Principal Players:** Charles Laughton, Robert Donat, Binnie Barnes, Elsa Lanchester and Merle Oberon. **Running time:** 97 minutes. **Released:** United Artists.

DINNER AT EIGHT

Having had such a great success the previous year with its all-star cast in *Grand Hotel,* MGM used the formula again in *Dinner at Eight.* It worked equally well here.

The star vehicle this time came from a stage play by George S. Kaufman and Edna Ferber which was enormously popular in New York. It was built around a dinner being given by a socialite for a pair of visiting British aristocrats. Before the affair begins, the script looks into the private lives of the guests, revealing humor as well as pathos.

Billie Burke plays the hostess, a flighty woman oblivious to the illness (heart trouble) of her banker husband, as well as to his troubles at the office. Lionel Barrymore is the husband, fighting to save his shipping line. Marie Dressler is cast as the retired actress down on her luck who wants to sell her shares in the Barrymore firm. Wallace Beery is the shrewd businessman seeking to get control of the shipping company, and Jean Harlow is his wife, a vulgar social climber. Only John Barrymore doesn't come to dinner; he is a former matinee idol who, when he is told he is through by his agent, commits suicide.

Superficially observed roles, all, but the talented cast gave the characters personal appeal and credibility. The Misses Dressler and Harlow steal the show.

The director was George Cukor, whom producer David O. Selznick brought over to MGM with him when he left RKO. It is a good, workmanlike job of handling material that is dialogue-heavy.

Producer: David O. Selznick. **Director:** George Cukor. **Scriptwriters:** Frances Marion and Herman J. Mankiewicz. **Principal Players:** Marie Dressler, John Barrymore, Wallace Beery, Jean Harlow, Lionel Barrymore, Lee Tracy, Billie Burke and Edmund Lowe. **Running time:** 113 minutes. **Released:** MGM.

Leslie Howard and Bette Davis in *Of Human Bondage,* the picture that catapulted Miss Davis to stardom. She was not even nominated for an Oscar, but received one a year later for *Dangerous.*

1934

The New Deal continued to overshadow the picture business. As the year began, General Johnson blasted Dr. A. Lawrence Lowell, distinguished educator, for declining to serve as Government representative on the motion picture "Blue Eagle" Code (not to be confused with the Production Code). Mrs. Frederick H. Bagley, of the Massachusetts Civic League, also refused to serve. Both opposed block booking, the trade custom of selling at one time films in large numbers, usually a studio's whole year output. The Federal Government began an investigation of all salaries over $150 a week.

A survey in Pelham, N.Y., found that parents and teachers and pupils had almost identical opinions on films. Favorites were *Little Women, The Invisible Man* and *Son of Kong*. Popular stars: Katharine Hepburn, Clark Gable. High school boys' favorites were Jean Harlow, Marie Dressler and Ruby Keeler; the girls' favorites were Leslie Howard, Bing Crosby and Robert Montgomery.

The Catholic National Legion of Decency campaign for decent movies, especially vigorous in Philadelphia, where all moviegoing was banned by Dennis Cardinal Dougherty, resulted in Joseph I. Breen, veteran newspaperman, being named to head studio relations of the Motion Picture Producers Association in Hollywood. Within a short time he became head of the industry's Production Code Administration, and for twenty years his strong voice and skill in suggesting creatively effective ways out of difficulties in scripts and rough cut films gave him more influence on film content than anyone else in the world.

"Our Movie-Made Children," a study stressing adverse influences, was widely circulated. John Casey, the former license commissioner of Boston, attacked the study saying that it was not typical as it was based on institutional and delinquent children. "I do not think the public should swallow such alleged 'researches' hook, line and sinker. It is humanly impossible, I feel, to separate the influences of motion pictures from all of the other influences that are conditioning factors in the lives of young people." Casey's view has been the industry's ever since.

Alexander Korda reported that the English film makers' prejudice against the American market was "rather imaginary and not based on true facts," citing the splendid reception by American audiences of his *The Private Life of Henry VIII.* Sam Goldwyn's campaign to make Anna Sten, the lead in *Nana,* a top-ranking star in the United States proved that there were limits to what publicity could accomplish. Martin and Osa Johnson brought home authentic pictures, with real sound, of darkest Africa. *It Happened One Night,* directed by Frank Capra and starring Claudette Colbert and Clark Gable, struck a near-mortal blow against the men's underwear business. Millions of men and boys stopped wearing underwear tops, à la Gable.

Film stocks closed the year up nearly 30 percent from the Depression low. Only Warners, of all the major companies, was down. The court decision upholding William Fox's Tri-Ergon sound patents (a decision reversed the following year by the Supreme Court) threatened the industry's economic health. Theatre remodeling got underway, with some new construction of small theatres in neighborhoods.

Stars of the year: Will Rogers, Clark Gable, Janet Gaynor, Wallace Beery, Mae West, Joan Crawford, Bing Crosby, Shirley Temple, Marie Dressler and Norma Shearer.

Robert J. Flaherty's documentary picture *Man of Aran.*

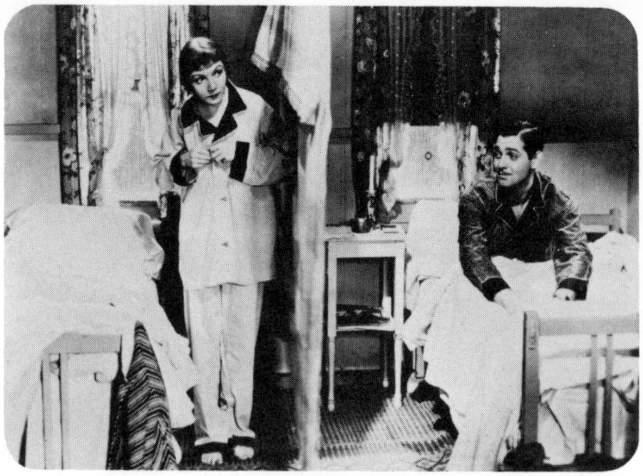

Claudette Colbert and Clark Gable in *It Happened One Night.*

MAN OF ARAN

The great documentary film maker Robert J. Flaherty had gone on a subarctic expedition to make *Nanook of the North* (1922); to the Samoan Isles for *Moana* (1926); and to the Polynesian Islands for *Tabu* (1932). He went to quite different territory for *Man of Aran:* the tiny Aran islands off the western coast of Ireland.

As a documentarian he had not been pleased with the intrusion of contrived plot elements into *Tabu*—something Paramount executives had insisted upon. In *Man of Aran* he returned to his earlier method, simply recording the day-to-day existence of a family on the island. The picture celebrates their courage in the unceasing battle against their environment—the barren land and the treacherous seas.

In a particularly compelling sequence the camera records the manner in which potatoes are raised: The islanders must overlay the rocky surface with seaweed, torturously gathered, and then cover it with soil accumulated little by little from rocky crevices.

As usual the Flaherty photography is superb, and the picture had a "prestige" success. Financed by Gainsborough, an English company, the film was released in the U.S. by Gaumont-British, who hoped it would continue the breakthrough in the American market begun by *The Private Life of Henry VIII.* It did not, of course.

Producer-Director-Photographer: Robert J. Flaherty. **Editor-Scenarist:** John Goldman. **Running time:** 77 minutes. **Released:** Gaumont-British.

IT HAPPENED ONE NIGHT

Contrary to a widespread impression, the famous director-writer team of Frank Capra and Robert Riskin did not begin their successful collaborations with *It Happened One Night.* They had already worked together on *Platinum Blonde* (a 1932 Jean Harlow vehicle), *American Madness* (1932) and *Lady for a Day* (1933).

With *It Happened One Night,* however, their joint efforts resulted in an amusing comedy of character and mild satire (kidding the caprices of the rich) that set records both at the box office and in the number of awards it won. Capra and Riskin were to continue making films at Columbia for the rest of the decade with similarly spectacular results—that is, the critics loved them (or most of them) and the public flocked to see them.

Claudette Colbert had been borrowed from Paramount to play another of those rebellious heiresses who were such popular characters in comedies of the day, and Clark Gable was secured from MGM to play the tough reporter who tries to get the exclusive story of her flight from her father to marry a man of whom the parent does not approve.

It was not so much the plot as the way it was handled that turned *It Happened One Night* into such a big success. Riskin's dialogue was glib and witty and Capra saw to it that it was delivered at a brisk pace and that the camera kept on the move. Miss Colbert and Gable played together smoothly.

Of Human Bondage with Leslie Howard and Bette Davis.

Both stars won Oscars; so did Capra and Riskin; and the film was named best picture—five awards in all. But the picture probably meant most of all to Harry Cohn, whose small studio it established as a leading force in the industry.

Producer: Columbia. **Director:** Frank Capra. **Scriptwriter:** Robert Riskin. **Principal Players:** Clark Gable, Claudette Colbert, Walter Connolly and Roscoe Karns. **Running time:** 105 minutes. **Released:** Columbia.

OF HUMAN BONDAGE

W. Somerset Maugham's autobiographical novel is a work of art, but you would never know it from the three films that have been made in Hollywood (the second was in 1946; the third in 1963). The first version is the most famous, primarily because it is the picture that established Bette Davis as a major star. Critics were lavish in their praise of her interpretation of the selfish waitress Mildred Rogers, and her grotesque makeup in the scene in which she is dying of syphilis foreshadowed a host of future films in which she would sacrifice glamour for realism.

Miss Davis had been called a promising actress on the basis of stage work when she went to Hollywood in 1930 at the behest of Universal. They put her into several mediocre films, and she suffered the same fate when she went to Warner Bros. until the studio agreed to lend her to RKO to play opposite Leslie Howard in *Of Human Bondage*. Even after that remarkable success she was relegated to "quickie" films, until her rebellion and flight to England. However, a court decision crushed her plans to make films there, as being in violation of her contract with Warners. Upon her repentant return in 1936 she made *Marked Woman* and *That Certain Woman,* among others, but it was not until 1938 and *Jezebel* that she really hit her peak. The rest, as they say, is history.

In the meantime she had won an Oscar for her performance in *Dangerous* (1935). She has always contended it was given her in compensation for having been passed over for *Of Human Bondage* the year before. She won a second Oscar for *Jezebel.*

Seen three decades after it first appeared, *Of Human Bondage* fails to hold up at all except for the Davis performance, where a great talent can be seen in an embryonic stage. The adaptation by Lester Cohen does not make credible the attraction that Mildred holds for the hero, and merely skims the surface of scenes that are powerful and moving in the book. The film also resorts to such tired cinematic devices of the day as using falling calendar leaves to indicate the passage of time.

In 1946 Mildred was played by Eleanor Parker, who was not temperamentally suited to it, and in 1963 Kim Novak was so inadequate that she almost turned the film into a parody.

Producer: Pandro S. Berman. **Director:** John Cromwell. **Scriptwriter:** Lester Cohen. **Principal Players:** Leslie Howard, Bette Davis and Frances Dee. **Running time:** 83 minutes. **Released:** RKO.

Fredric March, Charles Laughton and Norma Shearer in *The Barretts of Wimpole Street.*

The Thin Man with William Powell, Myrna Loy and Harold Huber.

THE BARRETTS OF WIMPOLE STREET

It has been hard for later generations to believe it, but in the early thirties the Rudolf Beiser play recounting the love affair and elopement of poets Elizabeth Barrett and Robert Browning was esteemed as high drama. Part of the aura of culture it achieved was due to the fact that Katharine Cornell, the First Lady of the Theatre, played in it on Broadway and then toured the country with the production.

When the film was released it was more popular with housewives and shopgirls than with intellectuals. It was and is an entertaining romance that had the benefit of a handsome production under the aegis of Irving Thalberg and the presence of three top stars. Thalberg cast his wife Norma Shearer as Miss Barrett, and borrowed Fredric March and Charles Laughton from Paramount to play the suitor, Browning, and her incestuously-inclined parent, respectively.

All three stars were Oscar winners, a point that MGM made much of in the advertising. Miss Shearer had won for *The Divorcee* (1930); March for *Dr. Jekyll and Mr. Hyde* (1931); and Laughton for *The Private Life of Henry VIII* (1932). March and Miss Shearer had co-starred the year before in *Smilin' Through.*

This is generally regarded as the best performance of Miss Shearer, whose warm and sincere manner was perfectly suited to the part. She was well-liked by the public and made many top films at MGM in the decade, but she was never a favorite of the critics, who found her Juliet a trifle too old and her Marie Antoinette more than a little overacted.

Producer: Irving Thalberg. **Director:** Sidney Franklin. **Scriptwriters:** Ernest Vajda and Claudine West. **Principal Players:** Norma Shearer, Fredric March, Charles Laughton and Maureen O'Sullivan. **Running time:** 109 minutes. **Released:** MGM.

THE THIN MAN

William Powell had played S. S. Van Dine's Philo Vance in two films and various other detectives less well known, but he really hit his stride when MGM cast him as Dashiell Hammett's Nick Charles. He was elegance personified, and he had the perfect sophisticated partner in Myrna Loy, as Nora, his spouse.

The case of the Thin Man itself was routine, but the dialogue sparkled with wit, and the situations, which sometimes became farcical, were consistently amusing.

Charles was no ordinary detective; he was retired and enjoying the good life—drinking, cavorting with his wife and playing with their dog. The carefree, credible relationship of the couple was a novelty in crime melodrama—an element that genre sorely needed.

So successful was this Charles adventure that MGM starred the two, along with the wirehaired terrier playing Asta, in five sequels.

Producer: Hunt Stromberg. **Director:** W. S. Van Dyke. **Scriptwriters:** Albert Hackett and Frances Goodrich. **Principal Players:** William Powell, Myrna Loy and Maureen O'Sullivan. **Running time:** 95 minutes. **Released:** MGM.

Jackie Cooper and Wallace Beery in *Treasure Island.*

Little Miss Marker with Dorothy Dell, Adolphe Menjou and Shirley Temple.

TREASURE ISLAND

Robert Louis Stevenson's classic adventure novel for boys has been a perennial favorite of moviemakers, who have filmed it no less than six times. There were four silent versions: in 1908, 1912, 1917 and 1920. The first sound version came in 1934, and Walt Disney turned out a remake in 1950, with Robert Newton as Long John Silver.

In 1934 that role was played by Wallace Beery, and Jackie Cooper was Jim. It was perfect casting, and the other actors were also aptly chosen for the famous roles: Lionel Barrymore as Billy Bones; Otto Kruger as Doctor Livesey; Lewis Stone as Captain Smollett; Nigel Bruce as Squire Trelawney; and Charles "Chic" Sales as Ben Gunn.

Victor Fleming, then one of the top directors at MGM, was assigned to the picture and it turned out to be his best accomplishment to date. He kept Beery's mugging to a minimum, and Cooper, the child star known for tearful parts, acquired a new and more "manly" image.

Producer: Hunt Stromberg. **Director:** Victor Fleming. **Scriptwriter:** John Lee Mahin. **Principal Players:** Wallace Beery and Jackie Cooper. **Running time:** 95 minutes. **Released:** MGM.

LITTLE MISS MARKER

Shirley Temple was only five years old when *Little Miss Marker* was released, but she was already a major star whose like has been seen neither before nor since. Her phenomenal career began in 1933 when she appeared in the Baby Burlesque series of short subjects. She stole *Stand Up and Cheer* from all the adults, including John Boles and Warner Baxter, and after that she was the star of all twenty-one of her pictures in that decade.

Those films, some made for Paramount but most for 20th Century-Fox, garnered a fortune for the tiny star and the studios. The public took the curly-haired, dimpled tot to their hearts, making her the number one box-office star in the country for four years in a row—1935 through 1938.

Little Miss Marker was an ideal vehicle for her. It is a sentimental Damon Runyon story populated by his familiar Broadway mugs whose hearts melt for the little child whose father has just committed suicide. Sorrowful Jones is the name of the gambler who takes her in hand against his better judgment, and eventually marries his girl friend to make a home for the youngster. Adolphe Menjou played Sorrowful.

As Miss Temple grew into her teens, her popularity subsided. There was a flurry of excitement when she got her first screen kiss in *Miss Annie Rooney* in 1942 (she was thirteen), and there were several pictures after that (*Since You Went Away, Kiss and Tell, That Hagen Girl,* etc.). But she never regained as a teenager and adult anything like the popularity she had as a child.

Producer: B. P. Schulberg. **Director:** Alexander Hall. **Scriptwriters:** William R. Lipman, Sam Hellman and Gladys Lehman. **Principal Players:** Adolphe Menjou, Dorothy Dell, Charles Bickford and Shirley Temple. **Running time:** 80 minutes. **Released:** Paramount.

Charles Laughton and Clark Gable in *Mutiny on the Bounty,* the classic epic of the sea and winner of the Academy Award as best picture of 1935.

1935

The trial in the Lindbergh baby kidnapping case provided newsreels that packed theatres, provoking a front-page controversy. David T. Wilentz, New Jersey Attorney General, charged that "these sound pictures were procured by trickery and in defiance of the court." Robert H. Cochrane, Universal Pictures executive, replied, "No apparatus has been concealed in the courtroom, not only because it is too cumbersome to conceal, but because no newsreel representative has done anything on the sly. All talk of photography by trickery is nonsense."

It was estimated that 10,000 theatres of 14,000 wired for sound got newsreels of the Hauptmann trial, some theatres getting the newsreels within one day of the court action.

Giveaways of dishes and other attendance lures were at a high. In Chicago, hundreds of theatres used giveaways two or three nights a week, some as often as five nights. Dishes or ovenware were purchased by the theatre owner at an average cost of ten cents each and exhibitors signed contracts with the dish distributors to use their products as premiums for a minimum of fifty-two weeks. This indicates the hold the custom had on the trade.

The *Register and Tribune* of Des Moines and sixty other newspapers carried a series of articles blasting Hollywood and stirring up criticism of all films. The studios had cooperated in the "research," believing that the aim was a serious study on "The Evolution of the Movie Industry." It came out as "Hollywood Unvarnished," with such newspaper catchlines as "Anatomy run riot" . . . . "Do you know what happens to chorus girls?" . . . . "How movies are faked" . . . . "The sins, scandals and loves of movie stars."

The successor to "Roxy" Rothafel as the country's leading theatre operator, W. G. Van Schmus, who had left Macy's to head Radio City Music Hall, had some advice for the industry: "Both Hollywood and New York might well wake up and serve the better taste of the American public. I do not mean the Park Avenue public. The Sweeneys have better taste than they have been credited with—and it is the Sweeneys that make our bread and butter."

Corporate turmoil was great. Mighty Paramount with 1,210 theatres (240 of which were overseas) was reorganized. Fox and the 20th Century Production Company of Darryl F. Zanuck merged to form 20th Century-Fox. Floyd Odlum's Atlas Corporation bought RKO. Republic was founded by Consolidated Film Industries. Jesse L. Lasky left Paramount, and Joe Brandt retired from Columbia.

Attendance averaged an estimated sixty-five to ninety million weekly. Annual production costs were at $180,000,000. Film stocks gained nearly 40 percent in the year.

Soviet films were shown in 152 U.S. theatres. Rumblings of trouble abroad increased as Germany banned or cut half of U.S. films.

Thomas E. Maloy, for eighteen years dictator of the projectionists' union in Chicago, was gunned down in Hollywood style. As he was driving along the Outer Drive opposite the World's Fair grounds in a big sedan, a smaller car raced alongside and two gunmen on the running boards let loose a hail of bullets.

Stars of the year: Shirley Temple, Will Rogers, Clark Gable, Fred Astaire, Ginger Rogers, Joan Crawford, Claudette Colbert, Dick Powell, Wallace Beery, Joe E. Brown and James Cagney.

Academy-Award winner Victor McLaglen (center) in *The Informer*, with Neil Fitzgerald and Joseph Sauers.

Les Misérables with Fredric March and Charles Laughton.

THE INFORMER

Hollywood has always been more or less disdainful of film critics, but on occasion they have proved useful. An instance in point is supplied by the box-office career of John Ford's *The Informer,* the first of his pictures to receive special notice by the more critical reviewers, although he had been making films since the 1920's.

The Informer was based on a novel by Liam O'Flaherty, a grim account of the "troubles" in Ireland in 1922, with the protagonist a traitor to the cause of the rebels. It was hardly commercial material, and the actor who played Gypo Nolan was Victor McLaglen—hardly a major audience draw.

It was not an expensive picture to make; all shooting was done indoors in a single set erected on two stages reproducing the Dublin streets and buildings. Costs charged directly to the picture, from acceptance of the final script to completion of the film, were only $285,000.

Knowing full well the help of the critics would be required, the studio put this slogan in its ads: "A Prediction: RKO-Radio is convinced that every critic in America will place it on his list of the Ten Best Pictures for 1935." Initial reviews were indeed excellent, but the film was released in May, seven months before ten best lists are compiled.

Predictably, business was spotty—a good engagement here and there, but many poor ones. Then came December and the ten best lists. The prediction was fulfilled. The newly organized New York Film Critics named *The Informer* best picture of the year and cited Ford as top director. (Later the film was nominated for an Oscar, but lost to *Mutiny on the Bounty.* However, both Ford and McLaglen won in their categories, as did Dudley Nichols for his screenplay and Max Steiner for his scoring.)

Belatedly, the public responded to the critical praise, and the film won a rash of new bookings which pushed its figures over to the profit side of the ledger. A *succès d'estime* had become a money film.

Producer: RKO-Radio. **Director:** John Ford. **Scriptwriter:** Dudley Nichols. **Principal Players:** Victor McLaglen, Heather Angel, Preston Foster and Margot Grahame. **Running time:** 91 minutes. **Released:** RKO.

LES MISERABLES

It was a year for great novelists on the screen. January had brought *David Copperfield;* June, *Vanity Fair* (*Becky Sharp*); September, *Anna Karenina;* and December, *A Tale of Two Cities.* April brought forth this adaptation of Victor Hugo's mammoth work, which had previously been made in at least two silent versions in the U.S. and by other film makers in both England and France.

(Other novels brought to the screen this same year included *The Three Musketeers, Alice Adams, The Last Days of Pompeii* and *Mutiny on the Bounty.* It was plainly a literary year.)

Darryl F. Zanuck produced *Les Misérables* for 20th Century Productions, the company he formed with

Mutiny on the Bounty with DeWitt Jennings, Ian Wolfe, Charles Laughton, Clark Gable.

Joseph M. Schenck in 1933 after he left Warner Bros. Direction was assigned to Richard Boleslawski, who is little remembered three decades later, although he had directed *Rasputin and the Empress* (1932) and *The Painted Veil* (1934) for MGM. He came to the United States from Poland in 1920 and also worked at Pathé and Columbia.

W. P. Lipscomb's screenplay was more faithful to the letter than the spirit of the book, but the picture was carried to success by two fine performances: Fredric March as Jean Valjean and Charles Laughton as Javert. It was one of the twelve top-grossing films of the year. A remake in 1952, with Michael Rennie and Robert Newton in the March and Laughton roles, was not well received.

Producer: Darryl F. Zanuck. **Director:** Richard Boleslawski. **Scriptwriter:** W. P. Lipscomb. **Principal Players:** Fredric March, Charles Laughton, Sir Cedric Hardwicke, Rochelle Hudson, Frances Drake, John Beal and Florence Eldridge. **Running time:** 105 minutes. **Released:** United Artists.

MUTINY ON THE BOUNTY

Frank Lloyd had turned *The Sea Hawk* into one of the great sea epics of the silent screen, so it was fitting that he be chosen by Irving Thalberg to make the first major example of the genre in sound. It became a classic, and far surpassed a remake twenty-seven years later by the same studio in a version whose only "improvement" over the original was the use of color photography.

Charles Nordhoff and James Norman Hall had written a trilogy (*Mutiny on the Bounty, Man Against the Sea* and *Pitcairn Island*) based on the true story of the English ship *H.M.S. Bounty* and the successful mutiny of part of her crew which took place in the late eighteenth century in the South Seas. The film covers only the first two books, detailing the motivations for the mutiny led by Master's Mate Fletcher Christian against the sadistically cruel Captain Bligh. The highly romanticized account includes an interlude in Tahiti where the crew cavorts with native girls, and the dramatic trial of Midshipman Byam and others, which exposed the barbaric naval code. The picture ends with the band of mutineers settling on Pitcairn.

It is an irresistible adventure story told on the screen with great sweep and narrative skill and acted unforgettably by the best talent Thalberg could muster. Legend has it that Charles Laughton did not want to play Bligh and had to be coaxed; it is one of his best screen performances, often hammy but even that is in key. Clark Gable is a dashing Christian—not very English, true, but a credible hero. Franchot Tone had one of his best roles, too, as Byam, and played it well.

The tremendous success of the picture led to a spate of sea films for years afterward, including, ironically, a remake of *The Sea Hawk* by another studio, Warner Bros. *Mutiny* won the Oscar as best film of 1935.

Producer: Irving Thalberg. **Director:** Frank Lloyd. **Scriptwriters:** Talbot Jennings, Jules Furthman and Carey Wilson. **Principal Players:** Charles Laughton, Clark Gable and Franchot Tone. **Running time:** 130 minutes. **Released:** MGM.

Nelson Eddy and Jeanette MacDonald in *Naughty Marietta.*

NAUGHTY MARIETTA

Already a favorite in the concert world, baritone Nelson Eddy became an idol of moviegoers after his appearance in Victor Herbert's operetta *Naughty Marietta* on screen. So strong was his impact on critics that his co-star, the already well established Jeanette MacDonald, was overshadowed in most of the reviews.

Not for long, however, because they soon became the most popular singing team in screen history. Operetta after operetta was a hit: *Rose Marie* (1936); *Maytime* (1937); *Girl of the Golden West* (1938); *Sweethearts* (1939); *New Moon* (1940); *Bittersweet* (1941); and *I Married an Angel* (1942). Eight films in all, before their vogue wore out.

Naughty Marietta is typical of their vehicles—the wispy plot is just an excuse for them to break frequently into song, which is what their public wanted.

In this film Miss MacDonald sang "Ah, Sweet Mystery of Life" and "Antoinette and Anatole" by herself, and "Chansonette" with a chorus. Eddy sang solo "I'm Falling in Love With Someone" and "Southern Moon," and both "Tramp, Tramp, Tramp" and "The Owl and the Polecat" with chorus. The stars dueted with "The Italian Street Song," and all voices blended in a finale medley of "Sweet Mystery" and "Tramp, Tramp, Tramp."

Producer: Hunt Stromberg. **Director:** W. S. Van Dyke. **Scriptwriter:** John Lee Mahin. **Principal Players:** Jeanette MacDonald, Nelson Eddy and Frank Morgan. **Running time:** 80 minutes. **Released:** MGM.

Miriam Hopkins (left) in *Becky Sharp,* with Ottola Nesmith and William Stack.

BECKY SHARP

An adaptation of Thackeray's novel *Vanity Fair,* this *Becky Sharp* was advertised as the film that "brings the miracle of living color to the screen." It was, indeed, the first full-length feature in the new three-color process known as Technicolor. (*The House of Rothschild* had its final scene in this process the year before.)

Some critics compared the emergence of *Becky Sharp* and color to *The Jazz Singer* and the coming of sound. They found its tones "naturalistic" and "exquisite"—all of which helped the film immensely at the box office. In point of fact, the use of color on the screen had a long way to go, although the designs of Robert Edmond Jones were often imaginative, and Rouben Mamoulian tried to use color dramatically.

As for the film's plot, it is a far from satisfactory dramatization of the great book. Thackeray analyzed his characters in depth; the movie makes stereotypes of them. (The critic on the New York *News* called Becky "the famous gold digger.")

Playing the lead was Miriam Hopkins, a former stage actress who enjoyed a minor vogue in films in the thirties in such pictures as *Design for Living* (1933), *These Three* (1936) and *Woman Chases Man* (1937). Her Becky Sharp was nowhere close to the one conceived by Thackeray.

Producer: Kenneth MacGowan. **Director:** Rouben Mamoulian. **Scriptwriter:** Francis Edward Faragoh. **Principal Players:** Miriam Hopkins, Frances Dee, Cedric Hardwicke, Billie Burke and Alison Skipworth. **Running time:** 72 minutes. **Released:** RKO.

Sig Rumann, Margaret Dumont and Groucho Marx in *A Night at the Opera.*

A NIGHT AT THE OPERA

The funniest picture the Marx Brothers ever made also turned out to be their most financially successful. Groucho, Chico and Harpo were at the top of their form in this spoof of grand opera which contains three sequences that not only epitomize their zany brand of farce but are among the funniest episodes ever put on film.

The first is the famous stateroom scene in which practically the entire cast gets into the act, squeezed into the tiny area like sardines. The second is the furniture shuttling sequence in which a detective is baffled by beds that seem to move themselves. The third is the hectic and hilarious climax at the opera dominated by Harpo, who not only substitutes "Take Me Out to the Ball Game" for the score to *Il Trovatore,* but swings on a flying trapeze like Tarzan. It is all much more amusing than it sounds in print.

Originally, the Marx Brothers were four; they started out as a vaudeville act with their mother and aunt billed as the "Six Musical Mascots." Later they toured as the Four Nightingales and finally became the Four Marx Brothers: Harpo (Arthur); Groucho (Julius); Chico (Leonard); and Zeppo (Herbert). They delighted Broadway with *Cocoanuts* and *Animal Crackers,* and Paramount brought them to Hollywood, where both were filmed virtually intact. *Monkey Business, Horsefeathers* and *Duck Soup* (which some critics think their best) followed. Then all but Zeppo went to MGM, where *A Night at the Opera* was their first picture.

A romance was considered obligatory in their films, and Kitty Carlisle and Allan Jones supplied it in this one and sang several songs, including the sentimental ballad "Alone." As usual, the madcap proceedings were also interrupted for Harpo to play the harp and Chico to do a turn at the piano. Margaret Dumont, the grande dame Groucho used as a foil, was on hand here, too, and added immeasurably to the fun.

Producer: Irving Thalberg. **Director:** Sam Wood. **Scriptwriters:** George S. Kaufman and Morrie Ryskind. **Principal Players:** Groucho, Chico and Harpo Marx, Kitty Carlisle and Allan Jones. **Running time:** 90 minutes. **Released:** MGM.

TOP HAT

The most popular dancing team in movies in the 1930's was that of Fred Astaire and Ginger Rogers; in fact, they had that field to themselves. They appeared in nine successful pictures together, from *Flying Down to Rio* in 1933 to *The Story of Vernon and Irene Castle* in 1939. Ten years later they were reunited in a tenth film, *The Barkleys of Broadway,* which made a lot of their fans nostalgic, but they called it a day after that as a film duo.

Top Hat is typical of their vehicles: The scale is intimate and the cast small; the dancing consists of several solos by Astaire and some numbers in tandem with Miss Rogers; and there are interludes for a slight plot that stresses comedy. There was usually at least one elaborate production number; here it was the fabulous "Picco-

Top Hat with Ginger Rogers and Fred Astaire.

David Copperfield with Freddie Bartholomew and W. C. Fields.

lino," a new dance that had its counterpart in the demonstrations of "The Continental" in *The Gay Divorcee.*

Top Hat and *Swing Time* and *Shall We Dance?* had an easy charm that other musicals of the time seemed to have to strain to achieve. That came from a carefree atmosphere, the speed with which everything moved so that the silly plot didn't bog down, and—most of all—the effervescent personalities of the two stars. Astaire was as debonair as he was light on his feet, and it didn't matter a whit that he couldn't really sing. Miss Rogers was lovely and appealing, and made the perfect dancing partner.

The music in *Top Hat* was by no less a songsmith than Irving Berlin and includes the famous classic "Cheek to Cheek."

Producer: Pandro S. Berman. **Director:** Mark Sandrich. **Scriptwriters:** Dwight Taylor and Allan Scott. **Principal Players:** Fred Astaire, Ginger Rogers, Edward Everett Horton and Helen Broderick. **Running time:** 102 minutes. **Released:** RKO.

DAVID COPPERFIELD

Several of Charles Dickens' novels had been transcribed to the screen in silent days, and only the year before Universal had released a sound version of *Great Expectations.* But the golden age for the nineteenth-century novelist on the screen commenced with this Hugh Walpole adaptation of *David Copperfield,* handsomely produced by David O. Selznick and directed by George Cukor with meticulous care.

Critics were impressed by how many of the episodes of the novel were put in the film and by how well they were joined together without the disjointed effect of so many plot-heavy films of the day. The two hours passed all too quickly, they said, and audiences agreed.

Casting is important in Dickens, but it is not too difficult: Many of the characters are "types" and one may simply choose accordingly. Even at that, it was a happy inspiration for the film makers to select W. C. Fields to play Micawber, the pauper with aristocratic manners. All the great comedian really had to do was to be himself, and that he did to perfection. The scene in which he denounces Roland Young as Uriah Heep ("the most consummate villain that has ever existed!") is a high moment of Dickens on the screen.

As David, young Freddie Bartholomew had the best role of his career and responded by giving his most moving performance.

Others who stand out in the aptly chosen cast include Edna May Oliver as Aunt Betsey and Lionel Barrymore as Dan Peggotty. Frank Lawton, an unknown, played the grown-up David.

Later that same year MGM released another film based on a Dickens classic. *A Tale of Two Cities,* with Ronald Colman as Sidney Carton, was also a big commercial success.

Producer: David O. Selznick. **Director:** George Cukor. **Scriptwriter:** Howard Estabrook. **Principal Players:** W. C. Fields, Lionel Barrymore, Maureen O'Sullivan, Madge Evans, Edna May Oliver, Lewis Stone, Frank Lawton and Freddie Bartholomew. **Running time:** 133 minutes. **Released:** MGM.

Hugh Herbert, Otis Harlan, James Cagney and Frank McHugh in *A Midsummer Night's Dream.*

A MIDSUMMER NIGHT'S DREAM

Numerous Shakespearean plays were filmed in the silent days (an entire book has been written on that subject alone), but the most lavish of the Hollywood productions in the sound era did not arrive until 1935. It was the comedy *A Midsummer Night's Dream,* and Warner Bros. went all out in every direction to assure it of commercial success.

Max Reinhardt, the noted stage entrepreneur, was hired to produce the film and co-direct it (since it was his first film, William Dieterle was assigned to assist). Initial bookings were in roadshow theatres only, with all seats reserved. The music of Mendelssohn, as arranged by Erich Wolfgang Korngold, accompanied the action. Spectacular ballets were included, directed by Bronislava Nijinska and Nini Theilade.

Believe it or not, the public was impressed and turned the film into a box-office hit. Not even the blank verse put them off, and they especially liked the beautiful girls and the dance pageantry.

Purists, on the other hand, were horrified, declaring that the production left nothing to the imagination but spelled everything out in explicit terms. The screen, they argued, should concentrate on realism and leave fantasy to the stage.

There were also lifted eyebrows over some of the casting: James Cagney as Bottom, Joe E. Brown as Flute, and Dick Powell as Lysander, in particular. Critics objected that they were highly contemporary screen personalities who simply could not inhabit the enchanted wood of Shakespeare.

Producer: Max Reinhardt. **Directors:** Reinhardt and William Dieterle. Play "arranged for the screen" by Charles Kenyon and Mary C. McCall, Jr. **Principal Players:** James Cagney, Joe E. Brown, Hugh Herbert, Frank McHugh, Olivia de Havilland, Mickey Rooney and Dick Powell. **Running time:** 132 minutes. **Released:** Warner Bros.

Gary Cooper and Jean Arthur in *Mr. Deeds Goes to Town,* Frank Capra's most famous film celebrating Americana.

1936

Motion pictures were coming out of the Depression this year. Attendance increased another 10 percent. Film stocks again gained dramatically on Wall Street. Additional sound stages were erected at most studios. Admission prices were raised, by as much as fifteen to twenty cents. Generally, grosses were the best in five years. Yet prices hit an all-time low at Plymouth, Ohio, where they went down to five cents. Rev. Joseph A. Daly, executive secretary of the Catholic National Legion of Decency, said attendance had risen 25 percent in the two years of Legion activity for a moral screen. He cited Shirley Temple and the late Will Rogers as box-office leaders. Mrs. Mary Harden Looram (who headed the women reviewers of the Legion for thirty-five years) said, "The industry seeks returns, the public seeks recreation, and the Church seeks respectability." Father Daly commented, "Those in the Legion are not bluenose reformers. To the industry decency means dollars. Dirt means deficits. We want to stand 100 percent behind the work Mr. Breen (head of the industry's code administration) is doing and we hope to sustain him in his valiant fight."

Hollywood looked for continuing gains as various key studio executives struggled for power. Studio heads created their own dynasties. It was the time of the all-powerful studio chief—Louis B. Mayer at MGM typified the breed. Producers paid $3,000,000 in the year for 614 stories considered suitable for filming.

Legislative activity involving films increased. In congress alone there were fourteen bills submitted affecting films, principally to outlaw block booking. In thirteen states a total of forty-eight bills were filed during the year. One seriously considered was a measure in New York to regulate the admission of minors to theatres. Some felt the state sought control and not just regulation.

One theatre was operating in the United States for every 8,234 persons. (In Europe the figure was one theatre for every 9,270.) A measure of the significance of these figures is that in 1970 in the United States there was only one movie theatre for every 20,000 persons. In 1936, the admission to movie theatres often exceeded in a week the total of the entire population of the country. In 1970 a good week's admissions would only be one-quarter of the population.

Barney Balaban became president of Paramount and J. Cheever Cowdin took control of Universal from Carl Laemmle. "Roxy" Rothafel and Irving Thalberg died.

San Francisco was the picture of the year. It was directed by W. S. Van Dyke, and starred Clark Gable, Spencer Tracy and Jeanette MacDonald.

With a narration by Pete Smith, MGM released a reel of 3-D anaglyph films called "Audioscopiks" which were viewed by audiences through red and green glasses. The footage had been bought by Fred Quimby, a producer of shorts for MGM, from J. F. Leventhal and J. A. Norling, 3-D pioneers. The reel had novelty appeal, but the system was of limited practicality because viewers became physically ill if they looked at anaglyphs too long. (The reception by one eye of images through a red filter and by the other of images through a green filter set up a physiological disturbance avoided in 3-D pictures years later through the use of clear polarized glasses.)

Stars of the year: Shirley Temple, Clark Gable, Fred Astaire, Ginger Rogers, Robert Taylor, Joe E. Brown, Dick Powell, Joan Crawford, Claudette Colbert, Jeanette MacDonald and Gary Cooper.

Louis Jouvet and Francoise Rosay (far right) in *Carnival in Flanders.*

CARNIVAL IN FLANDERS

In the era of silence, foreign films had flourished on American screens; then sound, with a few notable exceptions, tolled the death knell for pictures spoken in a foreign tongue. It got to the point where a distributor had to be a very brave fellow indeed to import a movie from abroad.

Fortunately a few had such courage, and to them is owed credit for a brief resurgence of the foreign film in the U.S. in the mid and late 1930's. *Carnival in Flanders* was one of the few outstanding French films to play in the U.S. in that decade—only in "specialized" theatres, however. The audience for it was small but appreciative.

In sophisticated and amusing fashion it asserts the superiority of the female of the species to the male. The setting is a Flemish town in 1616 (costumes and sets are elaborate). The mayor and board of aldermen are terrified when word is received of the approach of a Spanish duke with his military escort. In their cowardice they decide to play dead and hope for mercy. Annoyed and disgusted, the women of the town use their feminine wiles to make their own "conquests" of the Spaniards.

Three decades after its first showings in America, *Carnival in Flanders* has the stature of an early French sound classic.

Producer: Films Sonosres Tobis. **Director:** Jacques Feyder. **Scriptwriter:** Bernard Zimmer. **Principal Players:** Francoise Rosay, Jean Murat, Alermé, Louis Jouvet, M. Carmentier and Pierre Labry. **Running time:** 95 minutes. **Released:** American Tobis Co.

Paul Robeson, Hattie McDaniel, Irene Dunne and Charles Winninger in *Show Boat.*

SHOW BOAT

Every list of the great American musical comedies has to include *Show Boat;* to overlook it would be unthinkable. The book and lyrics are by Oscar Hammerstein II with music by Jerome Kern, and their high quality and brilliant integration (never before had songs flowed so naturally from the action) foreshadowed by more than a decade the famous series of musicals beginning with *Oklahoma!* that Hammerstein did with Richard Rodgers which were to be credited with revolutionizing the genre. *Show Boat* might have been written last year, it is so little dated.

There have been three successful film versions. Universal released the first in 1929, while the original Flo Ziegfeld production was still running on Broadway. Laura La Plante and Joseph Schildkraut played Magnolia and Gaylord on the screen, roles taken in 1936 by Irene Dunne and Allan Jones and in 1951 (an MGM remake) by Kathryn Grayson and Howard Keel. The third was the first in color.

Helen Morgan, who had played Julie on the stage, repeated the role in the second film version. No one has ever sung "Can't Help Lovin' That Man" quite so well as she. Ava Gardner was surprisingly good in the part in the 1951 version, but her singing voice was dubbed. Charles Winninger, the original stage Cap'n Andy Hawks, was in the second film, and Joe E. Brown took the part in the third.

Others in the cast of the 1936 version included Paul Robeson (singing "Ol' Man River"), Helen Westley,

The Great Ziegfeld with (at right) William Powell and Ray Bolger.

San Francisco with Clark Gable.

Donald Cook and Hattie McDaniel. A press release reported there were also a "Negro chorus of 200 voices, 50 dancing girls and 3,500 extras!"

Producer: Carl Laemmle, Jr. **Director:** James Whale. **Scriptwriter:** Oscar Hammerstein II. **Principal Players:** Irene Dunne, Allan Jones and Charles Winninger. **Running time:** 115 minutes. **Released:** Universal.

THE GREAT ZIEGFELD

Fabled showman Flo Ziegfeld himself had never put on a Broadway stage such a colossal spectacle as this screen version of his life and times. Here are some of the adjectives used to describe the film: grand, lavish, extravagant, glittering, ornate, opulent, brilliant, luxurious, breathtaking.

Other musicals, aided by color photography, have surpassed it since, but there is still an air of magnificence about this most ambitious and large-scaled musical of the 1930's. Best of the elaborately staged numbers is still "A Pretty Girl Is Like a Melody," in which literally hundreds of pulchritudinous females pose in tableaux. Audiences of the time repeatedly broke into applause.

The book recounts the personal as well as the professional life of Ziegfeld, including his two marriages. It shows him triumphant with four shows in New York in one season, and it shows him crushed by the market crash and struggling to get on his feet again.

William Powell played Ziegfeld in bravura style, and the wives were acted by Luise Rainer (Anna Held) and Myrna Loy (the young Billie Burke). Turns were taken by such top celebrities as Fanny Brice and Ray Bolger playing themselves, while other actors represented such Ziegfeld stars as Will Rogers, Eddie Cantor and Marilyn Miller.

The public loved it, even at roadshow prices, and it won the Oscar as best film of the year. Miss Rainer was chosen best actress, apparently on the basis of the famous telephone scene in which she congratulates Ziegfeld on his remarriage. Otherwise, it was not much of a part.

Producer: Hunt Stromberg. **Director:** Robert Z. Leonard. **Scriptwriter:** William Anthony McGuire. **Principal Players:** William Powell, Myrna Loy, Luise Rainer, Frank Morgan and Fanny Brice. **Running time:** 184 minutes. **Released:** MGM.

SAN FRANCISCO

This enormously popular picture has one of the best "special effects" sequences in the history of the American screen: a depiction of the San Francisco earthquake of 1906. As the city is destroyed by fire and explosion, the images are so powerfully realistic that the theatre itself seems to rock from the reverberations. The sequence runs for almost ten minutes, and three decades later it is still an impressive spectacle.

Other elements of this sentimental romance do not hold up as well—always excepting the star performances of Clark Gable, Jeanette MacDonald and Spencer Tracy. Gable was well established as a virile hero with soft

Mr. Deeds Goes to Town with Raymond Walburn and Gary Cooper.

emotions that a good woman could arouse, and the part of the lusty cafe owner was made for him. Miss MacDonald had already begun her films with Nelson Eddy (*Naughty Marietta* and *Rose Marie*) that were to make them one of the best-liked movie teams of the decade, and her role as a singer here was type casting. But Tracy had yet to break through into the top ranks, and his part as the kindly priest who befriends the lovers is the one that did it. Unassailable integrity and sincerity were the images Tracy projected, and audiences warmed to him.

Miss MacDonald was given several chances to display her vocal talents. Her numbers ranged from the ballad "Would You?" to "The Battle Hymn of the Republic," which she sang with a chorus of survivors looking down from the hills on the ruins of San Francisco and seeing a vision of the future city.

Producers: John Emerson and Bernard H. Hyman. **Director:** W. S. Van Dyke. **Scriptwriter:** Anita Loos. **Principal Players:** Clark Gable, Jeanette MacDonald, Spencer Tracy and Jack Holt. **Running time:** 115 minutes. **Released:** MGM.

MR. DEEDS GOES TO TOWN

As children of the Depression years, Americans were more positively responsive than they might have been in more affluent times to a film that advocated the philosophy that the rich should share their money with the poor. It was particularly attractive in the context of a comedy-drama that ingeniously mixed both elements in about equal measure and did not labor its social theme, which to some people sounded suspiciously like Socialism.

It was the third hit in a row for the director-writer team of Frank Capra and Robert Riskin, whose comic *It Happened One Night* had been a sleeper and whose sentimental *Broadway Bill* had stirred audiences. *Mr. Deeds* touched both emotions and was their biggest success to date.

The plot came from a story by Clarence Buddington Kelland which had appeared in the *Saturday Evening Post.* The part of the hero—a small-town hick who inherits a fortune from an uncle and has to prove his sanity in court when he tries to finance small farmers who have been failures—might have been written to the specifications of Gary Cooper. Capra recognized this and hired him in a collaboration that they were to resume five years later in *Meet John Doe,* which took on an entirely different social issue.

Romance was supplied to Longfellow Deeds in the shape of a tabloid reporter named Babe Bennett, whom Jean Arthur played in her familiar style—a winning mixture of a sophisticated cynic and a girl with a heart of gold. She was a favorite Capra heroine, and he also used her in *Mr. Smith Goes to Washington* and *You Can't Take It With You.*

Producer: Columbia. **Director:** Frank Capra. **Scriptwriter:** Robert Riskin. **Principal Players:** Gary Cooper, Jean Arthur, George Bancroft and Lionel Stander. **Running time:** 115 minutes. **Released:** Columbia.

Oscar Polk and Rex Ingram in *The Green Pastures.*

Hedy Keisler (Hedy Lamarr) in *Ecstasy.*

THE GREEN PASTURES

As a stage play, *The Green Pastures* had played 1,779 times in 203 cities in 39 states over a period of five years. The Marc Connelly work had won the 1930 Pulitzer Prize in addition. It was thus both a critical and commercial success.

Still, there was trepidation at Warner Bros. over the reception the film version might receive. Its presentation of legendary Biblical figures as Negroes was viewed by some as frivolous and even sacrilegious. And there was the Southern theatre market to consider, especially the Bible Belt.

Critics could—and did—hail the "courage" of the film makers, but that would have been small consolation in the face of a disastrous flop. Fortunately, the apprehensions proved mostly groundless. The film set records at many theatres, including Radio City Music Hall, and while Southern bookings were sparse, the picture did very well in the final accounting.

Connelly himself adapted his play to the screen with the aid of Sheridan Gibney (scriptwriter of *Anthony Adverse*), and few alterations were made in the original script. The play had been suggested by "sketches" written by Roark Bradford called *Ol' Man Adam an' His Chillun.* Several Biblical fables were strung together through a plot device that had a Negro Sunday school teacher telling the stories of De Lawd in heaven and incidents in the Old Testament. As he speaks, the stories are illustrated with all the characters, from Adam and Eve to Moses and Noah, portrayed as Negroes.

The approach is generally comic, and audiences enjoyed themselves. Warners had expected to get Richard Berry Harrison, who acted De Lawd on the stage, to make the film, but he died. Rex Ingram played the part in the movie and he also was Adam. Music was supplied by the famous Hall Johnson chorus of fifty-three male and female singers.

Producer: Warner Bros. **Directors:** Marc Connelly and William Keighley. **Scriptwriters:** Connelly and Sheridan Gibney. **Principal Players:** Rex Ingram, Oscar Polk, Eddie Anderson, Frank Wilson and George Reed. **Running time:** 90 minutes. **Released:** Warner Bros.

ECSTASY

A very young (fifteen) Hedy Lamarr scampered through the woodlands in the nude (the camera taking very long shots), and then simulated sexual intercourse (the camera remaining discreetly only on her face). It caused an international sensation and made a household word of a Czechoslovakian picture that was otherwise negligible on all counts.

Ecstasy was in trouble in the U.S. from the beginning. Customs held up the first print on moral grounds and then it was "inadvertently" burned by a U.S. Marshal. A new print said to be a different version was sent over from Prague and admitted without protest. On the basis of the notoriety it had gained, it got wide bookings here and did well. It did even better in reissue when Miss Lamarr had become well known to the American public

Three Smart Girls with Binnie Barnes, Charles Winninger, Nan Grey, Barbara Read and Deanna Durbin.

through such pictures as *Algiers* (her Hollywood debut in 1938), *White Cargo* (1942) and *Samson and Delilah* (1949).

Ecstasy was entered in the 1934 International Film Exposition in Venice where, as Terry Ramsaye put it, "It became for the Venetian show what Sally Rand was to the Chicago Fair." It also won the top prize that year.

Censors the world over were outraged by its brief excursions into nudity and sex, but no one was more persistent in seeking to ban it completely than Fritz Mandel, a German munitions magnate who married Miss Lamarr (then called Hedy Keisler) after she made the picture. Legend has it that Mandel bought up every available print and actively tried to have the film suppressed in countries where distributors would not cooperate in his plan.

Producer: Elekta Film Slavia. **Director-Scriptwriter:** Gustav Machaty. **Principal Players:** Hedy Keisler (later Hedy Lamarr), Albert Mog, R. Rogoz and Leopold Kramer. **Running time:** 81 minutes. **Released:** Jewel Productions, Inc.

THREE SMART GIRLS

Deanna Durbin was a little girl with a big soprano voice when Universal decided to make her into a movie personality. For her debut vehicle they chose *Three Smart Girls,* a slight comedy about three sisters who, upon learning that their divorced father is about to wed a gold digger, thwart those plans and reconcile him with his family.

Miss Durbin amazed film critics and audiences with the strength and power of such a voice in one so young. They also found her a pleasant and unpretentious actress.

The other two girls were played by Barbara Read and Nan Grey, neither of whom was heard of to any extent thereafter, although Miss Grey again appeared as Miss Durbin's sister in a successful sequel, *Three Smart Girls Grow Up* in 1939. (Helen Parrish replaced Miss Read, while Charles Winninger again played the father of the girls and Nella Walker their mother.)

Miss Durbin became one of the top stars at Universal, making an even bigger impact in her second picture, *100 Men and a Girl,* in which she played a young lady who cajoles Leopold Stokowski (portraying himself) into conducting a hundred unemployed musicians in a special symphonic performance.

A series of other hits followed *100 Men and a Girl* (*Mad About Music, That Certain Age,* etc.), but Miss Durbin was never really able to make the transition from child star to mature actress with success. She essayed dramatic roles in *Christmas Holiday* and *Lady on a Train,* but the critics were not impressed. Her last picture was a musical released in 1948, *Up in Central Park,* after which she retired from the screen and took up permanent residence in Paris.

Producer: Charles R. Rogers. **Director:** Henry Koster. **Scriptwriter:** Adele Comandini. **Principal Players:** Binnie Barnes, Alice Brady, Ray Milland, Charles Winninger, Nan Grey, Barbara Read and Deanna Durbin. **Running time:** 84 minutes. **Released:** Universal.

Greta Garbo and Robert Taylor in *Camille*.

Fury with Spencer Tracy.

CAMILLE

The legend of Greta Garbo is compounded of many things, from her "discovery" in Europe in 1925 by Louis B. Mayer (she had already made several Swedish and German films), to her abrupt retirement into self-imposed obscurity at the height of her career. But the essential quality is still the on-screen image—that of the eternal woman: feminine, beautiful, charming, yet always with an air of elusive mystery about her. The proud exterior obviously hid deep emotional scars.

The epitome of this image is to be found in *Camille,* based on the Alexander Dumas classic, often dramatized before but never given such an impressively handsome production as it had here from MGM. Garbo had excelled before, but in the role she played here, of the frivolous courtesan who falls in love too late, she surpassed herself.

Critics still argue whether she was a great actress as well as a great screen personality. *Camille* is sentimental claptrap, they point out, and the part is not all that challenging. Those who respond to the spell of Garbo find the question irrelevant.

Robert Taylor, then on the rise, was cast as Armand; he was handsome but unconvincing. Lionel Barrymore overacted outrageously as his father, but Henry Daniell was a brilliant Baron de Varville.

Camille not only has Garbo's best performance but it was one of her most financially successful films. Her last picture, *Two-Faced Woman* (1941), was attacked by church groups on the grounds that it was immoral, and the film suffered from editing made in an effort to appease those groups.

Producer: MGM. **Director:** George Cukor. **Scriptwriters:** Frances Marion, James Hilton and Zoë Akins. **Principal Players:** Greta Garbo, Robert Taylor and Lionel Barrymore. **Running time:** 105 minutes. **Released:** MGM.

FURY

German director Fritz Lang had established a world-wide reputation mainly on the basis of a silent film (the fantasy *Metropolis* set in the year 2100) and a sound one (*M,* the story of a child murderer) when he came to Hollywood in 1935. His first picture there was *Fury,* a trenchant indictment of mob rule that belonged to the socially crusading school of pictures that had produced *Scarface* and *I Am a Fugitive From a Chain Gang.* Lang co-authored the script as well as directed.

Public response was not as strong as it had been to those films of three years before, but it helped to launch Lang on a successful career in America. His second picture was a gangster melodrama regarded as a classic of the genre by many critics: *You Only Live Once* (1937), starring Henry Fonda and Sylvia Sidney, the latter of whom had the romantic lead in *Fury.*

The picture also supplied Spencer Tracy with his first major role, as the young man falsely accused of kidnapping who barely escapes murder by an enraged mob which dynamites the jail in which he has been incarcerated. Tracy won rave reviews, but the picture that

Modern Times with Billy Gilbert and Charlie Chaplin.

firmly established him as a leading star—*San Francisco*—was to come a month later.

Fury was one of the first films to be produced at MGM by Joseph L. Mankiewicz, who moved to the company in 1935 from Paramount where he had been a scriptwriter. (His others in 1936: *Three Godfathers, The Gorgeous Hussy* and *Love on the Run.*)

Producer: Joseph L. Mankiewicz. **Director:** Fritz Lang. **Scriptwriters:** Lang and Bartlett Cormack. **Principal Players:** Sylvia Sidney, Spencer Tracy, Walter Abel, Bruce Cabot and Walter Brennan. **Running time:** 90 minutes. **Released:** MGM.

MODERN TIMES

Sound pictures were nearly a decade old, and Charlie Chaplin had been absent from the screen for five years when he appeared in *Modern Times* in 1936. The master of silent comedy still refused to speak; his only concessions to the aural sense were a musical score which he composed (including a brief nonsense ditty sung by himself), and incidental noises and occasional voices.

Reviewing the picture at the time, Terry Ramsaye called it a compendium of all the major Chaplin themes and plots and detailed them as follows:

"The story, a waif of a wisp of a story, is the sentimental theme of *The Vagabond,* the most romantic of his earlier endeavors. Sequences that ensue are reminiscent of *The Floorwalker,* with its escalator, *The Rink,* with his acrobatic rollerskating and the most strikingly of all recalling the dope motivation of *Easy Street,* a Vincent Bryan notion of '17, in which our hero becomes a superman by falling on a hypodermic. This time the dope is in the salt shaker.

"Superimposed over it all, making it the authentic Chaplin complete, is the general theme of the triumph of the boob, ever under pursuit by Might and Power as depicted by the law and the police, from the Keystone Cops to the officers of modern times."

In a computer age the film's theme—man versus the machine—is as relevant as ever. The scene that drew the most laughs in 1936, in which the Little Tramp struggles with a feeding device, is just as funny over three decades afterwards, and just as pertinent. Chaplin's art is timeless.

Producer-Director-Writer: Charles Chaplin. **Principal Players:** Chaplin, Paulette Goddard, Henry Bergman and Chester Conklin. **Running time:** 87 minutes. **Released:** United Artists.

MY MAN GODFREY

Just a few months after *Mr. Deeds Goes to Town* was released, along came *My Man Godfrey,* another comedy with more on its mind than merely making the audience laugh. It, too, dealt with the extremes of wealth and poverty in the United States, and it also never belabored the message, which was there if the audience wanted to ponder it.

Godfrey is a tramp collected off an ash heap by a group of socialites out on a scavenger hunt. He is made

My Man Godfrey with Carole Lombard and William Powell.

a butler in a household full of eccentrics, whose lives he reforms or enriches in a number of ways before his true identity is revealed. Actually, he is the scion of a blue-blooded Boston family—which is cheating as far as the theme is concerned, albeit in a good cause. *Godfrey* is first-rate screwball farce—one of the funniest the thirties produced.

Like Mr. Deeds, Godfrey also shares his riches; at the end the city dump where he was found has been transformed into a night club manned by derelicts he met while incognito as one of their own.

William Powell played Godfrey; the actor was then at the height of his popularity, appearing in four other pictures in 1936, including *The Great Ziegfeld* and *After the Thin Man.* His casually sophisticated style was ideally suited to the role of hobo in disguise. His co-star was the vivacious Carole Lombard, who was always better as comedienne than tragedienne.

A remake of *My Man Godfrey* in 1957 with David Niven and June Allyson in the roles was a box-office failure. The material had dated; it was very much of its time.

Producer-Director: Gregory LaCava. **Scriptwriters:** Morrie Ryskind and Eric Hatch. **Principal Players:** William Powell, Carole Lombard, Alice Brady, Eugene Pallette, Gail Patrick and Mischa Auer. **Running time:** 95 minutes. **Released:** Universal.

Luise Rainer and Paul Muni in *The Good Earth,* dramatization of the great Pearl Buck novel, turned into a spectacular and moving film.

1937

In 1937, for the first time in seven years, all major groups in the film industry showed profits. The Great Depression was receding into memory, but already war clouds were filling the air in the Far East and in Europe. It was a confident President Roosevelt who was inaugurated for his second term in March. A former film company head, Joseph P. Kennedy, was selected to be U.S. Ambassador to the Court of St. James.

In theatres, the sale of candies and popcorn began to be significant, now estimated at over ten million dollars a year. Pressures from such leaders as Barney Balaban, president of Paramount, urged increased admission prices by theatres to help cover increased production costs in Hollywood. Partially to keep a closer eye on expenditures, Harry M. Warner, Warner Bros. president, moved his headquarters from New York to California.

Floyd Odlum, president of Atlas Corporation, which controlled RKO, issued a budget breakdown of a million-dollar film: Cast—$250,000; director—$100,000; extras—$50,000; assistant director—$20,000; cameraman—$15,000; lights—$20,000; cutters—$10,000; negative film—$10,000; tests—$12,000; insurance—$20,000; sound recording—$31,000; publicity—$20,000; make-up—$9,000; dramatic coaches—$2,000; crew and labor—$12,000; story preparation—$70,000; story costs—$50,000; costumes—$20,000; sets and art director—$125,000; stills—$4,000; and all indirect costs—$150,000.

Hit pictures included award-winner *The Life of Emile Zola,* which starred Paul Muni in the handsomely-mounted, carefully researched Warner Bros. production, and *The Great Ziegfeld,* released the year before. *Wee Willie Winkie* set a five-year record at the Roxy Theatre in New York City. *The Good Earth,* which had been in preparation four years, opened. Jean Harlow, aged 26, died of an illness contracted while making *Saratoga.*

Censorship forces were active. Censors in Kansas cut a *March of Time* issue. Congressman Martin Dies, acting on exhibitor complaints, called for an investigation of all phases of the motion picture business. To help improve public relations, the Motion Picture Producers and Distributors of America moved to make films available for school use. However, the overall family character of productions was indicated by Legion of Decency ratings: 1,160 films in unobjectionable categories; 98 in objectionable in part; and only 13—all made by independent companies—were condemned.

Tokyo, as part of its undeclared war on China, banned U.S. films. Japan, Italy and Germany formed a film bloc. Even England extended its quota system, designed to cut down the showing of U.S. films. All these developments made film company heads nervous because the foreign market was an important source of profits.

Some guild and labor groups in the industry were reluctantly recognized in the wake of a U.S. Supreme Court decision upholding the Wagner Labor Relations Act. Studio labor peace was expected, but the price was certain to be higher wage scales.

Stars of the year: Shirley Temple, Clark Gable, Robert Taylor, Bing Crosby, William Powell, Jane Withers, Fred Astaire, Ginger Rogers, Sonja Henie, Gary Cooper and Myrna Loy.

Freddie Bartholomew and Spencer Tracy in *Captains Courageous.*

The Dead End Kids in *Dead End.*

CAPTAINS COURAGEOUS

Spencer Tracy developed an accent for his role as Manuel, the Portuguese fisherman, in *Captains Courageous* and won his first Academy Award. The second came a year later—for his performance as Father Flanagan in *Boy's Town.* He is the only actor ever to win the Oscar two years in a row. (Luise Rainer and Katharine Hepburn accomplished the same feat in the "Best Actress" category.)

An adaptation of Rudyard Kipling's story of the Gloucester fishermen, *Captains Courageous* was extremely well received by critics as well as by the public. It is an adventure story of the sea, complete with exciting action sequences; yet it is much more than that. At its heart is a complex relationship between a man and a boy—between Manuel, the simple and practical-minded primitive, and Harvey, the sophisticated, spoiled brat he rescues from a fall from an ocean liner and instructs in his philosophy of life. In the process the boy discovers worthwhile qualities in himself which had been buried under spite and selfishness.

Tracy is magnificent, and Freddie Bartholomew is fine as the rich man's son. A small role went to young Mickey Rooney, who was shortly to become MGM's biggest star for several years.

Producer: Louis D. Lighton. **Director:** Victor Fleming. **Scriptwriters:** John Lee Mahin, Marc Connelly and Dale Van Every. **Principal Players:** Freddie Bartholomew, Spencer Tracy, Lionel Barrymore and Melvyn Douglas. **Running time:** 105 minutes. **Released:** MGM.

DEAD END

Sidney Kingsley's grim study of life on New York's East Side hardly seemed likely material for movie audiences of the 1930's, but Samuel Goldwyn was impressed by the play and felt that the fame it had gained in seven hundred Broadway performances, its controversial social elements and its own intrinsic dramatic power would prove successful on the screen. He was right—as usual—and his uncanny gift for sensing what would please motion picture audiences paid off again.

Once more he hired William Wyler, who had directed the film versions of the plays *Dodsworth* and *These Three* for him, to bring the stage play to the screen. Theirs was a collaboration that would continue its mutually profitable course into the forties with *The Little Foxes* (1941) and then after the war with *The Best Years of Our Lives* (1946).

This was a direct screening of the stage play, including its myriad of plots and subplots built around a bad boy from the other side of the tracks who comes home after ten years, unreformed, and finds things in the old home town pretty much the same. A good boy who used to best him in fights in their early days shoots the bad one dead.

As the play had done, the film used only a single set—a reproduction of a block along the East River where tenements hover beneath luxurious apartments. The film occasionally took the audience indoors, which the play never did.

Warner Bros. loaned Humphrey Bogart to Goldwyn

The Awful Truth with Cary Grant, Ralph Bellamy and Irene Dunne.

to play the villain, and he made a strong impact comparable to that he had made the year before as Duke Mantee in the film version of *The Petrified Forest.* The picture introduced the six Dead End Kids, brought to Hollywood from Broadway. They appeared thereafter in a series of pictures in which they were billed collectively as the Dead End Kids. The vogue for them did not last very long, and changing their names to the Bowery Boys didn't help matters.

Producer: Samuel Goldwyn. **Director:** William Wyler. **Scriptwriter:** Lillian Hellman. **Principal Players:** Sylvia Sidney, Joel McCrea, Humphrey Bogart, Wendy Barrie, Claire Trevor, Marjorie Main and the Dead End Kids. **Running time:** 90 minutes. **Released:** United Artists.

THE AWFUL TRUTH

The career of Leo McCarey spans the era of silence as well as sound; he began his career in 1918 as a writer, became an assistant director in 1920 and then proceeded to make comedies with Laurel and Hardy and Charlie Chase. In 1929, with sound in full sway, he made *The Sophomore* and thereafter sometimes produced as well as wrote and directed a great variety of films, from the comedy *Ruggles of Red Gap* (1934) to the sentimental drama *Going My Way* (1944) to the controversial anti-Communist film *My Son John* (1952).

One of his best dramatic films was Paramount's *Make Way for Tomorrow,* an honest treatment of the problems of old age. It came out the same year as his *The Awful Truth,* made for Columbia. *Tomorrow* died a horrible death at the box office; *Awful Truth* was a smash hit and is regarded by many as the definitive thirties' screwball comedy.

The slight plot comes from a play by Arthur Richman telling of two rich young married folk who get a ninety-day interlocutory divorce decree after an argument, but manage after many amusing complications to invalidate it by mutual consent just before midnight of the final day. The complications and their treatment give the picture its comic distinction.

The Awful Truth established Irene Dunne and Cary Grant as a popular romantic team, and they appeared thereafter in another comedy, *My Favorite Wife* (1940), and a tasteful soap opera, *Penny Serenade* (1941).

Producer-Director: Leo McCarey. **Scriptwriters:** Vina Delmar and Dwight Taylor. **Principal Players:** Irene Dunne, Cary Grant and Ralph Bellamy. **Running time:** 89 minutes. **Released:** Columbia.

MAYERLING

What really went on and why at the Mayerling hunting lodge on the fateful night of January 30, 1889, is a mystery that has fascinated film makers to the extent of at least three pictures on the subject. Several novels have also been based on the story of the tragic love affair of the Austrian Crown Prince Rudolph and his mistress Maria Vetsera, and now and again a "documented" book comes out purporting to introduce new evidence show-

Mayerling with Charles Boyer and Danielle Darrieux.

ing, for one example, that the hapless couple were murdered by paid assassins for political reasons.

This French film and a new version of the same title made in 1968 were both based on the novel *Idyl's End* by Claude Anet. The pictures adhere to the theory that the Baroness died at the hands of Rudolph, who then killed himself.

A lavishly made production, the first *Mayerling* was a big success in the few theatres in the country at the time that specialized in foreign pictures. Helping to attract such audiences to the English-titled film was Charles Boyer, who played Rudolph, but the highest critical plaudits went to Danielle Darrieux for her exquisite acting of the love-stricken Maria.

Anatole Litvak, the Russian-born director, made his international reputation with this film. He subsequently came to Hollywood where he directed *All This and Heaven, Too* and *Sorry, Wrong Number,* among others, with most critics feeling he hit his peak with *The Snake Pit* in 1949.

An interesting version, also French, was released in 1940; it was called *Mayerling to Sarajevo.* The 1968 *Mayerling* was directed and written by Terence Young with Omar Sharif and Catherine Deneuve as the lovers. It was in color and Panavision and expensively made, but observers who had seen both agreed it was far inferior to the original black-and-white version.

Producer: Nero Films. **Director:** Anatole Litvak. **Scriptwriters:** Joseph Kessel and J. C. Cube. **Principal Players:** Charles Boyer and Danielle Darrieux. **Running time:** 91 minutes. **Released:** Pax Films.

Barbara Stanwyck in *Stella Dallas.*

STELLA DALLAS

The great grandmother of all the noble heroines who suffered on radio and screen is *Stella Dallas,* the creation of Olive Higgins Prouty, whose only true rival in the field in the 1930's was Fannie Hurst, who wrote *Back Street,* among other tearjerker classics.

Stella had seen film incarnation earlier in 1925 when Belle Bennett portrayed the mill hand's daughter who marries out of her class and, aware that she is spoiling the chances of her own child to lead the rich, full life, nobly pretends to be an unworthy mother and turns the girl over to others. A decade later, Barbara Stanwyck played the role, and sound having arrived in the interim, she was able to speak the Prouty dialogue as well as gesticulate. It was her biggest role to date, and she made the most of it, winning new fans among female moviegoers.

John Boles portrayed the rich man the heroine weds and disappoints, and Anne Shirley was the daughter.

Stella Dallas has a classic soap opera scene that somehow sums up the gross sentimentality of the genre as none other can: The down-and-out heroine stands in the pouring rain outside the window of the mansion in which her daughter is being wed, watching the festivities with tears in her eyes. A policeman prods her to move on. Up with the music in the background, and fade out.

Producer: Samuel Goldwyn. **Director:** King Vidor. **Scriptwriters:** Victor Heerman and Sarah Y. Mason. **Principal Players:** Barbara Stanwyck, John Boles, Anne Shirley, Barbara O'Neil and Alan Hale. **Running time:** 104 minutes. **Released:** United Artists.

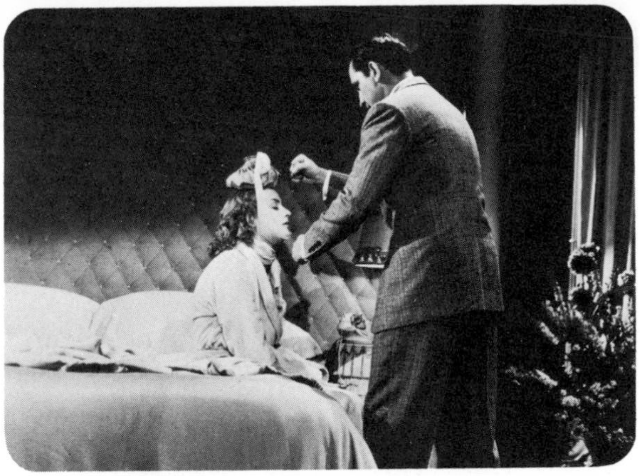

Carole Lombard and Fredric March in *Nothing Sacred.*

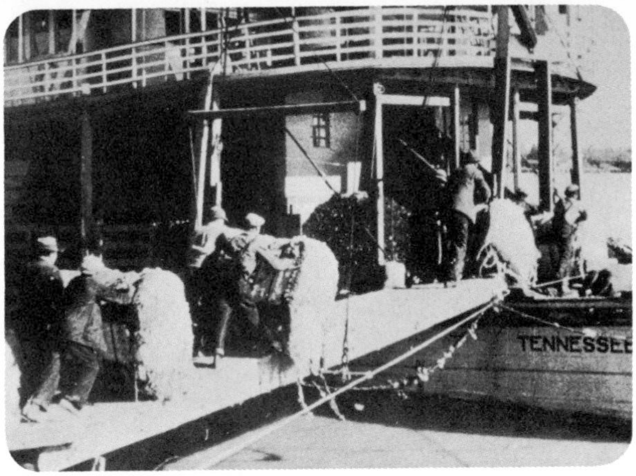

A scene from Lorentz' documentary film *The River.*

NOTHING SACRED

Ben Hecht had a high reputation as a journalist and a playwright when he went to Hollywood in 1930 to adapt with Charles MacArthur the screen version of their play, *The Front Page.* That was a hit, and so was *Twentieth Century* which they did a few years later (1934). Their forte was wise-cracking dialogue and characters that were caricatures.

In 1936 Hecht wrote on his own (from a story by James H. Street) what is one of the earliest and best examples of "black comedy"—*Nothing Sacred.* A situation which ordinarily would be treated solemnly, Hecht holds up to ridicule. A young girl is thought to be dying of radium poisoning. She is brought from Vermont to New York City by a reporter and enshrined as a heroine in the columns of his paper in a cynical effort to boost circulation. When it is learned she isn't really moribund, a fake suicide is arranged for the sympathetic public, and she and the reporter sail away disguised in sun glasses.

Even back then it was funny, and today it is even more appreciated for its satire and wit. Carole Lombard was the heroine in her most charming "mad-girl" performance. And the usually austere Fredric March was surprisingly good in a comic role as the enterprising newspaperman.

Producer: David O. Selznick. **Director:** William A. Wellman. **Scriptwriter:** Ben Hecht. **Principal Players:** Carole Lombard and Fredric March. **Running time:** 75 minutes. **Released:** United Artists.

THE RIVER

Film critics generally date the coming of age of the American film documentary by the work of Pare Lorentz—*The Plow That Broke the Plains* in 1936, and *The River* in 1937.

Both pictures were produced by Lorentz for the administration of Franklin D. Roosevelt, who wished to use the medium to explain various of his social programs to the public. *The Plow That Broke the Plains* dealt with what the government was doing to alleviate the plight of midwestern farmers driven out of their homes by drought and famine, and *The River* backed this up with a plea for flood control and soil conservation.

The documentaries were noted for the excellence of their photography and the eloquence of the commentary, written by Lorentz himself. Virgil Thompson, famed concert pianist and composer, composed an original musical score for *The River.*

At the urging of the Department of the Interior, Paramount Pictures agreed to distribute the film through its exchanges, and it had bookings in a number of large cities. It was a masterful blend of pictorial images, showing the river at its source and gradually increasing on its way to the sea and depicting the use of dams to control erosion and floods.

Lorentz produced a third film for the Government: *The Fight for Life* (1939). During World War II he also made a series of films for Government agencies.

Producer: Department of the Interior. **Director-Writer:** Pare Lorentz. **Running time:** 31 minutes. **Released:** Paramount.

Luise Rainer and Paul Muni in *The Good Earth.*

Jane Wyatt and Ronald Colman in *Lost Horizon.*

THE GOOD EARTH

Man against nature is a theme which knows no national boundaries, and, as were readers of the best-selling Pearl Buck novel before them, American moviegoers were sympathetic to the Chinese farmers in *The Good Earth.*

The battle against the locusts at the climax of the picture is one of the great spectacle scenes in film history, and audiences three decades later could be as overwhelmed by it as had been those when it first appeared in 1937.

This is one of the "prestige" pictures made at MGM under the aegis of Irving Thalberg, and he died shortly after completion of shooting. He never took screen credit for his pictures, but Louis B. Mayer ordered an inscription for this one which reads as follows: "To the memory of Irving Grant Thalberg we dedicate this picture, his last great achievement."

The Good Earth is a spectacle, but it is also a moving human drama of a man and his wife and the vicissitudes of their existence together. Paul Muni gave one of his best screen performances as Wang, the lowly farmer who rises in the world with the help of his faithful wife O-Lan, whom he mistreats and betrays until he discovers—too late—what he owes to her. As O-Lan, Luise Rainer earned her second Oscar.

Producer: MGM. **Director:** Sidney Franklin. **Scriptwriters:** Talbot Jennings, Tess Slesinger and Claudine West. **Principal Players:** Paul Muni, Luise Rainer, Walter Connolly and Tilly Losch. **Running time:** 125 minutes. **Released:** MGM.

LOST HORIZON

The highly successful team of Frank Capra and Robert Riskin had made their reputations on comedies—especially *It Happened One Night* and *Mr. Deeds Goes to Town.*

In *Lost Horizon,* they turned to quite different material—fantasy on an elaborate scale. The picture eventually did well (the press reaction was mixed), but Capra and Riskin returned to comedy thereafter (*You Can't Take It With You*).

Lost Horizon depicts a utopia, and thus the story, originally conceived by James Hilton, was close to the hearts of the socially-minded film pair. The picture took two years to make and cost $2,000,000, an enormous sum in those days.

A motley group of characters aboard a plane bound for Tibet is taken to a paradise called Shangri La when the plane crashes. It is a place where there is no sin, and where peace and contentment reign. Not appreciating what they have, the group leaves, but one of them, Robert Conway (played by Ronald Colman), tries to make his way back as the picture ends.

Shangri La became a household word—even for the President of the U.S. Asked where the planes which bombed Japan had originated from, Roosevelt said, "Shangri La."

Producer-Director: Frank Capra. **Scriptwriter:** Robert Riskin. **Principal Players:** Ronald Colman, Jane Wyatt, Edward Everett Horton, John Howard, Thomas Mitchell and Margo. **Running time:** 130 minutes. **Released:** Columbia.

Paul Muni in *The Life of Emile Zola.*

Roland Young and Cary Grant in *Topper.*

THE LIFE OF EMILE ZOLA

Biographical films enjoyed a vogue in the 1930's, mostly through the efforts of Paul Muni, a popular stage actor who made his film debut in *The Valiant* in 1928. He had huge success in the gangster film *Scarface* (1932) and the social drama *I Am a Fugitive From a Chain Gang* (1932).

In 1935 he portrayed Louis Pasteur and won an Academy Award; two years later, he played Emile Zola in a much better picture—better because the events of Zola's life were more susceptible to dramatization. Pasteur's achievements were all in the laboratory; Zola fought the hypocrites who denounced his novel *Nana* and went to court in his defense of Dreyfus. And what is more dramatically surefire than a courtroom trial? It won the Oscar as best film.

There were some critics who felt that the differences between Pasteur and Zola—and later, *Juarez* (1939)—as interpreted by Muni were largely ones of makeup. There were others who saw greater subtleties in his various interpretations. William Dieterle directed all three films with a strong flair for dramatic action.

Producer: Hal B. Wallis. **Director:** William Dieterle. **Scriptwriters:** Norman Reilly Raine, Heinz Herald and Geza Herczeg. **Principal Players:** Paul Muni, Gale Sondergaard, Joseph Schildkraut, Gloria Holden and Donald Crisp. **Running time:** 120 minutes. **Released:** Warner Bros.

TOPPER

The trick camera technique which had enabled Claude Rains to appear and disappear at will in *The Invisible Man* in 1933 was employed for this adaptation of the Thorne Smith story about a pleasure-loving married couple killed in a motor accident who are given a second chance to do something worthwhile. They pick as their good deed the emancipation of a henpecked banker (the title character of the film) who had been their friend in life.

The lens legerdemain intrigued and delighted audiences and almost stole the show. Roland Young was perfectly cast as Topper, the man brow-beaten by his society wife, played with the usual fluttering about by Billie Burke. The sophisticated ghosts were acted by Cary Grant and Constance Bennett.

There was really only one gag: complications aroused by the sudden appearance and disappearance of the couple to the embarassment of the hero. But audiences liked *Topper* well enough to inspire two sequels, *Topper Takes a Trip* (1939) and *Topper Returns* (1941). Young returned for both films, but Miss Bennett and Grant did not repeat their roles.

Producer: Hal Roach. **Director:** Norman Z. McLeod. **Scriptwriters:** Jack Jevne, Eric Hatch and Eddie Moran. **Principal Players:** Constance Bennett, Cary Grant, Roland Young and Billie Burke. **Running time:** 98 minutes. **Released:** MGM.

Grand Illusion with Jean Gabin (center) and Pierre Fresnay, Jean Renoir's masterpiece and the classic anti-war statement on film.

1938

This was the year when political implications became significant in certain U.S. films. With tension increasing in Europe and elsewhere, the U.S. films reflected the spirit of the times. There was debate, sometimes calm, sometimes angry, on the role of propaganda in films. There were those who asserted that messages were "for Western Union," wishing that entertainment films be entirely free of advocacy. An organization called Films for Democracy marshalled what later would be called "Left Wing" supporters.

After a few years of progress in economic recovery from the Great Depression, there was in 1938 a generally unfavorable economic climate, yet new theatre construction declined only 11 percent from the excellent mark set the year before. Altogether, 429 new theatres were built in the U.S., with an average seating capacity of around 750. In 1938 the average cost of a new theatre was $58,500, sharply down from the average of $85,000 in 1937. This was due to the generally poorer business conditions and to the fact that smaller theatres were being built.

Production costs had soared until important pictures were costing $23,200 per minute of screen time to make. Total story costs in Hollywood came to $2,730,000 for the year for 546 films.

New York critics picked a British film, *The Citadel,* as the year's best. A vote of women patrons showed that 89 percent thought that not a single picture released during the year was "offensively vulgar." Also, 78 percent voted that "films were becoming more entertaining." Their favorites were *Snow White and the Seven Dwarfs* (released late in 1937), *The Adventures of Robin Hood* and *In Old Chicago* (released in 1937). *Jezebel* was another outstanding film of the year.

The average film now cost $125,000. Between 50 and 250 prints were made for the domestic market, i.e., the U.S. and Canada. The average running time of a feature was $73\frac{1}{2}$ minutes. The longest was *The Firefly* at 131 minutes.

MGM lost a key plagiarism suit involving *Letty Lynton.* It was alleged that the film infringed the play *Dishonored Lady,* and $500,000 damages were awarded. This and other cases made all the major studios very sensitive on matters involving literary rights. Studios shunned unknown writers, preferring to get story material from produced plays, published books or from Hollywood writers under contract.

The Federal Government threw a bombshell at the film industry in the form of an antitrust suit against Paramount and seven other major film companies. The complaint charged combinations in restraint of trade, monopoly of production, distribution and exhibition. The Department of Justice asked for "divorcement," i.e., the separation of the theatre-owning and production-distribution activities. Also requested were bars on various restraints held to monopolize production. This aspect of the case involving Hollywood operations was quietly dropped. However, after delays caused by a trial consent decree and World War II, the case was finally tried and the film companies lost in the lower Federal Court and in the U.S. Supreme Court. Those whose complaints had interested the Department of Justice in the film industry were the smaller exhibitors who felt aggrieved by various trade practices.

Stars of the year: Shirley Temple, Clark Gable, Sonja Henie, Mickey Rooney, Spencer Tracy, Robert Taylor, Myrna Loy, Jane Withers, Alice Faye and Tyrone Power.

Virginia Weidler and Mickey Rooney in the film *Out West With the Hardys.*

OUT WEST WITH THE HARDYS

In 1937, MGM made a modestly-budgeted "B" picture called *A Family Affair,* in which the members of a typical middle-class American family called Hardy were introduced in a small town called Carmel. The father was a judge, and there were three children, Andy, Marian and Joan. Aunt Milly also lived with them in their typical American house.

In the first episode, the judge saved the people of Carmel from a group of greedy promoters who wanted to build a dam that would have caused the town to lose its water supply. The film proved so popular, outgrossing several "A" films of the day, that MGM turned it into a fourteen-picture series running from 1937 through 1946. MGM reports the total *Hardy* gross to be in excess of $73,000,000.

MGM also used these films to launch many contract players on the road to stardom. Among the alumnae of the series are Judy Garland, Lana Turner, Ava Gardner, Esther Williams and Kathryn Grayson, the latter two making their first appearances in *Hardy* pictures.

The film in the series that grossed the most in the thirties was *Out West With the Hardys,* the fourth to come along. Two possible reasons for its being the most successful are that the series had become well established by 1933, and that the plot was the equivalent of an old-fashioned western.

At bottom it was the story of the greedy rancher who controls his neighbor's water supply and puts a dollar a gallon price on it by way of forcing him to sell out at a giveaway price. Judge Hardy and family went west to the rescue of an old friend.

Later on in the series the film makers got serious and didactic, and some of the more conservative fans felt they had become too "adult." In one picture the judge lectured Andy on the desirability of sexual continence before marriage, and in another, the evils of excessive drink were attacked.

In the first episode (*Family Affair*) Judge Hardy was played by Lionel Barrymore and his wife by Spring Byington. In the second (*You're Only Young Once*), Lewis Stone replaced Barrymore and Fay Holden took over for Miss Byington. Stone and Miss Holden continued as regulars throughout the series along with Mickey Rooney as Andy, Cecilia Parker as Marian, Sara Haden as Aunt Milly, and Ann Rutherford as Polly.

In 1958, MGM tried to revive the series with a fifteenth picture, *Andy Hardy Comes Home,* in which Rooney succeeded Stone as father and judge, and Rooney's real-life son of eight years played his screen offspring. To identify the film with its predecessors, the Misses Holden and Parker came out of retirement to take over their old roles and Stone's portrait was shown several times as Rooney retired to his father's study to ponder his problems. *Andy Hardy Comes Home* was not a success. America was becoming more sophisticated.

Producer: MGM. **Director:** George B. Seitz. **Scriptwriters:** Kay Van Riper, Agnes Christine Johnston and William Ludwig. **Principal Players:** Lewis Stone, Mickey Rooney, Cecilia Parker, Fay Holden, Ann Rutherford and Sara Haden. **Running time:** 84 minutes. **Released:** MGM.

Leslie Howard and Wendy Hiller in *Pygmalion.*

Alexander's Ragtime Band with Ethel Merman.

PYGMALION

The man who finally persuaded George Bernard Shaw to permit his plays to be filmed was Gabriel Pascal, an international producer who had previously made films with his own units in Italy, France and Germany, as well as England. (He also played a leading role in his first big film, *Popoli Morituri.*)

It took some doing, as Shaw was very reluctant. Pascal was persuasive, and *Pygmalion* was a good choice with which to introduce the Irish dramatist to moviegoers.

MGM purchased the film for American distribution, and it was a surprise success, not being restricted to "art" theatres but playing the Astor in New York and similar theatres in other big cities.

It deserved its success, for it was an excellent job in all respects. Shaw himself wrote the screenplay (for which he won an Oscar), and the acting of Wendy Hiller, then a newcomer to the screen, as Eliza Doolittle, was inspired. No beauty in particular, she had a wistful charm and—more important—the acting skills to make the transformation from guttersnipe to lady. Leslie Howard was a dapper and likeable Higgins, and the entire cast, which included names renowned on the British stage, was first rate.

As nearly everyone knows, this is the property that inspired the mammoth stage success *My Fair Lady,* which was made into a film in 1964. There are those who prefer *Pygmalion* to the musical show.

Pascal continued to turn Shaw plays into films, making *Major Barbara* in 1944 and *Caesar and Cleopatra* (which he also directed) in the same year. He made *Androcles and the Lion* in Hollywood in 1951.

Producer: Gabriel Pascal. **Directors:** Anthony Asquith and Leslie Howard. **Scriptwriter:** George Bernard Shaw. **Principal Players:** Leslie Howard, Wendy Hiller, Wilfred Lawson and Marie Lohr. **Running time:** 96 minutes. **Released:** MGM.

ALEXANDER'S RAGTIME BAND

Irving Berlin had been writing hit songs for over a quarter of a century when, in 1938, Darryl F. Zanuck decided to build a musical around twenty-eight of them—twenty-six old ones and two written for the movie: "Now It Can Be Told" and "My Walking Stick."

The plot merely served to link the tunes together, it being a slight story of two boys and a girl and other members of a band which started in San Francisco and rose to a success crowned by an appearance at Carnegie Hall in the thirties.

Henry King had made *In Old Chicago* the year before for 20th Century-Fox with the same three stars: Tyrone Power, Alice Faye and Don Ameche. Miss Faye sang in both pictures, and in this one she was joined by no less than Ethel Merman (in a supporting role).

Both King pictures were great successes of the day.

Producer: Darryl F. Zanuck. **Director:** Henry King. **Scriptwriters:** Kathryn Scola and Lamar Trotti. **Principal Players:** Tyrone Power, Alice Faye, Don Ameche, Ethel Merman and Jack Haley. **Running time:** 105 minutes. **Released:** 20th Century-Fox.

Errol Flynn in *The Adventures of Robin Hood.*

You Can't Take It With You with Jean Arthur, Halliwell Hobbes, Dub Taylor, Spring Byington, Ann Miller and Mischa Auer.

THE ADVENTURES OF ROBIN HOOD

Up until 1938 the screen's most glamorous Robin Hood had been Douglas Fairbanks (*Robin Hood,* 1922). Then Errol Flynn played the role in this lavish Warner Bros. production and no one before or since has come close to matching him in masculine good looks, light-hearted air and romantic dash. It was his greatest triumph.

A similarly swashbuckling role had catapulted Flynn to fame in 1935 as the title character in *Captain Blood.* In England before that he had been on the stage in *Othello* and *The Constant Nymph* and also had done some film work there. He was always at his best in big adventure spectacles such as *The Prince and the Pauper* (1937) and *The Adventures of Don Juan* (1958). He was ill at ease in straight costume dramas like *The Private Lives of Elizabeth and Essex* (1939) and melodramas like *Cry Wolf* (1947).

But give him a trusty blade, and he was in his element. Under the robust direction of Michael Curtiz, he and Basil Rathbone (as the evil Sir Guy) performed one of the most vigorous and exciting sword duels in the history of the screen.

Olivia de Havilland, who had co-starred with Flynn in *Captain Blood* and *The Charge of the Light Brigade* (1936), was as lovely a Maid Marian as anyone could ask. Claude Rains was a wicked Prince John, Alan Hale a colorful Little John and Eugene Pallette a robust Friar Tuck.

William Keighley is credited as co-director; he started work on the picture, but Jack Warner replaced him when he was displeased with the early rushes.

Producer: Henry Blanke. **Directors:** Michael Curtiz and William Keighley. **Scriptwriters:** Norman Reilly Raine and Seton I. Miller. **Principal Players:** Errol Flynn, Olivia de Havilland, Ian Hunter, Claude Rains and Basil Rathbone. **Running time:** 102 minutes. **Released:** Warner Bros.

YOU CAN'T TAKE IT WITH YOU

"Do your own thing" was the keynote of the philosophy of rebellious youth in the 1960's. It was nothing new; the George S. Kaufman–Moss Hart play of the 1930's was dedicated to the same credo.

Members of the Sycamore family herein depicted do what they want to do on all occasions and like it—whether it be painting, dancing or what have you. They even manage to convert a stuffy old business tycoon to their way of life.

The property was surefire for the screen, and Frank Capra and scriptwriter Robert Riskin did not tamper much with the material. It was cast with the customary Capra shrewdness, the romantic leads going to Jean Arthur and James Stewart, who proved such a compatible pair that he put them together again in his *Mr. Smith Goes to Washington* the following year.

The dialogue did get oratorical now and then, including a monologue on the relative merits of Communism,

The Lady Vanishes with Dame May Whitty, Margaret Lockwood and Michael Redgrave.

Fascism and Americanism, with the last naturally winning the decision.

Capra won his third Oscar for direction, and the film was also cited as best picture of the year.

Producer-Director: Frank Capra. **Scriptwriter:** Robert Riskin. **Principal Players:** Jean Arthur, Lionel Barrymore, James Stewart and Edward Arnold. **Running time:** 125 minutes. **Released:** Columbia.

THE LADY VANISHES

Alfred Hitchcock entered the motion picture industry as a junior technician in 1920 and thereafter became a scriptwriter, production manager and art director at Gainsborough Studios. Then he found his true niche as a director. His first film in that capacity (without a collaborator) was *The Pleasure Garden* (1925). The following year he directed *The Lodger,* which was a thriller. That was to be the genre in which he became the specialist *par excellence.*

He was to make a number of such films in the decade from 1925 to 1935, but it was not until the mid-thirties that he became known to American audiences. Both *The Man Who Knew Too Much* (1934) and *The Thirty-Nine Steps* (1935) were well-liked here, but the most popular turned out to be *The Lady Vanishes.* It proved so successful, in fact, that it led to the inevitable overtures from Hollywood—which he accepted after doing one more picture in Great Britain, *Jamaica Inn,* which was more of a costume drama than a mystery.

The Hitchcock touch abounds in *The Lady Vanishes:* The little old lady who disappears from the train is not as innocuous as she seems, but is revealed as a spy; she and the other characters are introduced casually, but are quickly individualized; humor comes from character; and suspense mounts steadily. And the actors are firmly manipulated by a man who was not to be intimidated even by international stars.

Hitchcock's first Hollywood picture was for David O. Selznick: *Rebecca* in 1940. Then came the golden years and worldwide fame.

Producer: Edward Black. **Director:** Alfred Hitchcock. **Scriptwriters:** Sidney Gilliatt and Frank Launder. **Principal Players:** Michael Redgrave, Margaret Lockwood, Paul Lukas, Dame May Whitty, Googie Withers and Cecil Parker. **Running time:** 87 minutes. **Released:** Gaumont British.

BRINGING UP BABY

All the characters are more or less addled in this Howard Hawks comedy, which makes it the farce to end them all in the thirties. Some directors would have insisted upon at least one sane person for contrast and perspective—or as a comic butt—but not Hawks. This is one of his best jobs of direction; the fantasy world is beautifully sustained, and the picture is funny over thirty years later.

The baby of the title is not a child but a leopard, and the plot is wild. Katharine Hepburn plays a madcap heiress—a role she pretty well had the patent on by

Bringing Up Baby with May Robson, Katharine Hepburn and Charlie Ruggles.

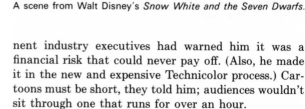

A scene from Walt Disney's *Snow White and the Seven Dwarfs.*

then—whose dog (played by Asta of *The Thin Man*) steals a bone an anthropologist (Cary Grant) needs to complete his dinosaur. Miss Hepburn also has a tame leopard which gets loose at the same time that a vicious one escapes from the local zoo. The complications roll up from there to a frantic ending.

Miss Hepburn and Grant played together more felicituously—and profitably—than they had in *Sylvia Scarlett* (1936). They were in two films together in 1938; the other was *Holiday,* a second film version of the Philip Barry romantic comedy made by Columbia.

Miss Hepburn had been slipping at the box office when these two films with Grant came out, and while they helped to restore her prestige somewhat, it was not until *The Philadelphia Story* in 1940 that she really hit her stride again.

Producer-Director: Howard Hawks. **Scriptwriters:** Dudley Nichols and Hagar Wilde. **Principal Players:** Katharine Hepburn, Cary Grant, Charlie Ruggles, Walter Catlett and Barry Fitzgerald. **Running time:** 100 minutes. **Released:** RKO.

SNOW WHITE AND THE SEVEN DWARFS

Walt Disney's first feature-length cartoon remains three decades later his most popular of that genre with audiences, and, most gratifyingly, the biggest grosser in the field. (The second is his *Jungle Book* of 1967.)

It was a bold step forward that the redoubtable showman took in making the Grimm fairy tale; prominent industry executives had warned him it was a financial risk that could never pay off. (Also, he made it in the new and expensive Technicolor process.) Cartoons must be short, they told him; audiences wouldn't sit through one that runs for over an hour.

This one ran eighty-two minutes, and the initial press and public reaction was such that not a single frame was cut. Originally released during the Christmas week of 1937, the film has been reissued several times over the past three decades, and the only other U.S. film that youngsters of all ages know so well is *The Wizard of Oz.*

As created by Disney and his talented staff, Snow White and the Prince are conventional figures; the picture is stolen by the Seven Dwarfs, who were even more cleverly individualized than the Three Little Pigs had been in the short released five years previously.

A special Academy Award was given to Disney for *Snow White,* which was recognized "as a significant screen innovation which has charmed millions and pioneered a great new entertainment field for the motion picture cartoon."

The success story which followed for the man who had started out in life as a commercial artist is too well known to bear repeating here. Disney made hit after hit, and his name on a film meant more dollars at the box office than that of many a star who has been forgotten.

Producer: Walt Disney. **Sequence Directors:** Perce Pearce, Larry Morey, William Cottrell, Wilfred Jackson, Ben Sharpsteen. **Story Adapters:** Ted Sears, Otto Englander, Earl Hurd, Dorothy Ann Blank, Richard Creedon, Dick Richard, Merrill De Maris and Webb Smith. **Running time:** 82 minutes. **Released:** RKO.

Grand Illusion with Erich von Stroheim (center).

GRAND ILLUSION

Seven years after Lewis Milestone's fine film version of Erich Maria Remarque's *All Quiet on the Western Front* was released, Jean Renoir's *Grand Illusion* appeared. Five decades after the actual event they still remain the two best sound films dealing with World War I.

The two pictures differ in their approaches to the anti-war theme; the Milestone film persuades the audience emotionally, while Renoir takes an intellectual tack. *Grand Illusion's* most crucial arguments come in long discussions between a German officer (Erich von Stroheim) and the Frenchman (Pierre Fresnay) who is his prisoner in a high-security German camp. As they reflect on their places in the scheme of things and what will happen to them when peace comes, there is a suggestion that the German at least really needs the conditions of wartime to keep secure his feelings of superiority and importance.

Obviously this philosophy disturbs Renoir, who also evinces pessimism about the ability of the "common men" (here, the foot soldier played by Jean Gabin) ever to be more than sheep, blindly following their leaders. Such threads, woven subtly into the fabric of the film, imply that war, however much one loathes it, is inevitable.

Highly praised by critics in America and elsewhere, *Grand Illusion* has become a staple of U.S. theatres that regularly play French classics.

Producer: Raymond Blondy. **Director:** Jean Renoir. **Scriptwriters:** Jean Renoir and Charles Spaak. **Principal Players:** Jean Gabin, Dita Parlo, Pierre Fresnay and Erich von Stroheim. **Running time:** 100 minutes. **Released:** World Pictures.

Clark Gable and Vivien Leigh in *Gone With the Wind,* one of the most publicized films of all time. It won nine Academy Awards.

1939

As war clouds gathered in Europe, the ideological content of the Hollywood product came under examination by assorted critics inside and outside the world of entertainment. By and large, the moviegoing public supported Americanism in films. Americanism was the theme of 43 features and 84 short subjects during the year, an output amounting to a third of the production of all the major studios. Propaganda films involved with foreign issues came under particular attack. One such was Walter Wanger's *Blockade,* concerning the Spanish Civil War. One writer said the film "toyed with an international political issue."

During the year the U.S. Army Signal Corps sharply increased its production of military training films and began to recruit Hollywood technical talent, usually by offering commissions in the Army Reserve. Experts asserted that a well-made film could do a better job of teaching a military subject such as "Cleaning the M-1 Rifle" than an instructor could do.

Gone With the Wind, one of the great landmark films, opened and the film trade would never be the same. The production by David O. Selznick was unusual in a number of respects: The cost made skeptics predict a huge loss; the running time of nearly four hours was said to be too long for patron comfort and enjoyment—as well as limiting the possible number of shows each day; and, lastly, many thought casting an unknown, Vivien Leigh, opposite Clark Gable was a mistake. Critics were wrong on all counts. Grosses were fantastic.

Hollywood worried about the effects on box office at theatres resulting from the appearance of movie stars on radio. Exhibitors in many parts of the country insisted that film players' radio participation hurt attendance, especially on Sunday, then the biggest grossing day. This also was the year when Orson Welles demonstrated the overwhelming power of a mass entertainment medium with his radio drama, *War of the Worlds,* which made half the people of the country think America was being invaded by the Martians!

The New York World's Fair was a great showcase for educational and advertising films. Altogether five hundred different films were on daily exhibit at the various buildings. New York's lively Mayor Fiorello LaGuardia launched a campaign to bring film production to New York. His appeals fell on deaf ears, as American film makers preferred to work, and play, in Hollywood.

Senator Matthew M. Neeley of West Virginia pushed for passage of his bill to outlaw block booking, while several state legislatures debated theatre circuit divorcement. Harry Hopkins, Secretary of Commerce, met with industry leaders, but denied that he was trying to influence Congressional consideration of the Neeley Bill.

On the censorship front, *Ecstasy* (first seen in the U.S. in 1936), starring Hedy Lamarr, was banned in a number of localities.

Hollywood companies entered the educational film field as Will H. Hays announced the formation of Teaching Film Custodians, with an initial library of six hundred films, at a meeting of the National Education Association.

Film correspondents and critics reached an all-time high of nine hundred. In Hollywood alone, 312 press representatives were accredited to the studios. Many of these wrote for overseas publications.

Stars of the year: Mickey Rooney, Tyrone Power, Spencer Tracy, Clark Gable, Shirley Temple, Bette Davis, Alice Faye, Errol Flynn, James Cagney and Sonja Henie.

Robert Donat and Greer Garson in *Goodbye, Mr. Chips*

GOODBYE, MR. CHIPS

Americans had been accused of being insular in the 1930's, refusing to give box-office support to imported films, as they had in the days of the silents. Even English pictures had rough going here, with a few notable exceptions. Shaw's Eliza Doolittle in *Pygmalion* became a beloved character, as did Mr. Chips, the schoolteacher hero of James Hilton's 1934 novel.

Technically, *Goodbye, Mr. Chips* was an American-English film; it was made in the British studios of MGM. The producer and director were Americans, but the cast was largely British. So, of course, were the school settings and the traditions observed there.

The conquest of America by Mr. Chips was due in large part to the performance of the role by Robert Donat, who won an Oscar. He had an actor's dream, being able to age from a shy youth to a benign old man and go through a love affair and marriage that were tragically ended by the early death of his bride. This lady was played by Greer Garson, introduced to American audiences here, and later to play the most popular British character of all—Mrs. Miniver. Late in 1969, MGM released a musical version of *Goodbye, Mr. Chips,* with a score by Leslie Bricusse that critics panned. Rave notices went to Peter O'Toole, however, for his fine performance in the title role.

Producer: Victor Saville. **Director:** Sam Wood. **Scriptwriters:** R. C. Sherriff, Claudine West and Eric Maschwitz. **Principal Players:** Robert Donat, Greer Garson, Terry Kilburn and John Mills. **Running time:** 114 minutes. **Released:** MGM.

Allen Jenkins, James Stewart, Marlene Dietrich and Brian Donlevy in *Destry Rides Again.*

DESTRY RIDES AGAIN

It was not only Destry who rode again in this amusing and profitable western. It was Marlene Dietrich.

In the late twenties *The Blue Angel* had made her an international star, but later roles and directors had tended to turn her into a clothes horse—a beautiful statue, striking to watch but lifeless.

They resurrected her in *Destry Rides Again,* first by putting her into a gaudy western saloon reminiscent of that nightclub in *The Blue Angel;* and secondly, by casting her as a singer and down-to-earth pal of the local bad man. They even let her have a hair-pulling fight scene with Una Merkel which had been widely publicized in advance in the press. Critics agreed that it was wilder, hotter and longer than they had been promised.

So much excitement was engendered by the triumphant return of Miss Dietrich that James Stewart, who played the title character, was almost overlooked. Destry was a meek but masterful young man who brings law and order to a frontier town without the aid of a six-shooter—up until the climax, when Frenchy (Miss Dietrich) stops a bullet meant for him. Stewart was Stewart, and to many people that was all that was necessary.

Producer: Joe Pasternak. **Director:** George Marshall. **Scriptwriters:** Felix Jackson, Henry Myers and Gertrude Purcell. **Principal Players:** Marlene Dietrich, James Stewart, Charles Winninger, Mischa Auer and Brian Donlevy. **Running time:** 94 minutes. **Released:** Universal.

John Wayne, George Bancroft, Donald Meek, Chris Martin, Thomas Mitchell and Andy Devine in *Stagecoach*.

Rosalind Russell, Norma Shearer and Joan Crawford in *The Women*.

STAGECOACH

John Ford's classic western has become such a legend, and has been copied and imitated so often, that some people have quite justifiably come to believe the plot was original back in 1939.

Actually it wasn't; the Dudley Nichols script used situations and characters that were long-established clichés. Apaches pursue a stagecoach, and the cavalry comes to the rescue. The wrongfully jailed hero shoots it out at dusk with three villains while the local population makes itself scarce. The same hero forgives the girl the indiscretions in her shady past. The city-slicker gambler turns out to have a heart of gold under his glittering exterior. The sheriff sets free the young man he ought to take to jail. And so on.

Several elements combined to make all these things and others look new and fresh in *Stagecoach:* Ford's vigorous direction and use of the Monument Valley backgrounds; Nichols' tightly constructed screenplay; and the excellent acting of the entire cast. John Wayne had been making westerns since 1930, but this was his best part to date and it launched him as a major star. Claire Trevor was the dance hall girl with a past; Thomas Mitchell, the drunken doctor; John Carradine, the gambler; George Bancroft, the sheriff; Berton Churchill, the fugitive embezzler; Louise Platt, the woman the stork overtakes en route; and Andy Devine, the coach driver.

A remake of *Stagecoach,* released in 1966, was a failure on almost all counts. A major error was inappropriate casting, with Ann-Margret in the Trevor role, Bing Crosby in the Mitchell one and so forth.

Producer: Walter Wanger. **Director:** John Ford. **Scriptwriter:** Dudley Nichols. **Principal Players:** Claire Trevor, John Wayne, Andy Devine, John Carradine, Thomas Mitchell, Louise Platt, George Bancroft, Donald Meek, Berton Churchill and Tim Holt. **Running time:** 97 minutes. **Released:** United Artists.

THE WOMEN

MGM faced a number of problems in bringing the Clare Booth Luce stage play—a rowdy and bawdy comedy—to the screen under the old Production Code. A reviewer summed up their success this way: "They took out the four-letter words, but they left in the spark. They didn't kill the points, and they added some. Some of the smirk went by the board but the wit is still there. It's a better picture than it was a play."

It had an all-star cast in the tradition of MGM films like *Grand Hotel* and *Dinner at Eight* although it was, of course, exclusively female. Norma Shearer, in the lead, had one of the few sympathetic roles. Characters of varying degrees of malice were played by Rosalind Russell, Joan Crawford, Mary Boland and Paulette Goddard, among others.

Producer: Hunt Stromberg. **Director:** George Cukor. **Scriptwriters:** Anita Loos and Jane Murfin. **Principal Players:** Norma Shearer, Joan Crawford, Rosalind Russell, Mary Boland, Paulette Goddard and Joan Fontaine. **Running time:** 133 minutes. **Released:** MGM.

Clara Blandick, Judy Garland, Margaret Hamilton and Charley Grapewin in *The Wizard of Oz.*

Tyrone Power in *Jesse James.*

THE WIZARD OF OZ

In her later years Judy Garland is said to have begun to disparage her role of Dorothy in *The Wizard of Oz* as a bore. She was probably expressing the half-conscious resentment of many performers to a role that gave them a public image they had a hard time shaking. (Some never do; she did.) She was probably also tired of being asked to sing "Over the Rainbow" wherever she went.

Yet this is the part that secured her claim to stardom at MGM and is the one by which she is known to generations not born when she played it, and by which she will be known to generations yet unborn. It is a television favorite, revived every year during prime time on a major network. No other film or star has enjoyed this kind of exposure.

The property first saw theatrical light when L. Frank Baum, adapting his own novel, wrote the book and lyrics for a musical that opened in New York City in January of 1903. There had also been a couple of silent film versions.

The MGM musical followed the book faithfully, but had new songs by Harold Arlen and E. Y. Harburg. The sets and costumes were imaginative, and the cast was delightful. In addition to Miss Garland, there were Frank Morgan as the Wizard; Ray Bolger as the Scarecrow; Jack Haley as the Tin Man; Margaret Hamilton as the Wicked Witch; and, best of all, Bert Lahr as the Cowardly Lion. The Munchkins were played by the Singer Midgets.

A foreward dedicated the picture to the "young in heart." There were—and are—millions of those.

Producer: Mervyn LeRoy. **Director:** Victor Fleming. **Scriptwriters:** Noel Langley, Florence Ryerson and Edgar Allan Woolf. **Principal Players:** Judy Garland, Frank Morgan, Ray Bolger, Bert Lahr, Jack Haley, Billie Burke and Margaret Hamilton. **Running time:** 102 minutes. **Released:** MGM.

JESSE JAMES

Tyrone Power—son of the famous actor of the same name—had been a stage actor briefly when 20th Century-Fox put him under contract and introduced him to motion picture audiences in *Girls' Dormitory* (1936). Thereafter he was cast in a variety of romantic leads: a series of romantic comedies with Loretta Young (*Love Is News*) and Sonja Henie (*Thin Ice*); biographical spectacles (*Suez* and *Marie Antoinette*); melodramas (*In Old Chicago*); and even a musical (*Alexander's Ragtime Band*).

He became one of Hollywood's biggest matinee idols, his peak years of popularity being 1938, 1939 and 1940.

It was in the middle year that he gave the firmest evidence to date that he could do something more than emanate charm and good looks—that, in fact, he could act. The role that offered the chance was that of the legendary outlaw, Jesse James. Power made the character real and plausible, creating neither a hero nor a villain, but a mixture of both.

Frank James, the brother, was played by Henry

Wuthering Heights with Laurence Olivier and Merle Oberon.

Clark Gable and Vivien Leigh in *Gone With the Wind.*

Fonda, who had less footage, but gave an equally stalwart performance.

Power continued to make pictures until 1958 when he died while filming *Solomon and Sheba.* (Yul Brynner replaced him.) Critics generally agree that Power's best performance as an actor is in *Nightmare Alley,* in which he plays an amoral opportunist who brings about his own undoing. His most swashbuckling performance was in *The Mark of Zorro.*

Producer: Darryl F. Zanuck. **Director:** Henry King. **Scriptwriter:** Nunnally Johnson. **Principal Players:** Tyrone Power, Henry Fonda, Nancy Kelly and Randolph Scott. **Running time:** 105 minutes. **Released:** 20th Century-Fox.

WUTHERING HEIGHTS

Emily Bronte's nineteenth-century novel should have been turned into a great movie. To anyone who has read the book, however, the film can never be more than a very good one, interesting for its shortcomings as well as its achievements.

The script of Ben Hecht and Charles MacArthur is fine in dramatizing and compressing the plot externals, but it misses the psychological depths. The direction of William Wyler brilliantly captures the eerie atmosphere of the Yorkshire Moors (recreated in the hills far north of Hollywood), but it fails in drawing sufficiently attuned performances from some of the players. The Heathcliff of Laurence Olivier is passionate, but Merle Oberon's Cathy is too reserved.

As for the Samuel Goldwyn production values, they are characteristically rich and polished. He even changed the period from Regency to Georgian, in order to have more colorful costuming, it is said.

Producer: Samuel Goldwyn. **Director:** William Wyler. **Scriptwriters:** Ben Hecht and Charles MacArthur. **Principal Players:** Merle Oberon, Laurence Olivier, David Niven, Flora Robson, Donald Crisp and Geraldine Fitzgerald. **Running time:** 105 minutes. **Released:** United Artists.

GONE WITH THE WIND

Too many legends have built up around *Gone With the Wind*—an historical film in more than one sense—to recount all of them here, but some are more to be treasured than others.

Item: The initial reluctance of producer David O. Selznick to buy the rights to the Margaret Mitchell novel, because several Civil War pictures, including *So Red the Rose,* had recently flopped.

Item: The search for an actress to play the leading role, which ended when agent Myron Selznick arrived on the set where Atlanta was being burned and introduced Vivien Leigh to his brother with the words, "I want you to meet Scarlett O'Hara."

Item: The threats of Southern ladies to boycott the film if Miss Leigh did not measure up to their specifications for a Dixie belle.

Item: The comment of director Victor Fleming: "I'm going to make this picture a melodrama."

Ninotchka with Greta Garbo and Melvyn Douglas.

Item: The lifting of Production Code restrictions to enable Clark Gable to say, when Scarlett asks what will become of her, "Frankly, my dear, I don't give a damn."

And so on. This astonishingly successful picture set records at box offices around the world—not only during its initial roadshow bookings in 1939 and 1940, but in five reissue engagements. At the end of the sixties, it was, along with *The Sound of Music,* one of the two top-grossing films of all time.

For the sixth go-around in 1967, MGM released the film in a 70mm version with six-track stereophonic sound. The 35mm print was blown up, almost frame by frame, and the sound track re-recorded into separate channels. The cropping necessitated by the change of image size sometimes resulted in heads cut off too sharply at the top and chins at the bottom in close two-character shots. These were minor irritations, however, and *Gone With the Wind* still cast its magic spell on audiences, retaining all its epic strength, and sweeping the spectator along with the majesty of its theme of reconstruction and rebirth after the devastations of war.

Its characters were always bigger than life, and now they have the stature of folk heroes. Gable was born to play Butler; this is the best performance of a great star. And Miss Leigh is so perfect as the vixen Scarlett it seems inconceivable that anyone else was even tested for the role. Olivia de Havilland's Melanie provides a classic example of how an actress can make a character sweet but never mawkish. Only Leslie Howard's performance as Ashley seems stilted three decades later.

So much of the film's talent has *Gone With the Wind.* Three of the four top stars, and Selznick and Fleming, were not around to see the "new" version in 1967. But they will be immortal as long as there are people to be entranced by expert storytelling on film.

Producer: David O. Selznick. **Director:** Victor Fleming. **Scriptwriter:** Sidney Howard. **Principal Players:** Clark Gable, Vivien Leigh, Olivia de Havilland and Leslie Howard. **Running time:** 220 minutes. **Released:** MGM.

NINOTCHKA

Ninotchka is the kind of title with which a picture may go into production, but which usually never reaches the theatre marquee. Somehow this one stuck, although all the ads contained the admonition, "Don't pronounce it—see it!" right after the title.

The ads for *Anna Christie* had announced, "Garbo talks!" and now, for *Ninotchka,* they proclaimed, "Garbo laughs!" She did unbend a little, to "flirt, dance, drink, howl, romance and kiss," to quote the ads again. But she was never as much at ease in lighthearted pictures as she was amid weightier surroundings.

The film was one of the first in which Hollywood took note of the existence of Soviet Russia (then an ally of Germany). The approach was satirical: Garbo was a dour, automaton-like Communist, a kind of ugly duckling transformed into a swan by Melvyn Douglas who used the magic of Paris to perform the trick.

The "Lubitsch touch," composed of subtle gestures and meanings, was still working beautifully at the time,

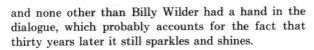

Mr. Smith Goes to Washington with Jean Arthur and James Stewart.

Mickey Rooney and Judy Garland in *Babes in Arms.*

and none other than Billy Wilder had a hand in the dialogue, which probably accounts for the fact that thirty years later it still sparkles and shines.

Producer-Director: Ernst Lubitsch. **Scriptwriters:** Charles Brackett, Billy Wilder and Walter Reisch. **Principal Players:** Greta Garbo, Melvyn Douglas, Ina Claire. **Running time:** 110 minutes. **Released:** MGM.

MR. SMITH GOES TO WASHINGTON

American democratic ideals are in trouble, but they will persevere as long as the idealists care. This is the simple message of Frank Capra's *Mr. Smith Goes to Washington*—a theme woven with the elements of popular entertainment as shrewdly as they had been in his earlier film, *Mr. Deeds Goes to Town*. In 1939 the American public heard the message loud and clear. The plot is simplicity itself: A young man gets into Congress on a pass, and stays to whip the "club" under their own rules. Scriptwriter Sidney Buchman filled it out with romance, suspense, topical references and fascinating characters.

The latter were played perfectly by a typically well-chosen Capra cast, topped by James Stewart, at his best as the naive freshman senator who learns the hard way. Also included were Jean Arthur as a disillusioned secretary, and in lesser roles, Guy Kibbee, Thomas Mitchell, Beulah Bondi and H. B. Warner.

Mr. Smith was the last picture Capra made for Columbia under a mutually profitable association that had produced a string of hits, including *It Happened One Night, Mr. Deeds Goes to Town, Lost Horizon* and *You Can't Take It With You.*

Producer: Columbia. **Director:** Frank Capra. **Scriptwriter:** Sidney Buchman. **Principal Players:** Jean Arthur, James Stewart, Claude Rains, Edward Arnold, Guy Kibbee, Thomas Mitchell and Beulah Bondi. **Running time:** 127 minutes. **Released:** Columbia.

BABES IN ARMS

In 1938 Mickey Rooney was the fourth most popular star in the country (according to *Motion Picture Herald*'s exhibitor poll) and second on the MGM lot only to Clark Gable, who was in second place in the poll. Judy Garland at the time was still "promising"; but *The Wizard of Oz* was not yet released.

Babes in Arms was a big hit; it helped to secure for Rooney the top box-office star position for 1939—a rating he held for both 1940 and 1941. Miss Garland made the list at tenth place in 1940 and 1941.

Both she and Rooney had come out of vaudeville, and that background served them well for this Rodgers and Hart musical about a group of youngsters from vaudevillian families who put on a successful show after their parents have failed in their attempt to make a comeback.

Producer: Arthur Freed. **Director:** Busby Berkeley. **Scriptwriter:** Jack McGowan and Kay Van Riper. **Principal Players:** Mickey Rooney, Judy Garland, Charles Winninger and Guy Kibbee. **Running time:** 95 minutes. **Released:** MGM.

Charles Chaplin and Jack Oakie in *The Great Dictator*, the film in which the great silent comedian finally spoke on the screen.

1940

Despite the blitzkrieg in Europe, Hollywood went right ahead with its plans to produce the usual five hundred features during the year. The economic uncertainties, however, resulted in substantial declines for major film companies' stocks. One factor was adverse developments abroad: The Nazis seized and banned Hollywood films in each dominated territory. Wherever they could apply pressures against Hollywood (and the U.S.) in a neutral country, e.g., Portugal, they did so.

On the domestic front, a project of James Roosevelt, son of the President, struck terror in the hearts of many theatre owners. Young Roosevelt championed a nickel-in-the-slot project for movies in taverns, cocktail lounges and shooting galleries. Showmen fought back by asking cities to set high license fees on the system's automatic 16mm projectors.

Both Bell Telephone Company and RCA demonstrated elaborate stereophonic sound systems employing multi-track recording and reproduction. The Bell demonstration was at Carnegie Hall and had no associated motion picture. The reproduction of sound, including its directional aspects, was so excellent that until the curtains were drawn to display a series of loudspeakers spread across the stage, hearers thought a live orchestra was playing. The RCA sound was for Disney's feature fantasy *Fantasia,* and the elaborate system was used for about a dozen engagements of the film. The recordings were made for *Fantasia* by Leopold Stokowski, who himself attended the first press demonstration of the sound system in New York. The great conductor had difficulty in controlling the sound mixing level, as he insisted in doing it personally. Keeping his eyes on his men and on a dial at the same time proved challenging.

A taste of more things to come (but which would be delayed by the war): RKO demonstrated large theatre television, and the Columbia Broadcasting System showed small color TV sets.

Charles Chaplin's first film in five years, *The Great Dictator,* went into release. The satire on the real dictators, Hitler and Mussolini, was well done and Chaplin displayed his mastery of many talents. Yet the cruel newspaper headlines of the day made it difficult for some to laugh, despite the ridicule and scorn of the film.

In New York's Federal Court the antitrust war between the giant film companies and the Department of Justice began. Film companies had impressive legal talent at their command, including Col. William J. Donovan, John W. Davis, former judge Thomas D. Thacker, Joseph Proskauer and others. Some negotiations for a consent decree began. Eventually, the companies were required to sell films in blocks of five (instead of a whole season's supply), and each film had to be screened for the trade in advance of selling. Also, a national arbitration system was established to deal with exhibitor grievances. Attorney General Robert H. Jackson said that the consent decree was not a final settlement of the Government's case, but only a truce. This proved to be a true prophecy.

State censors were proud that their operations made money. In New York, the censor board's annual operating budget was about $60,000 and its receipts ran (from fees charged to distributors) from $200,000 to $300,000. A film could be barred or cut on the ground that it was indecent, immoral, criminal, inhuman or sacrilegious.

Stars of the year: Mickey Rooney, Spencer Tracy, Clark Gable, Gene Autry, Tyrone Power, James Cagney, Bing Crosby, Wallace Beery, Bette Davis and Judy Garland.

Martha Scott and William Holden in *Our Town.*

OUR TOWN

About the time that Warner Bros. was getting *Kings Row* together, in which a small town was shown to be full of sinners underneath a respectable exterior, Sol Lesser was working on *Our Town,* based on the Thornton Wilder play in which small-town folk are shown to be noble and good.

Both pictures were popular in their day, but the one that gets revived the most and is held in greater critical esteem is *Kings Row.*

As a play, *Our Town* had been presented on a bare stage with the actors using a minimum of props. A narrator sat on the side of the stage to bind the action together and comment on it in a folksy, philosophical manner. The film used realistic sets, but retained the same narrator on screen, played by Frank Craven.

Wilder took a small New Hampshire town in the years before World War I and made it a microcosm of life. The romance of a boy and a girl, births and marriages and deaths in the families of the doctor and of the newspaper editor, are presented in cross section.

The cast included a young William Holden and, in minor roles, something of a who's who of character actors in Hollywood: Fay Bainter, Beulah Bondi, Thomas Mitchell, Guy Kibbee, Stuart Erwin, Frank Craven, Doro Merande and others.

Producer: Sol Lesser. **Director:** Sam Wood. **Scriptwriters:** Thornton Wilder, Frank Craven and Harry Chandlee. **Principal Players:** William Holden and Martha Scott. **Running time:** 90 minutes. **Released:** United Artists.

Henry Fonda, Jane Darwell and Russell Simpson in *The Grapes of Wrath.*

THE GRAPES OF WRATH

Films of social protest have been made almost since the birth of the medium, but none to date has ever surpassed John Ford's masterpiece, *The Grapes of Wrath.*

The Joad family has passed into American legend. Its members began life through the pen of John Steinbeck, who wrote a novel with the conscious purpose of drawing attention to the plight of the poverty-stricken Okies (the Oklahoma farmers driven out of their homes by drought and creditors) in the midst of the land of plenty. It was a literary work with a message, and it was sometimes uncomfortable in its sermonizing—a pitfall the film avoids.

Critic Edmund Wilson has called the structure of the book "cinematic"—so that when it came time to make the movie, he said, all they had to do was "pour" it onto the screen. He was right, which is not to disparage the fine job that Nunnally Johnson—at his best here—did in adapting it. He had to skip some minor incidents and skirt others, which he did intelligently.

The odyssey of the Joad family as it makes its way from the Dust Bowl to the "promised land" of California is told through a series of vignettes which always seem as real as truth, and sometimes achieve poetry. There is not a flaw in the casting or the performing.

There are many unforgettable scenes: The nostalgic return of Tom Joad (Henry Fonda) to the family homestead from prison; his dramatic meeting with Casey, the preacher who has lost his religion (John Carradine); the

Road to Singapore with Judith Barrett, Bing Crosby, Dorothy Lamour and Bob Hope.

The Great Dictator with Henry Daniell, Charlie Chaplin and Jack Oakie.

beautiful moment in which the mother (Jane Darwell) burns the letters and postcards that are her mementos of happier days on the night before the family departs. Possibly the most moving scene is the eloquent farewell between Tom and his mother in which he explains that he must leave the family because he has found his mission in life.

The great thing about *The Grapes of Wrath* is that it has not dated; it is as forceful and relevant today as it was when it first appeared.

Producer: Darryl F. Zanuck. **Director:** John Ford. **Scriptwriter:** Nunnally Johnson. **Principal Players:** Henry Fonda, Jane Darwell, John Carradine, Charley Grapewin, Doris Bowdon and Russell Simpson. **Running time:** 128 minutes. **Released:** 20th Century-Fox.

ROAD TO SINGAPORE

A Hollywood legend has it that the idea for the Bing Crosby-Bob Hope *Road* pictures originated after a golf match during which they, the director Victor Schertzinger, and producer Harlan Thompson had so much fun they decided it would be a good plan to prolong the foursome into a film production.

It could well be true; and even if not, the story gives an accurate reflection of the casual and improvisatory manner in which the pictures were made. *Road to Singapore* was the first and it set the pattern.

There was never a real plot—just the semblance of one to tie together a series of gags, Hollywood "in" jokes and slapstick situations. It was not unusual for a camel or a monkey suddenly to speak, and Hope and Crosby delivered frequent asides to the audience.

Singapore proved so successful it was followed by six more *Road* pictures, which gradually declined in popularity. The last was *The Road to Hong Kong* in 1962. Dorothy Lamour, who had been their female companion on the other trips, did not make the last one, although she turned up briefly at one point to get them out of a jam.

Producer: Harlan Thompson. **Director:** Victor Schertzinger. **Scriptwriters:** Don Hartman and Frank Butler. **Principal Players:** Bing Crosby, Dorothy Lamour, Bob Hope, Charles Coburn and Anthony Quinn. **Running time:** 83 minutes. **Released:** Paramount.

THE GREAT DICTATOR

A moment many American moviegoers had eagerly awaited finally came in 1940: Charles Chaplin spoke in a film. He had obviously waited not only for the right time but for something important to say.

His subject in *The Great Dictator* was the evil of fascism, but he did not labor the point until the very end of the film. His target was the foremost exponent of that philosophy, Adolph Hitler, and the ammunition was satire. Chaplin did the job with characteristic brilliance, building the story around a plot in which a Jewish barber who resembles the German tyrant is able to change places with him and take over the country.

The Philadelphia Story with James Stewart, Cary Grant and Katharine Hepburn.

Chaplin acted both roles. Early scenes in which the barber is a soldier in World War I evoked memories for some of *Shoulder Arms.* His comic imagination was at its peak in such scenes as the one in which the barber shaves a customer to the accompaniment of Brahms. The sharpest dig at Hitler came in a sequence in which he burlesqued the dictator's flamboyant and uninhibited exhortations. Chaplin spoke in gibberish.

There was considerable amusement, too, in a parody of Mussolini that was played by Jack Oakie, and in the comic business of Hitler trying to dominate this character.

Comedy, tragedy, satire, melodrama, slapstick and sentiment—and then suddenly, a sermon. At the end of the film Chaplin had the barber step out of character to deliver a speech on how to improve world conditions. It brought the audience up short.

The Great Dictator was the last film in which Chaplin employed his famous tramp character. It was also his last big commercial success in the United States.

Producer-Director-Writer: Charles Chaplin. **Principal Players:** Chaplin, Jack Oakie, Paulette Goddard, Reginald Gardiner, Henry Daniell and Billy Gilbert. **Running time:** 126 minutes. **Released:** United Artists.

THE PHILADELPHIA STORY

Few comebacks in the history of the film industry have been more triumphant and gratifying than the one made by Katharine Hepburn in *The Philadelphia Story.* Two years before, she and several other stars had been labeled "box-office poison" by a group of exhibitors who had done poor business with some of their films. The plucky lady picked herself up and went back to Broadway where her career had begun, starred in this Philip Barry comedy about Philadelphia's Main Line rich, and ran in it for a year.

The appearance of the movie version brought more critical plaudits for the talented actress, and business was better than ever. She was back on the top of the heap, and she stayed there.

The *Philadelphia* role was tailor-made for Miss Hepburn, giving her a chance to deliver witty and acerbic dialogue in her inimitable manner, to transform from a high-minded, cold and selfish woman to a gregarious and loving person, and to wear a ravishing modern wardrobe. She did it all in style.

The males—Cary Grant as the husband and James Stewart as a journalist—were overshadowed by Miss Hepburn, although Stewart did win an Oscar for best actor.

In 1957, MGM set the Barry script to music in a film called *High Society,* starring Bing Crosby, Frank Sinatra and Grace Kelly. Thanks to the stars, it made some money, but it was hardly an improvement over the original.

Producer: Joseph L. Mankiewicz. **Director:** George Cukor. **Scriptwriter:** Donald Ogden Stewart. **Principal Players:** Cary Grant, Katharine Hepburn, James Stewart and Ruth Hussey. **Running time:** 112 minutes. **Released:** MGM.

Spencer Tracy and Clark Gable in *Boom Town.*

Joan Fontaine, Laurence Olivier and Judith Anderson in *Rebecca.*

BOOM TOWN

MGM took its two top male stars of the day, Clark Gable and Spencer Tracy, who had previously been in *San Francisco* and *Test Pilot* together, co-starred them with Claudette Colbert, with whom Gable had appeared in *It Happened One Night,* and tossed in Hedy Lamarr in a profligate gesture. The result was *Boom Town,* one of those films tailor made for the personalities of the stars, and regarded by its makers to be guaranteed to do top box office. It certainly worked out that way.

Gable and Tracy had typically two-fisted roles, as strong men pursuing a fortune who go west to seek oil, meet, quarrel, join forces and start an association that endures with variations throughout the growth of the oil industry. Miss Colbert played a schoolteacher from the East who had gone west to marry Tracy, but met Gable and wed him instead. Miss Lamarr, in a minor role, rendered services to the men that seemed to go beyond strictly business.

The supporting cast was high-powered, too, including such stalwarts as Frank Morgan, Lionel Atwill, Chill Wills and Sara Haden.

Tracy, who had previously co-starred with Miss Lamarr in *I Take This Woman,* later made *Tortilla Flat* with her, but he and Gable never got together in a film again, nor did either star with Miss Colbert again.

Producer: Sam Zimbalist. **Director:** Jack Conway. **Scriptwriter:** John Lee Mahin. **Principal Players:** Clark Gable, Spencer Tracy, Claudette Colbert and Hedy Lamarr. **Running time:** 120 minutes. **Released:** MGM.

REBECCA

Alfred Hitchcock came to Hollywood to make films with the reputation of being England's top creator of suspense thrillers. (*The Thirty-Nine Steps* and *The Lady Vanishes* were two of his best known films.) He justified that reputation with his first American film, *Rebecca.*

It was based on a best-selling novel by Daphne du Maurier out of the "psychological" school. The heroine is a timid girl who, suddenly married to a wealthy aristocrat, nearly goes mad in her effort to emulate her husband's former wife—a high-spirited beauty whom she mistakenly believes her spouse still loves. The psychology is paper-thin, but the mood of a modern Gothic thriller was achieved by Hitchcock in his use of the rooms of the isolated castle called Manderley to suggest they were indeed haunted by the dead woman and that she was in fact a real threat to the heroine.

The leading role was played by Joan Fontaine in her first important appearance on the screen, and Laurence Olivier, who had portrayed Heathcliff in *Wuthering Heights,* was the mentally tortured husband. In the book the murder of his first wife was deliberate; the film turned it into a partial accident. The picture won the Oscar as best of the year.

Producer: David O. Selznick. **Director:** Alfred Hitchcock. **Scriptwriters:** Robert E. Sherwood and Joan Harrison. **Principal Players:** Laurence Olivier, Joan Fontaine, George Sanders and Judith Anderson. **Running time:** 125 minutes. **Released:** United Artists.

Dennis Morgan, Ginger Rogers, and Theodore Von Eltz in *Kitty Foyle.*

KITTY FOYLE

Just as the comedian traditionally longs to play Hamlet, so the song-and-dance girl pines to act Stella Dallas or the equivalent. Ginger Rogers, who had graduated from the film choruses of *Gold Diggers of 1933* and *42nd Street* to become the ballroom partner of Fred Astaire in *Flying Down to Rio,* shook off her dancing shoes with a vengeance to portray Kitty Foyle, the tough Irish girl from the wrong side of the tracks who falls in love with a rich man.

It was not Miss Rogers' first dramatic fling. Three years before she had been one of the aspiring actresses in *Stage Door,* and had given a good account of herself alongside such competition as Katharine Hepburn and Andrea Leeds. In *Kitty Foyle,* however, she was the single center of attention. It was a big challenge, and she met it well in the view of her industry colleagues. They gave her an Oscar for best female performance.

The critics, however, were less kind, and there was the usual resentment from admirers of other actresses who had been nominated for the honor. These included Bette Davis for *The Letter,* Joan Fontaine for *Rebecca,* Martha Scott for *Our Town* and Katharine Hepburn for *The Philadelphia Story.*

The public responded with enthusiasm to *Kitty Foyle,* the appetite of many having been whetted by the best-selling Christopher Morley novel on which the film was based. *Life* magazine had abetted the "want-to-see" mood by giving the film special treatment in two separate articles.

The Morley novel, which the author himself described as the "natural history of a woman," was handled faithfully by Dalton Trumbo in his screenplay. Trumbo did little to enhance the women's magazine fictional level of the original—a story so trite in its essentials that there was probably nothing that could be done with it.

Contributing to Miss Rogers' ability to dominate the movie was the casting of the two major male roles with bland actors. Dennis Morgan portrayed the Philadelphia Main Liner the heroine adores but is deserted by under family pressure, and James Craig was the suitor who loved her more than she loved him.

Miss Rogers went on to play other dramatic roles in such films as *Tender Comrade, I'll Be Seeing You, Storm Warning* and *Black Widow,* but she is most fondly remembered as the best dancing partner Fred Astaire ever had.

Producer: David Hempstead. **Director:** Sam Wood. **Scriptwriter:** Dalton Trumbo. **Principal Players:** Ginger Rogers, Dennis Morgan and James Craig. **Running time:** 105 minutes. **Released:** RKO Radio.

MY LITTLE CHICKADEE

Mae West may have been born too soon. She should have been at her peak in the 1960's when her skill at spoofing sex was badly needed to counteract the absurd excesses to which moviemakers went in the period. (She did return in 1970, in *Myra Breckinridge.*) Her heyday

Donald Meek, W. C. Fields and Mae West in *My Little Chickadee.*

instead was the early 1930's when her hilarious parodies of the sex game were taken too literally by the bluenoses. She was caught in the campaigns of the day to clean up the screens and became one of the first casualties. Her pictures became increasingly inhibited under the new rules, and her popularity diminished accordingly.

Then, in 1940, she joined forces with W.C. Fields, an old master at deflation of another kind, to write and act in *My Little Chickadee.* It evoked fond memories from moviegoers who could recall when both had seen better days

After three decades *My Little Chickadee* seems dated, and its stars are not at their best. But there is still amusement in it to stir laughter along with nostalgia, and younger moviegoers who have belatedly taken up both Fields and Miss West will tell you it is one of their favorites.

The script follows the outline of several staple western plots and the format is episodic, giving the effect of vaudeville turns for each star now and then. Anachronisms and slapstick abound.

Producer: Lester Cowan. **Director:** Edward P. Cline. **Scriptwriters:** Mae West and W. C. Fields. **Principal Players:** Mae West, W. C. Fields, Joseph Calleia, Dick Foran and Donald Meek. **Running time:** 83 minutes. **Released:** Universal.

Orson Welles and Ruth Warrick in *Citizen Kane,* Orson Welles' masterpiece and one of the most imitated and influential pictures in the history of the medium.

1941

This was the year when the motion picture industry was called upon to defend itself against charges that it had produced propaganda films to "incite the American people to war." From history's perspective, the whole matter may seem trivial and even ridiculous, but it was taken most seriously at the time.

Several United States Senators made the most vigorous charges of warmongering against Hollywood. Among them were D. Worth Clark and Gerald P. Nye. Senator Clark was chairman of the Commerce subcommittee, and he ordered public hearings. Wendell L. Willkie, defeated candidate for the Presidency, was engaged as special counsel to head the industry's defense. Will H. Hays, chairman of the industry association, stated, "No more false and shameful accusation could be made." Willkie also commented, "If you charge that the motion picture industry as a whole and its leading executives as individuals are opposed to the Nazi dictatorship in Germany, if this is the case, there need be no investigation. We abhor everything Hitler represents."

Senator Clark had listed seventeen films as "warmongering." These included *Escape, Foreign Correspondent* and *The Great Dictator*. Willkie retorted, "No legislative body of any kind has in this country a right to dictate, or seek to dictate, to this or any of the arts, except in the broadest terms of common decency. Further, there is no right even to suggest to the motion picture exhibitor what kind of pictures he should buy and present."

This whole matter faded when Senator Clark abruptly postponed the hearings in October, and the subject was dropped after the Japanese attacked Pearl Harbor on December 7, 1941. At the time, industry leaders were in Chicago for a "Unity Meeting." Never before or since was such unanimity achieved in the movie business. Immediately after receiving news of the attack, Will Hays issued a statement that the industry would provide a flow of wholesome entertainment as an essential contribution to military and civilian morale.

Also during the year, a major scandal involving the theatrical and projection union management, headed by George Browne and Willie Bioff, rocked the industry and caused some sleepless nights on the part of major company heads. The Federal Government charged that a million-dollar shakedown was involved.

Opposition to the showing of Axis films in the United States, prior, of course, to the war declaration, brought riots, censorship and complaints from the public and from exhibitors.

RCA demonstrated a theatre, the New Yorker in N.Y., wired for large-screen TV. Costs were estimated at $30,000 per theatre. Abram F. Myers, a leader of independent exhibitors, said, "There is no occasion for panic . . . . It's sound all over again but not so sudden or revolutionary."

Theatres began showing more and more defense shorts made by the U.S. Government. George Schaefer, national president of the Motion Picture Committee Cooperating for National Defense, said, "Ours is the only industry helping defense without profit." He referred to the cooperation not only of exhibitors but also of producers who made available, free of charge, prints of all features and shorts for use by the Army overseas and by the Navy on ships everywhere.

Stars of the year: Mickey Rooney, Clark Gable, Abbott & Costello, Bob Hope, Spencer Tracy, Gene Autry, Gary Cooper, Bette Davis, James Cagney and Judy Garland.

A scene from *The Stars Look Down.*

All That Money Can Buy with James Craig, Edward Arnold and Walter Huston.

THE STARS LOOK DOWN

British film makers had excelled in documentary in the 1930's far beyond any other nationality, but had lagged—except for some of the Hitchcock thrillers—in the entertainment field. Carol Reed's *The Stars Look Down* provided a breakthrough—a picture that combined the social realism of the English documentary school with a strong fictional story.

One of the few British pictures made before World War II that won worldwide critical acclaim, it established its director as a major international talent.

A grim recounting of life in a Welsh mining community (based on a novel by A. J. Cronin), it focuses on the conflict between labor and management over the formation of unions. The protagonist is a young miner who seeks to educate himself and lead his people in their efforts to better themselves. Thus, its general format was remarkably similar to that of John Ford's 1941 film *How Green Was My Valley,* which was an enormous commercial success. Theatre owners were reluctant to play the Reed film (released abroad in 1939) so close to the Ford one, and not only was it delayed in securing U.S. dates, but it did not fare well at those few theatres which finally did book it.

American audiences preferred the Ford approach, which mixed folksiness and sentimentality with the realism. Reed was unrelentingly serious.

The pictures are alike, however, in their creation of vivid characters. Michael Redgrave, in his first important screen role, was especially fine as the aspiring miner; Margaret Lockwood gave a brilliant performance as the foolish girl who is his ruination; and Nancy Price also shone as the mother who opposes her son over the issue of strikes. Emlyn Williams (author of *The Corn Is Green* and *Night Must Fall*) portrayed a mine owner in one of his frequent appearances as actor.

Producer: Grafton Films. **Director:** Carol Reed. **Scriptwriter:** J. B. Williams. **Principal Players:** Michael Redgrave, Margaret Lockwood, Emlyn Williams, Nancy Price and Cecil Parker. **Running time:** 97 minutes. **Released:** MGM.

ALL THAT MONEY CAN BUY

Wrote a trade journalist of the day: "This picture faces the hazard of being proclaimed an artistic triumph while faring in the field of commerce according to the state of the public appetite for fantasy, allegory and symbolism." That is a nice way of predicting a box-office dud, which *All That Money Can Buy* was.

It was also, however, a film far ahead of its time.

The story idea, which came from Stephen Vincent Benét, was imaginative: A struggle takes place between the Devil and lawyer Daniel Webster for the soul of a farmer who sold it to Satan for "seven years of everything that money can buy." The development on screen called on the audience for patience and the use of some imagination on their own, which not enough at the time were willing to supply.

William Dieterle directed it. (He had done the Emile Zola and Louis Pasteur biographical films for Warner

Back Street with Margaret Sullavan and Charles Boyer.

Bros. in the thirties.) For this film he emphasized pictorial composition to a greater degree than before; his images of the colonial New England sets were richly picturesque, but they did tend to slow the pace of the film.

Among the other pleasures of the picture are an amusing performance by Walter Huston as the roguish Satan (called "Mr. Scratch" here) and another in the grand style by Edward Arnold as Webster. The trial scene in which the fate of the farmer is decided (with the spirits of Benedict Arnold and other villains summoned forth to be the jury) is played with wit and élan.

During production the film was called *The Devil and Daniel Webster* (the name of the Benét story) and it was later shown in some theatres under that title. It also had for brief periods two other titles, *Here Is a Man,* and *A Certain Mr. Scratch.*

Producer-Director: William Dieterle. **Scriptwriter:** Dan Totheroh. **Principal Players:** Edward Arnold, Walter Huston, Jane Darwell, Simone Simon, Anne Shirley and James Craig. **Running time:** 107 minutes. **Released:** RKO.

BACK STREET

Fannie Hurst's old tearjerker novel has been made into a film three times (also in 1931 and 1961), but this is the best of the versions, by virtue of the superlative acting of Margaret Sullavan as Ray Smith (Schmidt in the original).

Miss Sullavan was an extraordinary stage actress who made her film debut in 1933 in *Only Yesterday.* In succeeding years she so enhanced a number of pictures with her luminous personality and sensuous, husky voice that many other actresses tried to imitate her. The titles stir fond memories for her admirers: *Little Man, What Now, Next Time We Love, Three Comrades, Shopworn Angel, The Mortal Storm,* right down to her last film, *No Sad Songs for Me* (1950).

She reached her zenith, however, in *Back Street,* in which she did what all the great actresses of the screen have done at one time or another: She took inferior material and raised it to the level of great art. The story tells of a woman who literally misses the boat on which she is to meet and wed her lover, encounters him years later when he is married, and accepts a niche in the "back street" of his life. The original novel is superficial and mawkish. Miss Sullavan imbued the story with her warm and charming personality and gave it depth by subtly indicating the changes in the woman over the years and her growth through happiness tempered by anguish and shame.

Charles Boyer was forced to play second fiddle as the hero, which he graciously did, as had John Boles in the first version with Irene Dunne. The 1961 film, which moved the story up in time and had lavish production values after the usual manner of Ross Hunter, was not a success.

Producer: Bruce Manning. **Director:** Robert Stevenson. **Scriptwriters:** Bruce Manning and Felix Jackson. **Principal Players:** Charles Boyer, Margaret Sullavan, Richard Carlson, Frank McHugh. **Running time:** 89 minutes. **Released:** Universal.

Donald Crisp, Roddy McDowall and Walter Pidgeon in *How Green Was My Valley.*

HOW GREEN WAS MY VALLEY

John Ford is a director with as large and impressive a body of work to his credit as any. His best westerns have never been equalled; nor indeed have his "family" films (*The Grapes of Wrath, Four Sons,* etc.), of which this is a primary example—and to some, the very best.

The source was a novel by Richard Llewellyn which had been on the best-seller lists. The film made from it is a classic example of a type of picture which has long appealed to audiences of all types: the saga of a family, told in episodic form, mixing the bitter with the sweet, and the crises with the quieter moments. Though the details may differ from what spectators have known in their own lives, the story produces a pleasurable nostalgic reaction that makes for strong identification.

Ford's many virtues as a film maker are in abundant evidence here: his sharp pictorial sense; his feeling for time and place and the traditions that are unique to them; and his firm grasp of character. In *How Green Was My Valley* he evoked the sadness of the passing of a way of life (that of the Welsh miners) and the breakup of the individual family that accompanies it.

He also inspired tremendously affecting performances from a large cast. The picture won seven well-deserved Oscars.

Producer: Darryl F. Zanuck. **Director:** John Ford. **Scriptwriter:** Philip Dunne. **Principal Players:** Walter Pidgeon, Maureen O'Hara, Donald Crisp, Anna Lee, Roddy McDowall, John Loder, Sara Allgood and Barry Fitzgerald. **Running time:** 118 minutes. **Released:** 20th Century-Fox.

Gary Cooper and Barbara Stanwyck in *Meet John Doe,* with Edward Arnold and city politicians.

MEET JOHN DOE

Behind many of the comedies of Frank Capra and Robert Riskin lay a concern for American democracy and its processes—about which they were usually optimistic. With *Meet John Doe,* however, the tone changed and became anxious. They hit out at a native brand of fascism in this picture, and they hit hard.

John Doe, played by Gary Cooper, is a "typical" American: As a bush-league ball player unemployed since his pitching arm went bad, he unwittingly becomes the head of a Golden Rule movement (whose motto is, "Love thy neighbor") and simultaneously the tool of a newspaper publisher of totalitarian beliefs. At the end the hero is discredited and thoroughly disillusioned, but the heroine—the newspaper columnist (Barbara Stanwyck) who got him into all the trouble in the first place—makes a speech to the effect that the movement he led has "existed from the beginning of time" and that the "little people will always be heard."

The message of the film was all the more effective from a commercial standpoint for being couched in terms of a light romance, with comedy to relieve the dramatics.

Capra and Riskin did their jobs as shrewdly as ever, but the public liked *Mr. Deeds Goes to Town* much better.

Producer-Director: Frank Capra. **Scriptwriter:** Robert Riskin. **Principal Players:** Gary Cooper, Barbara Stanwyck, Edward Arnold, James Gleason and Walter Brennan. **Running time:** 135 minutes. **Released:** Warner Bros.

Joan Leslie, June Lockhart and Gary Cooper in *Sergeant York.*

Orson Welles and Ruth Warrick in *Citizen Kane.*

SERGEANT YORK

Gary Cooper, who played all types of romantic leads, from a foreign legionnaire to Marco Polo, was primarily known and liked for his western roles. Yet his most popular part—and one that brought him an Academy Award—was that of the real-life Tennessee farmer who became a World War I hero when he singlehandedly captured 132 German soldiers in France in 1918.

Four writers, including John Huston, worked on the script which was based on the diary of Alvin York himself. They imbued it with local color, including the backwoods hill country, and a revival meeting at which the hero "gets religion" following an experience in a lightning storm. They also endowed it with a homespun philosophy extolling duty and heroism that endeared the film to the mass audience.

Howard Hawks directed it with expertise, making the battlefield scene tense and suspenseful and seeing to it that the triumphant return of the hero to New York to the acclaim of his countrymen was played at fever pitch.

Before York would consent to let his story be brought to the screen he stipulated two conditions: The facts must be kept accurate, and Gary Cooper must play the role.

Producers: Jesse L. Lasky and Hal B. Wallis. **Director:** Howard Hawks. **Scriptwriters:** Aben Finkel, Harry Chandlee, Howard Koch and John Huston. **Principal Players:** Gary Cooper, Walter Brennan, Joan Leslie and George Tobias. **Running time:** 134 minutes. **Released:** Warner Bros.

CITIZEN KANE

Citizen Kane was the first film of the young genius Orson Welles, who, when he came to Hollywood in 1940, had already conquered Broadway (with his Mercury Players in Shakespeare) and radio. (His overly realistic *War of the Worlds* depicting the invasion of the U.S. actually sent families scurrying from their homes.) *Kane* caused a sensation for two major reasons: Its story of the scandalous private and public life of an American newspaper publisher was rumored to be based on the career of an actual person, and it made bold and original use of cinematic techniques.

Many of the latter were not new with Welles, but his employment of them was so striking that it seemed at the time he had actually invented them. Since *Kane,* film makers have copied his methods of deep-focus photography (worked out with famed cinematographer Gregg Toland); odd angle shots; bizarre lighting; conversations overlapping from one sequence to the next; and other creative uses of sound—especially echoes, as in the famous Xanadu scenes. What was most distinctly his own was the film's brilliant narrative technique, such as the adoption of a *March of Time* form of documentary to sum up highlights of the hero's life at the start of the picture, and the intricately constructed flashbacks throughout.

In the opinion of most critics, Welles has never matched *Citizen Kane,* but his checkered career, from *The Magnificent Ambersons* (which followed *Kane,* in a studio-edited version not approved by Welles) to

The Maltese Falcon with Mary Astor and Humphrey Bogart.

The Little Foxes with Herbert Marshall and Bette Davis.

Chimes at Midnight (his version of the Falstaff story), has produced much to interest moviegoers.

Producer-Director: Orson Welles. **Scriptwriters:** Welles and Herman J. Mankiewicz. **Principal Players:** Welles, Joseph Cotten, Dorothy Comingore, Everett Sloane, Ray Collins, George Coulouris and Agnes Moorehead. **Running time:** 120 minutes. **Released:** RKO.

THE MALTESE FALCON

The forties produced many vintage private-eye thrillers, but none to match John Huston's version of the Dashiell Hammett novel featuring his Sam Spade character. It was an early representative of the genre, and it is the one by which all later ones have been measured.

This was the first film directed as well as written by Huston; he had previously collaborated on several screenplays, including those for *High Sierra* and *Sergeant York*. The Hammett plot is typically intricate, turning as it does around a search for a valuable gold falcon statuette and a band of thieves who constantly scheme to double-cross each other. The ending has the kind of irony that Huston has often favored since: Nobody gets the valuable prize.

Huston established a strong feeling of tension early in the film and held it throughout, alleviating it here and there with touches of humor, and punctuating it with unexpected violence.

Above all, there are the unforgettable characters, each cast with an unerring instinct. Others have played Sam Spade in films, but the role belongs forever to Humphrey Bogart. Mary Astor won an Oscar for *The Great Lie* in this same year; she could just as well have been cited for her protrait of the conniving Brigid O'Shaughnessy. Peter Lorre and Sydney Greenstreet made two of the most colorful villains in screen history, and Elisha Cook, Jr., added considerably to the fun as a trigger-happy but sensitive punk.

Producer: Hal B. Wallis. **Director-Writer:** John Huston. **Principal Players:** Humphrey Bogart, Mary Astor, Gladys George, Peter Lorre, Sydney Greenstreet and Elisha Cook, Jr. **Running time:** 100 minutes. **Released:** Warner Bros.

THE LITTLE FOXES

In the years that Bette Davis ruled the lot at Warners as their top female star (roughly 1938 to 1945), the brothers loaned her out to another producer only once. That was to Samuel Goldwyn for his filming of Lillian Hellman's Broadway success *The Little Foxes*, in which Miss Davis played the avaricious Regina Giddens.

It was directed by William Wyler, and demonstrates his skill at translating dramas from stage to screen virtually intact, and yet handling the transition so effectively that it does not emerge as a "photographed stage play." It is a skill involving the expert use of film syntax, upon which many learned essays have been written.

Miss Davis has written that she had disagreements with Wyler over the interpretation of the Giddens char-

Buck Privates with Lou Costello, the Andrews Sisters and Bud Abbott.

A scene from the "Nutcracker Suite" sequence in Walt Disney's *Fantasia*.

acter, as she wanted to repeat the approach used by Tallulah Bankhead on the stage, and he wished her to act it differently. As all good actresses should, she deferred to his wishes and consequently does not think too highly of her work here herself. It won her some of the best critical notices of her career.

The other members of the scheming Southern family, who exhibit pettiness, deceit, avarice, envy, conspiracy, theft and parental indifference, were played by many actors from the original New York cast. The result was one of the best ensemble performances a stage play has ever received on the screen.

Producer: Samuel Goldwyn. **Director:** William Wyler. **Scriptwriter:** Lillian Hellman. **Principal Players:** Bette Davis, Herbert Marshall, Teresa Wright and Richard Carlson. **Running time:** 115 minutes. **Released:** RKO.

BUCK PRIVATES

The comedy team of Bud Abbott and Lou Costello made its film debut—after success on the radio—in *Caribbean Holiday* in 1940, but it was not until the next year that they made it big. The picture was *Buck Privates,* released before the U.S. entered the war, although audiences were already extremely conscious of national defense measures.

This picture treated matters lightly—the Army and the draft, that is—which is the way a lot of Americans wanted it handled at the time. The story made no sense; it had to do with a number of doughboys who become ensnared in the processes of preparedness. Under the circumstances, sense was hardly required.

As a comedy team, Abbott and Costello carried on a tradition started by Laurel and Hardy, and were as popular in their day as the earlier duo had been in theirs. Abbott was the equivalent of the Laurel simpleton and Costello of the more sensible Hardy—at least superficially.

The Andrews Sisters, then an extremely popular singing group, appeared in *Buck Privates* and helped to make it a commercial hit.

Producer: Alex Gottlieb. **Director:** Arthur Lubin. **Scriptwriter:** Arthur T. Horman. **Principal Players:** Bud Abbott, Lou Costello, Lee Bowman, Jane Frazee and the Andrews Sisters. **Running time:** 84 minutes. **Released:** Universal.

FANTASIA

Two wrong ideas about *Fantasia* have somehow gained currency over the years. One is that the experimental film combining classical music with animated images lost a fortune for Walt Disney. The second is that the critics didn't like it.

The truth is that the picture, while its first engagements in 1940 were indeed disappointing, has been reissued successfully over the years to the point that it now actually shows a profit on the Disney accounting books.

The second truth is that, while there were the usual dissenters, the film was highly praised. Bosley Crowther

Here Comes Mr. Jordan with Rita Johnson, Robert Montgomery and Evelyn Keyes.

wrote, in *The New York Times* the day after the opening, "Motion picture history was made last night."

The film is built around eight musical selections played by the Philadelphia Orchestra under the direction of Leopold Stokowski. The sections are linked together through narration spoken by Deems Taylor.

By general consent the two best numbers are Stravinsky's "The Rite of Spring," in which the creation of the world is depicted, and Moussorgsky's "A Night on Bald Mountain," in which weird creatures including bats and gargoyles hold a black mass.

Fantasia also represents an early attempt to employ stereophonic sound with speakers placed on auditorium walls as well as behind the screen. The method—developed by RCA and called "Fantasound"—was used at the Broadway Theatre in New York and in a few other large cities, but was deemed too expensive for most exhibitors.

Producer: Walt Disney. **Story Directors:** Joe Grant and Dick Huemer. **Narration:** Deems Taylor. **Running time:** 135 minutes. **Released:** RKO Radio.

HERE COMES MR. JORDAN

War clouds hung over the nation, as well as most of the rest of the universe, and escapism was in demand by movie audiences. *Here Comes Mr. Jordan* took them farther away from reality than any other film of the year—to the spirit world, in fact, where a benevolent Claude Rains suavely acted as the emissary of the Almighty, abetted by Edward Everett Horton as a second supernatural agent.

At the time it was thought a bold step for moviemakers to treat life-after-death facetiously, and some in the industry predicted negative reactions to the film. The idea was handled with such good humor and taste, however, that audiences, far from disapproving, greatly admired the picture and turned it into a big hit.

The plot revolves around a prizefighter whose spirit is "taken" before it should have been by the two bungling heavenly personages. To rectify the error, they agree to return him to earth to live out his allotted span only to find that his body has been cremated. They then return his spirit to a murdered millionaire, and when that body is slain again, to the body of a boxer.

It is all highly fanciful but unexpectedly charming—thanks as much to the ingratiating performance of Robert Montgomery as the pugilist as to the witty and imaginative script. Shining in a supporting role was the always dependable James Gleason, portraying a fight manager who can't see the spirit of Mr. Jordan (Rains) but knows that it is there.

The success of *Here Comes Mr. Jordan* inspired all sorts of imitations by other film makers, none of whom ever quite captured its beguiling spell.

Producer: Everett Riskin. **Director:** Alexander Hall. **Scriptwriters:** Sidney Buchman and Seton I. Miller. **Principal Players:** Robert Montgomery, Claude Rains, Evelyn Keyes, Rita Johnson, Edward Everett Horton and James Gleason. **Running time:** 93 minutes. **Released:** Columbia.

The Lady Eve with Barbara Stanwyck and Henry Fonda.

THE LADY EVE

Preston Sturges is very much a film maker of the forties. In the thirties he had written scripts; then Paramount gave him the chance to show what he could do as director as well. He first came up with *The Great McGinty* in 1940, a spoof of politics that proved fresh and volatile, followed by *Christmas in July,* which kidded radio advertising contests and the "luck" it takes to win them. It was clever, too.

The third time, he really hit the jackpot with *The Lady Eve,* a delightful satire with an eternally popular target—sex. Gold digger chases rich man in this picture—and not only for money, but for revenge. An old story, yes, but Sturges made it sizzle and sparkle with flippant dialogue and comic situations that range from satire to slapstick.

Barbara Stanwyck not only looked more beautiful than ever as Eve, but under Sturges' guidance displayed a talent for comedy that won high critical praise. As Adam, the millionaire, the usually earnest Henry Fonda stepped out of character to participate in slapstick, both actively and passively. The two made an engaging team, and the subordinate characters were creatively drawn and vigorously played, too. Charles Coburn was a cardsharp; Eugene Pallete was a capitalist; William Demarest played a bodyguard; and Eric Blore was a confidence man.

A year later Sturges returned to the world of affluent America again in *The Palm Beach Story* and worked further variations on the subject that were equally entertaining. He also gave crooner Rudy Vallee a new lease on life as a comedian.

Producer: Paul Jones. **Director-Writer:** Preston Sturges. **Principal Players:** Barbara Stanwyck, Henry Fonda and Charles Coburn. **Running time:** 95 minutes. **Released:** Paramount.

James Cagney in *Yankee Doodle Dandy,* the high point in the career of Cagney, and a film exuding patriotism for Americans in wartime.

1942

Each month of the war brought increasing pressure on Hollywood and theatres throughout the country. At first there were blackouts or brownouts on both coasts, later a darkening of theatre marquees everywhere to save electricity. Studios lost more and more technicians and performers to military services. Local draft boards took varying views on the value of theatre employees to the national effort. Eventually, virtually all able-bodied young men left the theatres. National instructions were issued for air-raid procedures: Patrons were to remain in theatres during alerts or actual attacks.

President Roosevelt named Lowell Mellett coordinator of Government films. The latter said he wanted no screen censorship, but the Government ordered censorship on all features, shorts and newsreels, as well as still photos, in export or import. This effectively meant full censorship, as all productions were intended for export and some, such as newsreels and war stories, relied heavily on imported negatives.

Lew Ayres, as a conscientious objector, became a figure of national controversy. Nicholas Schenck, powerful head of MGM, known always for keeping out of the public eye, issued an open letter to Lew Ayres pointing out that the film star never ate "fish or meat or anything that had to be killed," but added, "Frankly, I must confess that I have never understood your position. It is a peculiarity beyond my personal comprehension."

Meanwhile, top stars flocked to the services. To the Army went James Stewart, Ronald Reagan, William Holden, Jeffrey Lynn and Burgess Meredith; to the Navy, Robert Montgomery, Douglas Fairbanks, Jr., Tony Martin, Gene Raymond, Wayne Morris; Sterling Hayden went into the Merchant Marine.

The war halted the building of new theatres, notably of drive-ins, of which seventy were operating and many more planned. Nelson Poynter, representative in Hollywood of the U.S. Office of War Information, called for fewer war films and more attention to the effects of the war on the common people. Lowell Mellett came out strongly against double bills for wasting needed film stock. Meanwhile, despite his earlier pledge to avoid censorship of films, he directed that his office review all scripts before production.

In spite of all, theatre business rose dramatically. War workers and soldiers on leave and others seeking recreation turned to theatres. It was cheap entertainment—theatres charged from twenty to forty cents for adults! Women theatre employees were seen more and more frequently. Theatres became centers of War Bond sales, but exhibitors continued to protest that there were too many war films.

Mrs. Miniver was a film universally liked. Some felt it did more than anything else to align the U.S. with Britain.

John Grierson, one of the founders of the British documentary film school, went to Canada to establish the Canadian Film Board. He and his staff directed most of their attentions to getting a wider and more influential distribution of British war-related short films in the United States. This unheralded, non-theatrical film activity was a significant factor in promoting a common understanding between Americans and their Allies, especially the British.

Stars of the year: Abbott & Costello, Clark Gable, Gary Cooper, Mickey Rooney, Bob Hope, James Cagney, Gene Autry, Betty Grable, Greer Garson and Spencer Tracy.

Greer Garson and Walter Pidgeon in *Mrs. Miniver.*

In Which We Serve with Noel Coward (center).

MRS. MINIVER

British film critics—and a portion of the general populace, too—snickered at Hollywood's rose-colored idea of a typical British family coping with the problems of the war. But Americans took *Mrs. Miniver* to their hearts and found it more convincing proof of the courage and integrity of their allies than *In Which We Serve,* which attracted a much smaller audience over here.

Mrs. Miniver had everything—humor, romance, suspense, tragedy and melodrama—all woven into vignettes in the day to day life of the family in a little English village. It also had Greer Garson as the redoubtable heroine (among her other exploits she captures a wounded Nazi flyer!) and Walter Pidgeon as her wise and witty husband. The two had previously co-starred in *Blossoms in the Dust,* and after *Mrs. Miniver,* they became such a popular team that they were cast together in *Mrs. Parkington, Madame Curie* and *Julia Misbehaves.* A sequel to *Mrs. Miniver,* starring both of them and called *The Miniver Story,* was released in 1950. It was not a similar success.

Mrs. Miniver won six Oscars, including best picture of the year. It was lavishly praised by most of the critics, probably more out of a sense of patriotic duty than from genuine conviction that it was a great work of art.

Producer: Sidney Franklin. **Director:** William Wyler. **Scriptwriters:** Arthur Wimperis, George Froeschel, James Hilton and Claudine West. **Principal Players:** Greer Garson, Walter Pidgeon, Teresa Wright and Richard Ney. **Running time:** 133 minutes. **Released:** MGM.

IN WHICH WE SERVE

The British film industry sent their American allies this film celebrating the British courage and tenacity in wartime. It was found moving and reassuring on both sides of the Atlantic in those troubled days.

Inspired by the documentary school of Paul Rotha and John Grierson, it was the work of—of all people—Noel Coward, known primarily for writing and acting in the most frivolous stage comedies of manners, with the exception of *Cavalcade.* This serious war film was a direct turnabout—and Coward not only wrote it and acted the lead, but produced it, composed the music for it and co-edited it (with David Lean)!

Actually, the hero of the film is not a man but a ship—the destroyer *Torrin.* The picture recounts her life and the lives of her men and their womenfolk back home, with flashbacks used for episodes dealing with the latter. No one man overshadows the others, from the captain to the petty officers and the ordinary seamen, all of whom recall the past as they face death on a float from the bullets of a Nazi plane. Warfare around Crete and the evacuation of Dunkirk were real events figuring in the story.

The film was praised at the time for its understatement of emotion and sentiment in an old British tradition, as well as for the documentary-like realism of many of its scenes.

Several actors and actresses who later were to become quite familiar to American devotees of British films appeared in this picture: John Mills, Bernard

Yankee Doodle Dandy with James Cagney.

Kings Row with Betty Field and Robert Cummings.

Miles, Celia Johnson, Kay Walsh, Michael Wilding and Richard Attenborough.

Producer-Writer: Noel Coward. **Directors:** Coward and David Lean. **Principal Players:** Coward, John Mills, Bernard Miles, Celia Johnson, Joyce Carey and Kay Walsh. **Running time:** 113 minutes. **Released:** United Artists.

YANKEE DOODLE DANDY

James Cagney's portrait of George M. Cohan is closer to pure Cagney than it is to the personality of the celebrated song-and-dance man, but it is nonetheless an irresistible characterization. Cagney is a much more versatile and talented actor than he is sometimes given credit for; this performance, for example, is a long way from *G-Men* (1935) and *Angels With Dirty Faces* (1937).

He sang and danced in *Yankee Doodle* with engaging skill, practically carrying it on his shoulders. The book is a mostly routine account of the life of Cohan from his birth on July 4, 1878, to his triumph on Broadway in the 1940's in *I'd Rather Be Right,* in which he mimicked President Roosevelt.

(A prologue to the film shows Cohan summoned to the White House, where he thinks the President is going to chastise him. Instead he greets him cordially and they reminisce about the past.)

The Cohan songs, from the title number through "Mary" and "Over There," are robustly staged and sung, and the dancing is lively and gay.

The film's makers envisioned it as serving to rouse the patriotic fervor of Americans in wartime, and it admirably served that purpose, while entertaining simultaneously. Cagney's real-life sister, Jeanne, played his screen sister, Josie Cohan.

Producers: Hal B. Wallis and William Cagney. **Director:** Michael Curtiz. **Scriptwriters:** Robert Buckner and Edmund Joseph. **Principal Players:** James Cagney, Joan Leslie, Walter Huston and Richard Whorf. **Running time:** 126 minutes. **Released:** Warner Bros.

KINGS ROW

The monumental task of preparing a screenplay from the Henry Bellaman best seller about sin in a small American town at the turn of the century fell to scriptwriter Casey Robinson. The novel—the *Peyton Place* of its day—was replete with such ingredients as sadism, incest, illicit love, homosexuality, suicide and murder. Robinson worked most of them in and hinted at others, coming up with a screenplay that not only was literate and dramatically powerful, but which received a Production Code certificate.

The management at Warner Bros. had qualms about the reception that might be given a period drama by a nation that had just gone to war, but they need not have. The picture was a tremendous success—a soap opera with class that provided the kind of escapism moviegoers wanted at the time.

In fact, the picture has held up well over the years—a testament to the skillful direction of Sam Wood,

Now, Voyager with Michael Ames (Tod Andrews), Gladys Cooper and Bette Davis.

which skirts both bathos and artificiality, and to the fine acting of a talented cast, two of whom did the best work of their careers. They are Ann Sheridan, the erstwhile "oomph girl," whose depiction of the tomboyish Randy was superb, and Ronald Reagan, the perennial juvenile, who gave a mature performance as the rake Parris. Robert Cummings, known mostly for light comic roles, was the young Doctor Drake to the life, and Betty Field was a poignant Cassandra. Smaller roles were also cast to perfection.

Producer: Hal B. Wallis. **Director:** Sam Wood. **Scriptwriter:** Casey Robinson. **Principal Players:** Ann Sheridan, Robert Cummings, Ronald Reagan and Betty Field. **Running time:** 130 minutes. **Released:** Warner Bros.

NOW, VOYAGER

Of the nineteen pictures Bette Davis made in the 1940's, none was more popular with her large audiences (mostly distaff) than this film based on a novel by Olive Higgins Prouty, the author of *Stella Dallas.*

It might have been just another soap opera: It was a variation on the ugly duckling theme, in which a frustrated spinster throws off the shackles of her tyrannical mother and becomes a "free" person through psychoanalysis and a therapeutic love affair with a married man. But Miss Davis touched it with the magic of her artistry and made the character come unforgettably alive.

According to her autobiography, she had more to do with *Now, Voyager* than simply performing in it. She says that she herself worked on the script as shooting progressed, taking out dialogue that had been written for the screenplay and replacing it with lines directly from the book. This tends to corroborate the impression many critics have that Miss Davis was constantly at work behind the scenes of her major films during her golden years at Warner Bros.

Certainly she dominates this movie with an acting tour de force that few screen actresses have ever matched. Never one to shun "deglamorization," she wore padding on her legs, pulled her hair back tight against her head and donned glasses to play the early ugly duckling scenes. And the transformation into a swan involved much more than tricks of makeup; Miss Davis made it come from within.

Producer: Hal B. Wallis. **Director:** Irving Rapper. **Scriptwriter:** Casey Robinson. **Principal Players:** Bette Davis, Paul Henreid, Claude Rains, Gladys Cooper, Bonita Granville and Ilka Chase. **Running time:** 120 minutes. **Released:** Warner Bros.

RANDOM HARVEST

James Hilton's novel had been a tremendous best seller, but bringing it to the screen presented a problem that turned out to be insurmountable. The book kept as a surprise the identity of the amnesia victim who is its hero; not until the end did the reader learn that the two men loved by the heroine were actually one and the same. The hero loses all recollection of his former life

Random Harvest with Ronald Colman and Greer Garson.

with a loving wife after a shellburst in World War I. He is nursed back to health by this same wife, although he thinks she is someone else.

It is very tricky, and in the film the same actor and actress had to play what amounts to four roles. Even with the climactic "twist" element missing, it became a very popular movie.

Part of that can be attributed to the appearance of Greer Garson as the woman of two personalities; after *Mrs. Miniver* she was top box-office. Her co-star this time was Ronald Colman, who brought his sincere manner and mellifluous voice to the dual male role.

Producer: Sidney Franklin. **Director:** Mervyn LeRoy. **Scriptwriters:** Claudine West, George Froeschel and Arthur Wimperis. **Principal players:** Ronald Colman, Greer Garson, Philip Dorn and Susan Peters. **Running time:** 126 minutes. **Released:** MGM.

Humphrey Bogart in *Casablanca,* one of the most popular of all the films made in the years of World War II and winner of the Academy Award as best picture of 1943.

1943

The grim realities of warfare in distant lands and on and over the oceans had certain echoes or reflections in the movie business. Notable was a recognition that the public needed more escapist entertainment and fewer war movies. Studios announced plans for the astonishingly high total of 110 musicals; fortunately, not all of them were made. At this time Paramount had nineteen musicals on its schedule; 20th Century-Fox, sixteen; and Universal International, fifteen.

A proposal of the Roosevelt Administration to impose a limitation on all salaries threw the industry into a crisis, for film stars, directors, producers and studio and home office executives were among the highest paid in all America. There was talk of a ceiling of either $25,000 or $67,000 on annual salaries. Charles Prutzman, general counsel and vice president of Universal Pictures, denounced the salary limitation plan on a national radio program, saying, "Compensation in America must be limited only by the abilities of our people." Hedy Lamarr sued MGM for refusing to increase her weekly paycheck from $1,500 to $2,000 as stipulated in her contract.

Senator—later, President—Harry S. Truman, as chairman of the Senate Special Committee Investigating the War Effort, heard testimony attacking the production of Army training films. The Signal Corps defended the record of its 437 Hollywood officers. The headline case involved Darryl F. Zanuck, then vice president in charge of production at 20th Century-Fox, who was commissioned a Colonel on January 4, 1941, and called to active duty on January 7, 1942. But until September 1, 1942, when he resigned his Fox post, he continued to draw $5,000 per week from the studio.

The Senate Judiciary Committee, under Joseph C. O'Mahoney of Wyoming, the Democratic majority leader, also studied films and the war.

Juvenile delinquency became a problem to theatres. The Office of War Information called theatre vandalism the most serious aspect of juvenile delinquency. The war-worker parents put children in theatres as a "baby-sitting" device. Older children earned "easy money" and spent it on shows. J. Edgar Hoover, FBI chief, cited the great upturn in juvenile crime figures. Monogram attempted to profit from the situation with its first film on the theme, *Where Are My Children?*

The War Manpower Commission ruled that theatre employees deferred as fathers, overage or 4-F (physically unfit) need not switch to war plants, but regulations otherwise tightened up for all in the eighteen to thirty-eight age bracket.

The trend to color on the screen was marked. Forty-nine color films were planned, with MGM, the leader, scheduling thirteen. A Technicolor commitment assuring use of the three-color Technicolor camera was highly prized. Farciot Edouart of Paramount Studios predicted that within three or four years after the end of the war all films would be in color. Advances in this and other technical areas were believed to be helped by the seizure of all enemy patents taken over by the U.S. Alien Property Custodian in accordance with a Presidential decree.

An industry worry was the threat of an increase of the Federal admission tax to 30 percent. Also, James Caesar Petrillo, the musician's union chief, after winning radio contributions to the Musicians Employment Fund, wanted assistance from Hollywood. He asserted that employment of a few hundred musicians in Hollywood kept thousands of musicians out of work, claiming that 10,000 lost their jobs when sound came into theatres in 1928 and 1929.

Premiums were still important attendance builders in some city neighborhoods and small towns, with dinnerware the most popular, a plate now costing about thirteen cents with a ticket instead of the ten-cent pre-war average. The war boom brought prosperity principally to big city first-run theatres and movie houses near military bases and big war plants.

Stars of the year: Betty Grable, Bob Hope, Abbott & Costello, Bing Crosby, Gary Cooper, Greer Garson, Humphrey Bogart, James Cagney, Mickey Rooney and Clark Gable.

Joseph Cotten, Teresa Wright and Macdonald Carey in *Shadow of a Doubt.*

SHADOW OF A DOUBT

A story of a murderer who intrudes into the home of his middle-class sister and her ordinary family (who accept him warmly, in their ignorance), *Shadow of a Doubt* could easily have been made right on the studio lot. But, wartime or no, Alfred Hitchcock took his cameras to a real small town—Santa Rosa, California.

The location shooting made all the difference. Hitchcock got into his film detailed views of dwellings, inside and out, and streets and bypaths that could never have been so effectively reproduced on a Hollywood backlot.

The sense of realism is important, for Hitchcock has never made a picture that so richly demonstrates one of his favorite ploys: the introduction of bizarre happenings into commonplace surroundings.

Characterizations run deeper in this picture than in most thrillers—even those of Hitchcock—and the relationship between the murdering uncle and the niece who adores him until she finds out the truth has subtle and intriguing ramifications. Joseph Cotten and Teresa Wright are excellent in these difficult roles.

To most audiences of the time, however, it was just a good mystery show, and they went to see it in large crowds, drawn by the magic of its maker's name as much as by anything else.

Producer: Jack H. Skirball. **Director:** Alfred Hitchcock. **Scriptwriters:** Thornton Wilder, Sally Benson and Alma Reville. **Principal Players:** Joseph Cotten, Teresa Wright, Macdonald Carey, Henry Travers and Patricia Collinge. **Running time:** 108 minutes. **Released:** Universal.

Katina Paxinou and Ingrid Bergman in *For Whom the Bell Tolls.*

FOR WHOM THE BELL TOLLS

"It is a great picture without political significance. We are not for or against anybody." So said Adolph Zukor in 1943, in answer to critics who condemned Paramount for filming Ernest Hemingway's novel about the Spanish Civil War, and to the government of General Franco which had sought to repress the picture. (It has still never been shown in Spain.)

Readers of the novel snickered at the gingerly manner in which the movie approached the Spanish conflict, calling the Loyalists, whom Hemingway championed, Republicans and never mentioning Franco by name.

It is a minor and not too relevant point. *For Whom the Bell Tolls,* while probably not "great," is a very good adventure movie with some enormously appealing characters that were very well played by a fine and colorful cast. Ingrid Bergman was probably miscast as Maria (too healthy and pretty), but her two big scenes—the one in which she recounts her rape by Nationalist soldiers, and her tearful farewell to her lover at the end—are played superbly. Gary Cooper was an impressive Robert Jordan; Katina Paxinou was the indomitable Pilar to the life; and Akim Tamiroff a thoroughly despicable Pablo. So it was with most of the rest.

Politics aside, *For Whom the Bell Tolls* was a very popular film.

Producer-Director: Sam Wood. **Scriptwriter:** Dudley Nichols. **Principal Players:** Gary Cooper, Ingrid Bergman, Akim Tamiroff, Arturo de Cordova, Vladimir Sokoloff, Mikhail Rasumny and Katina Paxinou. **Running time:** 165 minutes. **Released:** Paramount.

Dooley Wilson and Humphrey Bogart in *Casablanca.*

The Ox-Bow Incident with Anthony Quinn, Francis Ford, Dana Andrews, Henry Fonda, Frank Conroy and Jane Darwell.

CASABLANCA

Whenever a Humphrey Bogart Film Festival was held in the 1960's, the picture that nearly always drew the biggest crowds was *Casablanca.* For adults there was obviously nostalgia in viewing again a film they had hugely enjoyed in the war years. But what of the generation that knows Bogart movies only from television?

To them the great star of the forties and fifties has become a cult hero with whom they identify strongly. *Casablanca* offers the epitome of Bogart's image—the tough, cynical man of the world, who yet has retained some of the ideals of his youth.

Its fame has thus grown over the years, but *Casablanca* was a hit from the beginning. Part of its initial impact came from its being released after the Moroccan city had made the headlines as the site of a conference of the Allied powers. The film had nothing to do with that or the military exploits on the continent; it was set in 1941 when Casablanca was a stopping place for European refugees anxious to get to America.

Even at that, *Casablanca* does not really exist in a specific time or place; it is located in a never-never land in which movie good guys and bad guys play out a cat-and-mouse melodrama according to well-established rules. The love story also follows a familiar pattern. The heroine is torn between love and duty: Should she stay in Casablanca with her ex-lover, or go on to America with her husband, a Czech patriot?

The ending in which the lover forces her to do her duty is a typically romantic gesture which is the essence of the lasting appeal of the film. The cast could not have been bettered: Ingrid Bergman, Paul Henreid, Peter Lorre, Claude Rains, Sydney Greenstreet and Conrad Veidt—marvelous performers all, and except for Miss Bergman, all taking relatively small parts and making every moment count.

The magic of *Casablanca* so seduced the members of the Academy of Motion Picture Arts and Sciences that they gave it the Oscar as best film of the year and also cited the director and the screenplay writers.

Producer: Hal B. Wallis. **Director:** Michael Curtiz. **Scriptwriters:** Julius J. Epstein, Philip G. Epstein and Howard Koch. **Principal Players:** Humphrey Bogart, Ingrid Bergman and Paul Henreid. **Running time:** 102 minutes. **Released:** Warner Bros.

THE OX-BOW INCIDENT

Ads for *The Ox-Bow Incident* informed the public that it took nerve to make it and warned that nerve would be required to take it. It did indeed require courage to make this film in the middle of the war. It is a stark, slowly paced drama, set in 1885, of three men lynched for a crime it is later revealed they did not commit. The audience did not have equivalent nerve—which is to say that the picture died at the box office.

The setting is the Old West, but this is not a western. It is instead a strong dramatic preachment against mob rule, which is as effective in its quiet way as Fritz Lang's *Fury* (1936) was in its more flamboyant one.

The events move slowly, but as inexorably as fate

Hitler's Children with Tim Holt and Bonita Granville.

itself as the self-appointed posse closes in on three men in the darkness. It listens only briefly to their protestations of innocence and the doubts of a few members of the mob who are too weak and cowardly to press the issue. The ending, in which the truth of the hanged men's blamelessness is revealed, is devastating.

In his screenplay, Lamar Trotti preserved the essence of the Walter Van Tilburg Clark novel he adapted, and William A. Wellman directed without unnecessary adornment, so that the effect is of a legend given reality and truth.

There are any number of outstanding performances in the film, but most people seem to remember best that of doughty Jane Darwell as the evil shrew who is in the forefront of the call for blood. It was quite a contrast to her sympathetic portrait of Ma Joad in *The Grapes of Wrath.*

Producer-Writer: Lamar Trotti. **Director:** William A. Wellman. **Principal Players:** Henry Fonda, Dana Andrews, Anthony Quinn, Mary Beth Hughes, William Eythe, Henry Morgan and Jane Darwell. **Running time:** 75 minutes. **Released:** 20th Century-Fox.

HITLER'S CHILDREN

As soon as the U.S. got into the war, Hollywood dropped all restraints in its anti-Nazi movies, and few proved more popular than *Hitler's Children.* Made on a comparatively small budget, it was a real wartime "sleeper."

The fictionalized story was based on the factual book by Gregor Zeimer called *Education for Death.* Incorporated into the screenplay were demonstrations of such practices of National Socialism as the education of youth to deify Hitler and to glory in dying for him; the sterilization of men and women judged to be unfit or ill; the use of forced labor camps for women; and the barbaric behavior of the Gestapo.

The approach tended to be sensationalized, right down to the posters, which went out under the slogan "The truth about the Nazis from the cradle to the battlefront," and showed a Gestapo brute standing with a whip over a frightened girl whose clothes seemed to be falling off. "We know what to do to women who are not fit to be Nazi mothers," said the caption.

Events were tied together in the screenplay by having a German youth born in America (Tim Holt) fall in love with an American girl born in Germany (Bonita Granville). He is dedicated to Hitler; she is not and eventually converts him. In a melodramatic ending, he goes on a national radio hookup, ostensibly to confess his crimes against the state, but instead he makes a plea to the youth of the land to reach out for freedom. He is shot for his pains, and so is the girl when she rushes to his aid.

It all seems like arrant melodrama today, propaganda at its worst. But in 1943 it shook Americans up, which was what it was intended to do.

Producer: Edward A. Golden. **Director:** Edward Dmytryk. **Scriptwriter:** Emmet Lavery. **Principal Players:** Tim Holt, Bonita Granville, Kent Smith, Otto Kruger and H. B. Warner. **Running time:** 83 minutes. **Released:** RKO.

Charles Bickford (second from left), Jennifer Jones, and Vincent Price in *The Song of Bernadette.*

Heaven Can Wait with Don Ameche and Gene Tierney.

THE SONG OF BERNADETTE

They laid it on the line in a foreword to this film about the French girl who claimed to have had the Virgin Mary come to her in a vision: "For those who believe in God, no explanation is necessary; for those who do not believe in God, no explanation is possible."

It was wartime when the picture was released, and Americans were in the mood for a picture dealing with religious faith. It was a big commercial success, indicating that moviegoers of other faiths than Catholic found it reassuring and worthwhile. The Franz Werfel novel on which the picture was based had been a best seller.

Jennifer Jones' performance as the peasant girl who sticks to her story of the Virgin through rigorous questioning by skeptical clergymen (and eventually wins them over) was highly praised by such demanding critics as James Agee. (Bosley Crowther of *The New York Times* was one of the few holdouts.) She also won an Oscar for this, her first major role on the screen.

Producer: William Perlberg. **Director:** Henry King. **Scriptwriter:** George Seaton. **Principal Players:** Jennifer Jones, Charles Bickford, William Eythe, Vincent Price, Lee J. Cobb and Gladys Cooper. **Running time:** 165 minutes. **Released:** 20th Century-Fox.

HEAVEN CAN WAIT

A story celebrating the virtues of family life hardly seemed material suited to the impish Ernst Lubitsch "touch," but the mixture jelled to the satisfaction of both critics and audiences in *Heaven Can Wait.* The picture, in fact, was nominated for an Academy Award, but lost out to *Casablanca.*

While the family circle put on display in *Heaven Can Wait* was wealthy and lived in New York City, they could have been impecunious and inhabited a shack in Tennessee for all the difference it would have made as far as the theme of the story is concerned. That story recounts the domestic events in the life of a family—the romances, weddings, births, deaths—the vital statistics, as it were. The moral: Time in its passage changes only the individuals, never the family unit. The point is made in the Lubitsch manner—with subtlety and wit and no belaboring of the obvious.

At the center of the film is the character of Henry Van Cleve, who is shown from the time he is a babe in arms until his death at 70, at which point he arrives at the gates of hell but is turned away and told that members of families like the Van Cleves belong in heaven. Don Ameche played the role with versatility and charm, and garnered the best critical notices of his screen career. So, too, did Gene Tierney for her appealing performance as his wife. Laird Cregar made a roguish devil in the opening and closing sequences.

Lubitsch himself was highly praised for his use of color photography; James Agee said no one had ever before employed it with such "sensitivity and wit."

Producer-Director: Ernst Lubitsch. **Scriptwriter:** Samson Raphaelson. **Principal Players:** Gene Tierney, Don Ameche, Charles Coburn, Marjorie Main and Laird Cregar. **Running time:** 113 minutes. **Released:** 20th Century-Fox.

George Murphy (center) in *This Is the Army.*

THIS IS THE ARMY

From the proceeds of this film two million dollars were earmarked for Army and Navy Relief, so Americans on the home front could feel they were being patriotic as well as entertained when they went to the neighborhood theatre to see it.

It was a virtually intact cinematic adaptation of the Irving Berlin stage show, with a prologue added, recalling Berlin's musical *Yip, Yip Yaphank* of 1917, whose characters were the fathers of the soldiers in *This Is the Army.* The soldier players who had appeared on Broadway were joined by a number of Hollywood stars, who took part in a personal story staged between the production numbers. Berlin fans had a field day; there are nineteen of his songs, ranging from "Oh, How I Hate to Get Up in the Morning," which he himself sang in the film, to "This Is the Army, Mr. Jones."

The film is really just one big vaudeville show. Acts include Kate Smith singing "God Bless America" and one with Joe Louis punching a bag while Negro soldiers sing "What the Well-Dressed Man in Harlem Will Wear." Audiences loved it all.

Producers: Jack Warner and Hal B. Wallis. **Director:** Michael Curtiz. **Scriptwriters:** Casey Robinson and Capt. Claude Binyon. **Principal Players:** George Murphy, Joan Leslie, George Tobias and Alan Hale. **Running time:** 114 minutes. **Released:** Warner Bros.

Alexander Knox as Woodrow Wilson in the film *Wilson,* a biographical movie meticulously produced by Darryl F. Zanuck. It received six Academy Awards.

1944

Theatre stocks, bolstered by excellent business, enjoyed a boom on Wall Street. Major companies were valued at a total of $750,000,000, as against only $605,000,000 a year previously. The Federal Admission tax of 20 percent did not prove to inhibit attendance. Crowds flocked to almost any film. The quip was born, "All a theatre manager needs to do is open the doors and jump back quickly to avoid being crushed by the patrons."

The war itself continued with mounting fury. Many families were saddened by military deaths and injuries, but the economic mood of full employment and good wages kept theatres prosperous. For a time, films of Japanese atrocities were banned. Exhibitors again pressed for fewer war films and more musicals and comedies. Their accuracy in gauging trends in public taste was indicated by the record gross of Paramount's *Going My Way,* seven million dollars. Not surprisingly, Bing Crosby was voted the top box-office attraction in the FAME poll of exhibitors.

The industry was urged to organize, even to seek a voice at the peace table! A vain hope. The idea was proposed perhaps in recognition of the industry's non-profit support of the war effort. In each year of the war over two hundred films were provided without charge to the military for exhibition at overseas bases and on ships. No other industry made its product available to the Government gratis.

Terry Ramsaye, editor and film historian, charged that "war box-office prosperity has created a very real inflation—the inflation of the ego. Some leading picture makers and their pictures are getting too big for their breeches—which is to say the business of the motion-picture theatre." It was noted that wartime production costs at one studio had soared to an average of $1,600,000 per feature. Ramsaye applied to the current situation a remark made years previously by Mary Pickford: "This industry would be a lot better off if a lot of us went broke and had to go to work."

Hollywood studio leaders and film personalities formed the Motion Picture Alliance for the Preservation of American Ideals. This was a right-wing group set up to oppose the considerable Red activity in the industry.

The industry's technical organization, the Society of Motion Picture Engineers, called for leadership by the film industry in the development of television. This was a cry that fell on deaf ears, as most producers, distributors and exhibitors were much too busy with war prosperity in their own field to be worried about television, whose development had been arrested by the war. Few realized that the building of the great electronic manufacturing facilities for radar and other war-time applications would provide ready-made facilities as well as thousands of trained men to be put to work making television a commercial reality after peace arrived.

It is significant that in this year, marked by the Normandy invasion, and by some of the most violent battles of the war, few films touched on the war. Entertainment was the guide line. In some pictures, such as *The Song of Bernadette* (released the year before), the spiritual appeal of the film played a big part in its success.

Stars of the year: Bing Crosby, Gary Cooper, Bob Hope, Betty Grable, Spencer Tracy, Greer Garson, Humphrey Bogart, Abbott & Costello, Cary Grant and Bette Davis.

Geraldine Fitzgerald, as the second Mrs. Wilson, and Alexander Knox in *Wilson*.

Thirty Seconds Over Tokyo with Robert Walker, Van Johnson and Spencer Tracy.

WILSON

Darryl F. Zanuck's lavish biographical tribute to Woodrow Wilson, covering his years at Princeton and his career in politics through his election as President, stirred a hornet's nest of controversy in its day—a factor which, unfortunately, did not help it out at the box office as much as its makers had hoped.

It was released in the middle of an election campaign, while World War II was still raging on all fronts, and detractors of Franklin D. Roosevelt somehow interpreted it as propaganda for a fourth term.

Isolationists did not like its sympathetic attitude toward the League of Nations, which Wilson had so fervently supported, and they saw by implication an attempt to editorialize on behalf of a new such organization after the war. Others resented what they called a too idealized portrait of Wilson.

Others simply weren't interested in the subject matter, and found the two hours and a half devoted to it too much to take. A further problem was the casting of Alexander Knox in the title role. He was true to type—Wilson was rather colorless—but a more prepossessing actor would have given the character some much needed glamour.

Still, *Wilson* had—and has—its admirers, who like the film's serious attention to a period of American political life and the nostalgia induced by the meticulously detailed creation of the pre-twenties era, complete with songs of the day. It stands as yet one more instance of the fabled willingness of its producer to tackle the controversial, to take a commercial risk for something he felt worth doing. Zanuck supposedly said that if *Wilson* failed, he'd never make another picture without Betty Grable. Fortunately, he had his tongue in cheek.

Producer: Darryl F. Zanuck. **Director:** Henry King. **Scriptwriter:** Lamar Trotti. **Principal Players:** Alexander Knox, Charles Coburn, Geraldine Fitzgerald and Thomas Mitchell. **Running time:** 154 minutes. **Released:** 20th Century-Fox.

THIRTY SECONDS OVER TOKYO

Some terrific aerial sequences were the chief distinguishing features of this quasi-documentary about the bombing of Tokyo under the command of Lt. Col. Jimmy Doolittle (later Major General) and his fliers, complete with details of the long preparation for the mission and the travails of those airmen who were shot down and washed up on the coast of China. The film was based on a book by Lt. Ted Lawson, one of the fliers who survived the raid (at the cost of a leg). Robert Considine was his co-writer.

Spencer Tracy played Doolittle with his wonted air of integrity, and Lt. Lawson was acted by Van Johnson—still the very image of the all-American boy grown up.

Being released as it was so shortly before final victory, it was an extremely popular film.

Producer: Sam Zimbalist. **Director:** Mervyn LeRoy. **Scriptwriter:** Dalton Trumbo. **Principal Players:** Spencer Tracy, Van Johnson, Robert Walker and Phyllis Thaxter. **Running time:** 140 minutes. **Released:** MGM.

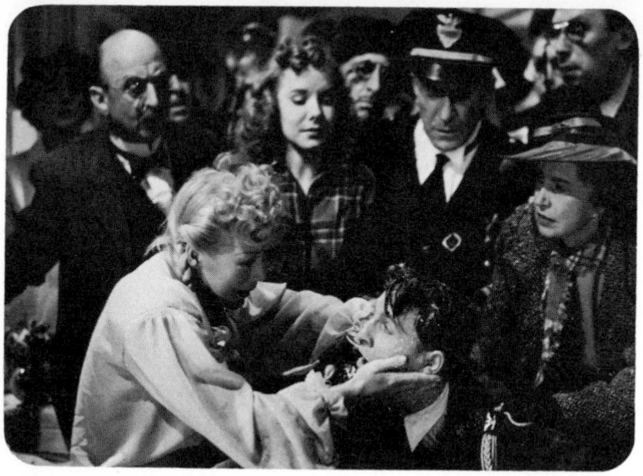

Betty Hutton (with Diana Lynn behind her) and Eddie Bracken in *The Miracle of Morgan's Creek.*

THE MIRACLE OF MORGAN'S CREEK

Writer-director Preston Sturges continued to maintain his unflagging pace of slapstick satire with *The Miracle of Morgan's Creek,* for which he conceived as imaginative an idea as any he had had.

It began with a situation that Hollywood usually treated seriously in those days: A small town girl (Betty Hutton) has a wild evening with a soldier and, in due time, finds herself pregnant. The soldier has long since departed town, so a local lad (Eddie Bracken) is called upon to rescue her good name.

At this point the plot really thickens in the Sturges manner: The hero has to leave town because he is wanted by military, state and federal authorities for impersonating a soldier, impairing the morals of a minor, abduction, forgery and bank robbery!

Obviously only a miracle can save the hapless pair, and Sturges supplies it in one of his funniest gags. The girl gives birth to sextuplets.

When the picture was released, exhibitors tried to keep the ending a secret, and advertising advised patrons they should definitely see the film from the beginning.

Sturges re-introduced briefly two characters from his 1940 film *The Great McGinty:* Brian Donlevy (McGinty) and Akim Tamiroff (The Boss).

Producer: Paramount. **Director-Writer:** Preston Sturges. **Principal Players:** Eddie Bracken, Betty Hutton, Diana Lynn and William Demarest. **Running time:** 99 minutes. **Released:** Paramount.

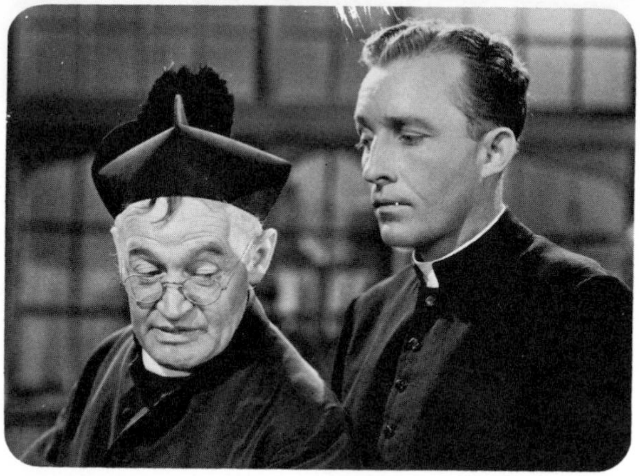

Barry Fitzgerald and Bing Crosby in *Going My Way.*

GOING MY WAY

Cynics scoffed when it was announced that the "non-actor," crooner Bing Crosby, would play one of the leading roles in this film about two Roman Catholic priests. Naturally he was to sing, but this was to be essentially a dramatic characterization.

Crosby showed them all—audiences, critics and his colleagues in Hollywood, the last of whom thought so much of his performance as Father O'Malley that they gave him an Oscar as best actor of the year.

His co-star Barry Fitzgerald, as the older clergyman, also won an Oscar. His was for best supporting actor, but he had also been nominated as best actor! This was the last time the same performer was nominated in two categories. Rules were tightened on the eligibility of players for starring or supporting awards.

Going My Way is built around the conflict between a conservative, tradition-minded pastor, and a young, progressive curate—a theme that was still relevant in the 1960's as the Church pursued a program of internal reforms.

Crosby was competent in this popular film, but he was really no competition, histrionically speaking, for Fitzgerald, who used a bag of acting tricks developed over the years to steal *Going My Way.* There isn't a dry eye in the house during the last scene, in which he is reunited with his ninety-year-old Irish mother.

Producer-Director-Writer: Leo McCarey. **Principal Players:** Bing Crosby, Barry Fitzgerald, Frank McHugh and Rise Stevens. **Running time:** 125 minutes. **Released:** Paramount.

Greer Garson and Walter Pidgeon in *Madame Curie.*

Un Carnet de Bal with Marie Bell and Louis Jouvet.

MADAME CURIE

The type of biographical film that had proved popular in the thirties was revived by MGM in this highly romanticized portrait of the famous woman scientist. Greer Garson endowed the discovery of radium with her warm, glowing personality, and Walter Pidgeon, who had co-starred with Miss Garson in *Mrs. Miniver,* played her husband, Pierre.

As much attention was given to the Curie's love affair and subsequent marriage as to their scientific endeavors together. This ensured box-office success.

Most of the critics, on the other hand, thought it was a very long two hours.

Producer: Sidney Franklin. **Director:** Mervyn LeRoy. **Scriptwriters:** Paul Osborn and Paul H. Rameau. **Principal Players:** Greer Garson, Walter Pidgeon, C. Aubrey Smith, Dame May Whitty, Robert Walker, Van Johnson and Margaret O'Brien. **Running time:** 124 minutes. **Released:** MGM.

UN CARNET DE BAL

Hollywood had tied a group of otherwise unrelated stories together with the single character of an eccentric millionaire who handed out a million dollars to different people in *If I Had a Million* in 1932. In *Un Carnet de Bal,* made in 1938, Julien Duvivier used both a character and an object to string together an episodic film. A lonely widow discovers the faded dance program of her first ball twenty years before, and decides to seek out the ten men who signed it, all of whom had professed to be in love with her at the time. Each visit brings disillusionment, and the ballroom she had remembered as belonging in a palace is revealed to be no more than a commonplace town hall.

Marie Bell of the Comedie Francaise played the heroine trying to rediscover her lost youth, and her search gave Americans a glimpse of practically all the outstanding French actors of the day: Louis Jouvet, Harry Baur, Raimu, Pierre Blanchar, Fernandel, and two actresses—Francoise Rosay and Sylvie.

In 1942, Duvivier made *Tales in Manhattan* in Hollywood, in which a tail coat was the unifying device for a multi-part film. The tail coat passed from hand to hand in episodes otherwise unrelated.

Producer-Director-Writer: Julien Duvivier. **Principal Players:** Harry Baur, Marie Bell, Pierre Blanchar, Fernandel, Louis Jouvet, Raimu, Francoise Rosay and Sylvie. **Running time:** 120 minutes. **Released:** Columbia.

DOUBLE INDEMNITY

One of three novels by James M. Cain to be made into films in the forties (the others: *The Postman Always Rings Twice* and *Mildred Pierce*), *Double Indemnity* comes closest to the unvarnished spirit of the original work, because it was co-written (with Raymond Chandler) and directed by Billy Wilder, whose pictures have never been exactly tolerant of human foibles.

There are no appealing characters in this melodrama,

Double Indemnity with Barbara Stanwyck and Fred MacMurray.

Since You Went Away with Jennifer Jones, Claudette Colbert and Shirley Temple.

in which a California femme fatale seduces an insurance salesman into helping her murder her older husband so she can collect on a double indemnity policy. Not even the murder victim or the insurance agent working to solve the case arouses any strong feelings of sympathy.

The public went to see it anyhow back in wartime 1944, and it still holds up well today, when its coldly analytical approach is even more widely appreciated.

The lack of passion extends to every element of the picture, including the love scenes between murder conspirators Barbara Stanwyck and Fred MacMurray, which are downright frosty.

The screenplay has been much praised for the terseness and wit of its dialogue.

Producer: Joseph Sistrom. **Director:** Billy Wilder. **Scriptwriters:** Billy Wilder and Raymond Chandler. **Principal Players:** Fred MacMurray, Barbara Stanwyck, Edward G. Robinson and Porter Hall. **Running time:** 106 minutes. **Released:** Paramount.

SINCE YOU WENT AWAY

The battlefield was viewed as realistically as possible in many of the war films of the mid-forties, but the home front was quite often looked at through rose-colored glasses, and never so much so as in David O. Selznick's *Since You Went Away.* He wrote the script as well as produced it.

The drama concentrated on the emotions of a wife whose husband is doing service overseas, with incidental episodic reactions in the home he left behind him. Not much plot—but plenty of sub-plots.

Comments made by Terry Ramsaye at the time on the film are amusing. "The home," he wrote, "which Mr. Selznick described as 'The American Fortress' is hardly typical or average American. It looks like about fifty thousand dollars worth of Greenwich, Conn., complete with lawns and garden. Also, despite some delays on the grocery bill, there's a scene which indicates that there is always Scotch on the sideboard."

By common consent, the best thing about the picture was the acting, with praise going to Claudette Colbert as the noble wife; Jennifer Jones and Robert Walker (married in real life but divorced in 1945) as one of the daughters and her army boy friend; Shirley Temple, making a return to the screen as the sub-adolescent daughter; and Monty Woolley as a testy old boarder.

Selznick adapted his script from a volume of letters, carrying the same title, that were taken mainly from a column in the *Dayton Journal Herald* by Margaret Buell Wilder.

Producer-Writer: David O. Selznick. **Director:** John Cromwell. **Principal Players:** Claudette Colbert, Jennifer Jones, Joseph Cotten, Shirley Temple, Monty Woolley, Lionel Barrymore and Robert Walker. **Running time:** 171 minutes. **Released:** United Artists.

Academy-Award winner Ray Milland in *The Lost Weekend,* Billy Wilder's brilliant adaptation of the Charles Jackson novel about an alcoholic.

1945

For the film trade, 1945 was a year of the beginning of transition and the beginning of the end of the war boom. Early in the year it was still unclear how long the war, at least in Japan, would last, and strict controls of the movie industry operations continued. The number of prints of each film was held at 285. The number of unreleased films hit a high of 189. Admission taxes hit an all-time high of $375,306,023. By year's end rationing was over, but supplies were hard to find.

The Government cracked down hard on those who flaunted restrictions. A theatre in Toledo that defied the curfew was refused film service by distributors on the request of the Government. The extent of the good business enjoyed by theatres was indicated by the fact that the Government's revenue from the ticket tax doubled from the year before.

Looking to the future, Charles Skouras, president of National Theatres, announced plans for prefab theatres for postwar construction. Donald M. Nelson, a former head of the War Production Board, became president of the Society of Independent Motion Picture Producers. In September, Will H. Hays turned over the reins of the Motion Picture Producers and Distributors of America, Inc. (soon to be renamed the Motion Picture Association of America, Inc.) to Eric Johnston, former president of the U.S. Chamber of Commerce.

The new association head faced a studio strike, a threat of a projectionist strike, problems of reopening foreign markets, and the resumption by the Government of its key trust suit before a Federal court, with Judges Augustus Noble Hand, Henry Warren Goddard and John Bright hearing the case.

As another portent of things to come, RCA demonstrated color television, but said that practical application was five years away—a considerable understatement, for color TV did not become widespread for twenty years. The Justice Department sued Paramount, Scophony and General Precision Instrument Co. as a theatre-TV monopoly in a futile action, as theatre-TV was not then or ever a significant factor in theatres.

Major exhibitors, including heads of leading circuits, asked for a ninety-minute maximum on the length of features, decrying the trend to longer films. This was done for two reasons: Increased film length cut down the number of shows a theatre could present each day; and long features made double bills impractical in many situations. Unquestionably, the amazing success of *Gone With the Wind,* three hours and forty minutes long when it was first released in 1939, was the prime factor in the trend to greater length. Another was the desire of the producer-distributor to obtain increased film rentals proportional to the increasing costs of production. A single feature could command a higher film rental, usually a percentage of box-office receipts, than parts of a double bill, one feature of which was rented for a fixed price.

Top box-office honors of the year went to Bing Crosby for the second year in a row, his film, *The Bells of St. Mary's,* being a hit attraction. Walt Disney, for the fifth year in a row, won the award for the best short in a poll of exhibitors. The industry itself was cited by the Federal Government for its services in the war effort. Bob Hope continued as radio's top performer and starred occasionally in films.

Stars of the year: Bing Crosby, Van Johnson, Greer Garson, Betty Grable, Spencer Tracy, Humphrey Bogart, Gary Cooper, Bob Hope, Judy Garland, Margaret O'Brien and Roy Rogers.

A Tree Grows in Brooklyn with Peggy Ann Garner and Ted Donaldson.

Dana Andrews and Richard Benedict in *A Walk in the Sun.*

A TREE GROWS IN BROOKLYN

Few novels since *Gone With the Wind* had appealed to such a wide American reading audience as Betty Smith's *A Tree Grows in Brooklyn.* Hollywood did itself proud in transferring the sensitive family saga to the screen, and the picture pleased a large audience.

The film was directed by Elia Kazan, a Broadway actor turned director. (He also played a supporting role in the 1940 James Cagney film *City for Conquest.*) In his first film project behind the camera, Kazan showed early what was to become his forte: an ability to get better performances from actors than they had ever given before.

Peggy Ann Garner, hitherto just another child star, was extremely touching as Francie, the little girl who longs to become a writer. Dorothy McGuire, the delightful *Claudia* of 1943, acquired new stature as an actress with her portrayal of the mother who becomes embittered as all her youthful hopes fade one by one. James Dunn did a beautiful job of performing the role of the father who drinks because he is a failure, and won an Oscar for it. And Joan Blondell never played so gay and winning a character as Aunt Sissy.

This is a sentimental picture certainly—but one of the best ever made.

Producer: Louis D. Lighton. **Director:** Elia Kazan. **Scriptwriters:** Tess Slesinger and Frank Davis. **Principal Players:** Dorothy McGuire, James Dunn, Peggy Ann Garner, Joan Blondell, Lloyd Nolan and Ted Donaldson. **Running time:** 128 minutes. **Released:** 20th Century-Fox.

A WALK IN THE SUN

Lewis Milestone's World War II film, *A Walk in the Sun,* is not on the same level with his great World War I picture, *All Quiet on the Western Front,* but it is nonetheless an interesting movie. It had the commercial disadvantage of being released a few months after *The Story of G.I. Joe,* a masterpiece to which it bears several superficial similarities.

As the Wellman film did, Milestone's picture follows one group of soldiers—the Lee Platoon of the Texas Division—on its first day on the beach at Salerno. It, too, avoids grand-scale battle scenes, and focuses instead on individual soldiers: the sergeant who cracks up under responsibility, the wise-cracking machine gunner, the cynical soldier, etc.

Individual sequences are quite effective in pointing up the ironies of war: The men can do nothing against a single plane which strafes them from above. The waiting and hiding that must be endured as they prepare to take a farm house that is held by the enemy are tensely conveyed.

Narration (both first- and third-person) is depended upon heavily but not redundantly, and a folk ballad is interpolated now and again for haunting comment on the action. The public was indifferent to the film, preferring *The Story of G.I. Joe.*

Producer-Director: Lewis Milestone. **Screenplay:** Harry Brown. **Principal Players:** Dana Andrews, Richard Conte, Sterling Holloway, Herbert Rudley, John Ireland and Lloyd Bridges. **Running time:** 117 minutes. **Released:** 20th Century-Fox.

Burgess Meredith (second from left) in *The Story of G.I. Joe.*

Joan Crawford and Jack Carson in *Mildred Pierce.*

THE STORY OF G. I. JOE

The best picture ever made about World War II (as of 1969 at least) was released in the year hostilities ended, and it conspicuously lacked spectacular battle sequences. Instead, *The Story of G. I. Joe* was just that—a portrait of the common, ordinary foot soldier who fought the war.

Three men worked on the screenplay, but, thanks also in large part to William Wellman's craftsmanlike direction, it comes across as if it were the product of one mind. And that is the mind of Ernie Pyle, the famous war reporter, on whose writings the film is based.

There is no story in the formal sense—just a series of small but potent incidents, as Company C of the 18th Infantry passes through Sicily, into Italy and on toward Rome, fighting for every hill along the way. They encounter a dog; a soldier goes berserk; a wedding takes place; the commandant of the company dies before they reach Rome and is buried while other companies get to the capital first. It all adds up to a true and moving depiction of how and by whom wars are fought.

The cast was headed by Burgess Meredith as Ernie Pyle and Robert Mitchum as a lieutenant, and included combat veterans of the campaigns in Africa, Sicily and Italy.

Producer: Lester Cowan. **Director:** William A. Wellman. **Scriptwriters:** Leopold Atlas, Guy Endore and Philip Stevenson. **Principal Players:** Burgess Meredith, Robert Mitchum, Freddie Steele, Wally Cassell and Jimmy Lloyd. **Running time:** 108 minutes. **Released:** United Artists.

MILDRED PIERCE

Early in 1968 an erudite American critic, in reviewing *The Graduate,* wrote that it was the first time an American film had shown a man having an affair with an older married woman and later with her own daughter. Obviously, he had never seen *Mildred Pierce.*

This vintage 1945 melodrama was daring in its own time not only for that plot development but for what James Agee referred to as its "constant attention to money and its effects." He thought this was not only somewhat revolutionary for a Hollywood film of the day but a good moral lesson for mass moviegoers.

The story, from a James Cain novel, tells of a woman who claws her way to the ownership of a chain of roadside restaurants, shedding a husband along the way, having affairs and then marrying one of the men. She does all in the interest of her daughter—who looks down her nose at her mother and all she stands for, and submits to the seduction of her stepfather.

Lurid and unsavory, yes, but *Mildred Pierce* had punch in 1945 and it still does today. It was more honest than most melodramas of its time, and the unpleasant events are firmly set in the colorful urban areas of southern California by director Michael Curtiz.

For her nicely shaded performance of Mildred, the Academy Award for best actress went to Joan Crawford.

Producer: Jerry Wald. **Director:** Michael Curtiz. **Scriptwriter:** Ranald MacDougall. **Principal Players:** Joan Crawford, Jack Carson, Zachary Scott, Eve Arden, Ann Blyth and Bruce Bennett. **Running time:** 111 minutes. **Released:** Warner Bros.

Hoagy Carmichael, Humphrey Bogart and Lauren Bacall in *To Have and Have Not.*

Ray Milland and Howard Da Silva in *The Lost Weekend.*

TO HAVE AND HAVE NOT

No male and female star team of the forties generated so much electricity as did Humphrey Bogart and Lauren Bacall (later to become husband and wife in real life) in this much-admired and successful melodrama. Based very loosely on the Ernest Hemingway book, little was left of the novel but the title. Warners remade it in 1950, calling it *The Breaking Point,* in a version that was somewhat more faithful to the original. John Garfield and Patricia Neal played the leads.

Most movie buffs prefer this version, which, while it may not have been Hemingway, was one of the most enjoyable melodramas of its decade. Director Howard Hawks gave it humor as well as tension.

Miss Bacall caused a sensation as the sexy siren who is more romantically aggressive than her prey (Bogart), and she had the best of the risqué lines. Critics compared her variously to Garbo, Dietrich and Mae West. But she was very much her own woman—not only here but in her later films.

That veteran scene-stealer, Walter Brennan, was at it again as a drifter, and Hoagy Carmichael made his film debut as a pianist in a Martinique cafe.

"Sheer entertainment" is a cliché phrase that critics are inclined to use too readily. *To Have and Have Not* is a picture that fully earns that description.

Producer-Director: Howard Hawks. **Scriptwriters:** Jules Furthman and William Faulkner. **Principal Players:** Humphrey Bogart, Lauren Bacall, Walter Brennan and Hoagy Carmichael. **Running time:** 100 minutes. **Released:** Warner Bros.

THE LOST WEEKEND

Until *The Lost Weekend* was made, alcoholics had generally been treated in films as comic figures, mostly in subordinate roles. The hero might get high on occasion (again for a humorous effect), but he would ordinarily regret it later (maybe because of a hangover). If he drank, it was sporadically, and he usually could hold it well.

Billy Wilder and Charles Brackett changed all that with their adaptation of the Charles Jackson novel. The alcoholic became for this film, if not the "hero," at least the protagonist. Alcoholism was depicted in all its ugliness, misery and horror—complete with delirium tremens, shown not with expressionistic camera tricks, but photographed in focus and head-on, as a bat devours a tiny mouse on a wall and the blood flows down. It was gruesomely effective.

The picture follows the book closely except for the motivation for Don Birnam's drinking. In the book he was a troubled bisexual; in the film he feels he is losing his powers as a writer. There was one other fundamental change: The movie has a happy ending, with Birnam resolving to quit the bottle and start his novel again.

Few sequences on the screen have shown degradation so uncompromisingly and so realistically as the one in which Birnam is caught stealing money from a woman's purse in a cocktail bar, and is exposed and humiliated. It was right out of the Jackson original, too, along with other powerful scenes too numerous to list.

But space must be given to Ray Milland's brilliant

The Bells of St. Mary's with Bing Crosby, Ingrid Bergman and Ruth Donnelly.

National Velvet with Mickey Rooney and Elizabeth Taylor.

performance, which won him an Academy Award. He was Don Birnam to perfection—the charm, the weakness and the anguish were all captured with unerring skill. Other Oscars included one for best picture, one to Wilder for his direction, and one to him and Brackett for their script.

Producer: Charles Brackett. **Director:** Billy Wilder. **Scriptwriters:** Brackett and Wilder. **Principal Players:** Ray Milland, Jane Wyman, Philip Terry, Howard Da Silva and Doris Dowling. **Running time:** 101 minutes. **Released:** Paramount.

THE BELLS OF ST. MARY'S

Bing Crosby portrayed in this picture a priest virtually indistinguishable from the one he played in *Going My Way*—a circumstance that led many people to think of this picture as a continuation of the first one.

In fact, James Agee called *The Bells of St. Mary's* an effort "to repeat the unrepeatable," but he couldn't have been more wrong from a commercial standpoint. *The Bells of St. Mary's* grossed over a million dollars more in the U.S. than had *Going My Way.*

The picture united three Oscar winners of the year before: Ingrid Bergman, who had won for *Gaslight;* and Crosby and director Leo McCarey, both of whom had been cited for *Going My Way.*

Following the leisurely and episodic style of *Going My Way, The Bells of St. Mary's* could get very cute on occasion—as when Miss Bergman, as the Sister Superior, instructs a boxer in boxing, and when Crosby reunites separated parents while vocalizing "In the Land of Beginning Again." Other moments, such as the farewell between the stars at the end, were more genuine.

Producer-Director: Leo McCarey. **Scriptwriter:** Dudley Nichols. **Principal Players:** Bing Crosby, Ingrid Bergman, Henry Travers and William Gargan. **Running time:** 126 minutes. **Released:** RKO.

NATIONAL VELVET

America fell in love with 12-year-old Elizabeth Taylor in *National Velvet* in 1945, and she was still a box-office favorite two decades later, although her career has had a full share of ups and downs. One critic wrote in 1968 that *National Velvet* was still her best picture.

Audiences were drawn to the film by Mickey Rooney and by the reputation of the Enid Bagnold novel, but when they left the theatre, it was the youthful Miss Taylor they were talking about. That, and one of the most exciting horse-race sequences ever filmed, the English Grand National Steeplechase in which the heroine rides her horse to victory.

Rooney was first-rate as the horse trainer with a shady past, and there were fine supporting performances from Donald Crisp, Anne Revere and Angela Lansbury.

Producer: Pandro Berman. **Director:** Clarence Brown. **Scriptwriters:** Theodore Reeves and Helen Deutsch. **Principal Players:** Mickey Rooney, Elizabeth Taylor, Donald Crisp, Anne Revere, Jackie Jenkins and Angela Lansbury. **Running time:** 124 minutes. **Released:** MGM.

Gene Kelly, José Iturbi, Frank Sinatra and Pamela Britton in *Anchors Aweigh.*

The Body Snatcher with Boris Karloff.

ANCHORS AWEIGH

A musical about two sailors on shore leave in Hollywood, *Anchors Aweigh* was four years ahead of *On the Town,* which added one sailor and two girls to the plot and moved the scene to New York. And Gene Kelly and Frank Sinatra starred in both.

On nearly all counts, *On the Town* is the more original and invigorating musical, but *Anchors Aweigh* is notable for some spectacular production numbers, best of which is the combined cartoon and live-action sequence in which Kelly's dancing partner is an animated mouse. Expert synchronization and timing achieved by Fred Quimby's cartoon department at MGM helped to make the feat a technical triumph; no one previously had combined cartoons and living actors with such a strong illusion of reality.

Producer: Joe Pasternak. **Director:** George Sidney. **Scriptwriter:** Isobel Lennart. **Principal Players:** Frank Sinatra, Kathryn Grayson, Gene Kelly, José Iturbi and Dean Stockwell. **Running time:** 143 minutes. **Released:** MGM.

THE BODY SNATCHER

Val Lewton won quite a fine reputation for himself in the 1940's by producing a series of weird and occult tales that achieved an effect of horror more through suggestion than through explicit sights. One of the most popular of these—if not the most highly praised—was *The Body Snatcher,* the source for which was a story by Robert Louis Stevenson. The director was Robert Wise.

It featured a trio of familiar menaces: Boris Karloff, Bela Lugosi and Henry Daniell. Karloff is cast as a murderous cabby who steals bodies from graves to sell to a doctor (Daniell) who has difficulty getting corpses to dissect in the teaching of surgery. The setting is nineteenth-century Edinburgh and, naturally, most of the dire happenings occur at night.

Karloff played this villain without any of the grotesque makeup he usually was required to put on for his screen roles.

Producer: Val Lewton. **Director:** Robert Wise. **Scriptwriters:** Philip MacDonald and Carlos Keith (pseudonym for Lewton). **Principal Players:** Boris Karloff, Henry Daniell, Bela Lugosi, Edith Atwater and Russell Wade. **Running time:** 77 minutes. **Released:** RKO.

KEYS OF THE KINGDOM

The Song of Bernadette (1943) having proven such a huge commercial success, 20th Century-Fox decided to tackle a religious theme again, using the A. J. Cronin best seller about an heroic priest. *Bernadette* made a star of Jennifer Jones, and *Keys of the Kingdom* did the same for Gregory Peck. (She won an Oscar; he was nominated, but lost.)

Peck was perfectly cast as the curate who fails in two assignments and then goes to China, where he ultimately succeeds in establishing a mission which survives

Keys of the Kingdom with Gregory Peck.

The Clock with Robert Walker (center) and Judy Garland.

a civil war and various other crises. The actor established an image of sincerity through a simple acting style that has served him well over the years—better in such films as this one, and *Twelve O'Clock High,* then in *Duel in the Sun* or *Moby Dick,* in which he was miscast.

The picture was one of the first Joseph L. Mankiewicz produced for 20th Century-Fox, where he had moved after a career as writer for MGM. He produced *Keys* and co-wrote the script.

Producer: Joseph L. Mankiewicz. **Director:** John Stahl. **Scriptwriters:** Joseph L. Mankiewicz and Nunnally Johnson. **Principal Players:** Gregory Peck, Thomas Mitchell, Vincent Price and Rose Stradner. **Running time:** 137 minutes. **Released:** 20th Century-Fox.

THE CLOCK

Arthur Freed and Vincente Minnelli, producer and director respectively, known for their exceptional achievements in the musical field, worked together on this song-less and simple story of a love affair between a soldier on leave in New York during the war and a girl he meets under the clock in Pennsylvania Station. The girl was played by Judy Garland, also known at the time exclusively for musicals, and the boy was Robert Walker. She proved enormously appealing as a dramatic actress, and he was boyish and endearing as the shy corporal from a small town who is overwhelmed by the sights and people of the big city.

Minnelli used sound—and the lack of it—with imagination: The words of the wedding ceremony are drowned out by a roaring elevated train, and a breakfast scene is played without any dialogue at all. The success of the film inspired Minnelli to tackle other dramatic scripts (*Undercurrent, Madame Bovary, Father of the Bride* and *The Bad and the Beautiful*).

In those days, Hollywood was not much for going on location, and huge sets were constructed at MGM for several New York scenes. They were meticulous in detail.

Producer: Arthur Freed. **Director:** Vincente Minnelli. **Scriptwriters:** Robert Nathan and Joseph Schrank. **Principal Players:** Judy Garland, Robert Walker, James Gleason and Keenan Wynn. **Running time:** 90 minutes. **Released:** MGM.

MEET ME IN ST. LOUIS

Is this the best period musical to be made in the forty-odd years of screen musicals? Admirers of Judy Garland and Vincente Minnelli insist that it is, and they have some sturdy arguments to support their views.

The script, based on a *New Yorker* series by Sally Benson, centers on a family living in St. Louis before and during its World Fair of 1904, and is full of episodes both comic and poignant. The nostalgic mood is splendidly achieved through sets and costuming that have a picture-book quality. The color photography gives it all a wonderfully romanticized glow. Minnelli stamped it with style.

Miss Garland was at the top of her form, but even

Meet Me in St. Louis with Joan Carroll, Lucille Bremer, Judy Garland, Hank Daniels and Margaret O'Brien.

The House on 92nd Street with (seated) Leo G. Carroll, William Eythe and Signe Hasso.

so, she had all she could do to keep Margaret O'Brien, playing her younger sister, from taking over the film in their scenes together. One of the most memorable episodes is Miss O'Brien's Halloween excursion, on which she becomes terrified while seeking tricks or treats. It evokes a moment in childhood that audiences still respond to with recognition and laughter.

Several of the Hugh Martin and Ralph Blane songs have become standards over the years and were associated with Miss Garland throughout her career: "The Trolley Song," a big production number; and "Have Yourself a Merry Little Christmas" and "The Boy Next Door," two ballads with a wistfulness that time has not dimmed.

Producer: Arthur Freed. **Director:** Vincente Minnelli. **Scriptwriters:** Irving Brecher and Fred F. Finkelhoffe. **Principal Players:** Judy Garland, Margaret O'Brien, Mary Astor, Lucille Bremer, Leon Ames and Tom Drake. **Running time:** 113 minutes. **Released:** MGM.

THE HOUSE ON 92ND STREET

Louis de Rochemont, the celebrated producer of the *March of Time* series, drew on the techniques developed for it to make this quasi-documentary purporting to be a re-enactment of an actual case out of FBI files, in which Nazi agents tried to steal data on the atomic bomb. The picture combined sequences filmed on real locations with the camera as a hidden observer, with sequences staged with actors, and used narration to bind it all together. Its success inspired a host of imitations in a new kind of semi-realistic school of film making—not quite documentary and not quite fiction, and no one could ever be sure where one began and the other left off.

Intentionally or not, *The House on 92nd Street* was a tribute to FBI methods, which were depicted as highly trained and skilled. The audience was shown how fingerprints are traced, how solvents are employed to bring out secret codes in apparently harmless letters, how film records of suspects are made through X-ray glass, etc.

Nor were the Nazi agents portrayed as simpletons and fools. In this picture they are well trained, efficient and ruthless—true to life.

The effect was to make the film highly credible and to cause many Americans to accept all of it as documented fact. Henry Hathaway's direction gave it a crisply realistic air, and the actors fit into the format perfectly.

Producer: Louis de Rochemont. **Director:** Henry Hathaway. **Scriptwriters:** Charles G. Booth, Barre Lyndon and John Monks, Jr. **Principal Players:** William Eythe, Lloyd Nolan, Signe Hasso, Leo G. Carroll and Gene Lockhart. **Running time:** 88 minutes. **Released:** 20th Century-Fox.

A SONG TO REMEMBER

Bringing the music of Brahms, Liszt and Tchaikovsky to the jukeboxes did not seem an especially noble endeavor to the intelligentsia, but it had proved

A Song to Remember with Paul Muni and Cornel Wilde.

profitable before to Hollywood moviemakers and so some of them did it again in *A Song to Remember.* This time it was Chopin who was given the glamor treatment and turned into a robust, handsome fellow in the person of Cornel Wilde. Likewise, writer George Sand became a ravishing beauty as acted by Merle Oberon. The historical-minded squirmed, along with the admirers of the composer, but average moviegoers were impressed and turned the picture into a hit.

In relating the life story of Chopin, the picture emphasized his chauvinism in regard to his native Poland and his romantic affair with the notorious Sand, who really did wear men's pants but probably with not the same élan as did Miss Oberon in the film. (Only Marlene Dietrich has donned slacks on the screen to more chic effect.) In the end, the screen Chopin must choose between loyalty to his country and his mistress; he opts, at the bidding of his old teacher (Paul Muni with a beard again), for the former, and dies while on a concert tour to raise money to free Polish patriots from prison.

The Chopin melodies were played on the sound track by no less an artist than José Iturbi, whose rendering of the "Polonaise" almost landed it on the Hit Parade.

Producer: Sidney Buchman. **Director:** Charles Vidor. **Scriptwriter:** Sidney Buchman. **Principal Players:** Paul Muni, Merle Oberon and Cornel Wilde. **Running time:** 113 minutes. **Released:** Columbia.

The Best Years of Our Lives with Donald Kerr, Hoagy Carmichael, Harold Russell and Dana Andrews, Samuel Goldwyn's timely film about veterans returning from the war. It won seven Academy Awards.

1946

Providing entertainment for a still war-weary public in the midst of the problems of conversion to peace was the major business of the year. *The Best Years of Our Lives,* Samuel Goldwyn's classic, caught the public mood and was a great success.

Problems of operation abounded: All 658 theatres in New York City were closed for a time in February, as a result of a tugboat strike which halted fuel deliveries to the city; studio musicians asked a doubling of their wages; various rail strikes caused delays in film deliveries; and a nationwide coal strike dimmed marquees.

In the main, admissions to theatres held remarkably steady. The public eagerly sought the lavish, loud and funny pictures which Hollywood was producing as an answer to the strains of the war. War themes were out. But a measure of the public's interest in good films was the trade estimate that fifty million persons saw one of the top films.

The Production Code was amended to permit films on drugs and drug addiction—over the strong protest of Harold Anslinger, U.S. Commissioner of Narcotics, who predicted that such action would arouse curiosity in drugs and lead to increased use and addiction.

The Code had a major test with Howard Hughes over *The Outlaw* . The Code seal was withdrawn on account of advertising abuse, and Hughes sued for antitrust violation. Eventually the court ruled that the Motion Picture Association was free to withdraw its seal, ending the first and only major threat to the industry's self-regulation system since its establishment in 1930.

Film company revenues hit all-time highs. Paramount estimated $21,792,000 for six months, four million more than made during the entire year of 1945. To no one's surprise there was a further rise in film stocks. No one yet took seriously the impeding impact on the box office of national television. The movies' key place as the public's favorite entertainment medium was soon to be challenged.

Theatres tried to look ahead, and organized the American Theatres Association as a successor to the War Activities Committee, under prominent circuit owner S. H. Fabian, and Ted R. Gamble, a Treasury Bond campaign executive.

The Federal Court ruled that films must be sold individually, and that distributors could not fix theatre admission prices. The sale of hundreds of theatres by the circuits was also ordered. In an important trust case in Chicago, the Jackson Park Theatre won a decision holding all Loop first-runs to a maximum of two weeks. The old order of long first-runs, then long waits before the next, lower-priced engagement, was on the way out.

Another trend which would become significant was indicated by the excellent acceptance of *Open City,* an Italian film. Soon Hollywood was to be challenged as never before by overseas products.

Theatre owners, of course, welcomed films from any source, provided only that they would attract patrons in profitable numbers. Other things being equal, many exhibitors preferred films from new sources in order to decrease their dependency on the major companies. The big producers had found that the shortage of prints, resulting from the wartime pinch, was actually helpful in creating a seller's market, and enabled them to charge theatres increased rentals.

Stars of the year: Bing Crosby, Van Johnson, Greer Garson, Betty Grable, Spencer Tracy, Humphrey Bogart, Gary Cooper, Bob Hope, Judy Garland, Margaret O'Brien and Roy Rogers.

Tyrone Power and Gene Tierney in *The Razor's Edge.*

THE RAZOR'S EDGE

The return of Tyrone Power to the screen after wartime service and the popularity of the Somerset Maugham book were chiefly responsible for the huge success enjoyed by *The Razor's Edge*. But one should not overlook the sumptuous production and the appeal of an all-star cast, including Gene Tierney, John Payne, Anne Baxter and Clifton Webb. And Herbert Marshall again played the narrator of the story—Maugham himself—as he had for *The Moon and Sixpence* four years before.

While the film has a spiritual theme—the Power character is in constant search of inner peace—the commercially shrewd Maugham did not neglect to pack into his story enough cliché incidents to make two films. There are romance, seduction, accidental death, alcoholism, murder, sudden poverty—a complete assortment of exciting elements.

The philosophical aspect of the hero's striving for contentment of soul never became too metaphysical; yet enough of it is there to persuade more impressionable members of the audience that they are being made to think while being entertained. Perhaps in the long run that is the real reason *The Razor's Edge* was such a hit as both book and film.

Producer: Darryl F. Zanuck. **Director:** Edmund Goulding. **Scriptwriter:** Lamar Trotti. **Principal Players:** Tyrone Power, Gene Tierney, John Payne, Anne Baxter, Clifton Webb and Herbert Marshall. **Running time:** 146 minutes. **Released:** 20th Century-Fox.

Aldo Fabrizi in *Open City.*

OPEN CITY

Roberto Rossellini fathered the neo-realist film movement in Italy which shook up the international industry in the late forties. The movement's artistic impact outweighed its financial one, although the latter was not inconsiderable. It all began with *Open City,* the newsreel-like document of the Resistance in Rome, which Rossellini had started filming before the Nazis had evacuated the Eternal City.

The film depicts the terror loosed by the enemy against the Italian underground movement between September, 1943, when the Germans occupied Rome, until the liberation that came in June, 1944. The script is based on actual incidents, and many of the scenes were re-enacted exactly where they occurred.

Rossellini showed the German cruelty in all its ugliness, and, as one reviewer described the torture scenes: "What Hollywood leaves to shadows and silhouettes, he puts in close-up."

Technically, the film is often clumsy, but the power of what the cameras recorded still comes across and makes such deficiencies unimportant. The cast was composed of non-professionals except for those in leading roles, who included Anna Magnani as an unmarried pregnant woman shot down in the streets, and Aldo Fabrizi as a priest sympathetic to the underground.

Producer-Director: Roberto Rossellini. **Scriptwriters:** Roberto Rossellini, Sergio Amidei and Federico Fellini. **Principal Players:** Aldo Fabrizi, Anna Magnani and Marcello Pagliero. **Running time:** 100 minutes. **Released:** Mayer-Burstyn.

Cary Grant, Ingrid Bergman, Leopoldine Konstantin and Claude Rains in *Notorious.*

NOTORIOUS

So much to-do was made over the long and impassioned kissing scene in *Notorious,* starring Cary Grant and Ingrid Bergman embroiled with a telephone receiver and cord, that it threatened to overshadow the fact that this was one of Alfred Hitchcock's best films of the 1940's. It had an intelligent script by Ben Hecht (better than the one he did for *Spellbound*), with characters in greater depth than those in the ordinary thriller. Nor was this achieved at the expense of suspense: There was plenty of that, too.

The love affair is one of the most realistic and convincing that Hitchcock has depicted. Miss Bergman is cast as the daughter of a German sentenced to jail for treason; Grant is an American intelligence officer who enlists her aid in exposing a German chemical cartel which is up to unknown deviltry in Rio. They fall in love, but when duty calls upon her to marry one of the villains to get valuable information, she does so. Her life is imperiled by slow poisoning when she is found out, and Grant rescues her in an exciting, gratifying ending.

Notorious contains one of Hitchcock's most famous camera tricks: The dazzling traveling shot in which the camera swoops down from the top of a staircase to a close-up of a key in the hand of Miss Bergman which she has stolen from her husband (Claude Rains) to give to Grant. It still takes the breath away!

Producer-Director: Alfred Hitchcock. **Scriptwriter:** Ben Hecht. **Principal Players:** Cary Grant, Ingrid Bergman and Claude Rains. **Running time:** 101 minutes. **Released:** RKO.

Jean-Louis Barrault and Arletty in *Children of Paradise.*

CHILDREN OF PARADISE

Masterpieces have their troubles getting made, but somehow it happens, and they survive. This most famous of all the film collaborations between director Marcel Carné and poet-scriptwriter Jacques Prévert (others include *Drôle de Drame* in 1937 and *Le Jour Se Lève* in 1939) was produced with very little money and under awkward conditions, being filmed during the last days of the Nazi occupation of Paris. (Legend has it that some of the actors were being sought by the Gestapo!) Its release to other countries was held up for as much as three years, for obvious reasons, and when it came to the U.S. in 1946, it had been cut by some thirty-four minutes.

Out of such adversity came art—one of the two or three great French films in the first four decades of sound that improves with the years. It evokes a time and a place vividly: the fabulous Boulevard du Crime in nineteenth-century Paris. It beautifully sustains a central mood throughout: Romanticism as a way of life is supremely defined by this film, whose characters are thrown this way and that by the vagaries of love, to which all else in life seems secondary.

And what characters! Types, of course, but types that come triumphantly alive through the magic of inspired acting: the sensitive mime of Jean-Louis Barrault; the vain and treacherous actor played by Pierre Brasseur; the lovely demimondaine of Arletty, adored by many men; the betrayed wife created by Maria Casares; and many more too numerous to list.

Henry V with Laurence Olivier.

Critics have carped that the film is not "cinematic," pointing out that, except for close-ups of details and the tracking shots through crowds, it could all be transferred right to the theatrical stage. Nevertheless they always end up praising the picture—a tribute to its spell.

Publicists in the U.S. called it "the French answer to *Gone With the Wind.*" Artistically, yes, but commercially, in America, no. The complete 195-minute version was finally shown here in 1960, and the picture still did not seem over-long.

Producer: Tricolore Films. **Director:** Marcel Carné. **Scriptwriter:** Jacques Prévert. **Principal Players:** Jean-Louis Barrault, Arletty, Pierre Brasseur, Pierre Renoir, Etienne Decroux, Leon Larive, Fabien Leris and Maria Casares. **Running time:** 195 minutes. **Released:** Alexander Korda.

HENRY V

Laurence Olivier's production of Shakespeare's play, in which he starred as well as directed for J. Arthur Rank, premiered in London late in 1944, where its portrait of a triumphant English king was seen as a harbinger of victory in the war. It had cost almost two million dollars.

It was not brought to the United States until after the war. United Artists acquired it and gave it a premiere in Boston, in the spring of 1946, under the sponsorship of the Theatre Guild. In its first year here it played sixty special engagements, many of them in legitimate theatres, on a two-a-day roadshow policy.

The Killers with Burt Lancaster and Ava Gardner.

Critics and the "specialized" audiences were enthralled by it. High praise went to the imaginative conception of the original for the screen, beginning with a performance of the play in the Globe Theatre in the time of Shakespeare and then moving back in history to the time of Henry the Fifth, and closing with another view of the audience at the Globe. There were also many laudatory phrases penned about the heroic stature of the Olivier performance. Nor were there many objections to his arbitrary inclusion of the Falstaff scene from *Henry IV* in *Henry V.*

Producer-Director: Laurence Olivier. **Scriptwriters:** Laurence Olivier and Allan Dent. **Principal Players:** Olivier, Renee Asherson and Robert Newton. **Running time:** 134 minutes. **Released:** United Artists.

THE KILLERS

The works of Ernest Hemingway have never fared too well on the screen, and all they took from his short story *The Killers* was its title—and the general idea of a man hiding in a small town who is tracked down by two gunmen and shot dead. The why and wherefore of the crime were dreamed up by Anthony Veiller, in terms of an insurance company investigator who follows a succession of clues that twist and turn, sometimes so confusingly it is hard to keep up without strain.

Still, *The Killers* is an absorbing melodrama, tautly directed by Robert Siodmak, and forcefully played by an interesting cast. Burt Lancaster made a strong im-

The Yearling with Jane Wyman, Claude Jarman, Jr., and Gregory Peck.

Gilda with Glenn Ford and Rita Hayworth.

pact as the murder victim in his screen debut (on loan from Paramount). Albert Dekker was the chief villain; Edmond O'Brien, the insurance man; and Ava Gardner was as lovely a double-crossing gun moll as any gangster melodrama ever had.

The picture was produced by the noted writer and columnist Mark Hellinger as his first for Universal. His top production to that time had been *High Sierra,* for Warner Bros.

Producer: Mark Hellinger. **Director:** Robert Siodmak. **Scriptwriter:** Anthony Veiller. **Principal Players:** Ava Gardner, Burt Lancaster, Edmond O'Brien, Albert Dekker and Sam Levene. **Running time:** 102 minutes. **Released:** Universal.

THE YEARLING

The Marjorie Kinnan Rawlings best seller about the people who pioneered the Florida frontier in the dangerous Everglade territory had a simple spirit and charm that were captured in the MGM film version to a remarkable degree. It was a tremendously popular "family picture" that all members could sit through without discomfort.

Child actors had often expressed love for animals on film before, but the affection that young Claude Jarman, Jr., displayed for the pet fawn of the title seemed the most deeply felt of all. The scene in which the yearling must be killed because he has been eating the crops was extraordinarily moving, thanks to the restrained hand of director Clarence Brown.

The parents were played by Gregory Peck and Jane Wyman, who were less successful than Jarman in giving naturalistic performances. This was not so much their fault, perhaps, as they inevitably brought to the film their well-defined screen images, while Jarman was a newcomer who seemed perfectly at home in the Florida swamp. They, on the other hand, were rather obviously tourists.

Producer: Sidney Franklin. **Director:** Clarence Brown. **Scriptwriter:** Paul Osborn. **Principal Players:** Gregory Peck, Jane Wyman and Claude Jarman, Jr. **Running time:** 135 minutes. **Released:** MGM.

GILDA

Musicals like *Cover Girl* and *You Were Never Lovelier* had helped to earn the title of "Love Goddess" for Rita Hayworth during the war, when she was a particular favorite of servicemen. But it was not until the year after hostilities had ceased that she was seen in the role that really epitomized her screen personality, the femme fatale in *Gilda.*

And this was not a musical, but a melodrama carefully tailored to the talents of the star, and curiously lacking in the incidental humor usually associated with the genre. Critics found some of the absurd goings-on unintentionally amusing, but the mass audience liked such elements as the exotic Buenos Aires setting, the sinister villainy of George Macready and the hot love affair between Miss Hayworth (the siren in black satin) and

The Spiral Staircase with Dorothy McGuire and George Brent.

Caesar and Cleopatra with Vivien Leigh and Claude Rains.

Glenn Ford (his first film since returning from the service).

Most of all, they were taken by Miss Hayworth's three songs (actually recorded by another woman, and dubbed in) and the sham striptease she did to the one called "Put the Blame on Mame." It set the screen to sizzling, and solidified her claim to top movie stardom.

Producer: Virginia Van Upp. **Director:** Charles Vidor. **Scriptwriter:** Marion Parsonnet. **Principal Players:** Rita Hayworth, Glenn Ford, George Macready and Joseph Calleia. **Running time:** 107 minutes. **Released:** Columbia.

THE SPIRAL STAIRCASE

Most of the better horror melodramas of the 1940's came from Val Lewton under the banner of RKO, but this was one from the same studio from another producer—Dore Schary. It had bigger production values than the Lewton pictures, and starred Dorothy McGuire, Ethel Barrymore and George Brent. It made more money, too.

Miss McGuire played a deaf mute employed as a maid in the stately mansion of the bedridden Miss Barrymore. An unknown killer has murdered three girls, all physically afflicted, and it is generally believed that Miss McGuire is next. The identity of the murderer is ultimately revealed to her and the audience, and the terror mounts relentlessly to the spine-tingling point at which the horrified girl recovers her voice.

The performances, especially that of Miss McGuire, are all first-rate, and the direction of Robert Siodmak is splendidly paced to build suspense.

Producer: Dore Schary. **Director:** Robert Siodmak. **Scriptwriter:** Mel Dinelli. **Principal Players:** Dorothy McGuire, George Brent, Ethel Barrymore and Kent Smith. **Running time:** 83 minutes. **Released:** RKO.

CAESAR AND CLEOPATRA

American fans of Vivien Leigh, Claude Rains and George Bernard Shaw went to see *Caesar and Cleopatra,* but not in sufficient numbers to pay off the six-million-dollar cost of the ambitious J. Arthur Rank presentation of Gabriel Pascal's production. At the time, it was the most expensive picture in the history of the British film industry.

Those who did see it certainly got their money's worth, even if the makers didn't. It is a visually opulent picture; costumes and settings reflect all the money spent. In fact, they are sometimes so overwhelming they threaten to obscure the Shaw dialogue.

That they don't is a tribute to the acting skills of Miss Leigh and Claude Rains in the title roles, and a cast of British character actors that includes Flora Robson, Francis L. Sullivan, Basil Sydney, Ernest Thesiger and Cecil Parker.

Producer-Director: Gabriel Pascal. **Scriptwriter:** G. B. Shaw. **Principal Players:** Claude Rains, Vivien Leigh, Stewart Granger and Flora Robson. **Running time:** 136 minutes. **Released:** United Artists.

Ann Todd and James Mason in *The Seventh Veil.*

The Best Years of Our Lives with Michael Hall, Myrna Loy (background), Teresa Wright and Fredric March.

THE SEVENTH VEIL

Psychiatry was not a new theme for the screen in 1946 (Hollywood's *Private Worlds* had appeared ten years earlier), but it was given a new lease on life by this popular British film. The veils of the poetic title referred to the "imponderable protections behind which the human mind shelters," or, put more simply, defense mechanisms.

Ann Todd played the neurotic heroine—a world-famous pianist tortured by the fear that she may lose the use of her hands. This comes from a traumatic childhood experience in which she had been caned on those hands on the eve of a pianoforte examination. James Mason portrayed her guardian, the man who devoted his life to the development of her genius. When he learns she plans to run away with a painter, he lashes at those same hands in a rage and drives her to attempt suicide.

Psychotherapy turns out to be quite simple: Under hypnosis the heroine has the seven veils of her mind lifted, and the light of self-knowledge—accompanied by a cure—floods in.

Do such pictures, as some critics have contended, attach a dangerous aura of glamor to neurosis? Probably—especially when the characters involved are such attractive ones as Miss Todd and Mason. (And what about Ingrid Bergman and Gregory Peck in *Spellbound?*) However, though there is no way to measure it, any damage to moviegoers is surely minimal.

The Seventh Veil represented a real breakthrough for Miss Todd, who has not had such a good part since. She is a talented lady who should have fared better in films. The screenplay of this picture won an Oscar.

Producer: Sydney Box. **Director:** Compton Bennett. **Scriptwriters:** Muriel and Sydney Box. **Principal Players:** James Mason, Ann Todd and Herbert Lom. **Running time:** 94 minutes. **Released:** Universal International.

THE BEST YEARS OF OUR LIVES

In 1946 many American war veterans were still struggling with the difficulties of readjustment to civilian life, and this was the timely subject tackled by producer Samuel Goldwyn, director William Wyler and writer Robert Sherwood in this film. No wonder it was so popular: It related the stories of three different men, told of their troubles with wives or sweethearts and employers, and gave each a happy ending!

The plot device had all three men returning to the U.S. on the same plane. One was an Air Force captain who had been a soda jerk; the second, a sergeant who had been a banking executive; and the third, a sailor from the wrong side of the tracks who had lost his hands in a bombing at sea. The audience was served up both laughter and tears over a running time that was just shy of three hours.

Terry Ramsaye, reviewing the film that year, thought occasional speeches of the actors "sound exactly like a collaboration of Archie MacLeish and Sherwood," and concluded the picture "is entirely in the tried and long-

The Jolson Story with Larry Parks.

My Darling Clementine with Henry Fonda and Victor Mature.

proved pattern which has made the American screen product successful merchandise. Art has its little moments, but merchandising is in happy control."

This was a minority opinion back then; most serious critics praised the picture lavishly. Time has proven the relatively restrained view of Ramsaye to be more exact.

The acting by Myrna Loy, Fredric March, Dana Andrews and others was very good, and Harold Russell, a former paratrooper who actually had lost his hands in the war, played the fictional equivalent with great skill. It was his first and only screen appearance, and won him an Oscar for best supporting actor.

Producer: Samuel Goldwyn. **Director:** William Wyler. **Scriptwriter:** Robert Sherwood. **Principal Players:** Myrna Loy, Fredric March, Dana Andrews, Teresa Wright, Virginia Mayo, Cathy O'Donnell, Hoagy Carmichael and Harold Russell. **Running time:** 172 minutes. **Released: RKO.**

THE JOLSON STORY

A generation brought up on the song styles of Bing Crosby and Frank Sinatra could hardly have been expected to respond to a singer whose forte was old-fashioned "belting," but respond they did to the voice of Al Jolson in this autobiographical film. The legendary vaudevillian of the twenties acquired new hordes of admirers when this film was released.

Jolson did not play himself on the screen—Larry Parks did that, with remarkable fidelity in looks and gesture—but the voice on the soundtrack was his, dubbed in while Parks mouthed the words. Almost every famous song Jolson sang is in the film, with the very obvious exception of "Sonny Boy." Settings for the numbers range from the balcony of a burlesque house, where Jolson worked as the stooge for a mediocre comedy act, to the stage of New York's Winter Garden Theatre, where he starred in a series of hits.

The songs are the film and vice versa. The plot gets very tiresome, particularly when it delves at length and repetitively into the old stage-versus-home life problems. Evelyn Keyes substituted for Ruby Keeler (Jolson's real-life wife for a time) in the film, with the character renamed Julie Benson.

Two years later Columbia made a sequel called *Jolson Sings Again,* which proved almost as popular as the original.

Producer: Sidney Skolsky. **Director:** Alfred E. Green. **Scriptwriter:** Stephen Longstreet. **Principal Players:** Larry Parks, Evelyn Keyes, William Demarest and Bill Goodwin. **Running time:** 128 minutes. **Released:** Columbia.

MY DARLING CLEMENTINE

Stuart N. Lake's 1931 novel, *Wyatt Earp, Frontier Marshal,* had been made into a motion picture by 20th Century-Fox twice before: in 1934, directed by Lew Seiler, and in 1939, directed by Allan Dwan. On both occasions it was called *Frontier Marshal.*

When John Ford returned from the service to do a film for the company, he chose this same property. A

Joseph Cotten and Jennifer Jones in *Duel in the Sun.*

study of the three pictures is very instructive. The first two are ably made "B" westerns. One does not wish to disparage them—as examples of their kind, they are good enough. *My Darling Clementine* is a masterpiece. It is the difference between directorial competence and genius.

Taking the same story materials—the slaying of two Earp brothers and the avenging of those deaths by the two surviving Earps, and the relationship of Wyatt Earp with Doc Holliday—Ford not only emphasizes character, but pays attention to details of frontier time and place that give his film a rare richness and complexity. The vastness of the western land hovers over all, revealed in horizon-deep shots of Monument Valley in black and white that have seldom—if ever—been matched for scenic beauty in any western. Ford is a cinematic poet.

Henry Fonda gave one of his two or three best screen performances as Wyatt Earp, and Victor Mature surprised everyone with his finely etched portrayal of the renegade doctor. Walter Brennan was unforgettable as the hateful Old Man Clanton.

Scripts for each of the three versions of the Lake book were by different writers: The first by William Conselman and Stuart Anthony; the second by Sam Hellman; and the Ford version by Samuel G. Engel (who also produced) and Winston Miller.

Producer: Samuel G. Engel. **Director:** John Ford. **Scriptwriters:** Samuel Engel and Winston Miller. **Principal Players:** Henry Fonda, Linda Darnell, Victor Mature and Walter Brennan. **Running time:** 97 minutes. **Released:** 20th Century-Fox.

DUEL IN THE SUN

Sex had been wedded with a western melodrama before (Howard Hughes' *The Outlaw*), but David O. Selznick was the first to do it with "taste" in his elaborately produced *Duel in the Sun.* He also spent the most money—six million dollars. Prior publicity had driven the public to fever pitch; they had been persuaded they were about to see another *Gone With the Wind.* It is hardly that, but *Duel* is still quite a show.

Selznick himself wrote the script (from a novel by Niven Busch, adapted by Oliver H. P. Garrett), and he cast Jennifer Jones in the role of a half-breed who, befriended by a rancher and his wife, becomes romantically involved with both their sons. One (Joseph Cotten) represents Soul, and the other (Gregory Peck) is Lust.

Censors of the day frowned upon the seduction scene between Peck and Miss Jones, in which, as one reviewer put it, "He takes her by storm in the most forthright display of virility illicitly triumphant an American camera has looked upon in years."

It all ends with a ludicrously overblown scene in which Peck and Miss Jones exchange bullets across a terrain of boulders, and then drag themselves toward each other for a final bloody caress, after which they expire! The American public flocked to see it.

Producer-Writer: David O. Selznick. **Director:** King Vidor. **Principal Players:** Jennifer Jones, Joseph Cotten, Gregory Peck, Lionel Barrymore, Lillian Gish, Walter Huston, Herbert Marshall and Charles Bickford. **Running time:** 136 minutes. **Released:** Selznick Releasing Organization.

Gentleman's Agreement with Dorothy McGuire and Gregory Peck, the most popular of the films of its period on race prejudice.

1947

This was the year that the issue of Communists in Hollywood boiled to a climax. Eric Johnston, Motion Picture Association president, told the House Un-American Activities Committee that "Reds suffered an overwhelming defeat when they attempted to take over Hollywood." But he rejected a suggestion by Representative John E. Rankin that subversive elements should be purged, saying, "I do not think that we are ready yet for concentration camps in America. A man has a right to make a living." Rankin threatened, "Unless the people in control of the industry are willing to clean house of Communists, Congress will have to do it for them."

Pressure continued, with Representative J. Parnell Thomas charging that "Some of the most flagrant Communist propaganda films were produced as a result of White House pressure." The industry took counsel with James F. Byrnes, former Secretary of State and "assistant President." In October; hearings were held, with Paul V. McNutt serving as the industry's special counsel. Industry spokesmen made a strong presentation of the rights of freedom of the screen, but the public relations effects were adverse. When nineteen Hollywood writers and directors became unfriendly witnesses, refusing to answer the House Committee's questions, criticism became general. (Ten of the witnesses eventually went to jail for contempt of Congress.)

In view of subsequent developments, notably the Presidential election of 1968, it is worth recording that one member of the House Un-American Activities Committee, Richard M. Nixon, found himself in a delicate spot. He was outspoken as an anti-Communist, but the film industry was influential in his California district. Mr. Nixon settled the matter by affably greeting the film industry representatives before the hearings opened, and then absenting himself for "pressuring business" elsewhere.

To repair the industry's public image, film makers met in New York under the leadership of Nicholas M. Schenck, president of Loew's, Inc., and issued a policy statement. It promised that no known Communist would be employed in the organized motion picture industry, and that the ten unfriendly witnesses cited for contempt of Congress would be discharged or suspended without compensation. The producers also called on Congress for legislation to assist the industry in ridding itself of subversive, disloyal elements.

The overwhelming majority of Congress had backed the contempt citations against Albert Maltz and Dalton Trumbo and then, by voice vote, approved censure of the others—Samuel Ornitz, John Howard Lawson, Ring Lardner, Jr., Lester Cole, Alvah Bessie, Henry Biberman, Edward Dmytryk and Robert Adrian Scott. The Hollywood talent guilds were reluctant to accept blacklisting but equally reluctant to rush to aid the "Unfriendly 10." Humphrey Bogart, who had made a trip to Washington on their behalf, stated that he "was not a Communist," but acknowledged that the trip was "ill-advised, even foolish."

On the censorship front, New York City had found a way of policing theatres—via licensing. Benjamin Fielding, City License Commissioner, said, "I can give the Mayor what he asked, a clean city. Censorship is repugnant to me. On the other hand, so are salacious pictures. There will be none, of any type, in theatres." *The Outlaw,* made by Howard Hughes, was the best-known film attacked by Fielding. In just a year, nineteen theatres had their licenses suspended for a day and two were shut completely.

Floyd B. Odlum, the president of Atlas Corporation, which controlled RKO Pictures, issued a breakdown of the admission dollar: 32¢ for film rental (20¢ of which went to production and 12¢ to distribution); 16¢ for theatre salaries; 15¢ rent; 11¢ profit; 6¢ income tax; and 20¢ for other operating expenses. Of production's 20¢, 4¢ went to talent; 7¢ sets; 1¢ story, 1¢ director; 1¢ tax; 4¢ studio overhead; and 2¢ profit.

Stars of the year: Bing Crosby, Betty Grable, Ingrid Bergman, Gary Cooper, Humphrey Bogart, Bob Hope, Clark Gable, Gregory Peck, Claudette Colbert and Alan Ladd.

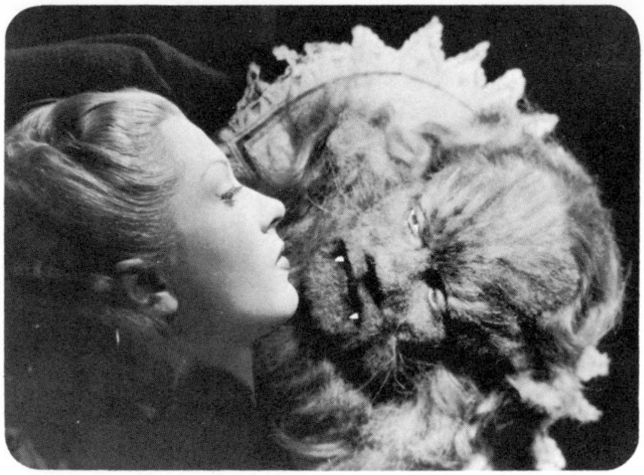

Josette Day and Jean Marais in *Beauty and the Beast.*

Robert Arthur, Dan Dailey and Betty Grable in *Mother Wore Tights.*

BEAUTY AND THE BEAST

The five feature films made by Jean Cocteau played to very limited audiences in the U.S., but the art theatre patrons who did see them found them interesting and provocative. His first full-length picture was *Beauty and the Beast,* which he made in 1946. It was released in the U.S. the following year.

Above all, the picture is visually exciting—its bizarre decor (especially in the haunted castle of the Beast), and the camerawork that recorded it are overwhelming. So much so, in fact, that some felt that the simple tale of the beauty who falls in love with a beast that turns into a Prince Charming got lost amidst the beautiful imagery.

Others will tell you that the Cocteau version of the old fairy tale is much more profound than that, and is full of symbolism and modern parallels worthy of prolonged study.

Actor Jean Marais, as made up by Christian Berard, was such an attractive Beast that some of the ladies were said to be disappointed when he was transformed into a handsome human.

Cocteau was a man of many talents—poet, novelist, essayist, playwright and artist, as well as a writer and director of motion pictures. His work has had great influence on other film makers in use of decor and camera setups.

Producer: Andre Paulve. **Director-Writer:** Jean Cocteau. **Principal Players:** Jean Marais, Josette Day and Marcel Andre. **Running time:** 88 minutes. **Released:** Lopert Pictures.

MOTHER WORE TIGHTS

Betty Grable had made her reputation as a pinup girl during World War II, mostly in modern musicals in which she showed her legs as frequently as possible. But one of her most popular pictures turned out to be this period piece (pre-World War I), a kind of "life with mother" set to music.

The nostalgic script was based on a book by Miriam Young, and Miss Grable's role was that of a dancer who retires to wed a comedian (Dan Dailey) and raise a family, and then goes back on the road with him when the two daughters reach school age. The plot ingredients were familiar, but there were a number of tender moments that endeared the picture to large audiences.

The music included six numbers alternating between the wistful and the gay, and Dailey made an excellent partner for the star.

Producer-Writer: Lamar Trotti. **Director:** Walter Lang. **Principal Players:** Betty Grable, Dan Dailey, Mona Freeman and Connie Marshall. **Running time:** 107 minutes. **Released:** 20th Century-Fox.

THE LAST ROUND-UP

Gene Autry was the King of the Cowboys back in the days when competition for the title was fierce among the heroes of all those westerns that Hollywood ground out by the week. He made his screen debut in 1934 (after success as a radio singer) singing with Mascot Pictures

The Last Round-Up with Gene Autry, Jean Heather (to his right), Carol Thurston (his left), and in bed, Bobby Blake.

Body and Soul with John Garfield (left).

(which later became Republic). His claim to fame was that he was the "first singing cowboy."

In *Motion Picture Herald's* yearly polls conducted to ascertain the top cowboy stars, Autry headed all comers from 1937 to 1942, and placed in the ranks from 1946 to 1954. He made the general popularity poll, too—from 1938 to 1942—becoming the first cowboy to do so.

Between 1942 and 1946, Autry was in the Air Force. In 1946 he formed Gene Autry Productions and moved from Republic to Columbia in 1947. His first picture for the new distributor was *The Last Round-Up,* and experts on the genre pronounced it his best, one of them remarking that it "achieves authentically and within logic such feats as combining an Indian uprising, a cattle stampede and a television broadcast in a normal story of the 1947 West!"

Producer: Armand Schaefer. **Director:** John English. **Scriptwriters:** Jack Townley and Earle Snell. **Principal Players:** Gene Autry, Jean Heather, Ralph Morgan, Carol Thurston and Mark Daniels. **Running time:** 77 minutes. **Released:** Columbia.

BODY AND SOUL

Of the three major prizefighting films of the 1940's, *Body and Soul* proved the most popular with the mass audience—probably because it was the most conventional in approach. (The others were *Champion* and *The Set-Up.*) This is true, at least, of the script of Abraham Polonsky, which shirked none of the clichés of the genre: maternal disapproval of the son for going into the boxing profession; the break with his sweetheart when he joins forces with racketeers; the final bout in which, although he has agreed to take a fall, he decides to win honestly; and the final reunion with the girl friend.

However, *Body and Soul* has several major talents doing top-flight work: John Garfield, giving one of his most dynamic performances in the lead; Robert Rossen, directing some of the best fight sequences on record; and James Wong Howe, photographing them with brilliance. Other merits are a lovely performance from the charming Lilli Palmer (as the girl friend), and a moving one from Canada Lee as an injured ex-champion.

These elements make *Body and Soul* worthwhile over two decades later.

Producer: Bob Roberts. **Director:** Robert Rossen. **Scriptwriter:** Abraham Polonsky. **Principal Players:** John Garfield, Lilli Palmer, Hazel Brooks, Anne Revere, William Contra and Canada Lee. **Running time:** 104 minutes. **Released:** United Artists.

CROSSFIRE

This Dore Schary production was the first in a cycle of Hollywood pictures dealing with anti-Semitism, and it set a high standard for frankness, sincerity and tact as it demonstrated that racial hatred can be as dangerous and fatal as a loaded gun.

It did so within the context of a suspenseful thriller. An ex-GI is murdered simply because he is a Jew. The killer is a soldier who tries to pin the crime on a colleague. In an exciting sequence, he finally breaks down.

Crossfire with William Phipps and Robert Ryan.

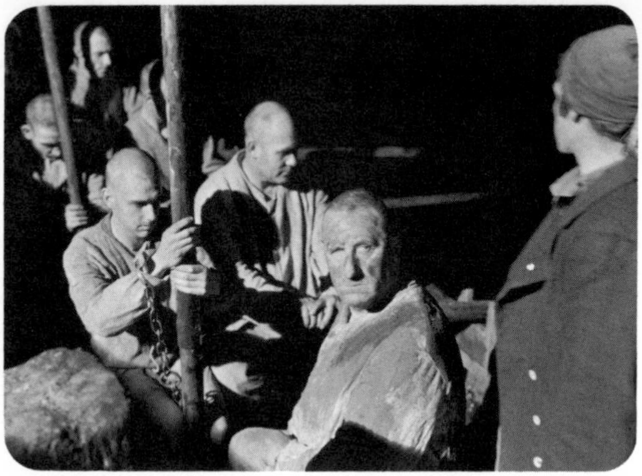

Great Expectations with Finlay Currie as the convict.

In the course of uncovering the murderer, the detective (Robert Young) states the theme explicitly, making the point that once the Irish were the subject of the same persecutions in the U.S. now visited on the Jews. Elsewhere, however, the message was never labored.

Of several fine performances, the best came from Robert Ryan as the murderous anti-Semite. He made the blood run cold with his impassioned delivery of such lines as one about the "Jew-boys who lived on easy street during the war while the white people fought in the front-line trenches."

Producer: Adrian Scott. **Director:** Edward Dmytryk. **Scriptwriter:** John Paxton. **Principal Players:** Robert Young, Robert Mitchum, Robert Ryan and Gloria Grahame. **Running time:** 86 minutes. **Released:** RKO.

GREAT EXPECTATIONS

What Laurence Olivier did for Shakespeare three times on the screen, David Lean did for Charles Dickens with this picture and *Oliver Twist* in 1948. If the Lean films are on the whole more successful adaptations, that is because the nineteenth-century novelist is more amenable to cinematic transition than the Bard of Avon.

Great Expectations is an artful compression into two hours' running time of the rambling novel. Its highlights of dramatic incident are shrewdly selected, and its eccentric characters brought to life through casting that is, for the most part, inspired.

John Mills played the hero, Pip; Martita Hunt created Miss Havisham, pining away in that cobwebbed mansion for forty years, mourning for a lost lover; Valerie Hobson was Estella, the girl Pip adores; Finlay Currie, the convict Magwitch; Francis L. Sullivan was seen as attorney Jaggers; Alec Guinness (in one of his first screen appearances) as Herbert Pocket. A very young Jean Simmons, by the way, played Estella as a child.

The picture had its American premiere at Radio City Music Hall, paving the way for engagements elsewhere in the U.S., outside the limited art theatre orbit.

Earlier film versions of *Great Expectations* include one directed by Stuart Walker for Universal in 1934, in which Francis L. Sullivan appeared in the same role he had later in Lean's version.

Producer: Ronald Neame. **Director:** David Lean. **Scriptwriters:** Ronald Neame, David Lean, and Kay Walsh. **Principal Players:** John Mills, Valerie Hobson, Bernard Miles, Francis L. Sullivan, Finlay Currie and Martita Hunt. **Running time:** 115 minutes. **Released:** Universal-International.

FOREVER AMBER

Kathleen Winsor was the Jacqueline Susann of her day, and her novel, *Forever Amber,* sold over two million copies. The elements exploited are the same—sensationalism and sex.

Amber was a pretty minx from seventeenth-century England who used her physical charms to advance from commoner beginnings to the castle of King Charles

Forever Amber with Linda Darnell and Cornel Wilde.

Odd Man Out with Fay Compton and James Mason.

himself. She did it bed by bed—a progression graphically detailed in the book.

The film recorded the same situations, but more discreetly. Had it been made in the 1960's, there undoubtedly would have been much more exposure of Linda Darnell (Amber) and her many boy friends (played by Cornel Wilde, John Russell, Glenn Langan and George Sanders) in their love scenes together.

The picture was lavishly produced, at a cost reputed to be almost six and a half million dollars.

Producer: William Perlberg. **Director:** Otto Preminger. **Scriptwriters:** Philip Dunne and Ring Lardner. **Principal Players:** Linda Darnell, Cornel Wilde, Richard Greene and George Sanders. **Running time:** 140 minutes. **Released:** 20th Century-Fox.

ODD MAN OUT

When Robert Alan Aurthur's *The Lost Man* was released in 1969, many critics seemed not even to notice that it was a paraphrase of Carol Reed's *Odd Man Out,* the picture which established him as a major director. The Irish Republican Army leader, played by James Mason, was replaced by a Civil Rights organizer, played by Sidney Poitier, and the locale was moved from Ireland to the U.S. But the central plot line was the same—a man shot in a robbery tries to elude the police and seeks aid along the way from a variety of people who respond to his plight in different ways.

But the difference in approach between the two films is more important than their similarities. The Aurthur picture is a good chase melodrama of its kind. The Reed version has the melodrama but something much more—a sense of poetry.

Reed makes of the flight of the fugitive a kind of tone poem, and the hero and the characters he meets become allegorical figures. The picture is splendidly acted in every role, but towering over all is the haunting performance of Mason as the doomed man.

Producer-Director: Carol Reed. **Scriptwriters:** R. C. Sherriff and F. L. Green. **Principal Players:** James Mason, Robert Newton, Robert Beatty, J. J. McCormick, Fay Compton, Cyril Cusack, Dan O'Herlihy and Kathleen Ryan. **Running time:** 116 minutes. **Released:** Universal-International.

SHOESHINE

A few months after Rossellini's *Open City* was released in America, it was followed by *Shoeshine,* and the second of the two great leaders of the neo-realist school in Italy was introduced here. Vittorio De Sica's film about two youths who become involved in a black market in postwar Rome is much more than a documentary on juvenile delinquency. It is a strong drama of friendship and betrayal that acquires the dimensions of real tragedy before it is over.

Shoeshine had respectable runs in a few U.S. cities, but it did not make the initial impact nor have the staying power of the more sensational *Open City.* De Sica's film was a disappointing commercial flop in Italy because it had to compete with the big American pic-

Shoeshine with Rinaldo Smordoni and Franco Interlenghi.

Gentleman's Agreement with John Garfield and Celeste Holm.

tures that were just beginning to be shown there again following the war.

De Sica was to make two more outstanding contributions to neo-realism (*Bicycle Thief* and *Umberto D*), but the movement soon fizzled out, and the Italian industry went back to making spectacles based on religious and mythical themes. De Sica himself turned to filming comedies with Sophia Loren. They also made a drama together which won them acclaim: *Two Women.*

Producer: Paolo W. Tamburella. **Director:** Vittorio De Sica. **Scriptwriter:** Cesare Zavattini. **Principal Players:** Rinaldo Smordoni and Franco Interlenghi. **Running time:** 93 minutes. **Released:** Lopert Pictures.

GENTLEMAN'S AGREEMENT

Crossfire had led the way in the exposure of anti-Semitism on the screen, but *Gentleman's Agreement* is the film that packed the theatres and took the awards. It won the Oscar as best picture of the year; Elia Kazan was chosen best director; and Celeste Holm got the supporting actress accolade.

Critics thought it much better than the Laura Z. Hobson best seller on which the script was based, crediting the literate script of Moss Hart, the expert Kazan direction and the fine playing of an all-star cast.

There were objections: The hero, a writer who poses as a Jew in order to do a report on anti-Semitism, seemed unduly naive when he ran into prejudice. It could be said in rebuttal, of course, that having knowledge of such practices and then being submitted to them oneself are two different matters.

A biting point was put across with special force with the introduction of June Havoc as a Jewish secretary harboring unconscious anti-Semitism against some of her own people.

In sum, *Gentleman's Agreement* hardly solved the issue, but it did touch a sore point on the American scene. The argument on the screen was that the answer is not in the hands of the rabble rousers but among the vast number of inherently good people who victimize themselves by indifference to the issue. The point is still relevant.

Producer: Darryl F. Zanuck. **Director:** Elia Kazan. **Scriptwriter:** Moss Hart. **Principal Players:** Gregory Peck, Dorothy McGuire, John Garfield, Celeste Holm, Anne Revere and Dean Stockwell. **Running time:** 118 minutes. **Released:** 20th Century-Fox.

Olivia de Havilland and Leo Genn in *The Snake Pit,* Anatole Litvak's controversial film about a mental breakdown and its cure. It was the forerunner of a flood of pictures on the subject.

1948

This was a period of readjustment for Hollywood. The war boom was over and the industry's image had been tarnished in the eyes of many as a result of the anti-Communist crusade of the year before. Costs had risen rapidly, but there had been no increase in quality. While stars began to get increased compensation, the product itself was cheapened. At the studios the ruling dynasties maintained a reign of terror. Privilege, abuse, favoritism and extravagance were dominant notes. Economically, the outlook was gloomy. Box-office receipts had declined from the peak of 1946. Britain had sharply cut the flow of dollars from film earnings. Government antitrust pressures increased, and the public became more selective in seeking good shows. The driving inspiration of showmanship had been dulled.

Studios did not know what type of films to make. There was a trend to remakes, with six such movies ready by mid-year and twenty-seven more planned. Some of the films were issued under the original titles; others had new ones to fool, if possible, the public. Important remakes included *Quo Vadis, Down to the Sea in Ships, Carmen, The Scarlet Pimpernel, Little Women* and *The Three Musketeers.* Story purchases were down, with prices for film rights of novels off 40 percent to 50 percent from earlier levels. A book's film rights now rarely brought over $50,000.

However, two trends which later became important started: Hollywood became increasingly interested in production abroad; and the easing of war-time restrictions opened the way to more films in color.

Exhibitors' interest in drive-in theatres increased. There were 350 in operation in the spring, and another hundred or more opened during the summer. Circuits became concerned at the decline in attendance by children. The average admission price had risen to over 35¢. (For comparison: In 1929 it had been 30¢; 1933, 20¢; 1940, 24¢; 1945, 30½¢.) The public began to question the value of double bills.

Exhibitor spokesmen were articulate in decrying the growing length of Hollywood features. Among theatre owners there was virtual unanimity that features, especially the better-quality films, should be kept under ninety minutes in length. Robert J. O'Donnell, a Texas circuit operator known as "Mr. Exhibitor," said, "The recent deluge of two-hour and two-hour-and-ten-minute pictures and in some instances longer, is a very definite mistake."

Concern increased about television. Exhibitors flirted with theatre television. The Paramount Theatre in New York showed Governor Thomas E. Dewey's acceptance speech after his nomination for President at the Republican National Convention in Philadelphia. Also, the Louis-Walcott prize fight was telecast to a few theatres. Twentieth Century-Fox began selling an edition of its newsreel to television.

Grosses of foreign films declined 45 percent from the recent peak. Joseph Burstyn, partner of Arthur Mayer in Mayer-Burstyn, pioneers in foreign film importation, said, "There is room for only four to five really good films from Europe in this country. Too many old and unworthy pictures have been and are being brought in." At this time the major New York circuits—and most others throughout the country—simply refused to book foreign language films.

Stars of the year: Bing Crosby, Betty Grable, Abbott & Costello, Gary Cooper, Bob Hope, Humphrey Bogart, Clark Gable, Cary Grant, Spencer Tracy and Ingrid Bergman.

Lew Ayres and Jane Wyman in *Johnny Belinda.*

Philip Dorn, Irene Dunne and June Hedin in *I Remember Mama.*

JOHNNY BELINDA

Jane Wyman had enjoyed a steady but not very distinguished career since her debut in films in 1936, mostly as a comedienne, with *The Yearling* and *Lost Weekend* the most notable exceptions. Then she was given the chance of a lifetime by producer Jerry Wald, in the role of the deaf mute in *Johnny Belinda.* She rose to the occasion magnificently.

The script was adapted from a stage play by Elmer Harris and is on the heavily melodramatic side, including the rape of the heroine by the drunken town bully, the slaying of her father by this same man and, finally, her killing the bully when he tries to claim his child and take it from her.

The violence of the story was in strong contrast to the setting, which is a small community on Cape Breton Island near Nova Scotia. Opening reels of the film were slowed down considerably as the camera recorded the scenic beauty of the island and the surrounding sea.

The Wyman performance is incandescent. Without a word to speak the actress might have been expected to chew the scenery with gestures, but she never did. The innocence and the beauty of the character were all written in her eloquent face. She won an Oscar, and seldom has it been so justified.

Producer: Jerry Wald. **Director:** Jean Negulesco. **Scriptwriters:** Irmgard von Cube and Allen Vincent. **Principal Players:** Jane Wyman, Lew Ayres, Charles Bickford, Agnes Moorehead and Stephen McNally. **Running time:** 102 minutes. **Released:** Warner Bros.

I REMEMBER MAMA

In the school of "tender" and "heart-warming" episodic films about the ups and downs of a family, George Stevens made a minor masterpiece in *I Remember Mama.* It was his first postwar film and revealed him to be even more firm in his craftsmanship than before.

The film was an adaptation of a stage play by John van Druten, who, in turn, had drawn upon *Mama's Bank Account,* a series of short stories by Kathryn Forbes about an American-Norwegian family. The format was a series of incidents, revolving around the mother and father, their four children, an uncle, three aunts and the boarder, a broken-down actor. Crises occur: the illness of one daughter, the graduation of another, the marriage of a middle-aged sister, the death of the uncle. The problems were those faced by most families everywhere, and audiences of all sorts were quick to comprehend and appreciate the film.

Under the meticulous direction of Stevens, Irene Dunne gave a tremendously moving performance as the wise and gentle Mama—her Norwegian accent was technically perfect, but the greater achievement was in her projection of a person who was good without being pious, and strong without being domineering. There were other fine performances but hers was supreme.

Producer: Harriet Parsons. **Director:** George Stevens. **Scriptwriter:** DeWitt Bodeen. **Principal Players:** Irene Dunne, Barbara Bel Geddes, Oscar Homolka, Philip Dorn, Sir Cedric Hardwicke, Rudy Vallee and Edgar Bergen. **Running time:** 137 minutes. **Released:** RKO.

Edward G. Robinson and Claire Trevor in *Key Largo.*

Hamlet with Laurence Olivier.

KEY LARGO

Seldom in screen history has a Broadway play undergone such transformation on film as Maxwell Anderson's *Key Largo.* What had been a philosophically pretentious drama on the stage, written in blank verse, was changed into a gangster melodrama, written in straightforward and realistic prose.

Outwardly some of the characters remained the same, but the hero, whom Anderson had made a cynical veteran of the Spanish Civil War, was turned into a disillusioned army officer of World War II. The central situation was similar: The hero arrives at Key Largo looking for relatives of a friend slain in the war, only to find them—a chair-bound old man and his daughter—kept prisoners in the hotel they own by a racketeer operating a counterfeit ring out of Cuba.

Key Largo was not a great play, but the movie is a first-rate example of this type of gangster melodrama. Humphrey Bogart was in fine form as the man who has lost his ideals but recovers them in time to kill off the gangsters one by one. Lauren Bacall, although more subdued than she had been in *To Have and Have Not,* was still an intriguing female. Lionel Barrymore played the father, and there was memorable acting by Claire Trevor as the bibulous moll of the head of the gang, who won an Academy Award for her supporting role.

The gangster chief was portrayed by Edward G. Robinson, who stole the film. As a ruthless hood deported from the U.S. ("like I was a dirty Red or something"), he put on a terrific show and handled expertly the transition from vicious killer to a trembling coward when a hurricane strikes the island, threatening all their lives. John Huston directed the film with his usual flair for melodramatic tension.

Producer: Jerry Wald. **Director:** John Huston. **Scriptwriters:** Huston and Richard Brooks. **Principal Players:** Humphrey Bogart, Edward G. Robinson, Lauren Bacall, Lionel Barrymore and Claire Trevor. **Running time:** 101 minutes. **Released:** Warner Bros.

HAMLET

Like *Henry V* before it, the J. Arthur Rank production of *Hamlet* was brought to the U.S. under the august auspices of the Theatre Guild, with a grand opening in Boston on the night of August 18, 1948. The film, along with *The Red Shoes,* released the same year, was part of Rank's ambitious program to attain new world significance for the British film industry—and to make some money in the American market.

Hamlet, alas, was mostly a *succès d'estime*—doomed to art house engagement in the U.S.

Shakespeare did eventually make a breakthrough to the mass audience in the 1960's, but it took Elizabeth Taylor and Richard Burton in *The Taming of the Shrew* to do that, along with Franco Zeffirelli's *Romeo and Juliet.*

Laurence Olivier's interpretation of *Hamlet,* both as director and actor, won much praise from the critics, although some felt he bore down a little too hard on the Oedipal relationship with his mother (the kiss he gave Eileen Herlie as Gertrude was full on the lips), and

The Red Shoes with Moira Shearer and Robert Helpmann.

Red River with Joanne Dru, John Wayne and Montgomery Clift.

purists denounced truncations of the original text. His reading of the soliloquies was impressively clear and articulate, although one was now and again distracted from the meaning by a too-fluid movement of the camera to sights other than the speaker.

Shakespeare still presents problems to film makers, but Olivier solved many of them here with high imagination. His handling of the play scene was perhaps the most cinematic. Hollywood was very impressed by *Hamlet* and gave it five Oscars.

Producer: Filippo Del Guidice. **Director:** Laurence Olivier. **Principal Players:** Olivier, Jean Simmons, Eileen Herlie, Basil Sydney, Felix Aylmer, Terence Morgan and Norman Wooland. **Running time:** 153 minutes. **Released:** Universal-International.

THE RED SHOES

With this picture and *Hamlet,* J. Arthur Rank in 1948 continued his determined drive to capture the American film market. The key to his failure lies in the types of pictures with which he sought to make inroads: both this and *Hamlet* were for special audiences, not the masses.

In fact, *The Red Shoes* had less of a potential patronage than *Hamlet;* its major appeal obviously was to balletomanes, or a select group *within* a select group. The story, such as it was, was subordinate to the dancing—which those qualified to appraise said was superb.

Over two hours were consumed to relate the sad tale of a middle-aged impresario (Anton Walbrook) who takes a dancer (Moira Shearer) to develop as his prima ballerina, only to lose her when she falls in love with a youthful composer (Marius Goring) attached to the company. The young couple leave, but she later returns to the ballet and, torn between her love of dancing and her love of the composer, she ends her life by jumping in front of a train.

Far more interesting than the story were the details of the world of the ballet itself, which were recorded in an obviously careful and expensive production on a broad scale. The costuming was stunning, and the camera work in the ballet sequences noteworthy.

Miss Shearer proved a better dancer than actress, but Walbrook was impressive.

Producers-Directors-Writers: Michael Powell and Emeric Pressburger. **Principal Players:** Anton Walbrook, Marius Goring and Moira Shearer. **Running time:** 133 minutes. **Released:** Eagle-Lion.

RED RIVER

"In twenty-five years, just three," said the ads, *"The Covered Wagon, Cimarron,* and now, *Red River."* It was not an idle boast; Howard Hawks' western truly deserves the appellation, "great."

It centers, as do so many of his films, around a conflict between two strong men. Here they are John Wayne, as a tough-minded, rugged individualist who singlehandedly builds a cattle empire in the unbroken reaches of Texas; and Montgomery Clift, as his foster

A still from Carl Dreyer's *Day of Wrath*.

The Snake Pit with Olivia de Havilland and Betsy Blair.

son, who teams that same ruggedness with gentler qualities of leadership. The climax is a grueling cattle drive to open the Chisholm Trail from Texas to Kansas, with the two protagonists at odds on the hazardous journey as to which cattle market they will take the herd, Kansas City or Abilene.

Strong emphasis on characterization gives the film tightness and unity. And the photography, most of it taken on location in Texas, is a strong contributing factor to the excellence of the film.

Wayne played his part with customary vigor, but the stronger impression was made by young Clift, whom the film made an important new star.

Producer-Director: Howard Hawks. **Scriptwriters:** Borden Chase and Charles Schnee. **Principal Players:** John Wayne, Montgomery Clift, Joanne Dru and Walter Brennan. **Running time:** 125 minutes. **Released:** United Artists.

DAY OF WRATH

The setting is seventeenth-century Denmark, and the heroine is a young woman married to an older man whose death she wishes for aloud when she falls in love with a younger man. When the husband dies, she is accused of witchcraft, and after a period of inquisition and torture she comes to believe the truth of the charge herself, and accepts her fate at the stake without resistance.

This is a real horror story, much more frightening for adults than anything out of the Frankenstein-Dracula school. The great Danish director Carl Dreyer evoked in this film all the terror of a mind being twisted and brainwashed, in a powerful picture that is still as relevant as Orwell's *1984*.

But influential critics panned it when it was released here in 1948—they thought the pace too slow and ponderous. Since then it has been a favorite of film-society members and other buffs.

Dreyer's pictures never did well commercially in the U.S., and *Day of Wrath* was no exception. But this and his classic silent film, *Passion of Joan of Arc,* made his place in screen history secure.

Producer-Director: Carl Th. Dreyer. **Scriptwriters:** Dreyer, Poul Knudsen and Mogens Skot-Hansen. **Principal Players:** Thorkild Roose, Lisbeth Movin, Sigrid Neiiendam and Preben Lerdoff. **Running time:** 100 minutes. **Released:** Brandon Films.

THE SNAKE PIT

Much controversy was stirred by this example of a Hollywood "problem" picture, part of it revolving around the question of whether a mental breakdown was a proper subject for a fictional film, and part of it around the film's treatment of the subject, which some deemed overly sensational.

There was concern in particular over laughter aroused in audiences at the expense of the mentally unbalanced shown going through enigmatic rituals and routines—all unaware, and unable to help themselves. And an overhead shot of a sequence in which several inmates go

Paisan with Gar Moore and Maria Michi.

through a weird dance like "snakes in a pit" was found offensive.

On the other hand, the film did call attention to crowded conditions existing in many of the nation's hospitals. The line between dramatic integrity and exploitation is very thin and hard to define.

On one point, however, there was no disagreement: Olivia de Havilland gave a superb performance as the woman who becomes psychotic, is sent to an asylum and is eventually cured.

Producers: Anatole Litvak and Robert Bassler. **Director:** Litvak. **Scriptwriter:** Frank Partos. **Principal Players:** Olivia de Havilland, Mark Stevens and Leo Genn. **Running time:** 108 minutes. **Released:** 20th Century-Fox.

PAISAN

Roberto Rossellini followed his powerful *Open City* with *Paisan,* a six-part film, again dealing with the war in Italy. It did not have the same impact on American audiences that the first picture did, but there were many critics who thought it a superior film, possessing a more sensitive feeling for the characters involved and the effects of the war upon them than the first work had managed.

The six individual stories are skillfully connected with a commentary on the northward advance of the Allied armies. Sequences range from the comic (a drunk American Negro M.P. is robbed of his boots by a street boy) to the poignant (a prostitute picks up a drunk American soldier, only to discover that she had encountered him some time earlier in Rome before her downfall) and the melodramatically exciting (partisan activities in Florence).

Rossellini's career has been mostly downhill since his two war masterpieces, although there were sparks of the early genius in *Generale Della Rovere,* released in the U.S. in 1961. It was not a commercial success.

Producer-Director: Roberto Rossellini. **Scriptwriters:** Roberto Rossellini and Sergio Amidei. **Principal Players:** Carmela Sazio, Robert Vanloon, Dots M. Johnson, Alfonsini, Maria Michi, Gar Moore and Harriet White. **Running time:** 120 minutes. **Released:** Mayer-Burstyn.

THE TREASURE OF SIERRA MADRE

John Huston's classic statement on the lust for gold and its consequences was hailed as a powerful picture when it first appeared, and it was given credit as a giant step forward in realism, Hollywood style. It had Humphrey Bogart as star, and he was then at the peak of his popularity. It had a lot of action and suspense. It should have been a tremendous box-office success.

Surprisingly, it wasn't, and the experts could come up with nothing better in explanation than that it lacked appeal for women because there was no romance.

Part of the trouble undoubtedly lay in the excessive length of the picture, with Huston taking too much time in the beginning to bring his major characters together

The Treasure of Sierra Madre with Tim Holt and Humphrey Bogart.

for the trip into the Mexican wilderness in search of gold. Also, there was uncertainty about which were the good guys and which the bad; audiences in those days liked to be sure about such things from the beginning. (Eventually Bogart is established as the heavy, but he had played many such roles before. This was not a switch in image.)

For those with patience, however, *Sierra Madre* did—and still does today—offer nuggets of pure gold in such treasures as the performance of Walter Huston as the eccentric old prospector, the direction of John Huston, which is as strong in developing character as in establishing milieu, and the ironic ending in which the gold is snatched out of the hands of the survivors by a whirlwind. Huston's best film ever, say many, and it is hard to argue the matter.

Producer: Henry Blanke. **Director-Writer:** John Huston. **Principal Players:** Humphrey Bogart, Walter Huston, Tim Holt and Bruce Bennett. **Running time:** 126 minutes. **Released:** Warner Bros.

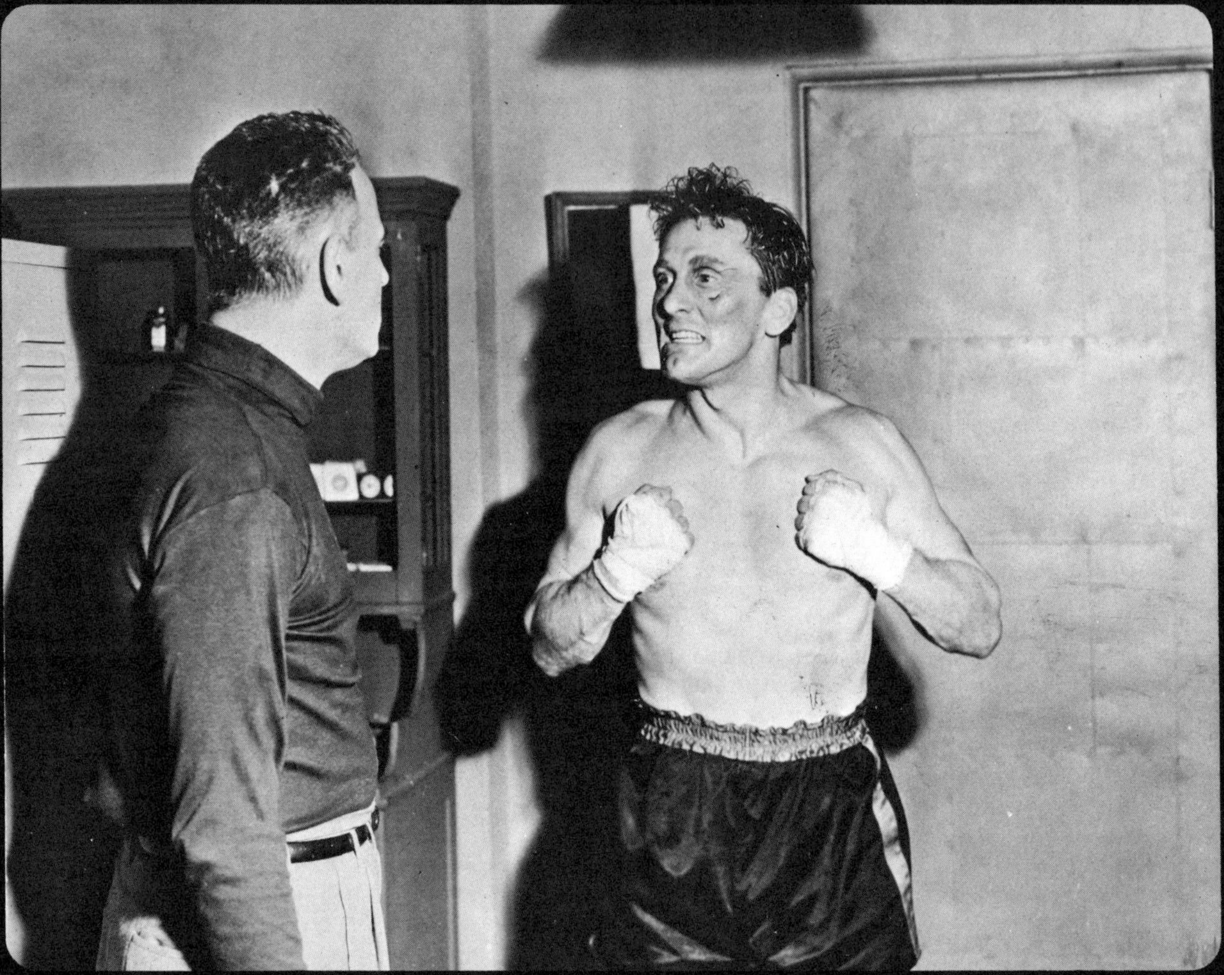

Kirk Douglas in *Champion,* the Stanley Kramer film which made Douglas a star and its producer one to reckon with in Hollywood.

1949

Film stocks generally increased an average of 25 percent in value during the year. Only Paramount, on account of divorcement of its theatre holdings, declined. The new year began with excellent holiday business, topped by *On the Town,* with receipts of $172,000 in a week at the Radio City Music Hall in New York City.

Film industry public relations, as usual, were in a sorry state. After long soul-searching, the industry attempted to respond with the formation of the Council of Motion Picture Organizations (COMPO) to lead public relations campaigns. On a more direct basis, COMPO was to spearhead the drive for the reduction and elimination of the 20 percent Federal tax on theatre admissions.

The name of Joseph L. Mankiewicz, well-known director and screen writer, became a household word on account of his scathing attack in *Life* magazine on theatre owners for sloppy operations.

Al Lichtman, industry pioneer and prominent in production and distribution for many years, attacked double bills as the main cause of the hue and cry raised by critics and some patrons against bad pictures. A deeper part of the reason was that Hollywood had not yet found a response to the public's desire for improved product. A portent of increased appeal of theatre product in the years ahead was the announcement by Eastman Kodak of a new, improved color process.

The inauguration of Harry S. Truman was the first major event to be seen on the new NBC-TV network. Home television increased extensively. It was estimated that 40 percent of the population of the United States lived within range of TV stations. Ninety-eight stations were on the air in fifty-eight major cities. Four million sets had been installed.

Exhibitors attempted to help find better films by proposing the formation of the National Exhibitors Film Company, under the leadership of Si Fabian, exhibitor leader and circuit head. It was proposed that the major circuits raise ten million dollars as a revolving fund to increase the number of quality films made each year.

Gael Sullivan, head of the Theatre Owners of America, suggested a Festival Month to win back theatre patrons.

Many eyes were on the foreign film market. During the year, 192 foreign films were imported into the United States. Also, U.S. film earnings suffered with the revaluation of the pound sterling from $4.03 (where it had been pegged all during the war years) to $2.80.

The five major film companies—Paramount, Loew's, Inc., Radio-Keith-Orpheum, 20th Century-Fox, and Warner Bros. Pictures, Inc.—continued plans to divorce theatre operations as required by the Supreme Court. All details were to be completed by 1952.

Montgomery Clift, Kirk Douglas and Betty Garrett were leading "Stars of Tomorrow." Jack Benny, once again, was the year's top radio star.

Stars of the year: Bob Hope, Bing Crosby, Abbott & Costello, John Wayne, Gary Cooper, Cary Grant, Betty Grable, Esther Williams, Humphrey Bogart and Clark Gable.

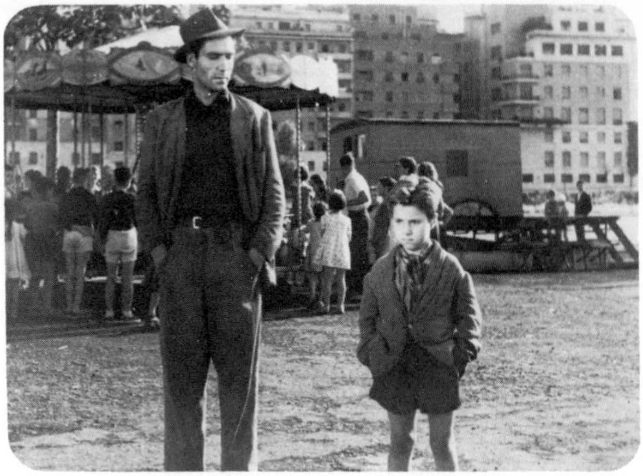

Lamberto Maggiorani and Enzio Staiola in *The Bicycle Thief.*

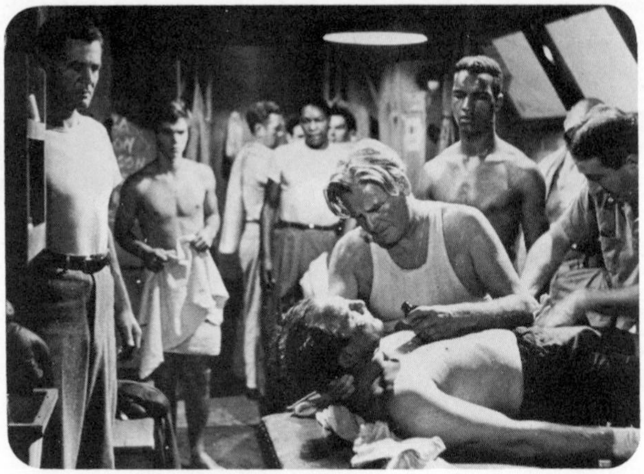

Robert Ryan, Darryl Hickman, Wallace Ford (as the handler) and James Edwards (standing) in *The Set-Up.*

THE BICYCLE THIEF

It is ironic and amusing to recall today that this early Vittorio De Sica work, while highly praised by most critics on artistic grounds, was denounced by political voices from both right and left. To the former it was "communistic" because it made society and environment the real villains in the plight of a workman who faces loss of his job and starvation when his bicycle is stolen. On the other hand, leftists denounced it because the "hero" did not take positive action to correct the injustices to which he was subjected in a capitalist society.

This was the second film made by De Sica and scriptwriter Cesare Zavattini to achieve commercial success in the U.S., *Shoeshine* having been the first (1947).

The U.S. distributor sought a Code seal for the film but was denied it because of one scene in a brothel and a second in which the young son of the protagonist urinates againt the wall.

As he did in other of the "neo-realistic" films in the beginning of his career, De Sica used unknowns to play the leading roles, choosing them in many instances right from the street.

The picture received a special Academy Award voted by the board of governors who proclaimed it "the most outstanding foreign language film released in the United States during 1949." (An Oscar for the best film from abroad was not made an official category until 1956.)

Producer-Director: Vittorio De Sica. **Scriptwriter:** Cesare Zavattini. **Principal Players:** Enzio Staiola and Lamberto Maggiorani. **Running time:** 90 minutes. **Released:** Mayer-Burstyn.

THE SET-UP

Less popular with audiences than *Body and Soul* (1947) and *Champion* (1949), this prize fight film is in some respects better than either.

For one thing, its characters are more credible and more deeply explored. The hero is an aging fighter who won't admit that the time has come to retire and only quits the ring when he is beaten up by hoodlums for refusing to lose a "fixed" fight. Robert Ryan was superb in the difficult role of the stubborn fighter, and Audrey Totter was also fine as the wife who wanted him to quit before it was too late.

Equally important was the direction of Robert Wise, the film editor (*Citizen Kane*) turned director (who many years later was to make *The Sound of Music*). The fight scenes were long and gory—but uncommonly realistic.

The public did not respond. *The Set-Up* apparently was just too downbeat for them.

Producer: Richard Goldstone. **Director:** Robert Wise. **Screenplay:** Art Cohn. **Principal Players:** Robert Ryan, Audrey Totter, George Tobias, Alan Baxter and Wallace Ford. **Running time:** 72 minutes. **Released:** RKO.

PINKY

In 1949, Hollywood turned from dealing with racial prejudice against the Jews to that directed against the Negro. The cycle included four pictures of which *Pinky*

Pinky with Jeanne Crain and Ethel Waters.

was the third to go into release. (*Home of the Brave* and *Lost Boundaries* preceded it in that order, and *Intruder in the Dust* followed.)

Pinky had the biggest production budget of the quartet, and it was personally produced by Darryl F. Zanuck, then production head of 20th Century-Fox, in a long tradition of making films of a controversial or commercially risky nature (which is often the same thing). He selected as his director Elia Kazan, who had performed in a similar capacity for Zanuck's *Gentlemen's Agreement,* a popular 1947 film on the subject of anti-Semitism.

Some critics felt that *Pinky* stacked the cards a bit too much in its own favor by giving the heroine skin light enough for her to pass as white. And instead of a Negro actress of light pigmentation they chose Jeanne Crain, a Fox contract player who had been in the musical version of *State Fair.*

The plot resolution was unusually honest for films of those days: The heroine who has returned South after passing for white as a nurse in the North rejects her doctor Yankee suitor (played by William Lundigan) on the grounds that his love for her is based on tolerance rather than a genuine conviction of racial equality. The supporting cast included Ethel Barrymore as an eccentric landowner who wills her estate to Pinky, and Ethel Waters as the latter's illiterate grandmother.

Producer: Darryl F. Zanuck. **Director:** Elia Kazan. **Scriptwriters:** Philip Dunne and Dudley Nichols. **Principal Players:** Jeanne Crain, Ethel Barrymore, Ethel Waters and William Ludigan. **Running time:** 120 minutes. **Released:** 20th Century-Fox.

John Hodiak, George Murphy, Marshall Thompson, Ricardo Montalban and Don Taylor in *Battleground.*

BATTLEGROUND

World War II had been over for five years, and the U.S. public was ripe for this nostalgic look back, with its glorification of the ordinary foot soldier. The setting was Bastogne and the Battle of the Bulge, but it could have been innumerable other places and innumerable other campaigns in Europe. The "heroes" could have belonged to any military squad almost anywhere.

The fact that the men were all stock types contributed to the tremendous popularity enjoyed by this film; veterans of the war could see characteristics of the comrades with whom they had served in at least one or two of the actors on the screen. Van Johnson was the nonchalant and woman-conscious soldier; John Hodiak, the cynical columnist from Missouri; Ricardo Montalban, the Mexican to whom snow at first hand is new; George Murphy, the overage soldier, discharged but unable to get out; Bruce Cowling, the tough squad leader; Jerome Courtland, the Kentucky mountaineer who sleeps happier in his socks; James Whitmore, the hard-as-nails, tobacco-spitting platoon sergeant; Douglas Fowley, the wise guy with the clicking false teeth; Marshall Thompson, the shy, youthful replacement; and so on. And Leon Ames played the inevitable "Holy Joe" who reminds the men why they are fighting, and asks each to pray according to his own religion.

Battleground supplies an example of the war film in which the entire group is the hero; no one soldier emerges in triumphant heroism above any of the others. The war itself is seen only in photographic montages,

On the Town with Frank Sinatra, Jules Munshin and Gene Kelly.

and some critics complained at the time that the snow was quite obviously studio-made.

There were also objections from some quarters that the squad selected for emphasis was ordinary and had apparently rendered no service beyond the routine duties of a rear-guard action. In fact, the men seemed totally unaware of what country they were in and were even less certain of the part they were playing in mighty events.

Perhaps that was the point of screenplay writer Robert Pirosh, who, incidentally, was at Bastogne himself. His script won an Oscar.

The performances are generally apt, and the direction of William A. Wellman serviceable. Dore Schary produced, this being the first film he took screen credit for since his appointment as head of production at MGM in 1948.

Producer: Dore Schary. **Director:** William A. Wellman. **Scriptwriter:** Robert Pirosh. **Principal Players:** Van Johnson, John Hodiak, Ricardo Montalban and George Murphy. **Running time:** 118 minutes. **Released:** MGM.

ON THE TOWN

A new era in screen musicals was launched with this film, although not everyone recognized it at the time. Perceptive critics of the day saw what *On the Town* had that was different: It used the film medium in an extraordinarily creative way. It relied heavily on dance and ballet, but they were photographed with more imaginative placement of the camera than before. Both dancing and singing were cleverly integrated into the book; the show was never stopped cold to introduce a big production number.

Audiences may not have been aware of *how* it was being done, but they loved it, finding its exuberance infectious. Its success paved the way for *An American in Paris,* (with its lengthy ballet sequence), *Singin' in the Rain, The Band Wagon* and *Gigi,* all produced by Arthur Freed for MGM.

The plot was flimsy even for a musical show—three sailors on leave meet three girls, and romance blooms—but co-directors Stanley Donen and Gene Kelly paced it so swiftly nobody has time to notice. New York backgrounds—all shot on location—were cleverly employed, from the Empire State Building to Grant's Tomb, to the Statue of Liberty and back again. Especially amusing was the satirical gag in which the floor show was always the same at the various night clubs visited by the seamen and their dates.

Everything was inspired, from Leonard Bernstein's music from the stage show to the book by Adolph Green and Betty Comden, who also wrote the Broadway script. The players were perfectly matched: Kelly with Vera-Ellen; Frank Sinatra with Betty Garrett; and Jules Munshin with Ann Miller.

Producer: Arthur Freed. **Directors:** Gene Kelly and Stanley Donen. **Scriptwriters:** Betty Comden and Adolph Green. **Principal Players:** Gene Kelly, Frank Sinatra, Betty Garrett, Ann Miller, Jules Munshin and Vera-Ellen. **Running time:** 98 minutes. **Released:** MGM.

Ann Sothern and Linda Darnell in *A Letter to Three Wives.*

Champion with Kirk Douglas (center).

A LETTER TO THREE WIVES

Joseph L. Mankiewicz began his film career as a writer for Paramount in 1929 and followed this with a post at MGM as producer. Then, in 1943, he moved to 20th Century-Fox and began to direct films.

It was for that studio he made his two masterpieces—*A Letter to Three Wives* and *All About Eve*—writing and directing them, but leaving the production reins to others.

The script of *A Letter to Three Wives* is a model of ingenious construction and scintillating dialogue. It is built around the device of having an unmarried woman (never shown but heard offscreen in the voice of Celeste Holm) send a letter jointly to three married friends informing them that she has left town with one of their husbands—which one, she doesn't say. Then each of the three recipients reflects on her past life, and each finds reason to believe she is the one whose spouse has deserted her.

Jeanne Crain is worried because she is a country girl who feels out of place with the high society friends of her husband (Jeffrey Lynn); Ann Sothern is upset because she has become the domineering breadwinner of the family, making more money as a radio writer than her schoolteacher husband (Kirk Douglas); and Linda Darnell is perturbed because she feels her spouse (Paul Douglas) is aware she married him for his money.

Stock character types all, but neatly disguised by the Mankiewicz gift for witty and literate dialogue. The actors were shrewdly cast by him, and all did well, with Linda Darnell standing out from the rest in the best performance she had ever given.

Producer: Sol C. Siegel. **Director-Writer:** Joseph L. Mankiewicz. **Principal Players:** Jeanne Crain, Linda Darnell, Ann Sothern, Kirk Douglas, Paul Douglas, Barbara Lawrence and Jeffrey Lynn. **Running time:** 103 minutes. **Released:** 20th Century-Fox.

CHAMPION

Many fans of the genre thought Robert Rossen's *Body and Soul* (1947) had been the last word in fictional prizefighting films, but this low-budget Stanley Kramer production found a wide audience. It is typical of the "offbeat" films which Kramer made early in his career. *Champion,* in fact, was his first production, an area of film making to which he turned after doing research at MGM and editing. It was also his initial collaboration with Carl Foreman, who was to do screenplays for some of Kramer's most notable pictures.

Mark Robson had been directing films since 1944 (*Isle of the Dead* and *Roughshod,* among them), but *Champion* is the film that brought him to the ranks of major talent.

It was also a lucky picture for Kirk Douglas, whom producer Hal Wallis had brought to Hollywood from Broadway in 1945. His performance as the title character—a bounder who makes his way to the top of the prizefight game at the expense of friends and relatives, as well as foes—was lavishly praised, and not least for the refusal of actor and director to seek sympathy from

They Live by Night with Cathy O'Donnell and Farley Granger.

a character which plainly deserved none. Douglas was nominated for an Oscar, but lost out to Broderick Crawford (*All the King's Men*).

The Foreman script was based on a Ring Lardner story of the same title. Applauded also was the low-key, black-and-white photography of Frank Planer, which helped immensely to catch the aroma of the prizefight ring with sharpness and authority.

Producer: Stanley Kramer. **Director:** Mark Robson. **Scriptwriter:** Carl Foreman. **Principal Players:** Kirk Douglas, Marilyn Maxwell, Arthur Kennedy and Paul Stewart. **Running time:** 99 minutes. **Released:** United Artists.

THEY LIVE BY NIGHT

This is one of those small "quality" films turned out in the forties which baffled film distributors as to how they should be merchandised. The title was changed several times (it was even reviewed in the trade press as *The Twisted Road,* and called *Your Red Wagon* at another point), and its release was postponed for over a year after completion.

None of the title maneuvers really worked; *They Live by Night* was too grim for the average moviegoer of the time. It is important as the first major film of Nicholas Ray, who had assisted Elia Kazan when the latter made his directorial debut in Hollywood with *A Tree Grows in Brooklyn.*

The story of two young lovers (played by Farley Granger and Cathy O'Donnell) fleeing from the police

Intruder in the Dust with Claude Jarman, Jr., and David Brian.

(he has escaped from prison) was more than reminiscent of such melodramas of the thirties as *You Only Live Once,* in which Sylvia Sydney and Henry Fonda were the doomed pair. But the Charles Schnee screenplay either avoided the usual clichés or made them fresh through incisive characterizations. And Ray's direction was not only strongly atmospheric, but drew from his two young leads the best performances of their careers.

Producer: John Houseman. **Director:** Nicholas Ray. **Scriptwriter:** Charles Schnee. **Principal Players:** Farley Granger, Cathy O'Donnell and Howard Da Silva. **Running time:** 95 minutes. **Released:** RKO.

INTRUDER IN THE DUST

Hollywood's racial cycle of the 1940's had already brought forth three films when *Intruder in the Dust* appeared. It may have been late in the game, but it was a strong drama (based on a William Faulkner novel) that made its points about race prejudice with more subtlety than had the earlier pictures. Unfortunately, its belated appearance—and possibly its uncompromising approach—worked against it at the box office.

Humanity at its worst—lynch law and mob rule—was shown without flinching by producer-director Clarence Brown, who directed what is probably one of the most horrible, as well as the most gripping, sequences that has ever been recorded in an "entertainment" motion picture. This is the long passage in which the Jefferson townsfolk drive ferociously to the jailhouse to await the

The Fallen Idol with Bobby Henrey and Ralph Richardson.

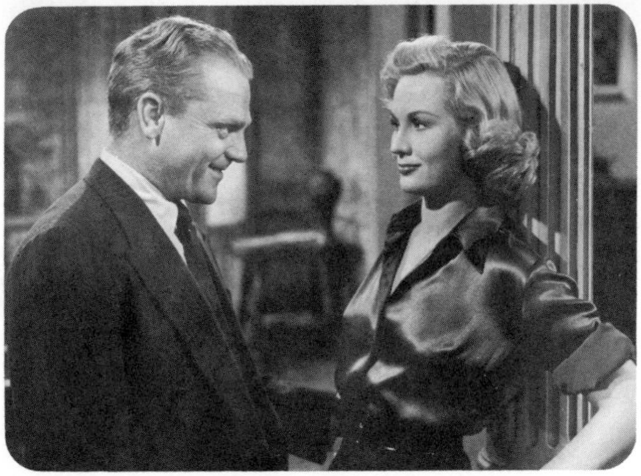

White Heat with James Cagney and Virginia Mayo.

lynching of a Negro accused of murdering a white man. The loud-speaker is blaring with jazz music; children eat ice cream; a mother carrying a child inquires when the activities will begin; and a group of men play cards to while away the waiting period. An air of suppressed excitement and ghoulish anticipation hangs over the crowded town.

The characters are among the most memorable in screen history and are acted with extraordinary power: Juano Hernandez as the Negro farmer whose proud manner further alienates whites who are eager to convict him for a crime he didn't commit; Claude Jarman, Jr., as the white lad befriended by Hernandez; David Brian as the defense lawyer who reluctantly takes the case; and Elizabeth Patterson as the doughty old lady who unearths evidence as to the real murderer.

Producer-Director: Clarence Brown. **Scriptwriter:** Ben Maddow. **Principal Players:** David Brian, Claude Jarman, Jr., Juano Hernandez, Porter Hall and Elizabeth Patterson. **Running time:** 87 minutes. **Released:** MGM.

THE FALLEN IDOL

Whatever happened to Bobby Henrey, the delightful youngster who gave such a superlative performance in this Carol Reed thriller? The French ambassador in London leaves his son in the care of a butler. The boy comes (wrongly) to suspect that the butler has murdered his wife. Young Henrey portrayed emotions ranging from childish glee to terror with a charm and virtuosity that had the critics raving about him. Then he disappeared from the film scene.

It was Reed's skillful handling of young Henrey that helped earn him a reputation as a "child's director" almost beyond compare. That his touch has survived over the years was proved as recently as *Oliver!* (1968) in which he guided Mark Lester to give an unaffected and appealing performance as the Dickens character.

But the Reed hand is equally adept at bringing special qualities to the suspense film, most notably in creating a strong sense of milieu and imbuing even his minor characters with strong personalities. In the leads, as the butler and the embassy secretary, Ralph Richardson and Michele Morgan managed to hold their own in their scenes with Henrey.

Producer-Director: Carol Reed. **Screenplay:** Graham Greene. **Principal Players:** Ralph Richardson, Bobby Henrey, Jack Hawkins, Michele Morgan and Sonia Dresdel. **Running time:** 94 minutes. **Released:** Selznick Releasing Organization.

WHITE HEAT

James Cagney gunned his way to fame playing a hoodlum in the thirties. Since then, he had played perfectly respectable citizens, such as George M. Cohan. In 1949, he suddenly turned to crime again, in a picture that harked back to his early prison melodramas. This was *White Heat* and, if anything, it was more brutal and violent than any picture Cagney had starred in before.

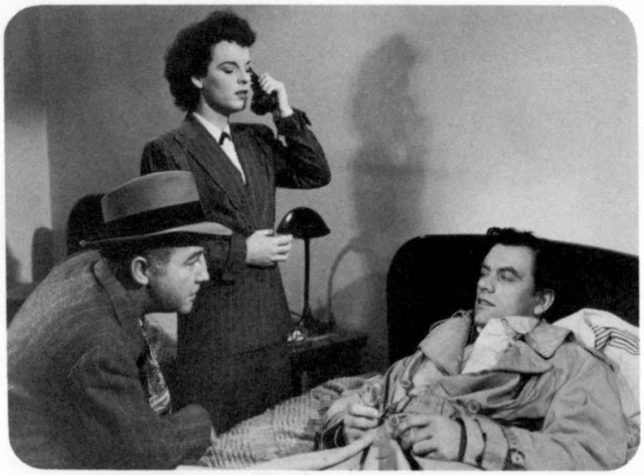

All the King's Men with Broderick Crawford, Mercedes Mc-Cambridge and John Ireland.

Certainly he never played a more frightening and vicious character than this Cody Jarrett, a gang leader dominated by his psychopathic mother (Margaret Wycherly) who wants to put him "on top of the world." In one scene, an escaping convict locked in the compartment of a car asks for air; the Cagney answer is to ventilate it with bullet holes. In another, he tries to fight his way out of a police trap by sending two of his colleagues as decoys to certain death. He also slaps his moll (played by Virginia Mayo) around now and again.

It was a terrific performance and well-received, but Cagney never portrayed such a gangster again. After all, what could have followed *White Heat*?

Producer: Louis F. Edelman. **Director:** Raoul Walsh. **Scriptwriters:** Ivan Goff and Ben Roberts. **Principal Players:** James Cagney, Virginia Mayo, Edmond O'Brien and Margaret Wycherly. **Running time:** 114 mintues. **Released:** Warner Bros.

ALL THE KING'S MEN

An idealistic politician comes out of the backwoods of a southern state intoxicated by his ability to spellbind rural voters, eventually rises to the governorship and is finally corrupted by the power he has acquired. Hardly a new story, but it was told with considerable power by Robert Rossen in this picture, doing triple duty as writer, director and producer. It won the Academy Award as best picture of the year, and two others: for Broderick Crawford as best actor, and Mercedes McCambridge as best supporting actress.

The script was based on the Pulitzer Prize-winning novel by Robert Penn Warren, and literary critics noted it was thinly disguised fiction dealing with the life of Huey Long, or at least suggesting certain parallels in the career of the late governor of Louisiana. The film tends to corroborate the impression, and nowhere so much as at the end when Crawford, playing Willie Stark, is slain in the corridors of the state capitol and his assassin is then killed on the spot.

Crawford, an able actor who heretofore had played mostly unrewarding roles in "B" pictures, rose spendidly to the occasion with this major role. He nailed down all the nuances of the part—craftiness, brutality, hypocrisy, fanaticism, sarcasm—with skill. Such a part never came his way again. Miss McCambridge also gave a sharp edge to her depiction of his unscrupulous aide-de-camp, using a rasping voice for effective delivery of some cleverly sarcastic dialogue.

Producer-Director-Writer: Robert Rossen. **Principal Players:** Broderick Crawford, Joanne Dru, John Ireland, John Derek and Mercedes McCambridge. **Running time:** 109 minutes. **Released:** Columbia.

THE HEIRESS

Stories about the ugly duckling female who turns into a swan, whether through plastic surgery or the ministrations of a good man who loves her, have always been popular fodder for screenplays. A tale in which this fails to happen—one in which the duckling

The Heiress with Montgomery Clift and Olivia de Havilland.

remains plain and discovers that men are only interested in her for her money—is much more realistic, but obviously less appealing. Surprisingly, it turned out to be successful for *The Heiress.*

The heroine, who is sister under the skin to numerous others in countless novels and plays, first saw light of day in the novel *Washington Square,* by Henry James. This was adapted into a play by Ruth and Augustus Goetz which had a profitable run on Broadway in 1946–47.

It didn't really seem like film material, mostly for the psychological reason stated above. But it was entrusted to William Wyler, Hollywood's most proficient transferer from stage to screen of the day, who once more remained faithful to both spirit and letter of the original and yet utilized the more fluid medium to fullest effect.

Olivia de Havilland, one of Hollywood's prettier actresses, was de-glamorized to portray the introverted and physically unattractive heroine and gave a performance so emotionally powerful she was justly rewarded with her second Academy Award. The role of the phlegmatic father who cruelly belittles his daughter for his own reasons went to Ralph Richardson instead of Basil Rathbone, who had played it on Broadway. However, Richardson had acted it on the London stage, and he was splendidly arrogant and astringent in the film. (Wendy Hiller had the de Havilland role on Broadway.)

Unfortunately, Montgomery Clift was miscast as the fortune-hunter suitor; he simply lacked the guile the role required. Much better was Miriam Hopkins, who was amusing as the flighty aunt who interferes in the romance of her niece to the regret of both.

Producer-Director: William Wyler. **Scriptwriters:** Ruth and Augustus Goetz. **Principal Players:** Olivia de Havilland, Montgomery Clift, Ralph Richardson and Miriam Hopkins. **Running time:** 120 minutes. **Released:** Paramount.

Orson Welles in *The Third Man,* the picture which established director Carol Reed on the international scene and also made the zither famous.

1950

This year, marked by the outbreak of the Korean War in June, was the first in which television showed a significant adverse effect on theatre box offices. The attendance declines in the period from the end of the war boom in 1947 through 1949 could be attributed to the readjustment to peace conditions. From 1949 to 1950, the number of TV sets sold doubled to 8,000,000, and 70,000,000 American citizens were in the range of TV stations. A major impetus to television was the linking up of 72 stations in 42 major markets by the Long Lines Department of the American Telephone and Telegraph Company. Altogether the network extended 17,000 miles. An indication of more intense TV competition in the future was the Federal Communication Commission's abortive authorization of the CBS color television system, a mechanical method supplanted after the Korean War by the electronic color system championed by RCA.

During the year, major initial efforts were made to use the power of TV to attract audiences to movie theatres. In one test a reported 25 percent of the theatre patrons for one first-run film engagement were attracted by TV ads. Soon TV joined radio and newspaper space as a regular form of film advertising. When films were judged to have a particular appeal to the young, it became customary to increase the proportion of the ad budget spent on TV.

Although by now the crop of World War II babies should have had a beneficial effect on theatre attendance, experience soon showed that a generation brought up on television would not acquire the movie-going habit of weekly attendance. One leading exhibitor, Robert M. Weitman, managing director of the Paramount Theatre in New York (and later head of production at MGM and Columbia in Hollywood), said, "The young must be introduced to and encouraged in the movie habit." It was a vain hope.

Much talk in the trade also was expended—and little action taken—on the subject of how to regain the "lost audience" of adults. The industry launched a national attendance-building drive with the slogan "Movies Are Better Than Ever." It was a flop because it was evident to potential patrons that the statement was untrue: Only a minority of movies were better. Public relations also suffered from public outcries at the torrid Ingrid Bergman-Roberto Rossellini romance, because people expected a star to reflect in private life the character often played on the screen. Senator Edwin Johnson of California attempted to capitalize on the scandal and called for Federal film censorship, as if that would affect the private lives of the film makers.

The independent producers in Hollywood were having their troubles. Stanley Kramer was especially pessimistic, saying, "Independent film financing has 'dried up.' It's a dead issue." Other independents sought the shelter of a strong financial backer, usually a major studio. Jerry Wald and Norman Krasna signed an independent production deal with the famed millionaire and sometime movie producer Howard Hughes.

During this year, British films made some headway in the United States, spurred by J. Arthur Rank, the flour miller turned film magnate during World War II.

Rank felt that British pictures should be popular everywhere, not just for money but for the greater glory of Britain. Meanwhile, French and Italian imports lost ground. Few foreign films could compete for American audience attention with such domestic hits as *Annie Get Your Gun, Cheaper by the Dozen, Cinderella, Father of the Bride* and *Samson and Delilah.*

The Motion Picture Association set up a Foreign Film Advisory Unit to help importers, an appreciated diplomatic gesture.

Stars of the year: John Wayne, Bob Hope, Bing Crosby, Betty Grable, James Stewart, Abbott & Costello, Clifton Webb, Esther Williams, Spencer Tracy and Randolph Scott.

Anna Magnani in *The Miracle (Ways of Love)*.

THE MIRACLE (WAYS OF LOVE)

The genesis of the Italian film *The Miracle* and the profound effect it had on motion picture censorship in the United States are far more interesting and, for that matter, historically important than the forty-minute film itself.

The idea for the story came from no less a film personage than Federico Fellini, who was a talented writer of scripts long before he turned director and became internationally famous as the maker of *La Dolce Vita*. Fellini brought the plot to Roberto Rossellini who was looking for properties in which to star Anna Magnani, who had won acclaim with her brilliant performance under his direction in *Open City*. Rossellini decided to make a two-part film as a showcase for his star.

Under the joint title of *L'Amore* (*Love*) he put an adaptation of Jean Cocteau's *The Human Voice* (a long monologue a woman recites to the lover who is leaving her) and *The Miracle*. This was the way *The Miracle* was released in Italy, where, surprisingly, it produced very little adverse reaction from censors or clergy! It tells the simple story of a mentally retarded peasant woman who is seduced by a wandering shepherd whom she believes to be St. Joseph. When she becomes pregnant, she declares it was through immaculate conception and she is taking part in a miracle. The villagers scorn and abuse her and throw her out, so she goes off alone to give birth in the ruins of a church. (Fellini himself played the shepherd, incidentally, his first and only screen acting effort.)

In the U.S., Joseph Burstyn, a leading importer of foreign pictures, packaged *The Miracle* with two short French movies under the general title of *Ways of Love*. He opened it at the Paris Theatre in New York City on December 12, 1950, and the forces of history were set in motion.

A furor broke out: The city commissioner of licenses said he found it "officially and personally blasphemous"; Cardinal Spellman denounced it from the pulpit and called for a Catholic boycott of any theatre playing it; the Paris Theatre was picketed and counter-picketed by groups with different views on the film.

At last the Board of Regents took action and revoked the license it had originally given the film on the grounds it now found it to be "sacrilegious." An appeal failing in New York courts, Burstyn went to the U.S. Supreme Court, which, in May of 1952, made the famous decision which put motion pictures under the free speech and free press guarantees of the First and Fourteenth Amendments. *The Miracle* was thus cleared for public exhibition.

Nobody ever seems to remember anything about the other two parts of *Ways of Love*. For the record, they were *A Day in the Country,* based on a short story by Guy de Maupassant and directed by Jean Renoir, and *Jofroi,* based on a story by Jean Giono and directed by Marcel Pagnol.

Producer-Director: Roberto Rossellini. **Scriptwriters:** Rossellini and Tullio Pinnelli. **Principal Players:** Anna Magnani and Federico Fellini. **Running time:** 40 minutes. **Released:** Joseph Burstyn.

Deborah Kerr, Richard Carlson and Stewart Granger in *King Solomon's Mines.*

KING SOLOMON'S MINES

Some twenty years after *Trader Horn,* MGM sent a huge production company to Africa again—this time with a script based on the famous novel by H. Rider Haggard. Again, the lure of adventure in little known places worked its spell on the American public. This was one of the big hits of the year.

Art it wasn't, except for a few shots of the exotic countryside and the wild life inhabiting it, but it was a stirring and sturdy tale in the time-honored tradition of handsome and brave heroes and beautiful and helpless heroines, all handled with an eye for thrills, climaxes and the box office. One sequence in particular had audiences gasping: a stampede of wild animals desperately trying to escape a brush fire. Countless westerns had shown cattle on a celluloid rampage, but this time, people saw zebras, giraffes, elephants and rhinos race across the screen. The difference counted.

Portraying Haggard's big-game-hunter hero, Allan Quartermain, was Stewart Granger. He dominated the other actors, including Deborah Kerr, a pleasant but conventional heroine, and Richard Carlson, who always seemed to be trailing the other two around and never established a clear identity of his own.

The color photography of Robert Surtees was a big asset, and he won a much-deserved Oscar for his work.

Producer: Sam Zimbalist. **Directors:** Compton Bennett and Andrew Marton. **Scriptwriter:** Helen Deutsch. **Principal Players:** Deborah Kerr, Stewart Granger and Richard Carlson. **Running time:** 102 minutes. **Released:** MGM.

Bette Davis, Gary Merrill, Anne Baxter and George Sanders in *All About Eve.*

ALL ABOUT EVE

Well aware that 20th Century-Fox had an extraordinary picture in Joseph Mankiewicz's *All About Eve,* but one that might be hard to sell to the public because of its "intelligent" subject matter, the company devised a special plan for showing it in theatres. They called it "scheduled performances," and explained that the policy was to make it possible for moviegoers to see the picture "the only way it should be seen—from the beginning." Patrons were advised that tickets could be purchased in advance; that a seat would be assured for all; and that no one would be seated after the start of any of the four daily performances.

The policy was really a variation of roadshow exhibition practices, but without specific seats being assigned to ticket buyers. It didn't work out too well in 1950, but it was later used for roadshow pictures when they left downtown theatres and went to the neighborhoods for subsequent release. As such, it is still in use today.

Actually, the Fox people and theatre owners who booked the film needn't have worried. *Eve* may have been sophisticated—one trade reviewer called it "the best sophisticated drama ever to have come out of Hollywood"—but its appeal was not restricted to the carriage trade.

Mankiewicz has been accused of writing stage plays as opposed to film scripts, and then photographing them. It is certainly true that his forte is witty dialogue, and the whole of this film about stage people is conversational. It bristles with satirical observations, subtle

The Asphalt Jungle with Jean Hagen, Sterling Hayden and Marilyn Monroe.

references, glib parlance, trade talk, irony and wisecrack, with a dash of double entendre here and there for full measure. Many of its epithets and bon mots are still quoted nearly twenty years later by admirers of the movie who esteem them as the ultimate in wit.

All About Eve reached new heights in other things, too—especially acting. After a run of terrible roles in worse pictures (*Beyond the Forest* had been the nadir), Bette Davis bounced back with formidable resiliency and demonstrated anew her right to the title of movie star *par excellence*. Her portrayal of a stage star turned forty and having a difficult time adjusting to the onslaught of age was a grandly showy performance on the surface, and it had great depth in its complexity of emotional range. She was nominated for, but did not receive, an Academy Award (possibly because she already had two).

Anne Baxter was never better than she was in playing the title character, a fan of the great actress who worms her way into the star's good graces to further a boundless ambition. George Sanders surpassed all his previous portraits of wicked bounders gifted with gab with his performance as an unscrupulous Broadway critic. Even Celeste Holm, although bland compared with the other actresses, was effective as the playwright's wife, and Hugh Marlowe, though equally bland, was also good. Gary Merrill played the stage director who loves the aging star, but is put off by her petty jealousies and tantrums, with more skill than he displayed before or since. In a small role, Thelma Ritter shone with customary brilliance. Marilyn Monroe had a bit role as a starlet whom Sanders referred to as a "graduate of the school of Copacabana" in a typical Mankiewicz epithet.

Producer: Darryl F. Zanuck. **Director-Writer:** Joseph L. Mankiewicz. **Principal Players:** Bette Davis, Anne Baxter, George Sanders, Celeste Holm, Gary Merrill and Hugh Marlowe. **Running time:** 138 minutes. **Released:** 20th Century-Fox.

THE ASPHALT JUNGLE

John Huston reaffirmed his superb ability at tense melodrama (*The Maltese Falcon, Key Largo,* etc.) with his direction of this hard-hitting story of crime in a big American city, taken from a novel by W. R. Burnett.

Basically the subject was a familiar one (the burglarizing of a jewelry store), but it was set apart by the credibility and range of the characterizations. This had the effect of lending additional credulity to the dramatic situations in which they were involved.

Participants in the crime are introduced individually and then slowly drawn together: Sam Jaffe as a polite jewel thief with an eye for young girls; Sterling Hayden, petty criminal and strong-arm man; Louis Calhern, prominent lawyer, philanderer and double-crosser; James Whitmore, hunchbacked lunchroom operator; Barry Kelley, crooked police officer; and Marc Lawrence, bookie and go-between for the criminals.

To Hayden went much deserved praise for his surprisingly fine performance; he redeemed himself from the stigma of a series of poor films. Jaffe, a stage actor who had not gone far in Hollywood, was also lauded for

Kind Hearts and Coronets with Alec Guinness.

Born Yesterday with Broderick Crawford (center) and Judy Holliday.

the originality of his playing of an unregenerated criminal with an instinct for the nicer things in life. In fact, everybody was highly effective—including two actresses in minor parts, Jean Hagen and Marilyn Monroe. Miss Monroe made such a strong impression as the doll-like mistress of Calhern that *The Asphalt Jungle* and Huston are credited with setting her career in stride.

Producer: Arthur Hornblow, Jr. **Director:** John Huston. **Scriptwriters:** Huston and Ben Maddow. **Principal Players:** Sterling Hayden, Louis Calhern, James Whitmore, Sam Jaffe and Jean Hagen. **Running time:** 112 minutes. **Released:** MGM.

KIND HEARTS AND CORONETS

Alec Guinness played eight roles (including a female) in this J. Arthur Rank production, and thereby endeared himself to art theatre audiences seven years before the great mass audience "discovered" him in *The Bridge on the River Kwai* (1957). He had already been seen in a bit role in *Great Expectations* (1946), and in England his performance as Fagin in David Lean's *Oliver Twist* had won acclaim, but it was not to be released here until 1951—and then to be quickly withdrawn because of objections that the portrayal was anti-Semitic.

The great Guinness show of versatility (he was especially amusing as a suffragette) sought to draw laughs from mass murder—much in the spirit of the American play and film *Arsenic and Old Lace.* Dennis Price, a star in England who never became popular in the U.S., had the leading role as the lad who gains a dukedom by methodically eliminating all possible heirs. In a clever final twist, he got his just desserts immediately after attaining his goal.

The supporting cast was a virtual Who's Who of top-flight British character actors who seemed thoroughly to enjoy poking fun at eccentric English "types."

Producer: Michael Balcon. **Director:** Robert Hamer. **Scriptwriters:** Robert Hamer and John Dighton. **Principal Players:** Dennis Price, Valerie Hobson, Joan Greenwood, Alec Guinness, Audrey Fildes, Miles Malleson, Olive Morton and Hugh Griffith. **Running time:** 101 minutes. **Released:** Eagle Lion.

BORN YESTERDAY

With *Born Yesterday,* Judy Holliday leaped into the front ranks of screen talent. She had played the lead in the Broadway play, when Jean Arthur left the original company while it was still in out-of-town tryouts. It established an image for her—the lovable dumb blond—that she was never quite able to shake in subsequent films, try though she did. It also won her the 1950 Best Actress Oscar over such formidable competition as Bette Davis (*All About Eve*) and Gloria Swanson (*Sunset Boulevard*).

In fact, Miss Holliday bested other actors in her own picture; her co-stars, Broderick Crawford and William Holden, were competent but overmatched. It was her show all the way.

Albert Mannheimer's script deviated from Garson Kanin's play only in minor concessions to screen usage,

Sunset Boulevard with Gloria Swanson.

retaining most of the sometimes salty dialogue. Miss Holliday is the mistress of millionaire junkman Crawford, who hires newspaper reporter Holden to coach her in good manners and behavior. The basic plot thus had overtones of *Pygmalion,* but it was very much up-to-date in the way it utilized that situation in a 1950 Washington, D.C., setting. There was even a message of sorts about such matters as honesty, democratic principles, integrity and good citizenship.

George Cukor's direction was characteristically smooth.

Producer: S. Sylvan Simon. **Director:** George Cukor. **Scriptwriter:** Albert Mannheimer. **Principal Players:** Judy Holliday, Broderick Crawford and William Holden. **Running time:** 104 minutes. **Released:** Columbia.

SUNSET BOULEVARD

Hollywood as a citadel of scandal has long been a favorite American myth, and Billy Wilder exploited it rather shamelessly in *Sunset Boulevard.* Let the critics point out that the protagonists were hardly typical denizens of the place—she was a "has-been" actress of the silent era, and he, a "never-was" scriptwriter. The audience saw it as an exposé of that sinful community in California, and relished it as such.

Gloria Swanson made a triumphant return to the screen in this justly celebrated picture. Her role was written larger than life, and she played it that way on a grand scale. There are some unforgettably powerful scenes, such as the one in which she talks of the past: "I'm big. It's the pictures that have got small. We didn't need dialogue. We had faces then." Or that final grandiose moment in which she descends the stairs of her baroque mansion, thinking in her confused state that she is on a movie set: "I'm ready for my close-up, Mr. DeMille."

There are numerous other scenes that linger in the memory years after the film first appeared: the visit to the men's shop where the heroine orders clothes tailored for her young lover (William Holden in one of his best performances); the funeral of her pet monkey presided over by the still-menacing Erich von Stroheim as her butler and chauffeur; and the visit to Paramount Studios to see Cecil B. DeMille (who played himself in the film).

Sunset Boulevard is a cruel and cynical film in many ways, but it is a work of art.

Producer: Charles Brackett. **Director:** Billy Wilder. **Scriptwriters:** Brackett, Wilder and D. M. Marshman, Jr. **Principal Players:** William Holden, Gloria Swanson and Erich von Stroheim. **Running time:** 110 minutes. **Released:** Paramount.

FATHER OF THE BRIDE

The ritual of marrying off a daughter—American style, circa 1950—was gently parodied in this extremely popular picture which owed the greater part of its success to a superb performance by Spencer Tracy as the much put-upon head of a typical U.S. family whose only

Father of the Bride with Joan Bennett and Spencer Tracy.

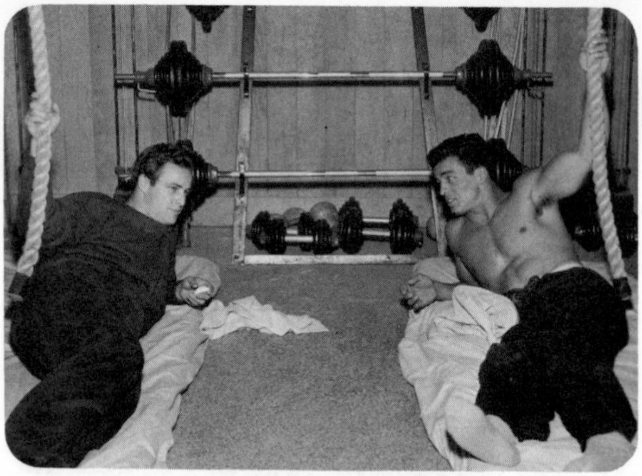

The Men with Marlon Brando and Arthur Jurado.

daughter falls in love and weds. Indeed, the Tracy skill at underplaying for humorous effect was never so memorably demonstrated as here.

Based on a best-selling book by Edward Street, given a vastly larger readership in reprint form in *Readers Digest,* the picture was just what the public of the time wanted in entertainment: It was good-natured, heartwarming and down-to-earth. All the intricate machinery surrounding the marriage rite—the engagement party, wedding announcements, church ceremony, rehearsals, morning coats, caterers, trousseaus, etc.—was incorporated into the script by Frances Goodrich and Albert Hackett in clever and often hilarious detail. Elizabeth Taylor was the daughter set to wed; Don Taylor played the object of her affections; and Joan Bennett was the bride's mother.

Pandro S. Berman produced, and Vincente Minnelli directed. Formidable company all, but it was Tracy's picture hands down.

Producer: Pandro S. Berman. **Director:** Vincente Minnelli. **Scriptwriters:** Frances Goodrich and Albert Hackett. **Principal Players:** Spencer Tracy, Joan Bennett, Elizabeth Taylor and Don Taylor. **Running time:** 93 minutes. **Released:** MGM.

THE MEN

Marlon Brando, who had made an indelible mark on Broadway history with his brilliant performance as Stanley Kowalski in Tennessee Williams' play *A Streetcar Named Desire,* was to enact that role on the screen—but not until 1951. He made his motion picture debut instead in 1950, in this Stanley Kramer production, *The Men,* in which he played a paraplegic veteran of World War II.

Brando had the benefit of first-rate talent to assist him in his entry into the new medium: The screenplay was by Carl Foreman and the direction by Fred Zinnemann.

The script was an earnest, thoughtful one set in a hospital for paraplegics and detailing the methods by which the inmates sought to adjust to their handicap and make a new life for themselves.

Inevitably the characters were stereotypes: Jack Webb was the intelligent and cynical ex-soldier; Richard Erdman, the one with a joke for every occasion; and Arthur Jurado played the serious fellow of Mexican extraction.

The central character, played by Brando, was defeated, hopeless and bitter. In finding himself, this paraplegic passes through pain, resentment, resistance, hopelessness and self-pity until he finds the courage within himself to rise above his physical disability.

It was a juicy role, and Brando played it to the emotional hilt, making an electrifying impact on American audiences. Kramer, Foreman and Zinnemann aside, *The Men* is primarily remembered today as the picture which introduced Brando to the screen.

Producer: Stanley Kramer. **Director:** Fred Zinnemann. **Scriptwriter:** Carl Foreman. **Principal Players:** Marlon Brando, Teresa Wright and Everett Sloane. **Running time:** 85 minutes. **Released:** United Artists.

Valli and Joseph Cotten in *The Third Man.*

THE THIRD MAN

Sir Carol Reed has made all types of pictures—biography (*The Young Mr. Pitt*), musical (*Oliver!*) and drama (*The Stars Look Down*)—but most of his admirers prefer his thrillers, and he has never made a better one than *The Third Man,* set in postwar Vienna, where it was filmed. American audiences loved it; the only complaints were about the amount of German dialogue spoken throughout—a captious objection, for care was taken in all instances either to provide a translation of sorts or to make it clear through the situations what was being said.

Graham Greene wrote the screenplay, and it was one of his best "entertainments" (the expression he uses to distinguish his work in this genre from his more "serious" novels). The characters were vivid and uncommonly well-acted. Joseph Cotten was cast as the American who comes to Vienna to visit a friend, and remains to expose the fellow as a villainous black marketeer (sumptuously acted by Orson Welles). Valli (who later added her first name, Alida) portrayed the mistress of the Welles character who remains in love with him despite his nefarious activities. Trevor Howard was seen as the British intelligence officer pursuing Welles, and Bernard Lee was his assistant.

The story grips the attention from the start and seldom lets up. But what lingers years afterward in the minds of those who saw it in 1950 are two aspects that are incidental to the overall picture: war-torn Vienna, which somehow becomes an important "character" in the film, and the sounds made by that hypnotic instrument, the Austrian zither—which were then entirely new to most American ears. They still play the zither in Viennese cafes in New York, and "The Third Man Theme" is almost always on the program.

An Oscar went to Robert Krasker for his black-and-white cinematography.

Producer-Director: Carol Reed. **Scriptwriter:** Graham Greene. **Principal Players:** Joseph Cotten, Valli, Orson Welles and Trevor Howard. **Running time:** 104 minutes. **Released:** Selznick Releasing Organization.

Kim Hunter, Vivien Leigh and Marlon Brando in *A Streetcar Named Desire,* the most successful of all the transferences of Tennessee Williams' plays to the screen.

1951

President Harry Truman hailed the cooperation of the motion picture industry with various public causes in a White House talk with Edward Arnold, actor, just prior to the national television and radio call for national emergency mobilization for the Korean War. Eric Johnston, president of the Motion Picture Association, took a leave of absence to become director of the Economic Stabilization Agency, with supervision over the country's wage and price control policies.

The Korean War did not impose any serious difficulties on the movie business, either in the studios or theatres. There was a $5,000 limitation on what could be spent on remodeling a theatre during the year, but there were no restrictions on equipment or maintenance. While some items were in short supply, there was no concern about film stock. In 1950, the shift had been made from cellulose nitrate (actually chemically related to gun-cotton and dangerous to handle or store) to cellulose acetate (triacetate), so-called safety stock which was non-explosive and slow burning.

In some respects the war was a boon to the movie industry as it cut off the expansion of television competition. The Federal Communications Commission's freeze on licenses for new TV stations, originally imposed as a result of the confusion on what type of color would be best, was continued "for the duration." In January in Chicago, Zenith conducted tests of its Phonevision system, installed with the reluctant cooperation of the Illinois Bell Telephone Company in 300 homes in the Chicago area. Results of this, as with other early pay-TV systems, were inconclusive.

Theatres continued to test TV shows. While the first large-screen theatre television system had been installed in June, 1948, growth was slow. By the end of 1951, only thirty-three theatres in seventeen cities had large-screen television equipment. The problem was primarily the difficulty of securing program material of wide appeal which was not simultaneously available on home TV sets. Many exhibitors felt that theatre TV would be essentially limited to prize fight championships and a few other sports events. At this period, only half the TV stations on the air were showing a profit.

Once again the House Un-American Activities Committee attacked the film industry, listing over three hundred persons as "identified as members of the Communist Party."

The Department of Justice was the focal point for more talks on consent decrees flowing out of the anti-trust decisions in the key suit filed in 1938. Paramount Theatres and Paramount Pictures were separated in 1950. In 1951, RKO began separate operations of the theatres and the production-distribution activities. The other three of the "Big Five" defendants were in advanced talks on implementing the Court "divorcement" orders.

A group headed by attorneys Arthur Krim and Robert Benjamin took control of United Artists from Mary Pickford and Charles Chaplin. This company was to prosper in the years ahead as most of the other major companies went through a variety of management crises.

Chinese films topped the list of imported pictures, with 77 seen during the year by the New York censors. This compared with 60 British films, 36 from Germany, 23 Italian and 27 from France.

Stars of the year: John Wayne, Martin & Lewis, Betty Grable, Abbott & Costello, Bing Crosby, Bob Hope, Randolph Scott, Gary Cooper, Doris Day and Spencer Tracy.

Jerry Lewis (center) and Dean Martin in *At War With the Army*.

A Streetcar Named Desire with Vivien Leigh and Kim Hunter.

AT WAR WITH THE ARMY

Dean Martin and Jerry Lewis, the latter as comedian and the former as straight man and singer, joined forces in 1946 at the 500 Club in Atlantic City, from whence they went on to become an extremely popular duo in theatres as well as night clubs. In 1949 they made their motion picture debut in *My Friend Irma,* a comedy which they stole from its stars John Lund, Marie Wilson and Diana Lynn. They pulled the same trick again in a sequel the following year called *My Friend Irma Goes West,* and after that they played second fiddle to no other performers.

In their third film, *At War With the Army,* the pattern was set for a series of co-starring pictures in the 1950's, in which Lewis usually played a simpleminded bungler and Martin his exasperated but always loyal buddy. Their relationship was in a comic tradition going back to Laurel and Hardy and Abbott and Costello. In fact, *At War With the Army* bears strong resemblance in format—comedy routines, gags, and a wisp of a plot—to *Buck Privates,* which had made Abbott and Costello famous. In turn, the Abbott and Costello picture had among its antecedents the silent comedy *Behind the Front,* starring Wallace Beery and Raymond Hatton.

The highlight of *At War With the Army* was an amusing imitation of Bing Crosby and Barry Fitzgerald in a singing sequence from *Going My Way.*

Over a dozen films followed, with which Martin and Lewis built up a large and dedicated audience of fans. They included *That's My Boy, The Stooge, Sailor Beware, Scared Stiff,* etc. Their last picture together was *Hollywood or Bust,* in 1956, after which they went their separate ways.

Producer-Writer: Fred F. Finklehoffe. **Director:** Hal Walker. **Principal Players:** Dean Martin, Jerry Lewis and Polly Bergen. **Running time:** 92 minutes. **Released:** Paramount.

A STREETCAR NAMED DESIRE

Drama critics are generally divided among themselves as to whether this or *The Glass Menagerie* is Tennessee Williams' best play. In 1950, *Menagerie* was brought to the screen in such a fashion as to result in both artistic and commercial disaster. But Hollywood redeemed itself the following year with a superb version of *Streetcar* that has deservedly become a movie classic—and one that was successful at the box office as well.

We say "Hollywood"—actually, the talents that made *Streetcar* such a success on film were those who had created it so well on the New York stage, including director Elia Kazan and actors Marlon Brando, Kim Hunter and Karl Malden. Even several of the bit players were recruited from Broadway for the film.

The notable exception was Vivien Leigh, who was selected instead of Jessica Tandy to play Blanche Du Bois. Miss Tandy, a highly acclaimed stage actress, was nonetheless unknown to most movie audiences. Miss Leigh had acted the role on the London stage, however, and she was so brilliant in the film that admirers of Miss Tandy could hardly object.

Audie Murphy in *The Red Badge of Courage.*

Indeed, Blanche is a once-in-a-lifetime role for an actress, and Miss Leigh surpassed all her previous work in this picture, including her great Scarlett O'Hara. It is something of an irony that an English actress should have played the two most famous Southern belles in American fiction.

The bitter tragedy of the mental disintegration of the heroine (one of the "dispossessed in life whose experiences had unfitted her for reality," in the apt description of critic Brooks Atkinson) was counterpoised by comic touches in the characterization of Stanley Kowalski, played by the remarkable Marlon Brando, who made the role famous—and vice versa. Kazan interwove the disparate elements with extraordinary skill and with the attention to melodramatic realism for which he is noted. In some quarters he was criticized for "stagey" film direction, which was absurd in the face of the powerful emotional effect created by the screen images under his guidance.

The playwright himself wrote the screenplay from an adaptation by Oscar Saul. Miss Leigh won an Oscar, and other Academy Awards went to Miss Hunter (best supporting actress) and Malden (best supporting actor). Richard Day was also cited for his art direction, as was George James Hopkins for his set decoration. Alex North's haunting musical score is one of the best ever written for a film.

Producer: Charles K. Feldman. **Director:** Elia Kazan. **Scriptwriter:** Tennessee Williams. **Principal Players:** Vivien Leigh, Marlon Brando, Kim Hunter and Karl Malden. **Running time:** 122 minutes. **Released:** Warner Bros.

THE RED BADGE OF COURAGE

A book—Lillian Ross' *Picture*—has been written about the making of this adaptation of the classic Stephen Crane novel about the Civil War by producer Gottfried Reinhardt and director John Huston. It supplies extremely intriguing reading. Its revelation of methods of production under the great studio czars of the 1930's and 1940's helps to explain the fragmentized nature of the film, which was frantically edited and re-edited before being released, in futile efforts to make it more "commercial."

Miss Ross never does answer the question as to whether or not a potentially great movie was ruined in the process, perhaps because no one can be sure. What is on the screen has flashes of brilliance, particularly in the battle scenes, which capture all the confusion and horror of war through an accumulation of vivid details. But the central theme—the acceptance by the young soldier hero of the necessity of fighting after a cowardly defection—is lost in the erratic continuity and superficial treatment of the struggle of the protagonist within himself.

Part of the trouble lies with the actor selected to play the central role of the Youth—Audie Murphy, the much-decorated real-life soldier of World War II. He gave a wooden performance which failed to reflect the inner feelings of the character. Bill Mauldin, the cartoonist, turned actor to play the Loud Soldier, but the best acting came from John Dierkes as the Tall Soldier.

Red Badge remains one of those legends of Hollywood

The Great Caruso with Mario Lanza (center).

A Place in the Sun with Montgomery Clift and Shelley Winters.

film making—a well-intended film by an important director that failed to come off. The reasons, as revealed in the Ross book, are as historically interesting as the film itself.

Producer: Gottfried Reinhardt. **Director-Writer:** John Huston. **Principal Players:** Audie Murphy, Bill Mauldin, John Dierkes and Royal Dano. **Running time:** 69 minutes. **Released:** MGM.

THE GREAT CARUSO

Can opera be turned into movie box office? Skeptics—and there were many—said no, but they were proved wrong by producer Joe Pasternak with this biography of the legendary Italian singer.

It also made a big star, for a time, of Mario Lanza, who had made something of a splash in *That Midnight Kiss* two years before. In *Caruso* he dominated the film—not by any subtle acting, which was beyond him, but by virtue of an overpowering tenor voice. His selections were as wide-ranging as they were numerous—from the "Vesti la Giubba" from *I Pagliacci* to the "Miserere" from *Tosca* and on to the popular ballad "Because."

Other operatic stars were enlisted for the picture: Dorothy Kirsten had the second feminine lead, and there were also Jarmila Novotna, Teresa Celli and Blanche Thebom. Opera buffs were also treated to brief sequences from *Aïda, La Bohème, Rigoletto, Martha, Cavalleria Rusticana, La Gioconda* and *Lucia di Lammermoor.*

In addition, the Bach-Gounod "Ave Maria," some liturgical singing and several Italian folk songs were to be heard. It was a lot of music!

The story hit the highlights of Caruso's life, from his arrival in this country from Italy, his early rejection by critics, his marriage to the daughter of a wealthy patron of the Metropolitan Opera (played by Ann Blyth), to his great triumphs, followed by the loss of his voice and death. Plainly, the story had what the mass audience likes—romance, conflict and sentiment. And moviegoers didn't mind all that singing a bit—in fact, they obviously enjoyed it.

Producer: Joe Pasternak. **Director:** Richard Thorpe. **Scriptwriters:** Sonya Levien and William Ludwig. **Principal Players:** Mario Lanza, Ann Blyth, Dorothy Kirsten and Jarmila Novotna. **Running time:** 109 minutes. **Released:** MGM.

A PLACE IN THE SUN

Theodore Dreiser's novel *An American Tragedy* is monumental, not only in its size and scope, but in its reputation with literary critics. It was written in the twenties and was based on a real murder trial that occurred early in the century. It is somewhat reportorial in approach, and is highly critical of a society that could condemn to death a young man who had committed murder in intent but not in actuality.

A film version made in 1931 by Paramount, directed by Joseph von Sternberg, was hotly denounced by Dreiser himself as destroying his true purpose by placing

Alec Guinness and Stanley Holloway in *The Lavender Hill Mob.*

the primary blame on the hero rather than on environment and circumstance.

Would Dreiser have approved George Stevens' 1951 film? It is not a faithful adaptation in any sense; it moves the time up to the fifties and changes the name of the hero from Clyde Griffith to George Eastman. The question of moral responsibility is left hanging; it is deliberately vague.

Such speculations are really irrelevant in view of the film's powerful depiction of the intensities of youth: the love affair of the poor hero and the rich girl, idealized yet completely convincing; and the tragedy of the poor girl he makes pregnant and drives to desperate measures.

Elizabeth Taylor gave two of her best performances under the direction of Stevens (the other was in *Giant*), and this is the better of the two. Montgomery Clift, that most sensitive of the male stars of the 1950's, was perfection as the Clyde-George character, and Shelley Winters was almost unbearably poignant as the girl who is accidentally drowned.

A female film critic of the day said that American audiences would never accept a film in which an innocent man was sent to the electric chair for a crime he didn't commit. She was wrong; it was an enormous box-office success. Critical acclaim was generally ecstatic, and the film won six Oscars: direction, writing, cinematography, costume design, editing, music.

Producer-Director: George Stevens. **Scriptwriters:** Michael Wilson and Harry Brown. **Principal Players:** Elizabeth Taylor, Montgomery Clift and Shelley Winters. **Running time:** 122 minutes. **Released:** Paramount.

THE LAVENDER HILL MOB

Alec Guinness was the most popular of the British character actors with U.S. art theatre audiences in the early 1950's, and *The Lavender Hill Mob* was a particular favorite of that clientele, who liked to watch the British poke fun at themselves. The general tone was gentle satire; there was a funny chase scene right out of Mack Sennett; and the whole was held together by Guinness' brilliant characterization of a timid bank clerk who almost succeeds in committing the perfect crime.

T.E.B. Clarke's screenplay had a typically ingenious gimmick: Guinness and his fellow conspirator (the droll Stanley Holloway) steal gold from a bank and melt it down into souvenir Eiffel Towers for shipment to France! It almost works until a careless French clerk sells the towers as souvenirs, and this leads to that mad chase sequence with Guinness and Holloway trying to elude the confused London police force.

Both Guinness and Clarke were nominated for Academy Awards for *Lavender Hill Mob;* the actor lost, but the writer won.

Other Guinness comedies that were popular in the 1950's include the following: *The Man in the White Suit, The Captain's Paradise, The Ladykillers* and *The Horse's Mouth.*

Producer: Michael Balcon. **Director:** Charles Crichton. **Scriptwriter:** T.E.B. Clarke. **Principal Players:** Alec Guinness, Stanley Holloway and Sidney James. **Running time:** 82 minutes. **Released:** Universal.

Georges Guétary, Gene Kelly and Oscar Levant in *An American in Paris.*

AN AMERICAN IN PARIS

MGM's musical experts, producer Arthur Freed and director Vincente Minnelli, took a daring gamble for Hollywood with *An American in Paris:* They inserted a lengthy ballet at the climax of the picture that ran for over twenty minutes. The ballet depicted the Parisian romance of the hero (Gene Kelly) against backdrops and settings that were reproductions of famous paintings of Paris scenes.

Thus, MGM brought "culture" to the movie masses, accustomed to something different in their musical fare—and the masses loved it. For several years afterward, a ballet sequence (although a much shorter one) was *de rigueur* for the American musical.

While *An American in Paris* is sometimes referred to as having "revolutionized" the Hollywood musical, the extensive use of ballet to tell the story was actually its major innovation. Otherwise the basic elements were the same as before. The plot was flimsy: Ex-G.I. Kelly remains in Paris after the war, falls in love with Leslie Caron, who is already engaged to Georges Guétary, etc. The score was mostly composed of old favorites by George and Ira Gershwin: "Nice Work If You Can Get It," "Embraceable You," "I Got Rhythm" and "'s Wonderful." Among the few new tunes, "Our Love Is Here to Stay" was outstanding. Comic relief was supplied in typical dead-pan fashion by Oscar Levant, whose big scene was a daydream in which he envisions himself as the piano soloist in a great symphony he is conducting simultaneously. As his imagination gains free reign, he appears as the entire string section, the tympanist, cymbalist, etc., and turns up at the conclusion of the symphony as the leader of the claque. (This sequence, incidentally, is another example of how to dress up longhair stuff for the average moviegoer and make him like it.)

For all its trite plot elements, *An American in Paris* has a perennial freshness about it. The color production is tasteful and often dazzling; Kelly is a delight, especially in the sequence in which he conducts an English lesson for the neighborhood children to the tune of "I Got Rhythm"; Miss Caron was an altogether winning new face as the heroine; and some even found the other newcomer, Guétary, full of Gallic charm. (Miss Caron went on to bigger roles, but not he.)

Seven Oscars were won by the picture, including one for best film of the year and one for Alan Jay Lerner for his story and screenplay (this was thirteen years before *My Fair Lady* became a film). Also cited were the cinematography, art direction, set decoration, costume design and musical scoring.

The Academy voted a special award that same year to Kelly "in appreciation of his versatility as an actor, singer, director and dancer, and specifically for his brilliant achievements in the art of choreography on film." If you count that one, *An American in Paris* garnered eight Oscars!

Producer: Arthur Freed. **Director:** Vincente Minnelli. **Scriptwriter:** Alan Jay Lerner. **Principal Players:** Gene Kelly, Leslie Caron, Oscar Levant and Georges Guétary. **Running time:** 113 minutes. **Released:** MGM.

The African Queen with Humphrey Bogart and Katharine Hepburn.

THE AFRICAN QUEEN

It was a highly unlikely idea to co-star Katharine Hepburn with Humphrey Bogart—to pair the queen of screwball comedy and serious drama with the most famous of the gangster heroes. It had to work very well or not at all.

Fortunately for Sam Spiegel, the producer, and John Huston, the writer-director, it turned out to have been a happy inspiration all around. *The African Queen* delighted a huge public, and won for Bogart his first and only Academy Award.

He certainly deserved it. His performance as the unkempt, slipshod, bibulous riverboat captain, who is talked into an act of heroism (blowing up a German gunboat blocking East African waters) by a missionary woman, was a comic creation of high skill. Some of his fans professed to have taken a bit of time to get used to him in this new type of role, but before it was over, they were impressed.

Miss Hepburn's assignment as a straitlaced and inhibited British missionary was also a departure for her, and she managed the transformation to an emotionally responsive woman with conviction as well as wit. Indeed, the two great stars had real "chemistry" together; they not only amused the audience, but made it believe in and accept the love affair that developed between the two disparate characters.

The script was based on a novel of the same name by C. S. Forester, and Huston was assisted in adapting it to the screen by James Agee, the former film critic. It was filmed entirely on location in Africa.

Producer: Sam Spiegel. **Director:** John Huston. **Scriptwriters:** John Huston and James Agee. **Principal Players:** Humphrey Bogart, Katharine Hepburn and Robert Morley. **Running time:** 106 minutes. **Released:** United Artists.

Charlton Heston, Betty Hutton and Cornel Wilde in *The Greatest Show on Earth,* Cecil B. DeMille's definitive movie spectacle about the circus.

1952

The Communist issue overshadowed the industry this year. The House Un-American Activities Committee issued a formal report charging that after the 1947 hearings, steps had not been taken "to check Communism within the industry." Eric Johnston attacked the report as "misleading and unfair." Some of the members of the Congressional committee indicated that they had not read the report carefully enough before approving its publication. However, Senator Richard M. Nixon had no qualms, stating, "The demonstrated activity of Communists within the motion picture industry is a matter of concern to the members of Congress and loyal Americans everywhere." Nixon specifically praised Howard Hughes' bizarre action in closing down the RKO Radio studio to screen out Reds. Hughes announced: "My determination is to make RKO one studio where the work of Communist sympathizers will not be used."

The record shows that Howard Hughes was more interested in selling the studio than in making films. In a baffling transaction, he sold control to a group headed by Ralph E. Stolkin and A. L. Koolish. But within a few weeks these men withdrew, when *The Wall Street Journal* and other publications published information about unsavory backgrounds.

The Red issue kept popping up. The American Legion published an article by J. B. Matthews in its national magazine titled, "Did the Movies Really Clean House?" Roy M. Brewer, international representative of the International Alliance of Theatrical Stage and Screen Employees, on behalf of the Hollywood AFL Film Council, called on the House Un-American Activities Committee to introduce legislation barring the importation of films made abroad by Communists or Communist sympathizers. The film *Encounter,* made in Italy with Paul Muni, was singled out for criticism.

The Supreme Court, in *The Miracle* case, struck out sacrilege as a ground for censorship. A comment by Justice Douglas indicated that the Mutual Film case of 1915 (which said films were not part of the press) would soon be overturned: "Expression by means of motion pictures is included in the free speech and free press guarantee of the First and Fourteenth Amendments." A key decision in Ohio declared newsreel censorship unconstitutional. Judge Frank W. Wiley of the Toledo Municipal Court stated, "From the 1952 viewpoint, it appears that self-censorship (on the part of the industry) has removed much of the possibility for evil that existed in the earlier years" (when courts approved censorship). In a significant civil rights decision, the U.S. Supreme Court held that the State of Texas could not bar the exhibition of *Pinky.*

Theatre owners worried more over the future, as the FCC authorized 2,053 TV channels in 1,291 communities. Prior to that time, only 108 stations were in operation. Exhibitors felt the effects of TV competition, especially on Sunday nights, and called for at least a five-year clearance between sale of "A" quality films to TV and three years on "B" films. The Department of Justice countered with a suit compelling major companies to sell features to TV broadcasters and to all 16mm outlets. Spyros Skouras, president of 20th Century-Fox, said, "This threatens our existence as an industry."

Milton Rachmil, head of Decca Records, showed the way to increased diversification within the entertainment field by his acquisition of Universal Pictures. Well-known exhibitor Si Fabian acquired control of Stanley Warner theatres. An era ended when William J. German obtained from Eastman Kodak the franchise for sale of professional 35mm film, previously held by Jules Brulatour under a unique agreement with George Eastman.

Notable films included Cecil B. DeMille's *The Greatest Show on Earth* and *This Is Cinerama.*

Stars of the year: Martin & Lewis, Gary Cooper, John Wayne, Bing Crosby, Bob Hope, James Stewart, Doris Day, Gregory Peck, Susan Hayward and Randolph Scott.

Gary Cooper in *High Noon.*

Singin' in the Rain with Gene Kelly and Jean Hagen.

HIGH NOON

As a producer and writer, and later as a director, Stanley Kramer has most often sought to combine good picture making with good editorializing. *High Noon,* which he produced after *Home of the Brave* and *The Men,* remains the most successful demonstration of his method.

Its extraordinary performance at the box office started a Hollywood trend toward so-called adult westerns—that is, those which subordinate the traditional action elements to development of a serious theme. In *High Noon,* a sheriff performs a dangerous job in the face of apathy and cowardliness from the rest of the community. He stands alone, an oasis of heroism and loyalty to duty in a desert of moral indifference.

The "message" is plain. But it is delivered unaffectedly and in imaginative cinematic terms—the crane shot of Gary Cooper all alone in the middle of the deserted town awaiting the killer is deservedly famous. Fred Zinnemann directed and Carl Foreman wrote the script. The title song, a ballad by Dimitri Tiomkin with lyrics by Ned Washington, was effectively used throughout the film to tie the action together, and later became popular on its own.

Two newcomers appeared in the film: Grace Kelly, as Cooper's Quaker wife, and Katy Jurado, as a half-Mexican woman in love with him in the past. Miss Jurado had the bigger role and carried it off well. Both ladies have since disappeared from the film scene—the former to Monaco, of course.

Cooper won the Academy Award for best performance of the year, and Tiomkin was cited for best musical score as well as best song. A fourth Oscar went to Elmo Williams and Harry Gerstad for editing.

Producer: Stanley Kramer. **Director:** Fred Zinnemann. **Scriptwriter:** Carl Foreman. **Principal Players:** Gary Cooper, Thomas Mitchell, Lloyd Bridges, Katy Jurado and Grace Kelly. **Running time:** 85 minutes. **Released:** United Artists.

SINGIN' IN THE RAIN

The best movie musicals have nearly always been those written directly for the screen, and one of the best of these best is *Singin' in the Rain.* It is everything a movie musical ought to be.

Adolph Green and Betty Comden (of *On the Town* fame) had the inspiration for the ingenious story and script, fixing the place at Hollywood in the days immediately before the celluloid revolution precipitated by the Brothers Warner and *The Jazz Singer,* with full credit to the pioneers in sound and their pioneering sound picture.

Gene Kelly is cast as the matinee idol of the silent era, and Jean Hagen is his glamorous opposite number. Loosely modeled after Bushman and Bayne and other famous romantic teams of the early days in films, they live off the fat of the land and the adulation of their public. Along comes sound, and panic sets in.

The book is never weighty, but is certainly less gossamer than is usual in musicals. It goes on to show how

Claire Bloom and Charlie Chaplin in *Limelight*.

the crisis was survived, with Kelly moving on to happier days with Debbie Reynolds (never better than here) as his singing co-star.

Hollywood and its legendary exaggerations come in for a good deal of spoofing, some of which is barbed and most of which is innocuous. Quite a few of the secrets of picture making as practiced back in 1927 are revealed, making for both interest and amusement.

The title song, which Kelly sings and dances to delightfully, was first heard in *Hollywood Revue of 1929,* "You Are My Lucky Star" comes from *Broadway Melody of 1936.* Altogether, there are thirteen numbers by Nacio Herb Brown and Arthur Freed, plus two others, for a total of fifteen songs, plus snatches of memorable oldies like "Should I?" and "The Wedding of the Painted Doll" in a montage sequence tracing the development of film musical numbers from the days of the immortal Busby Berkeley.

The production numbers are first-rate, too, the biggest being "Gotta Dance" in which Kelly, Cyd Charisse, and Donald O'Connor give in to that urge backed by what looks like the entire population of Culver City.

Praise is due all participants in this film, from Kelly, who starred and co-directed with Stanley Donen, to Arthur Freed, who produced, in addition to contributing most of the song lyrics. They don't make movie musicals like this one any more.

Producer: Arthur Freed. **Directors:** Stanley Donen and Gene Kelly. **Scriptwriters:** Adolph Green and Betty Comden. **Principal Players:** Gene Kelly, Donald O'Connor, Debbie Reynolds and Jean Hagen. **Running time:** 103 minutes. **Released:** MGM.

LIMELIGHT

Seldom has the American public turned so against one of its former idols with such venom as it did on Charlie Chaplin. *Limelight,* as had *Monsieur Verdoux* before it, suffered the consequences at the box office. That is too bad, for the film represents many facets of the Chaplin talent and is, in addition, a kind of summation of his personal philosophy of life.

As writer, Chaplin used a slim story line, but built on it a firm dramatic structure, mixing normally opposing elements with superb ease: drama with comedy, vaudeville with ballet, and wisecracks with philosophical discussion. As director he managed the changes with finesse.

But it is as actor that he shone most brilliantly here, playing the role of a British music-hall artist who, while his own career is fading, nurses a talented young dancer back to health and paves her way to stardom. (Claire Bloom, brought over from England, was extremely moving in this difficult role.) He played dramatic scenes with genuine pathos; he did a routine with Buster Keaton that is hilarious; and he demonstrated once again his unparalleled mastery of the art of pantomime. And not only did he produce, write and star in the picture. He composed the musical score, the main theme of which is so popular it is still played regularly over radio stations eighteen years later.

Regrettably, Chaplin did not choose to end his extraordinary career with this masterpiece. In England he wrote, directed and starred in a film called *A King in*

This Is Cinerama with Gathering of the Clans in Scotland.

New York which has never been shown in the U.S., and in 1966—also in Britain—he wrote and directed a film for Universal called *A Countess From Hong Kong.* It reflected only a pale shadow of the old Chaplin, and fared at the box office accordingly.

Producer-Writer-Director: Charles Chaplin. **Principal Players:** Charles Chaplin, Claire Bloom and Sydney Chaplin. **Running time:** 143 minutes. **Released:** United Artists.

THIS IS CINERAMA

No one who was not actually there on the night that Cinerama was unveiled to the public—September 30, 1952, at the Broadway Theatre in New York—can hope to realize the tremendous impact that the new three-camera, three-projector process had upon the first audience. It was, in a word, terrific.

To moviegoers accustomed to looking at a little picture of moving images looming distantly out of surrounding blackness, it was downright devastating to have that world of the screen spread out vastly and move in on them, to become so dominating and intimate that one was scarcely outside of it.

The first-night audience was fascinated. After an introduction of standard projection, it was swept up into the big world of Cinerama and taken on a roller coaster ride. Many people became quite dizzy.

Equally realistic was a trip by air across America, which was like sitting in the front cabin of the plane.

The two-hour program of *This Is Cinerama,* which was narrated by Lowell Thomas, also included the dance of the priestesses from *Aïda;* a helicopter view of Niagara Falls; the Long Island Choral Society singing "The Messiah"; Venetian boatmen in gondolas; the Gathering of the Clans in Scotland; a bullfight and native dances in Spain; the triumphal march from *Aïda* performed by the La Scala Opera Company in Milan; the Vienna Boys Choir singing; a tour of the Tyrol in Wolfgang; and the Water Carnival at Cypress Gardens in Florida.

Strictly routine travelogue material, of course, but so impressive on the huge Cinerama screen(s).

This Is Cinerama was followed by *Cinerama Holiday* (1955), which tried unsuccessfully to tie the travelogue pieces together with a semblance of a plot. A bobsled ride down a Swiss mountainside at St. Moritz substituted for the roller coaster and the audience was taken on another plane ride, this time in a Navy jet.

Three more travelogues followed with grosses becoming progressively less. Then, in 1962, MGM produced the first "story" film in Cinerama, *The Wonderful World of the Brothers Grimm,* followed by *How the West Was Won.* Both were enormously successful at the box office, but the three-camera, three-projector process was discarded shortly thereafter for a one-camera, one-projector method. Films made today and presented in Cinerama look like all the other pictures in 70 mm. The true Cinerama is apparently gone for good.

Producers: Lowell Thomas and Merian C. Cooper. **Running time:** 120 minutes. **Released:** Cinerama.

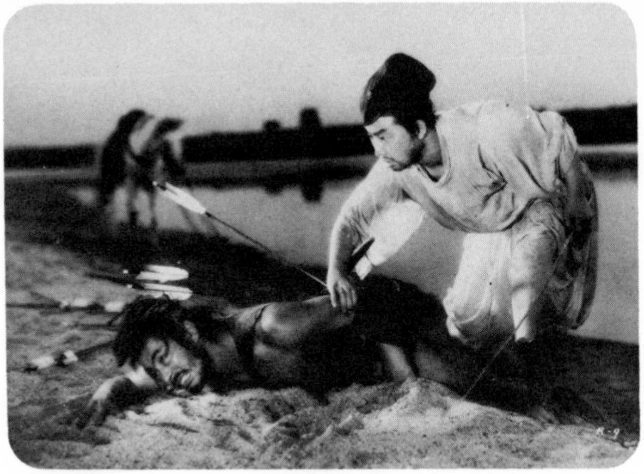

Toshiro Mifune (left) in *Rashomon.*

Breaking the Sound Barrier with Ralph Richardson (left).

RASHOMON

Americans (except perhaps for a few film scholars) knew little or nothing of Japanese motion pictures until *Rashomon* appeared in 1952. That opened the floodgates to films from that prolific industry, the best of which are generally agreed to be those of Akira Kurosawa, the director of *Rashomon.* (The worst: a series of mediocre science fiction movies, featuring King-Kongish gorillas and other monstrosities.)

Rashomon had caused a sensation at the Venice film festival in 1951, and the raves of critics no doubt helped to encourage its acquisition for the American market by RKO Radio. It turned out to be a huge success in art-house theatres.

The plot and its construction were as unique as the brilliantly created medieval forest setting in which the events took place. A crime has been committed: A bandit has seized a nobleman and his wife traveling through a forest. He rapes the woman before her husband's eyes. Later, the husband is found dead.

The story is recounted four times: through the eyes of the bandit, the wife, the dead man (speaking through a medium) and an eyewitness—an old woodcutter who relates his version of the happenings to three other men with whom he has taken refuge from the rain.

The audience is never told explicitly which character is telling the truth. *Rashomon* seems to suggest that no one can ever be sure just what the truth is.

As fascinating as the story and its construction is the cinematic skill with which Kurosawa put it on the screen. His fast-tracking shots through the forest, for instance, have been much imitated by moviemakers all over the world.

Hollywood has also paid Kurosawa the supreme compliment of remaking two of his pictures: *Rashomon* became *The Outrage* (1964) and *Seven Samurai* (1956) was turned into *The Magnificent Seven* (1960).

Producer: Jingo Minoura. **Director:** Akira Kurosawa. **Scriptwriters:** Akira Kurosawa and Shinobo Hashimoto. **Principal Players:** Toshiro Mifune, Machiko Kyo and Masayuki Mori. **Running time:** 90 minutes. **Released:** RKO Radio.

BREAKING THE SOUND BARRIER

The notable achievement of director David Lean in this picture was the skillful balancing of the excitement of the conquest of the speed of sound by jet planes with the human drama surrounding it. Neither element overshadowed the other as usually happens in such films; both were given their due and beautifully counterpointed.

The photographic effects were breathtaking at the time and indeed still are, even in these days when one can view the moon on television: full throttle descents from 40,000 feet, as the plane shudders and throbs in the attempt to break through the sound barrier; the grandeur of a jet flight from London to Cairo at incredible heights; the awesome sight of a strewn field and a deep crater in the earth when a pilot attempting the

The Greatest Show on Earth with Charlton Heston and Betty Hutton.

Forbidden Games with Georges Poujouly and Brigitte Fossey.

breakthrough fails; and the stirring spectacle of a jet plane in full flight.

In the meantime, the human drama of the effect of the ceaseless quest of individuals attains comparable power. It is built around the conflict between a plane manufacturer and his daughter who loses both her husband and her brother in the efforts directed by her father to break the sound barrier. Her parent seems hard and unfeeling to her; actually he is waging his own interior battle, and when she comes to an understanding of this and the compulsion that drives him, they are reunited in an eloquent climactic sequence.

The performances by Ralph Richardson and Ann Todd were in the best British tradition of understatement of emotion. The script of Terence Rattigan is probably his finest work for the screen, and Malcolm Arnold's musical score helped build up the emotional power of this remarkable film.

Producer-Director: David Lean. **Scriptwriter:** Terence Rattigan. **Principal Players:** Ralph Richardson, Ann Todd and Nigel Patrick. **Running time:** 115 minutes. **Released:** United Artists.

THE GREATEST SHOW ON EARTH

Never a favorite of the critics, Cecil B. DeMille, that showman extraordinaire, garnered the best reviews of his career when he turned from the religious spectacle to the circus. The public, of course, always flocked to see his pictures, and this one was no exception—to put it mildly.

Cooperation of the Ringling Brothers-Barnum and Bailey Circus was obtained in shooting the film, which was made with all the DeMille flair for size, thrills, color and splash. The cast was typically stellar.

A sign of the times and how they change: In 1952, eyebrows were raised in some quarters over the introduction of the subject of euthanasia (James Stewart was wanted by the police for killing his hopelessly ill wife), and over the frankness with which Gloria Grahame expressed her libidinous interest in Charlton Heston in some scenes.

Producer-Director: Cecil B. DeMille. **Scriptwriters:** Fredric M. Frank, Theodore St. John and Frank Cavett. **Principal Players:** Betty Hutton, Cornel Wilde, Charlton Heston, James Stewart, Dorothy Lamour and Gloria Grahame. **Running time:** 153 minutes. **Released:** Paramount.

FORBIDDEN GAMES

Not since *Children of Paradise* in 1946 had a French film come to the U.S. as highly praised abroad as did *Forbidden Games.* American critics concurred (the film had won the Grand Prize at Venice), and art theatres had one of their biggest hits of the early fifties.

It is an anti-war film with a difference; it shows the effects of war on the minds of children. The heroine is a five-year-old girl who sees her parents killed right before her eyes by a strafing German plane during the exodus from Paris in 1940. Her dog is also killed and, when she is taken in by a peasant family, she persuades

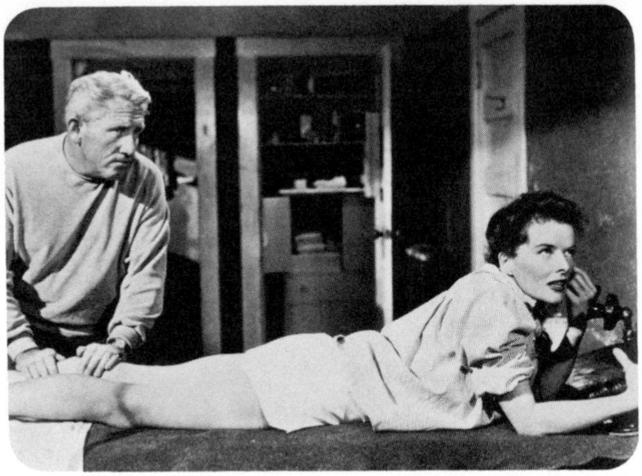

Pat and Mike with Spencer Tracy and Katharine Hepburn.

the fourteen-year-old son to help her conduct a burial ceremony. Death soon becomes an obsession with the two of them, and they build up an animal cemetery, marking the graves with crosses they have stolen from the churchyard. Eventually, their "games" are exposed, and the girl is dispatched alone to an orphanage.

What it all means—the corruption of innocent children by adults, and an explosion of the myth of the "pure" French peasant—has been much written about by critics, whose theories vary, but they all concur in two points. They admire the direction of René Clément, and the extraordinary performance of little Brigitte Fossey in the difficult role of the girl. Her emotional range was remarkable in one so young: She moved from displays of fear and self-confidence to girlish coquetry with flawless ease.

Producer: Robert Dorfman. **Director:** René Clément. **Scriptwriters:** Clément, Jean Aurenche and Pierre Bost. **Principal Players:** Brigitte Fossey, Georges Poujouly, Lucien Hubert, Suzanne Courtal and Jacques Marin. **Running time:** 89 minutes. **Released:** Times Film Corp.

PAT AND MIKE

Katharine Hepburn and Spencer Tracy made nine films together, from *Woman of the Year* in 1942 to *Guess Who's Coming to Dinner* in 1967. Many critics feel this film, which came ten years after their first pairing, is the best.

Tracy acts the part of a sports promoter willing to play it slightly offside if there is a faster buck in it that way. Miss Hepburn is a super-athlete, with golf and tennis her specialities. From absolutely no romantic interest in each other in the beginning, they proceed in a business arrangement which leads, to no one's surprise, to their falling in love.

A slight plot indeed, but it is bolstered by sprightly dialogue supplied by Ruth Gordon and Garson Kanin, and by slick direction from George Cukor.

The Hepburn-Tracy team was beloved by the American public which flocked to see them in such other comedies as *Without Love, State of the Union* and *Adam's Rib,* but did not care for them as much in their excursion into serious drama in *Keeper of the Flame.* The contrasting images of the stars—her cool sophistication set against his down-to-earth practicality—were better suited to comic exploitation.

Producer: Lawrence Weingarten. **Director:** George Cukor. **Scriptwriters:** Ruth Gordon and Garson Kanin. **Principal Players:** Spencer Tracy, Katharine Hepburn, Aldo Ray and William Ching. **Running time:** 95 minutes. **Released:** MGM.

COME BACK, LITTLE SHEBA

William Inge's play about a frumpy housewife and her alcoholic husband—the playwright's first big success on Broadway—has not held up too well over the years, but the performance of Shirley Booth, marking her screen debut in a repetition of her stage role, is still one to treasure. It won her an Academy Award.

Students of the thespian art would do well to study

Come Back, Little Sheba with Philip Ober, Burt Lancaster, Edwin Max, Lisa Golm and Shirley Booth.

the role and the skill with which Miss Booth moves from the comic to the tragic, sometimes actually fusing the two. A silly woman who dreams of her lost dog Sheba finally comes to a firmer understanding of herself and the husband who resents having been forced to marry her twenty years earlier. Director Daniel Mann focused the camera on Miss Booth almost constantly, and what emerged was as full a portrait of a woman as has ever been captured on the screen.

Unfortunately, Burt Lancaster was miscast as her middle-aged weakling husband. Put in the film for commercial purposes, he was not able to overcome the handicap of his youth and vitality, which shone through the makeup.

Producer: Hal B. Wallis. **Director:** Daniel Mann. **Scriptwriter:** Ketti Frings. **Principal Players:** Burt Lancaster, Shirley Booth, Terry Moore and Richard Jaeckel. **Running time:** 99 minutes. **Released:** Paramount.

Alan Ladd and Brandon de Wilde in *Shane,* George Stevens archetypal western and the high point in Ladd's career.

1953

It was in this year that the motion picture screen, first in the United States and then throughout the world, burst out of the proportions originally set by Thomas Edison. The ratio of screen width to height, expressed as 1:33, represented the 3-by-4 size picked by Edison, who had wanted something as close to square as would be practical.

The size revolution had been touched off the year before with the debut of Cinerama—a deeply curved triple screen requiring three projections. For some time in 1953, there was a question whether the changes would result in 3-D (stereoscopic) effects, or whether the new format would simply be a wider screen than had been used in the past.

This was also the year in which 3-D or stereographic movies captured the public fancy on a wide scale. Years before (in 1936) anaglyphs using red and green glasses had enjoyed a brief whirl. But at that time the industry quietly buried the subject, saying: "The public will never wear special glasses."

But 1953 saw tens of millions of glasses employed by the public to view *Bwana Devil,* an independent production by Arch Oboler with crude but sometimes fascinating 3-D effects. This set off a chain reaction. The 3-D films were characterized by poor plots, inferior production values and atrocious stereoscopic effects. Exploited as a fad, 3-D died quickly—but not without helping to set the stage for the wide-screen development which became almost universal.

A twenty-year-old French anamorphic (image-squeezing) system was resurrected by Spyros P. Skouras, then the head of 20th Century-Fox. The name CinemaScope was coined, and the entertainment world was taken by storm with the first picture, *The Robe.* Exhibitors spent millions for expansion lenses to project the squeezed prints onto very wide screens. New impact was also given through sound with the use of magnetic soundtracks.

But apart from 3-D, CinemaScope and stereophonic sound, 1953 was a notable film year. A "has-been" singer made a comeback as an actor when Frank Sinatra appeared in *From Here to Eternity,* and the ancient screen genre of the western came into new distinction with *Shane.* Censors had nightmares over *The Moon Is Blue,* though only a year later it was difficult to recall what the controversy was all about. Screen fare was unusually diverse; such charming films as *Lili* and *Roman Holiday* were among the most popular.

Films reflected the general emotional uplift of the country resulting from relief that the long, hard war in Korea was over—an achievement credited importantly to a familiar figure in newsreels of the preceding decade, General Dwight D. Eisenhower, who was inaugurated President in 1953. Adolph Zukor, chairman of the board of Paramount Pictures, and the last surviving person properly entitled to be called an American screen pioneer, celebrated his fiftieth anniversary in the industry. It had been a long road for him from 1903 and the U.S. release of Sarah Bernhardt in *Queen Elizabeth.* The road ran on and on. In July, 1969, he was honored in a full-page ad in *The New York Times* by Gulf and Western, Paramount's new owner.

Stars of the year: Gary Cooper, Martin & Lewis, John Wayne, Alan Ladd, Bing Crosby, Marilyn Monroe, James Stewart, Bob Hope, Susan Hayward and Randolph Scott.

Marilyn Monroe, Betty Grable and Lauren Bacall in *How to Marry a Millionaire.*

HOW TO MARRY A MILLIONAIRE

The second picture to be made in CinemaScope and the first comedy in the new process, this film also served to confirm an aspect of the talent of Marilyn Monroe that some had underrated: ability as a comedienne. As one of three models in New York City whose prime aim in life is to marry a rich man (the other two were played by Betty Grable and Lauren Bacall), she was delightful, especially in situations built around the character's myopia. (She heeded Dorothy Parker's famous axiom about men never making passes at girls who wear glasses.)

Special efforts were made to show off CinemaScope and give the customer his money's worth. In a prologue, the full 20th Century-Fox studio symphony orchestra was shown under the direction of Alfred Newman, playing his composition "Street Scene." This blended into the main titles and credits. The orchestra appeared on stage again at the end of the film.

In addition, the action was moved about the streets of New York to show views of the city in the screen's new dimensions, and there were scenes of snow-covered mountains and views taken from airplanes landing on unusually broad and lengthy air strips.

William Powell, one of the big stars of the 1930's, had a supporting role in the picture.

Producer-Writer: Nunnally Johnson. **Director:** Jean Negulesco. **Principal Players:** Marilyn Monroe, Betty Grable and Lauren Bacall. **Running time:** 96 minutes. **Released:** 20th Century-Fox.

Brandon de Wilde, Van Heflin and Alan Ladd in *Shane.*

SHANE

George Stevens' *Shane* won an immediately favorable reception from public and critics alike when it first appeared in 1953, and it has been successfully revived several times since. Whenever devotees of the western discuss the great ones of the genre, *Shane* is usually among the first to be mentioned.

The basic story has served as the plot for many an inferior western since the early days of the medium, it being the well-worn tale of homesteaders trying to farm a grant of land against the wishes of the cattle ranchers who want the range unfenced and free. The characters are stock types: the stubborn farmer (Van Heflin); the unscrupulous rancher (Emile Meyer); the "good" gunfighter on the side of the angels (Alan Ladd); and the "evil" killer aiding the villains (Jack Palance).

But Stevens took these materials and used them with such skill that, although the individual elements were hackneyed, the cumulative effect was new and overwhelming. The result was the creation of pure myth.

Shane is notable in the career of Alan Ladd as having provided him with his best role—an occasion to which he rose admirably. And, to date, it is the last screen appearance of the great comedienne of the thirties and forties, Jean Arthur, here in a straight dramatic role which she played beautifully.

Producer-Director: George Stevens. **Scriptwriter:** A. B. Guthrie, Jr. **Principal Players:** Alan Ladd, Jean Arthur, Van Heflin, Brandon de Wilde and Jack Palance. **Running time:** 118 minutes. **Released:** Paramount.

Montgomery Clift (center) and Frank Sinatra in *From Here to Eternity.*

Roman Holiday with Gregory Peck and Audrey Hepburn.

FROM HERE TO ETERNITY

The previous year had seen the advent of Cinerama; 1953 was to be the year of CinemaScope and 3-D. Yet the picture that was chosen as best of the year by many critics and the Academy was not even in color: It was the film of James Jones' best-selling novel about life in the U.S. Army prior to Pearl Harbor.

The reason was obvious: It was a modern reaffirmation of Shakespeare's theory that the play is the thing.

In this instance, it had taken more courage than usual to bring the "play" to the screen; producer Buddy Adler, director Fred Zinnemann and scriptwriter Daniel Taradash were faced with problems in transferring the Jones work to celluloid that were formidable indeed, under the strictures of the Production Code.

Yet they succeeded; they eliminated the G.I. profanity, transformed the New Congress Club from a brothel to a bar, and laundered some of the more excessive aspects of violence and sex. In the process, they retained both the essence of Jones' full-bodied and all-too-human characters and the spirit of his outraged denunciation of "Old Army" tactics that crushed the individual spirit.

The picture won eight Oscars in all, including ones for Zinnemann and Taradash. Frank Sinatra was cited as best supporting actor for his portrayal of Maggio, the cocky Italian-American soldier who defies a sadistic prison guard and is killed. (Sinatra's career was sagging at the time, and this picture revitalized it.) Donna Reed was also a winner (best supporting actress) for her performance as a dance-hall hostess. (She had been a prostitute in the book.) There were other worthy performances from Burt Lancaster, Deborah Kerr and Montgomery Clift. In fact, the whole cast could hardly have been bettered.

Commercially, as well as artistically, *From Here to Eternity* had few peers in its day.

Producer: Buddy Adler. **Director:** Fred Zinnemann. **Scriptwriter:** Daniel Taradash. **Principal Players:** Burt Lancaster, Montgomery Clift, Deborah Kerr, Frank Sinatra and Donna Reed. **Running time:** 118 minutes. **Released:** Columbia.

ROMAN HOLIDAY

Audrey Hepburn made her screen debut with a walk-on role in the British picture *Laughter in Paradise* in 1951; two years later she became a major Hollywood star in *Roman Holiday.* William Wyler was the producer-director who selected her to play a princess who kicks up her heels in Rome by touring it incognito in the company of an American journalist (acted by Gregory Peck). Miss Hepburn won an Oscar for her performance, which made her new stardom official.

The picture was photographed on location in Rome, and part of its appeal was a tour of many of the famous landmarks of the city.

Producer-Director: William Wyler. **Scriptwriter:** Ian McLellan Hunter and John Dighton. **Principal Players:** Gregory Peck, Audrey Hepburn and Eddie Albert. **Running time:** 110 minutes. **Released:** Paramount.

Michael Rennie, Victor Mature and Richard Burton in *The Robe.*

A scene from *Bwana Devil.*

THE ROBE

CinemaScope, the new film process using anamorphic lenses (see introduction), represented a tremendous gamble for the company that sponsored its introduction—20th Century-Fox. Therefore, Spyros Skouras, the president, and Darryl F. Zanuck, his production head, considered for a long time before selecting the property with which they would launch the new technique.

They finally chose Lloyd C. Douglas' novel *The Robe,* which had such elements of popular appeal as a religious subject, romance and spectacular scenes. A fictional account centering upon what happens to a number of persons who come into possession of the garment taken from Christ at the time of the crucifixion, it had been a best seller some dozen years before. Producer Frank Ross had long wanted to bring it to the screen, and finally the time seemed ripe.

With CinemaScope and the Lloyd book as box-office magnets, it was not deemed necessary to cast the film with major stars. Richard Burton, then virtually unknown, was hired for the romantic lead, and his co-stars were Jean Simmons, Victor Mature and Michael Rennie—none of them ever in the running for top box-office status.

The gamble paid off; both CinemaScope and *The Robe* were a hit. (The New York *Daily News,* in an unprecedented move, gave the picture eight stars—four for the process and four for the story!)

Seen today, *The Robe* appears to many as just another inflated spectacle in which the characters are swamped by the pomp and circumstance. But when it made its debut, it was awe-inspiring, thanks to the "modern miracle you see without the use of glasses" (as the ads described CinemaScope).

Producer: Frank Ross. **Director:** Henry Koster. **Screenwriter:** Philip Dunne. **Principal Players:** Richard Burton, Jean Simmons, Victor Mature, Michael Rennie and Jay Robinson. **Running time:** 135 minutes. **Released:** 20th Century-Fox.

BWANA DEVIL

Produced, directed and written by Arch Oboler, this film has historical importance for one reason only: It was the first feature-length dramatic film made especially for three-dimensional projection. As such it enjoyed a huge success; audiences were not averse to donning the spectacles necessary to produce the 3-D effect. Later the novelty wore off, and films designed for three dimensions were released in two, or "flat."

For the record, the film was set in Africa, and the plot concerned a couple of lions which put a stop to the building of a railroad by devouring the workmen, until the animals were killed by a white engineer. Robert Stack starred as the latter character, and Barbara Britton and Nigel Bruce were the other principal players. The film was denied a Production Code seal because of a frank love scene between Stack and Miss Britton.

Producer-Director-Writer: Arch Oboler. **Principal Players:** Robert Stack, Barbara Britton and Nigel Bruce. **Running time:** 79 minutes. **Released:** Natural Vision.

Yves Montand in *Wages of Fear.*

William Holden, Maggie McNamara and David Niven in *The Moon Is Blue.*

WAGES OF FEAR

Two films from France dominated imports from that country in the decade of the 1950's, and both came from the same producer-director, Henri Clouzot. *Wages of Fear* arrived first in the U.S.; *Diabolique* was to follow.

Clouzot took the novel *Le Salarie de la Peur* by Georges Arnaud and turned it into a brilliant exercise in cinematic suspense, as well as a study in greed and fear—with an ending that pointed up the irony of fate.

The setting is a small village in Central America where the major business is oil, run by U.S. interests. The plot centers around an offer made by the American company to four men of various nationalities—two Frenchmen, one Italian and one Dutchman—to drive two trucks loaded with nitroglycerine over hazardous roads to the fields. Only one man survives the journey, but he, too, is killed in an accident on the way back.

The original version of the picture ran for over two hours, but it was cut to 106 minutes for the American market, most of the deleted footage being from the early part of the film, expanding the characterizations of the four principals. The complete version was finally released in the U.S. in 1967, but it did not repeat the success of the first.

Wages of Fear is also significant as the first film in which the large American public saw Yves Montand, who played one of the two Frenchmen.

Producer-Director-Writer: Henri Clouzot. **Principal Players:** Yves Montand, Charles Vanel, Peter Van Eyck and Folco Lulli. **Running time:** 106 minutes. **Released:** International Affiliates.

THE MOON IS BLUE

Erosion of the Production Code of the industry was a slow process, but the first really severe damage dates from this picture based on a Broadway bedroom farce by F. Hugh Herbert.

Otto Preminger, who had staged the enormously successful play, also directed (and produced) the movie, making it as close an approximation of the original as possible.

Thus, for the first time, American movie audiences could see and hear for themselves the type of sex comedy that Broadway audiences had been accustomed to for years. Any that had previously reached the screen at all had undergone considerable expurgation. This factor, and the controversy surrounding the picture, helped turn it into a big hit of the year.

Unable to obtain a Code Seal, which was denied equally on grounds of subject matter and treatment (the seduction of a virgin, handled frivolously), as well as language (the phrase "professional virgin" was found offensive), the distributors released it anyway. Thus the Code was dealt a debilitating blow.

Today, *The Moon Is Blue* seems mild indeed in its treatment of sex, including its discussion of methods of seduction (a comparison of its merits and demerits), which shocked some people in 1953.

Producer-Director: Otto Preminger. **Scriptwriter:** F. Hugh Herbert. **Principal Players:** William Holden, David Niven and Maggie McNamara. **Running time:** 99 minutes. **Released:** United Artists.

Lee J. Cobb and Marlon Brando in *On the Waterfront,* Elia Kazan's famous exposé of union racketeering in which Brando gave one of the screen's top all-time performances.

1954

This year marked the low point in four decades of film making in Hollywood. Releases fell 22 percent from the year before. Productions made in Hollywood totalled only 232. This may be compared with 369 features in 1950; 470 in 1940; and 503 in 1935.

The gloom in all branches of the industry was moderated by two factors. First, a reduction in the Federal Admissions Tax from 20 percent to 10 percent on all tickets over 50¢ was passed by Congress. This meant that approximately half the theatres in the United States, some 9,000, now paid no Federal Admission Tax at all. In towns with populations under 7,500, the prevailing average admissions were: adults, 40¢ and children, 14¢; in cities over 100,000, the average was 54¢ for adults and 16¢ for children.

The second encouraging factor was of more interest, directly, to producers and distributors than to American theatre owners: The foreign market for U.S. films was the best since World War II. Actually, this increasing source of revenue to the major companies was important in sustaining even the low level of production at Hollywood. Without the foreign revenues, U.S. exhibitors would have been in even more desperate shape. What was happening was that film taste was becoming increasingly international. A film successful on Broadway or Bad Axe, Michigan, was likely to be a success in Paris, Timahoe or Timbuktu.

On the other side of the coin, there was a slowly growing acceptance of foreign films by U.S. audiences. Many of the imported films not only had problems getting booked by exhibitors and attracting moviegoers, but they also had to overcome some formidable legal obstacles. It is disputable whether censor boards were more strict on imports than Hollywood releases. In any event, it was a group of films from abroad which brought landmark court decisions overriding the censors. In the process, full freedom of the screen was gradually achieved.

In 1954, the Supreme Court cleared the way for the exhibition of two films, *M* and *La Ronde.* These decisions struck down the censors' use of "immorality" as a standard of objection. The Supreme Court held that "immorality" was too vague a term to restrict exhibition of a film. These decisions, following the earlier ones on *The Miracle* and *Pinky,* pointed the way to a growing sentiment of extending to films the same constitutional protection as that enjoyed by the press.

In a film of the same name, Bing Crosby sang what had already become one of the most popular songs of all times, "White Christmas." A standard since its appearance in *Holiday Inn* in 1942, the constant repetition of the song on innumerable radio programs unquestionably was a promotional factor in helping the motion picture. *20,000 Leagues Under the Sea* was another film that delighted millions. It profited from the huge audience of the Walt Disney television show. Audrey Hepburn was selected by exhibitors as the top "Star of Tomorrow." *On the Waterfront* was a success with both critics and the public. It ushered in a trend to increased realism in some American films.

Nicholas Schenck, president of MGM when Loew's Theatres was formed into a separate company, as required by the consent decree settling the Government's antitrust suit, repeated a classic remark, "Some years ago I said that there is nothing wrong with this industry that good pictures cannot cure. This still goes!" The only trouble was that it was very difficult to make a good picture.

Two deaths made members of the industry think back to a less troubled time, often referred to as the "Golden Age of Hollywood." Will H. Hays, president from 1922 to 1946 of the industry association often referred to as the "Hays Office"; and Terry Ramsaye, author of *A Million and One Nights,* a history of the silent screen, and a long-time editor and writer on film subjects, died during the year.

Stars of the year: John Wayne, Martin & Lewis, Gary Cooper, James Stewart, Marilyn Monroe, Alan Ladd, William Holden, Bing Crosby, Jane Wyman and Marlon Brando.

Judy Garland in *A Star Is Born.*

A STAR IS BORN

Judy Garland had been absent from the screen for four years when she returned in a blaze of glory in *A Star Is Born,* singing and dancing better than ever before, and giving a dramatic performance that fulfilled the promise she had shown almost ten years earlier in *The Clock* (1945).

The vehicle selected for her return did not at first glance seem an auspicious one. It was a remake of David O. Selznick's 1937 film of the same name. The first *A Star Is Born* was an original script by Dorothy Parker, Alan Campbell and Robert Carson, and although it was a well-deserved success in its day, its contrived plotting (the rise of one star simultaneously with the fall of another) and its sentimental backstage look at Hollywood seemed too much of another era, and not especially suited to updating.

The fears were ungrounded. Moss Hart did a new script, modernizing the Hollywood milieu carefully, treading lightly in the sentimental areas, and integrating music into the story with ease by making the heroine a musical comedy star. He even retained the heroine's immortal final line of dialogue: As she steps up to the microphone at a Hollywood benefit for her first public utterance since the death of her husband, she introduces herself not as Vicki Lester but with the greeting, "Hello, everybody, this is Mrs. Norman Maine." Along with everything else, it worked beautifully.

Miss Garland, in the role created by Janet Gaynor, was simply magnificent, whether singing the haunting ballad "The Man That Got Away" or playing an emotional scene with Charles Bickford (as her producer), in which she pleads with him to help her husband make a comeback. Under the tactful direction of George Cukor, she dominates the picture, but not so much that it ever becomes just a one-woman show.

James Mason played the old Fredric March role of the husband whose career goes on the skids as his wife's ascends under his guidance. It is often referred to as his finest performance.

When first released in New York, at two theatres and advanced admission prices, *A Star Is Born* ran for three hours and two minutes. Reviewers and critics were virtually unanimous in praising the film, also pointing out that it was so entertaining it did not seem nearly so long as it actually was. But exhibitors in other cities complained to the distributor about the film, which they regarded as too long, both for their audiences to sit comfortably through, and to play an adequate number of performances each day.

Cuts totaling twenty-eight minutes were made in deference to the showmen but to the annoyance of many others, including the influential *New York Times* critic, Bosley Crowther. He said the deletions turned *A Star Is Born* into quite a different picture from the one he had seen first, and he refused for that reason to include it on his Ten-Best list.

Producer: Sidney Luft. **Director:** George Cukor. **Screenplay:** Moss Hart. **Principal Players:** Judy Garland, James Mason, Jack Carson and Charles Bickford. **Running time:** 155 minutes. **Released:** Warner Bros.

James Stewart in *Rear Window.*

REAR WINDOW

Always eager to experiment with film technique (in *Rope* it was with the continuous reel-long take, with no cuts or dissolves; in *Lifeboat* it was confining the action to a single set), Alfred Hitchcock here set himself a new problem. He shot the entire picture from the restricted viewpoint of its hero, a magazine photographer laid up with a broken leg in his Greenwich Village apartment. From his window, he spies on his neighbors and eventually comes to suspect—rightly—that one of them is guilty of murder.

The audience is allowed to see only what James Stewart, playing the hero, sees: the funny and poignant moments in the lives of the tenants, none of whom bothers ever to pull down his shades. Stewart views them all through field glasses and telescopic camera lenses.

For some of the critics all this was too contrived and didn't work out well, but the public disagreed, being enchanted by the story idea as well as by the star appeal of Stewart and Grace Kelly, whose cool beauty was never so attractively displayed as here.

Helpful support was supplied by Thelma Ritter, in a typical role as a talkative masseuse with a tart opinion on every subject from marriage to psychiatry to murder.

Producer-Director: Alfred Hitchcock. **Scriptwriter:** John Michael Hayes. **Principal Players:** James Stewart, Grace Kelly, Wendell Corey and Thelma Ritter. **Running time:** 112 minutes. **Released:** Paramount.

Humphrey Bogart, Robert Francis and Van Johnson in *The Caine Mutiny.*

THE CAINE MUTINY

Stanley Kramer, who had sprung to fame at United Artists by producing such pictures as *Champion* and *Home of the Brave,* left that company to go to Columbia in 1951. There he made a series of small but often interesting films that, unfortunately, never found very large audiences (*Death of a Salesman, Member of the Wedding, The Juggler,* etc.). His last picture under the Columbia arrangement was *The Caine Mutiny,* which, ironically, turned out to be a huge box-office success. (He was to return to Columbia over a decade later to make *Ship of Fools* and *Guess Who's Coming to Dinner.*)

The source of this film was a novel by Herman Wouk which won a Pulitzer Prize and was turned into a Broadway play called *The Caine Mutiny Court Martial,* which, as the title indicates, confined itself to only a part of the novel—the climactic trial sequence.

The U.S. Navy objected to the film being made, because the Navy asserted—incorrectly—that there never had been a mutiny in its history, and it did not like a Naval officer being portrayed as a coward, in the person of the fictional Captain Queeg. Scriptwriter Stanley Roberts sought to get around this by indicating, during and after the court martial, that while Queeg (played by Humphrey Bogart) may have been a sick man, he was basically a good officer who had been victimized by subordinates. The character played by Fred MacMurray, Lt. Keefer, worked on the suspicions and uncertainties of Queeg's executive officer (Van Johnson), until the latter, convinced it was the only way to

Mr. Hulot's Holiday with Jacques Tati (left).

20,000 Leagues Under the Sea with James Mason, Kirk Douglas, Peter Lorre, and Paul Lukas.

save the minesweeper *Caine* and the men aboard it, relieved Queeg of command at the height of a typhoon, believing that he was acting within Naval regulations.

Special effects for the storm at sea were excellent, and the all-star cast performed competently with a special nod to José Ferrer for his performance as the attorney for the junior officers charged with mutiny. The film was nominated for an Oscar as best of the year, but the award went to another Columbia release, *On the Waterfront.*

Producer: Stanley Kramer. **Director:** Edward Dmytryk. **Scriptwriter:** Stanley Roberts. **Principal Players:** Humphrey Bogart, José Ferrer, Van Johnson and Fred MacMurray. **Running time:** 125 minutes. **Released:** Columbia.

MR. HULOT'S HOLIDAY

Famed as actor and pantomimist in his native France, Jacques Tati never acquired similar popularity in the U.S., although he was much admired by art theatre patrons in the 1950's. This picture is generally considered the best example on film of his skill. He produced, directed, co-authored and starred in it! (*Jour de Fête* had been seen in 1947, and *Mon Oncle* was to come in 1958.)

None of his pictures had any plot, and this was no exception, being a film of visual comedy and sight gags. Tati appeared as a likable if pompous boob on vacation at the seashore, and from the vantage point of his quadruple film-making role, he poked fun at certain character "types"—the couple who collect sea shells, the retired British colonel who takes charge of organizing recreational groups, an old maid and a stout businessman. The picture won the Grand Prize at the Cannes Festival.

Producer-Director-Writer: Jacques Tati. **Principal Players:** Tati, Nathalie Pascaud, Michele Rolla and Valentine Camax. **Running time:** 85 minutes. **Released:** G-B-D International Films.

20,000 LEAGUES UNDER THE SEA

The CinemaScope cameras had been taken underwater earlier (*Beneath the 12-Mile Reef* in 1953), but never so effectively as in this Walt Disney adaptation of the Jules Verne novel. The most impressive sequence was of the battle between a giant squid and the crew of the submarine *Nautilus,* but there was plenty of visual excitement as well in a tour of the wonders of the deep, given the heroes by the villainous Captain Nemo. Not surprisingly, the film won an Oscar for its special effects.

Richard Fleischer directed an all-male cast headed by Kirk Douglas, James Mason, Paul Lukas and Peter Lorre. Fleischer made an even better science fiction film over a decade later—*Fantastic Voyage,* which was not, however, as commercially successful as *20,000 Leagues.*

Producer: Walt Disney. **Director:** Richard Fleischer. **Scriptwriter:** Earl Felton. **Principal Players:** Kirk Douglas, James Mason, Paul Lukas and Peter Lorre. **Running time:** 128 minutes. **Released:** Buena Vista.

Howard Keel and Jane Powell in the film *Seven Brides for Seven Brothers.*

Three Coins in the Fountain with Maggie McNamara and Jean Peters.

SEVEN BRIDES FOR SEVEN BROTHERS

The new era for creative film musicals that had been launched in 1949 with *On the Town,* reached its highest point with *Singin' in the Rain* in 1952, but picked up new speed with *The Band Wagon* in 1953, and hit another peak with this delightful example of the genre a year later. Since *Brides,* however, first-rate musicals written directly for the screen have been hard to come by; most of those in the 1960's were adaptations of "safe" Broadway hits. *Brides* is a picture to treasure.

The idea for the film, in which a family of American farmers apply coercive tactics in order to secure brides for themselves, patterned after the treatment Caesar's legions gave the Sabine women, came from a story by Stephen Vincent Benét ("The Sobbin' Women"). It was freshly and amusingly developed for the screen by Albert Hackett, Frances Goodrich and Dorothy Kingsley. Johnny Mercer supplied some catchy tunes—"When You're in Love," "Wonderful, Wonderful Day," "Bless Your Beautiful Hide" and "Goin' Courtin'."

Stanley Donen directed with his usual aplomb, but the real hero of the occasion was Michael Kidd, whose dances—especially a hoe-down number performed at a barn raising—were brilliantly original.

Jane Powell and Howard Keel were the nominal stars and they sang with gusto, although both were a bit wooden in the emotional scenes toward the end. The other brides were played by six charming newcomers—Julie Newmeyer, Nancy Kilgas, Virginia Gibson, Rita Kilmonis, Norma Doggett and Betty Carr—none of whom, alas, was ever heard from again. Adolph Deutsch and Saul Chaplin shared an Oscar for their scoring.

Producer: Jack Cummings. **Director:** Stanley Donen. **Scriptwriters:** Albert Hackett, Frances Goodrich and Dorothy Kingsley. **Principal Players:** Howard Keel and Jane Powell. **Running time:** 103 minutes. **Released:** MGM.

THREE COINS IN THE FOUNTAIN

As a travelogue in color CinemaScope, this picture had solid merit; as a romantic comedy it was lacking in originality and wit. The virtues of the first element were sufficient to overcome the deficiencies of the latter, and *Three Coins in the Fountain* was responsible for new influxes of tourists to Italy to see for themselves the lovely vistas shown in the film.

The John Patrick screenplay had a simple structure: Boy meets girl, loses her and then wins her—all in triplicate. The girls were played by Dorothy McGuire, Jean Peters and Maggie McNamara; the boyfriends by Clifton Webb, Louis Jourdan and Rossano Brazzi.

The picture opens with a view of Rome, and Frank Sinatra singing the title song—a melody that became as popular as the movie, and won an Oscar for best song.

Producer: Sol C. Siegel. **Director:** Jean Negulesco. **Scriptwriter:** John Patrick. **Principal Players:** Clifton Webb, Dorothy McGuire, Jean Peters, Louis Jourdan, Maggie McNamara and Rossano Brazzi. **Running time:** 102 minutes. **Released:** 20th Century-Fox.

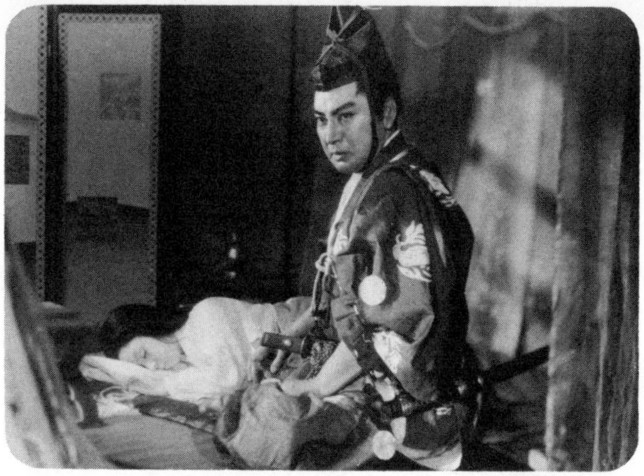

A scene from the Japanese film *Gate of Hell.*

Rod Steiger and Marlon Brando in *On the Waterfront.*

GATE OF HELL

Two Academy Awards—one for best foreign film and one for color costume design—went to this picture set in twelfth-century Japan. It should also have been cited for its cinematography, art direction and set decoration, which are superb.

Many Hollywood film makers have been accused of overwhelming a simple story with elaborate production values. The Japanese managed to turn that vice into a virtue, here.

The plot is concerned with the lust of a feudal warlord for a woman married to another. Thinking to win her by killing off the husband, the warrior plunges his sword into a sleeping figure—which turns out to be the wife, who has deliberately sacrified herself that her husband might be spared. Overcome with remorse, the warrior begs the husband to slay him, but the husband refuses, and the warrior goes off to become a monk.

Possibly this Oriental soap opera has deeper meaning for the Japanese than for Americans. The latter, however, could find compensation for lack of emotional inspiration in the dazzling color compositions, which were like fine Japanese prints come to life, and in the physical excitement of some frenzied battle scenes.

Gate of Hell also won the Grand Prize at the 1954 international film festival at Cannes.

Producer: Masaichi Nagata. **Director-Writer:** Teinosuke Kinugasa. **Principal Players:** Kazuo Hasegawa, Machiko Kyo and Isao Yamagata. **Running time:** 89 minutes. **Released:** Edward Harrison.

ON THE WATERFRONT

A stickler for realism in milieu as well as in human behavior in his plays and films, Elia Kazan carried his methods to their ultimate expression in what many consider his finest picture, *On the Waterfront.* Intended as an exposé of union racketeering on the docks of New York and New Jersey, as well as a crime thriller, it was more successful in the latter aim than the former, which tended to be superficial and unconvincing.

Highly praised by the critics, who mostly ignored or glossed over its failings, the picture won no less than eight Oscars: for best picture, best actor (Marlon Brando), best supporting actress (Eva Marie Saint), direction (Kazan), writing (Budd Schulberg), cinematography (Boris Kaufman), editing (Gene Milford) and art direction (Richard Day).

Surely the best-deserved of these was the one that went to Brando, who had been bypassed in 1951 for his performance in *A Streetcar Named Desire.* This was in many ways an even greater performance, the role of the not-too-bright, but earnest and well-meaning ex-prize fighter being more complex and realistic than that of Stanley Kowalski. Brando's big scene in the taxicab with Rod Steiger (as his brother, the lawyer to a corrupt labor leader), in which he sums up the disillusionment of an entire wasted life, was masterfully played.

Producer: Sam Spiegel. **Director:** Elia Kazan. **Scriptwriter:** Budd Schulberg. **Principal Players:** Marlon Brando, Eva Marie Saint, Rod Steiger and Karl Malden. **Running time:** 108 minutes. **Released:** Columbia.

Ernest Borgnine (right) in *Marty,* the Academy-Award winner which started a trend in Hollywood of adapting television plays to the movie screen.

1955

This year, exhibitors raised a hue and cry for more features, and when producers showed no indication of increasing production, exhibitors themselves tried to organize to make films.

There were many reasons for the steady and alarming decline in Hollywood activity. As a result of the divorcement of the five major national exhibition circuits from production and distribution, the five largest studios no longer had large, guaranteed markets. In former days, with cross-licensing and franchise deals between the five major companies, even a poor film was assured of thousands of engagements. Under the new system, with circuits independent of film making, and with films sold one by one, theatre by theatre (at least in theory), a really bad picture might get few theatre bookings. This meant that there was no "bottom" to the potential gross, and as a result, conditions deteriorated to the point at which only one feature in five was profitable.

The leading stars and a number of prominent directors, producers and writers put additional pressure on the studios. These film makers began to demand higher and higher participation deals. They did not want to work for set salaries but wanted guaranteed revenues and a "piece of the action," i.e., a partnership in the film's net or, in some cases, the gross. This development ran up the cost of production to astronomical figures, and also caused increased delays. This was, of course, an essential change in what had been a simple employer-employee relationship. Enjoying a participation, a personality wanted to have a say in everything, from script and costumes to advertising copy and distribution policy.

James Stewart's early films made on participation were reported to be the most profitable for any actor up to that time. Marlon Brando was another leader in insisting on "tough" partnership deals, demanding—and getting—a control never previously enjoyed by any actor who was not his own producer, like Charles Chaplin.

Senator Estes Kefauver caused film industry leaders many anxious moments with hearings in Los Angeles and in Washington on the relationship between films and juvenile delinquency. Millions of words of testimony produced no unanimous conclusions, and the debate continued on and on.

Another Washington figure of influence at this time was H. J. Anslinger, Commissioner of Narcotics, who repeatedly said, "Dope films make addicts." Eventually a number of "dope" films were made, but no one has proved in this area, nor in any other, a causal relationship between scenes in a film and the subsequent conduct of spectators.

This year the first conglomerate took a position in the U.S. film industry. General Tire, run by members of the O'Neil family, took over RKO and promptly did two things: First, produced fifteen unsuccessful theatrical films—they were too expensive to be "small" films and not good enough to be "blockbusters"; and secondly, sold the large RKO backlog of features to television. This opened the floodgates for a rush of such sales. It made irrelevant the hard-won Federal Court victory in which Judge Leon H. Yankwich ruled that the film companies could not be required (by the Department of Justice) to sell films to television.

The Council of Motion Picture Organizations, popularly known as COMPO, in which all facets of the industry were represented, took an audience poll with these results: Best Picture of the Year, *Mister Roberts;*

Best Actor, James Dean in *East of Eden;* Best Actress, Jennifer Jones in *Love Is a Many Splendored Thing;* Most Promising Newcomers, Tab Hunter in *Battle Cry* and *The Track of the Cat,* and Peggy Lee in *Pete Kelly's Blues.*

Oklahoma! was brought out in the Todd-AO process, a system using a wide-angle lens, wide film and multi-magnetic tracks for stereophonic sound.

Stars of the year: James Stewart, Grace Kelly, John Wayne, William Holden, Gary Cooper, Marlon Brando, Martin & Lewis, Humphrey Bogart, June Allyson and Clark Gable.

Ernest Borgnine and Esther Minciotti in *Marty.*

Henry Fonda and James Cagney in *Mister Roberts.*

MARTY

In 1955, Hollywood turned to its erstwhile enemy, television, for source material. One of the first properties that had already been seen on TV was Paddy Chayefsky's *Marty.* He himself rewrote and expanded it for the theatrical version and also acted as associate producer.

It was made on a very low budget and turned out to be a real sleeper, not only captivating large audiences, but also winning the Oscar as best picture of the year. Hollywood was caught by surprise, but recovered quickly and started exploring other TV playlets for possible reincarnation on the big screen.

An Oscar also went to Ernest Borgnine, who previously had been seen only as a minor heavy. As the lonely Bronx butcher who has almost given up all thoughts of romance until he meets a girl as unhappy as he, Borgnine proved he could create a warm and sympathetic character as well as villainous ones.

Outstanding among the elements in the film were those showing Borgnine at home with his Italian mother who objects to his interest in the girl; the quiet unfolding of communication between ordinary hero and heroine; and sequences of domestic mother-in-law trouble involving Borgnine's aunt and married cousin.

Chayefsky also won an Oscar for his screenplay, and Delbert Mann was similarly cited for his direction.

Producer: Harold Hecht. **Director:** Delbert Mann. **Scriptwriter:** Paddy Chayefsky. **Principal Players:** Ernest Borgnine, Betsy Blair, Esther Minciotti and Augusta Ciolli. **Running time:** 91 minutes. **Released:** United Artists.

MISTER ROBERTS

Drama critic George Jean Nathan once dismissed this Thomas Heggen-Joshua Logan stage hit as a "boys' school play gone to sea," but it was a spectacularly long-running show on Broadway, and the motion picture did equally well. The major change in its translation from stage to screen was the deletion of some of the bawdier language.

The setting is a Navy supply ship doomed to stagnation in the back waters of the war in the Pacific, and the title character is an intelligent and efficient young officer who longs to get into combat. Henry Fonda repeated his Broadway role on the screen. His chief antagonist is the captain of the ship—a petty-minded tyrant whom James Cagney played on film with some of the old gusto and mannerisms he brought to his legendary portrayals of hoodlums.

Overshadowing both of them in the picture was Jack Lemmon as Ensign Pulver, a flighty fellow assigned to laundry and morale boosting, who longs for the romantic adventures he had in civilian life. His broadly comic performance won Lemmon the Oscar as best supporting actor.

Two directors worked on the picture, with Mervyn LeRoy taking over the reins from John Ford after the latter became ill.

Producer: Leland Hayward. **Directors:** John Ford and Mervyn LeRoy. **Scriptwriters:** Frank Nugent and Joshua Logan. **Principal Players:** Henry Fonda, James Cagney, William Powell and Jack Lemmon. **Running time:** 123 minutes. **Released:** Warner Bros.

Vera Clouzot and Simone Signoret in *Diabolique.*

I'll Cry Tomorrow with Susan Hayward and Richard Conte.

DIABOLIQUE

Having frightened American audiences out of their wits with *The Wages of Fear,* Henri-Georges Clouzot followed that suspenseful melodrama with this mystery film, which ends in unmitigated horror. True Grand Guignol, in fact.

He began his assault on the audience's nerves early with a gruesome murder, then baffled them as to the whereabouts of the corpse, and finally built up to his blood-curdling and surprising climax.

Clouzot also developed here several plot gimmicks that have been much copied by other film makers—including a murder that is not really a murder and a twist in the ending which reveals that one of the conspirators in the slaying has been double-crossed.

The cast included Simone Signoret as a cold-blooded murderess; Vera Clouzot as a weak-willed one; and Paul Meurisse as their odious victim (though not really).

Producer-Director: Henri-Georges Clouzot. **Scriptwriters:** Clouzot and G. Geronimi. **Principal Players:** Simone Signoret, Vera Clouzot, Paul Meurisse and Charles Vanel. **Running time:** 107 minutes. **Released:** United Motion Picture Organization.

I'LL CRY TOMORROW

Lillian Roth did not spare the sordid details of her own private life and singing career, both of which were ruined by alcoholism, in the book she wrote with two collaborators, Mike Connolly and Gerold Frank. And MGM did not soften the unpleasant aspects of her story in transferring *I'll Cry Tomorrow* to the screen.

Essentially it is a soap opera, a sad tale of many domestic and professional crises which has a typical happy ending, courtesy of Alcoholics Anonymous. But the picture was given unusual integrity by two factors: a stunningly realistic performance by Susan Hayward as Miss Roth, and direction by newcomer Daniel Mann that avoided bathos most of the way.

Part of Miss Roth's problem was an ambitious "stage mother," and this role was played in three dimensions by the brilliant Jo Van Fleet. She made the woman despicable and pathetic at the same time.

In contrast, the men in Miss Roth's screen life were stock types: Don Taylor, the weak one; Richard Conte, the sadist; Eddie Albert, the sympathetic rehabilitator; and so on.

Producer: Lawrence Weingarten. **Director:** Daniel Mann. **Scriptwriters:** Helen Deutsch and Jay Richard Kennedy. **Principal Players:** Susan Hayward, Richard Conte, Eddie Albert, Jo Van Fleet, Don Taylor and Ray Danton. **Running time:** 117 minutes. **Released:** MGM.

RIFIFI

Jules Dassin is the one who started it all, with *Rififi*—started the endless series of films in which all the steps in the planning, execution and consequences of a difficult robbery are shown in explicit detail. Although an American director (*Reunion in France, Canterville*

Rififi with Perlo Vita (Jules Dassin) in the background, center.

Rebel Without a Cause with James Dean (center).

Ghost, Brute Force, etc.), he made this picture in France. Subtitles did not keep it from being highly successful in the U.S.

The robbery itself (of a jewelry store) is depicted in a twenty-minute sequence completely devoid of any dialogue or background music. The only sound effects are those provided by the four thieves working at their trade. Critics thought the episode a tour de force.

Dassin also played one of the leads in the film, a safecracker imported from Italy, but he chose to be credited in this capacity as Perlo Vita.

"Rififi," by the way, is French slang, roughly translated as "trouble" or "brawl."

Producer: Rene G. Vuattoux. **Director:** Jules Dassin. **Scriptwriters:** Jules Dassin, Auguste le Breton and Rene Wheeler. **Principal Players:** Jean Servais, Carl Mohner, Robert Manuel and Perlo Vita. **Running time:** 118 minutes. **Released:** United Motion Picture Organization.

REBEL WITHOUT A CAUSE

As another entry in the juvenile delinquency sweepstakes, *Rebel Without a Cause* broke new ground by focusing not on the teenagers of the slums, but on the children of the well-to-do. It did not cause the uproar *Blackboard Jungle* did—perhaps because it was released later in the same year.

What set it apart also were three remarkable performances from James Dean, Natalie Wood and Sal Mineo, playing youngsters whose parents neglect them in different ways. Their portrayals were poignant and true to life.

Unfortunately, the script of Nicholas Ray (who also directed) tended to make the issue of blame a matter of black and white. The children were all misunderstood, and the parents all guilty of sins (either of omission or commission) against their offspring.

The picture was released a few weeks after the tragic death of James Dean in an automobile accident. His final film, *Giant,* was released a year later. *Rebel* proved that an extraordinary acting career could have been expected of him, had he lived.

Producer: David Weisbart. **Director-Writer:** Nicholas Ray. **Principal Players:** James Dean, Natalie Wood, Jim Backus, Ann Doran, William Hopper, Rochelle Hudson and Sal Mineo. **Running time:** 111 minutes. **Released:** Warner Bros.

PATHER PANCHALI

Indian films were virtually unknown in the Western world when Satyajit Ray burst on the international scene in 1956 at Cannes with *Pather Panchali* (*Song of the Road*), which was voted the "best human document." From here, it went on to win awards at San Francisco and Vancouver, and to be acclaimed by the world's critics.

Its initial reception in the U.S., however, was not auspicious. Some of the more influential reviewers found its slow pacing and deliberate accumulation of detail oppressive and boring, as it recounted the struggles of

A still from Satyajit Ray's *Pather Panchali.*

The Blackboard Jungle with Glenn Ford.

a peasant family to survive. Not until the other two films of the Ray trilogy appeared—*The Unvanquished* in 1957 and *The World of Apu* in 1959—did the first one get its due recognition. In recent years, the three films have been booked in American theatres as a unit. It makes for a long, but rewarding, afternoon and evening.

Ray based the scripts for the first two films on a two-volume novel by Bibhuti Banerji, but the film maker let his own imagination run free for the final film, *Apu.* And some critics thought that picture the best of the three.

Producer-Director-Writer: Satyajit Ray. **Principal Players:** Kanu Banerji, Karuna Banerji, Subir Banerji, Runki Banerji and Umas Das Gupta. **Running time:** 122 minutes. **Released:** Edward Harrison.

THE BLACKBOARD JUNGLE

American schools were already in trouble in 1955, as was sharply brought to public attention in this film depicting conditions in a big-city vocational school, showing it to be a breeding ground for hoodlums. The strongest response the picture evoked at the time was not outrage at the frightening situation exposed, but indignation that it should be shown in theatres abroad. Claire Booth Luce, then Ambassador to Italy, was in the forefront of political figures who demanded that it not be released in other countries, on the grounds that it presented an unflattering image of the U.S.

The screenplay was built around the experiences of a young teacher (excellently played by Glenn Ford) in his first job at a run-down high school in a slum area. His students were undisciplined and aggressively hostile, and their abuse was both verbal and physical, the latter consisting of beating him up, after he has had jailed a student caught in an attempted rape. Finally he is able to get through to one black student, awakening in him a dormant sense of decency. Sidney Poitier played this role, in one of his earliest screen performances.

Although the picture did not probe very deeply into the causes of the school crisis, it pointed up aspects of the problem in vividly melodramatic terms. One telling comment from Ford's dialogue concerned salaries of educators: "A teacher makes the same as a soda jerk and no more than a prostitute."

Producer: Pandro S. Berman. **Director-Writer:** Richard Brooks. **Principal Players:** Glenn Ford, Anne Francis, Louis Calhern, Richard Kiley, Sidney Poitier, Vic Morrow and Rafael Campos. **Running time:** 101 minutes. **Released:** MGM.

THE NIGHT OF THE HUNTER

To be anomalous is to deviate from the general rule or norm, and if ever a film epitomized that description, it is *The Night of the Hunter.*

One wonders how such a strange and symbol-laden script (adapted by the critic James Agee from a novel by Davis Grubb) ever was produced in Hollywood. Basically, it is a suspense tale of two youngsters running from a killer, but the emphasis was on the character-

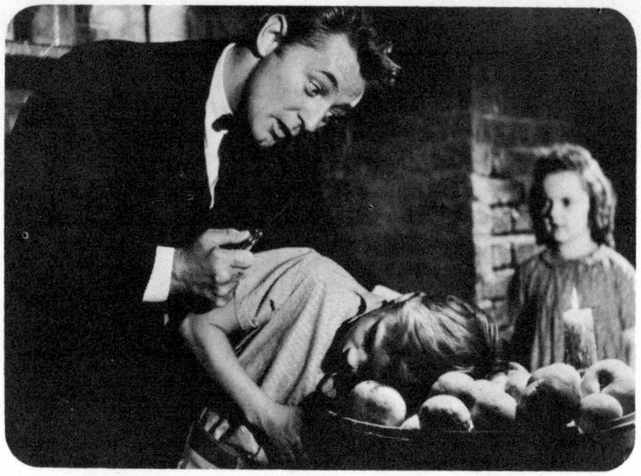

The Night of the Hunter with Robert Mitchum, Billy Chapin and Sally Jane Bruce.

Umberto D with Carlo Battisti and Maria Pia Casilio.

izations of these three and others involved briefly in their story. The story ultimately was subordinated also to the creation of a sombre and ominous mood.

In fact, Charles Laughton, whose first and only film directorial job this was, showed himself a master of atmosphere. A majority of the scenes were staged at night, and the evocation of impending horror was superb.

For another unconventional aspect, Robert Mitchum was cast "against type" as the murderer with a religious fixation. It was his most unusual role, and he performed commendably.

Not surprisingly, the film did not do well commercially, and its admirers place it among the select few pictures that were ahead of their time.

The producer was Paul Gregory, the stage entrepreneur who had brought *Don Juan in Hell, John Brown's Body* and *The Caine Mutiny Court Martial* to Broadway. Laughton had directed all three stage ventures.

Producer: Paul Gregory. **Director:** Charles Laughton. **Scriptwriter:** James Agee. **Principal Players:** Robert Mitchum, Shelley Winters, Lillian Gish, Evelyn Varden, Peter Graves, Billy Chapin and Sally Jane Bruce. **Running time:** 93 minutes. **Released:** United Artists.

UMBERTO D

Although *Umberto D* was completed and released abroad in 1952, it did not reach the U.S. until late in 1955. The major reason: Old age as subject matter has never been box-office material, and probably never will be.

It is one of three great films directed by Vittorio De Sica; the others are *Shoeshine* and *Bicycle Thief.* Like them, it is a "slice-of-life" movie photographed primarily on the streets of an Italian city (in this instance Rome), with non-professionals in the leading roles. Also, like the others, it tells a simple story of a crisis in the life of one of the "little people" of the world. Umberto Domenico Ferrari (the protagonist's full name) is an old man of seventy, a former government employee who has been retired on a pension which is inadequate for his needs. His problem is a commonplace but desperate one—to obtain enough money to pay his overdue rent bill since he has been threatened with eviction by his landlady. In the end he fails and is forced out into the street, completely alone and friendless except for his mongrel dog.

Out of this very ordinary situation, De Sica has made an extraordinary picture which is notable for its penetrating characterization of a courageous old man with human failings and virtues that everyone recognizes as true. (Carlo Battisti is marvelous in the part.) And through this character, De Sica eloquently conveys both the pathos and the triumph of the aged everywhere—the loneliness, fatigue and fear of illness, balanced by courage, dignity and will to survive.

Producer-Director: Vittorio De Sica. **Scriptwriters:** Vittorio De Sica and Cesare Zavattini. **Principal Players:** Carlo Battisti, Maria Pia Casilio and Lina Gennari. **Running time:** 89 minutes. **Released:** Edward Harrison.

Cantinflas and David Niven in *Around the World in 80 Days,* Mike Todd's all-star extravaganza based on the Jules Verne classic and one of the first films in Todd-AO.

1956

Following the initial sale in 1955 of major company features to television by RKO, 1956 witnessed a veritable avalanche, to the consternation of theatre owners. More than 2,500 major motion pictures became available for broadcast to home TV sets. Exhibitors had lost their campaign to restrict such showings. The only remaining important bar was union-made—all the films offered to TV had been produced not later than 1948, because the unions insisted on the right to participate in TV rentals (on terms not yet negotiated) of all major features made after 1948.

Senator Estes Kefauver released a seventy-one page report of his subcommittee of the Senate Judiciary Committee, which held extensive hearings on films and juvenile delinquency in 1955. The Senator, then a darling of many and reputed to have Presidential ambitions, deplored excessive brutality in films and criticised what he considered objectionable advertising. He urged producers to exercise increased responsibility on both counts. Those interested in freedom of the screen were pleased that Senator Kefauver rejected censorship as both undesirable and impractical. He cited the value of the industry's motion picture Production Code and suggested stricter adherence to it. Exhibitors welcomed the report's call for a curb on excessive screen violence.

The Fund for the Republic, financed by Ford Foundation money, published a six-hundred-page study by John Cogley of blacklisting in the motion picture industry. This brought back unpleasant memories of one of the stormiest years of the industry so far as public relations were concerned—1947, when the House Un-American Activities Committee, headed by Representative J. Parnell Thomas (who had succeeded Martin Dies in that post), held hearings on Communist activity in Hollywood. The Fund for the Republic's report asserted that the heads of the major film companies under the leadership of Eric Johnston, president of the Motion Picture Association, had acted in a compound of "fear and shame." The report gave a good summary of the efforts of Communists—essentially unsuccessful efforts—to penetrate Hollywood, but it lacked proper historical perspective. Despite persistent efforts, Communists never succeeded in getting material that would further Communism into released Hollywood films.

The importance of records as a source of promotion for films received increased recognition, with the record of "The Song From Moulin Rouge" being credited with significant publicity value. The film industry was learning that the largest audience segment for pictures was in the same age group that gave the greatest attention to music and records.

The major companies, which had enjoyed extraordinarily long stability in top corporate management, entered upon a period of rapid change which has continued to the present. The first step was taken on a road which led, some years later, to the retirement from the industry of one of the best-known names. In 1956, Jack Warner, the last active member of the four Warner brothers, sold control of the company to a group organized by famed banker Serge Semenenko. The Warner Bros. feature backlog was sold for television to a company headed by Eliot Hyman. In 1967, Hyman merged Warner Bros. with his company, Seven Arts, and in 1969, sold out to Kinney, a conglomerate which began in the parking lot business.

In other significant corporate changes, Joseph Vogel succeeded Arthur M. Loew, a son of Marcus Loew, as head of MGM. Arthur Loew had held the presidency only a brief time after succeeding Nicholas M. Schenck, who had held the post for twenty-eight years.

Despite excellent box-office returns for such films as Mike Todd's *Around the World in 80 Days* in the Todd-AO wide-screen process, Cecil B. DeMille's remake of *The Ten Commandments,* and *Giant,* produced by Henry Ginsberg and directed by George Stevens, most films lacked strong appeal. Al Lichtman, industry pioneer, said fresh ideas and sweeping changes in policy were needed to insure the future of the American film. No one, inside or outside the industry, who was aware of what was going on could disagree.

Stars of the year: William Holden, John Wayne, James Stewart, Burt Lancaster, Glenn Ford, Martin & Lewis, Gary Cooper, Marilyn Monroe, Kim Novak and Frank Sinatra.

Elvis Presley in *Love Me Tender.*

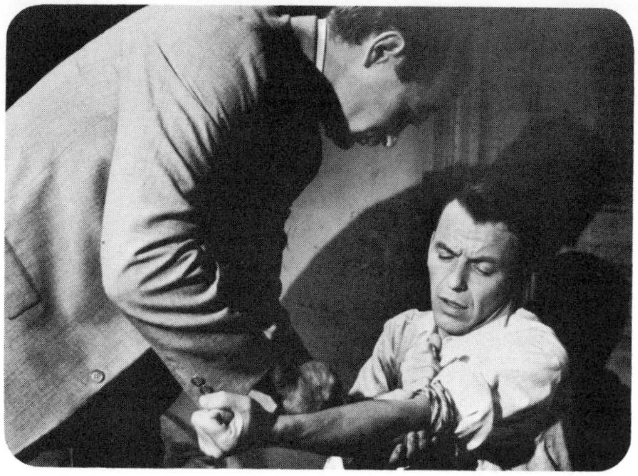

The Man With the Golden Arm with Darren McGavin and Frank Sinatra.

LOVE ME TENDER

What would otherwise have been an obscure western of 1956, relegated to the lower half of double bills, was a box-office sensation instead. This was due entirely to the presence in it of Elvis Presley, the man who, if he did not, as some admirers claim, invent rock 'n' roll, at least is the one who set that musical school on the road to success.

Love Me Tender was one of the top-grossing pictures of its year, and was responsible for landing Presley among the top ten moneymaking stars (*Motion Picture Herald* poll) of 1957. He disappeared from the list for three years after that, but in 1961 he ranked tenth, and stayed on in the five years after that. (His peak was at fifth place in 1962.)

So dependable was he at the box office for almost a decade that legend has it theatre owners told film distributors the pictures didn't really need titles. Just send them out with numbers (1, 2, 3, etc.), they said, but keep them coming.

The debut role of Presley was not as tailored to his special talents as later ones were to be; it was that of a young farmer who has married the girl his older brother loved when word came falsely that the latter was dead. Elvis even died at the end, in order to pave the way for the true lovers to get together. However, the action was frequently stopped for him to do his singing act with the guitar, meanwhile punctuating the music with twistings of the hips. He sang the title number, "Poor Boy," and "Let Me," to the delight of his numerous youthful fans. If he couldn't act, so what?

In later pictures, Presley played a modern-day swain hotly pursued by girls and pursuing same. A few titles to jog the memory: *Kid Galahad, Girls! Girls! Girls!, Viva Las Vegas* and *Paradise, Hawaiian Style.*

Producer: David Weisbart. **Director:** Robert D. Webb. **Scriptwriter:** Robert Buckner. **Principal Players:** Richard Egan, Debra Paget and Elvis Presley. **Running time:** 89 minutes. **Released:** 20th Century-Fox.

THE MAN WITH THE GOLDEN ARM

Otto Preminger's "pioneering" film about dope addiction deserves little more than a footnote in film history as yet another of the pictures that played their part in shaking up the Production Code, indirectly causing several revisions in it, and ultimately precipitating its abandonment.

The Preminger violations here were to show the use of narcotics by an addict (Frank Sinatra receiving arm injections from a dope peddler) and the violent effects upon him (including a harrowing "cold turkey" cure).

For all the "realism" of the Preminger movie, it had a typically phony happy ending: The hero is cured and walks into the night with the somewhat tarnished girl of his dreams (Kim Novak, no less), to a hopeful future.

Producer-Writer: Otto Preminger. **Scriptwriters:** Walter Newman and Lewis Meltzer. **Principal Players:** Frank Sinatra, Eleanor Parker and Kim Novak. **Running time:** 119 minutes. **Released:** United Artists.

Yul Brynner, Rita Moreno and Deborah Kerr in *The King and I.*

Giant with James Dean.

THE KING AND I

Chronologically, *South Pacific* was written and staged by the team of Rodgers and Hammerstein two years before *The King and I,* but the former musical's stage engagements across the country ran longer and thus held up production and release of the film version until 1958.

The King and I was based on a 1944 novel by Margaret Landon which had previously been made into a non-musical motion picture (in 1946, by 20th Century-Fox), starring Irene Dunne and Rex Harrison. In the stage musical, Gertrude Lawrence, in the last role of her career, was Anna; her co-star was the then unknown Yul Brynner, who became an overnight sensation and—luckily for him—was hired to do the movie musical. His co-star in the film was Deborah Kerr.

The filmed *King and I* is very faithful to the stage play—perhaps slavishly so. Walter Lang directed straightforwardly, using the big screen (CinemaScope 55) with a minimum of cinematic imagination.

But the performances and the songs were triumphant over all. Brynner had made the part of the King of Siam so completely his own in New York that it was unthinkable anyone else should have done the film. He won a much-deserved Oscar and has since had a fairly steady career in films, but never after was he fortunate enough to get such a once-in-a-lifetime role. Miss Kerr was charming, as always, although her songs had to be dubbed.

The music is as much a delight today as it was then: "I Whistle a Happy Tune," "Hello, Young Lovers," "Getting to Know You," "We Kiss in a Shadow," "Shall We Dance?" and so on.

Producer: Charles Brackett. **Director:** Walter Lang. **Scriptwriter:** Ernest Lehman. **Principal Players:** Deborah Kerr, Yul Brynner and Rita Moreno. **Running time:** 133 minutes. **Released:** 20th Century-Fox.

GIANT

For the picture to follow his two masterpieces, *A Place in the Sun* (1951) and *Shane* (1953), George Stevens selected a novel by the popular author Edna Ferber about modern Texas ranchers and oilmen. Commercially, it was the most successful of his pictures.

The time lapses between the films in this period of his career are indicative of the painstaking methods that Stevens brings to his craft. It is reported that he shot scenes for the three pictures above from every conceivable angle, and then took the extensive footage into the editing laboratory, where he personally selected the frames to be used in the final print from the many photographed. Obviously, this is an expensive production method (Hitchcock, for instance, edits his films as he shoots them), and the three Stevens' films were costly. But all paid off handsomely at the box office.

Giant is an appropriate name for the film in several respects: It runs for three hours and twenty-one minutes; the story spans thirty years; an all-star cast was headed by Elizabeth Taylor, Rock Hudson and James

Gregory Peck (left) in *Moby Dick.*

Dean; and the Texas settings were vast and overpowering. Like the Ferber novel, the plot line traveled in many channels, carrying sub-themes and secondary plots along the way. Also, like the original, the film was not always flattering to Texans—particularly the *nouveau riche.*

Miss Taylor, whom Stevens had inspired to give her best performance in *A Place in the Sun,* was very good in the early parts of the film as the high-spirited girl from the East who marries Hudson and goes to Texas with him. However, she had to age three decades, and she did not grow old very gracefully or convincingly in the film. Hudson gave one of his better performances as the rich rancher, but he, too, was best in the early episodes. To make it unanimous, James Dean was excellent in the youthful phase of his portrayal, but less credible as an older, drunken oil king. This, by the way, was the fast-rising actor's last picture; he had completed it just before the car crash that took his life.

Co-producer of the film with Stevens was Henry Ginsberg, who headed Paramount Studios from 1940 to 1950. Stevens has made only three films since *Giant: The Diary of Anne Frank* (1959), *The Greatest Story Ever Told* (1965) and *The Only Game in Town* (1969). Ginsberg has produced nothing since *Giant;* in fact, he is no longer in the film business, but is an executive consultant in commercial and industrial financing.

Producers: George Stevens and Henry Ginsberg. **Director:** George Stevens. **Scriptwriters:** Fred Guiol and Ivan Moffat. **Principal Players:** Elizabeth Taylor, Rock Hudson and James Dean. **Running time:** 201 minutes. **Released:** Warner Bros.

MOBY DICK

Attempts have been made to film Herman Melville's great allegorical novel three times; this version by John Huston comes closest to success in solving the difficult problems of transposition. The first two both starred John Barrymore: a silent version called *The Sea Beast,* in 1926, and a sound version in 1930 called *Moby Dick.* Great liberties were taken with the book on both occasions—Barrymore being a matinee idol, there had to be a love story. In 1926, the romantic interest was supplied by Dolores Costello, and in 1930, by Joan Bennett. The Huston film has no women in major roles.

It has other virtues, including some of the best sea and ship material ever photographed. The whales, both live and studio-made, are impressive—and sometimes it is hard to tell which is which.

Something of the spirit of the whaling men and their philosophy is given in the early part of the picture in a long but fascinating sermon delivered by Orson Welles as Father Mapple. But the story does not tarry long ashore. All the rest takes place on the *Pequod* and in its small whaling skiffs. The methods, difficulties and dangers of whaling are shown in interesting detail.

Of the defects in the Huston version—some serious, some not—the worst is the wooden performance of Gregory Peck as Captain Ahab. He seemed neurotic, in a small, non-deadly way, but never a man possessed.

As is well known, Huston likes to work in Ireland, so he went to Youghal to find a substitute for New Bedford. The New England whaling men in the film were really

Around the World in 80 Days with David Niven, Charles Boyer and Cantinflas.

English actors and Welsh and Madeira Island fishermen. The whale hunts were conducted off the coasts of Madeira and the Canary Islands. Every effort was made to re-create the conditions of the nineteenth century, with the whaling ship outfitted in as authentic a manner as possible.

Of special interest is the fact that Technicolor printing process was used by Huston for the first time in a quarter of a century. Before the usual three colors are printed by the Technicolor imbibition process, a low contrast silver image is printed to improve definition. Also the color values are "desaturated." This results in a realistic, muted type of color which gives the aura of historical paintings. It was extremely effective for *Moby Dick.*

Producer-Director: John Huston. **Scriptwriters:** John Huston and Ray Bradbury. **Principal Players:** Gregory Peck, Richard Basehart, Leo Genn and Orson Welles. **Running time:** 116 minutes. **Released:** Warner Bros.

AROUND THE WORLD IN 80 DAYS

The troubles that plagued the legendary producer Michael Todd in making this film (especially in securing financing and in inducing top stars to appear in walk-on roles as a special favor to him) were enormous and endless, and the successful result was a tribute to his resilience as well as his talents of persuasion. An extravaganza based on the Jules Verne story, it was the second film to be shot in Todd-AO. (*Oklahoma!* was the first.)

When first shown to the press in October of 1956, it was an unknown quantity, but reactions were immediately enthusiastic from the reviewers and the public response was tremendous. Fashions in films change, however, and when it was reissued to theatres in 1967, *80 Days* did not do well.

Part of the original appeal of the picture was surely its all-star cast and the guessing game it afforded the audience in trying to identify some fifty personalities as they popped up suddenly and then just as quickly disappeared. Noel Coward was a London employment agency manager; Frank Sinatra a piano player; Marlene Dietrich the mistress of a Barbary Coast dive; Ronald Colman an Indian railroad official; Beatrice Lillie a religious revivalist leader, etc.

The incidents were strung together by a plot line in which David Niven was an English gentleman who makes a bet with members of his London club that he can circle the globe in eighty days flat. Cantinflas, the Mexican comedian, played his manservant.

Of great appeal, too, was the travelogue element in the picture, which was shot in twenty-five locales around the world.

The film won five Oscars, including one for best picture of the year.

Producer: Michael Todd. **Director:** Michael Anderson. **Scriptwriters:** James Poe, John Farrow and S. J. Perelman. **Principal Players:** David Niven, Cantinflas, Robert Newton and Shirley MacLaine. **Running time:** 178 minutes. **Released:** United Artists.

Karl Malden and Carroll Baker in *Baby Doll.*

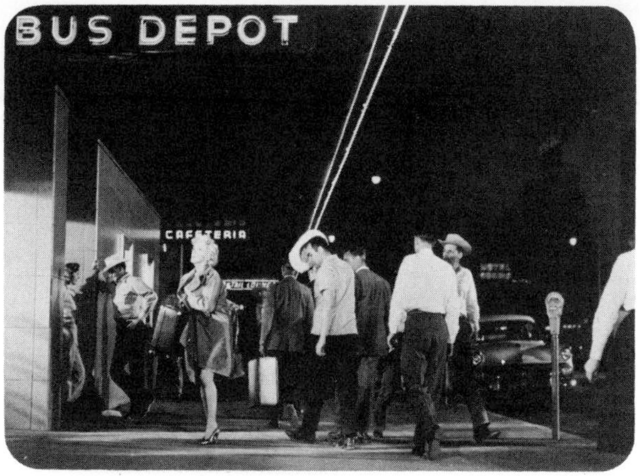

Bus Stop with Marilyn Monroe (center).

BABY DOLL

Playwright Tennessee Williams and director Elia Kazan, whose teaming had been so felicitous in the filming of the play *A Streetcar Named Desire* (a relationship carried over from the Broadway stage), joined forces to make a second film together five years later. The Williams script was an extension of his one-act play, *27 Loads of Cotton;* the setting was again the Deep South, although lower down on the social scale than the decaying gentility of *Streetcar.*

Carroll Baker and Karl Malden had their first film-starring roles in *Baby Doll,* she in the title part as a teen-aged bride whose marriage could not be consummated until she was twenty, and he as the frustrated bridegroom anxious to rid his wife of her virginity right away, although he had agreed to the restriction. Eli Wallach was introduced to the screen as the third central character, a cotton-gin owner who seduces the heroine as an act of revenge against her husband after the latter burns down his mill.

Aside from the importance of *Baby Doll* to the careers of these three actors (all of whom were lavishly praised), the picture has another historical distinction: It became the first film of a major Hollywood studio to be condemned by the Legion of Decency.

It was charged by the Legion and others that the picture was in flagrant violation of the Production Code through, among other things, its depiction of details of the crime of arson and its use of such words as "wop," "dago" and "nigger."

In defense, Kazan said he had done his best "to get on film what I felt in the South. Not the way things should be . . . but the way they appeared to me there and then." He added: "I wasn't trying to be moral or immoral, only truthful." Warner Bros. backed him up and released the picture without cuts. It was in due course withdrawn from theatrical release, with the rights reverting to Kazan. It was reissued in 1969.

Producer-Director: Elia Kazan. **Scriptwriter:** Tennessee Williams. **Principal Players:** Karl Malden, Carroll Baker and Eli Wallach. **Running time:** 114 minutes. **Released:** Warner Bros.

BUS STOP

Marilyn Monroe had been absent from the screen for a whole year when *Bus Stop* was released. In the interim she had secured herself a new husband (Arthur Miller) and had been instructed in the histrionic art by Lee Strasberg, prime exponent of the Method, a school of acting in which the performer buries himself deeply in the role and draws upon his own psychological experiences as a basis for those of the character he portrays. The Method has admirers and detractors.

Some observers had expressed fears that Miss Monroe might be ruined by exposure to such "arty" ideas, but these proved groundless. On the contrary, her performance as "Cherie," the wistful saloon singer pursued by a gruff young cowboy who falls in love with her at first sight, is generally regarded by critics as the best she ever gave. There were objections from some

The Bad Seed with Patty McCormack and Henry Jones.

quarters that she tended to imitate the mannerisms of Kim Stanley, who had performed the part on the stage. These came mostly from people who never did think Miss Monroe to be anything but a sex symbol.

George Axelrod adapted the William Inge play to the screen, rearranging the action so that events which had taken place only in the single diner set on stage could occur naturally elsewhere. He moved the action to a ranch, a dance hall, a rodeo and the countryside.

The picture also served to introduce Don Murray to the screen. He gave a personable performance as Virgil, the cowboy who has to learn that some women prefer gentleness in a man.

Miss Monroe made *Bus Stop* as the first of four pictures she agreed to do in a newly renegotiated contract with 20th Century-Fox. This pact specified that her films would be directed by one of six "suitable" talents. The six included Joshua Logan (of *South Pacific* fame).

Producer: Buddy Adler. **Director:** Joshua Logan. **Screenplay:** George Axelrod. **Principal Players:** Marilyn Monroe, Don Murray, Arthur O'Connell, Betty Field and Eileen Heckart. **Running time:** 96 minutes. **Released:** 20th Century-Fox.

THE BAD SEED

Although *The Bad Seed* had been a huge success as a Broadway play (adapted by Maxwell Anderson from the novel by William March), there was considerable skepticism that a motion picture made from it would please more than a small portion of the public. Again the cynics were wrong; *The Bad Seed* was a smashing commercial hit.

True enough, the subject matter hardly seemed palatable for the mass audience—it is the story of an eight-year-old murderess! Repeating their Broadway roles were Patty McCormack as the unique villainess, and Nancy Kelly as the mother who discovers she has given birth to a monster. Neither was exactly a box-office personality of note, although Miss Kelly was a veteran film actress (*Women in Bondage, Song of the Sarong, Murder in the Music Hall,* etc.)

Critics praised the acting—including that of Eileen Heckart as the mother of a boy who is one of the child's murder victims—but did not like the ending in which the child murderess was punished by being struck by lightning and killed, whereas in the play the child had lived.

Critics also objected to the epilogue in which Miss Kelly takes Miss McCormack over her knee for a well-deserved spanking, after they have taken curtain calls together.

The advertising slogan was typically misleading: "A hidden shame out in the open—and the most terrifying rock-bottom a woman ever hit for love." The love, of course, was that of a mother for her little girl, but the ads showed a woman's feet entering a room where a man lies cowering on the floor.

Producer-Director: Mervyn LeRoy. **Scriptwriter:** John Lee Mahin. **Principal Players:** Nancy Kelly, Patty McCormack, Henry Jones and Eileen Heckart. **Running time:** 127 minutes. **Released:** Warner Bros.

Friendly Persuasion with Richard Eyer, Gary Cooper, Dorothy McGuire and Phyllis Love.

FRIENDLY PERSUASION

The 1950's were a prolific period for William Wyler, and the titles give evidence of his remarkable aptitude in handling all types of material: the moralizing melodrama, *Detective Story* (1951); the serious drama, *Carrie,* from Theodore Dreiser's book (1952); the charming love story, *Roman Holiday* (1953); the suspense thriller, *Desperate Hours* (1955); and then, in 1956, *Friendly Persuasion,* a comedy-drama about a Quaker family in southern Indiana during the Civil War. (A western and a spectacle were still to come in the decade—*The Big Country* and *Ben Hur.)*

The source of *Friendly Persuasion* was a book by Jessamyn West celebrating the life of those gentle idealists, the Quakers, pointing out what is unique about them (their quaint customs) and what is universal (their humanity).

Her book was based on the experiences of an actual family.

Episodic in construction, the screenplay ranged from sequences illustrating Quaker practices (in church and at home) and slapstick (an encounter with Marjorie Main as a farm owner with three man-hungry daughters), to serious drama (when the older son leaves to join the war). Wyler handled all parts expertly, and tied them into a well-integrated whole.

Gary Cooper gave one of his best performances as the father of the family (called Birdwell on the screen), whether a scene called for dramatic emotional power or quiet humor. Dorothy McGuire played his wife with warm conviction, and newcomer Anthony Perkins was fine as the rebellious older son.

Producer-Director: William Wyler. **Principal Players:** Gary Cooper, Dorothy McGuire and Anthony Perkins. **Running time:** 139 minutes. **Released:** Allied Artists.

Sessue Hayakawa and Alec Guinness in *The Bridge on the River Kwai,* David Lean's "psychological" war film which won seven

1957

Pessimism was rife in 1957. It was the year when the entertainment industry's prophets of doom were their most strident. One example: Edwin Silverman, a Chicago exhibitor, predicted, "All major Hollywood studios, with the possible exception of one, will close within the next six months."

Early in the year Paramount Newsreel died, a victim of television competition and increased costs. Within a short time, all five of the weekly U.S. newsreel companies gave up theatrical service. Patrons always had loved newsreels more than distribution and exhibition executives. Despite their significance in screen journalism, especially in promoting national interests, newsreels were just a "step-child," having never been adequately financed. To the average exhibitor, newsreels were program fillers; to the average film salesman, newsreels were a "sweetener" to throw in for almost nothing when making a deal for features.

The mightiest of the old-line major companies, Loew's, Inc., went through a stormy year resisting corporate raiders. The first challenge was made by Joseph Tomlinson, a real-estate operator, who before the end of the year got Louis B. Mayer and Sam Briskin to join his faction. It was a sorry end for Mayer, long the head of MGM, who died a few months after Joseph Vogel won a victory by vote of the stockholders.

An industry characterized by little research over its long history received some enlightenment on its lost audience from an unexpected source, *The Saturday Evening Post.* That magazine financed a study of moviegoing which reported some shocking figures: 26 percent of the people questioned between the ages of 10 and 19 did not go to movies; 10.7 percent of those aged 20-34; 12.2 percent of those 35-44; 18.1 percent of those 45-54; and 33 percent of those aged 55 or over. It was also reported that only 17.1 percent of those questioned attended a movie theatre once a week or oftener; 12.2 percent went two or three times a month; 14.3 percent, once a month; and a startling 25.2 percent went once a year or less. This documented what the box-office receipts had shown—enthusiasm for films was at a low.

Meanwhile, a spectre of television with its own box office, pay TV, haunted many in exhibition, but was viewed with keen anticipation by Hollywood. Paramount's Telemeter, a home coin-box system, was demonstrated. Even more significant was extensive testing of pay TV in Bartlesville, Oklahoma. The sponsor was the principal theatre operator in the area. There, patrons of the toll TV service were charged $9.50 per month, plus an installation charge of $33 to $35. In contrast, the average family in Bartlesville then was paying only about $2.50 per month for admission to theatres. In Washington, the Federal Communications Commission approved a three-year test of toll TV using the air waves. The O'Neil General Tire interests promptly applied for permission to test a system of pay TV in Hartford, Conn.

The Supreme Court perplexed followers of censorship decisions by ruling that obscenity is not protected by the Constitution, but it left unclear what, in a film, might constitute obscenity. The Supreme Court's so-called Roth Rule indicated that anything would be approved provided it had "the slightest redeeming social importance."

Stars of the year: Rock Hudson, John Wayne, Pat Boone, Elvis Presley, Frank Sinatra, Gary Cooper, William Holden, James Stewart, Jerry Lewis and Yul Brynner.

E. G. Marshall, Don Murray, Philip Abbott, Jack Warden and Larry Blyden in *The Bachelor Party.*

The Ten Commandments with John Derek, Debra Paget, Yvonne de Carlo and Charlton Heston.

THE BACHELOR PARTY

Another of the "little" pictures of the 1950's that first saw the light of day as television scripts, and then were remade for the theatrical screen, *The Bachelor Party* is one of the very best of the school. Again, the writer was Paddy Chayefsky, author of *Marty,* the most commercially successful and accoladed of all the "TV films."

Chayefsky himself expanded his original script of *The Bachelor Party,* as he had done for *Marty.* What he likes to do is to take a particular social custom (as he also did in *The Catered Affair*) and make it a crisis in the lives of the people involved. Under the stress of that crisis, their true selves are revealed.

In this story, four young men who work together in a bookkeeping office take one of their colleagues who is about to be married out for an evening on the town. The event begins as a lark. But underneath their surface joviality, all of the men are concealing a variety of weaknesses and fears. Before the bachelor party is over, each has discovered some important truths about himself as well as his friends.

A key to the success of the Chayefsky films, second only to the strong scripts he wrote, was the casting of the roles, which in this instance was apt in every case. Of the men, Don Murray, E. G. Marshall and Jack Warden were outstanding, and Carolyn Jones headed the distaff contingent with a hilarious portrayal of a Greenwich Village "existentialist."

In one memorable episode the camera observed the comic reactions of the men to a stag movie. The audience was never shown what they saw. Imagine how they would have handled this scene in 1969!

Producer: Harold Hecht. **Director:** Delbert Mann. **Scriptwriter:** Paddy Chayefsky. **Principal Players:** Don Murray, E. G. Marshall, Jack Warden and Philip Abbott. **Running time:** 93 minutes. **Released:** United Artists.

THE TEN COMMANDMENTS

Cecil D. DeMille was so entranced with the story of Moses and the Ten Commandments, as recorded in the Scriptures, that he brought it to the screen twice. In 1923 he made a silent version, part of which was devoted to a modern story recounting the consequences of breaking the ten rules in the twentieth century. His 1956 version, made on a much vaster scale and in color and VistaVision, stuck strictly to the Biblical story (with an embellishment here and there, of course), letting the spectator read modern parallels into it if he so desired.

This second version was the most commercially successful of all the many pictures made by this producer-director with the "touch of gold." Few showmen in the history of the screen have so had their pulse on what the public wanted to see and when. Sophisticated critics scoffed more harshly than ever at *The Ten Commandments,* but the public paid them no attention.

This film reveals the artistic strengths and weaknesses of DeMille. Of the first, the most important is his ability at handling scenes of spectacle. The Exodus in this picture is an awe-inspiring sight of thousands of people,

Sweet Smell of Success with Burt Lancaster.

animals, fowl, conveyances, sights, sounds and confusions spreading out across a vast desert. The film is lavish in special effects, as the Pillar of Fire, the parting of the Red Sea and the delivery of God's words to Moses on Mount Sinai. All this is quite a show.

The major weakness of this film (and most of DeMille's others) is in the handling of characterizations and actors. There is almost no subtlety anywhere; everything is put over in broad strokes with little left to the imagination. And the actors—sometimes very good ones—all tended to perform in a stilted, exaggerated style that seriously dates the film. Seen ten years later (it was reissued in 1966) the virtues and defects of this picture seemed more sharply at odds than ever.

Producer-Director: Cecil B. DeMille. **Scriptwriters:** Aeneas MacKenzie, Jesse L. Lasky, Jr., Jack Gariss and Fredric M. Frank. **Principal Players:** Charlton Heston, Yul Brynner, Anne Baxter, Edward G. Robinson, Yvonne de Carlo, Debra Paget and John Derek. **Running time:** 219 minutes. **Released:** Paramount.

SWEET SMELL OF SUCCESS

1957 was quite a year for films telling the "inside story" about the private lives of prominent personalities in show business. There had already been *The Great Man* and *A Face in the Crowd,* which purported to expose the venal nature of radio and television stars who present a hypocritical face to the public. *Sweet Smell of Success* turned to another aspect of the Broadway scene—the double-dealing and chicanery engaged in by press agents to secure the favor and support of the powerful gossip columnists of the New York newspapers. *Success* was the best of the three pictures.

For actor Tony Curtis it marked a big turning point in his career; his role of a publicity promoter was that of an unmitigated heel. Curtis justified the confidence of producer James Hill in casting him "against type" by giving a brilliant performance. As the unprincipled press agent, he at one point acts as a procurer in order to induce a columnist (Burt Lancaster, also playing a cad) to print a "smear item."

The British director Alexander Mackendrick showed an uncommon understanding of the nuances of the Broadway night-life scene.

Producer: James Hill. **Director:** Alexander Mackendrick. **Scriptwriters:** Clifford Odets and Ernest Lehman. **Principal Players:** Burt Lancaster and Tony Curtis. **Running time:** 96 minutes. **Released:** United Artists.

AND GOD CREATED WOMAN

Certain film stars are always identified with one picture in particular; in it they create an image they can never quite shake off. So it is with Brigitte Bardot and *And God Created Woman.*

In fact, the lady has never had a film to equal this one in popularity, in America or anywhere else. It caused a sensation when it was released here; exposure of the Bardot figure in various stages of dress and undress was the reason.

Surely the outraged censors and moralists could not

And God Created Woman with Brigitte Bardot.

The Bridge on the River Kwai with Geoffrey Horne, Jack Hawkins and William Holden.

have objected to the moral of the tale, which was ponderously conventional. The heroine had married one man to be near his brother, who was the man she really loved, but at the end she came to her senses (courtesy of a beating by her husband) and piously returned to home and hearth.

U.S. gross for *Woman* is reputed to be near $4,000,000; the only French film before or since to surpass it is *A Man and a Woman.* By the mid-1960's, Miss Bardot had pretty much faded from the international film scene, but the image she created—the undraped female with animalistic morals to match—stays vivid and undimmed.

Producer: Raoul J. Levy. **Director:** Roger Vadim. **Scriptwriters:** Vadim and Levy. **Principal Players:** Brigitte Bardot, Curt Jurgens, Jean-Louis Trintignant and Christian Marquand. **Running time:** 101 minutes. **Released:** Kingsley International.

THE BRIDGE ON THE RIVER KWAI

Before it opened in America, *The Bridge on the River Kwai* had a premiere in England, where it was greeted with the kind of ecstatic notices that producers dream about. These opinions were supported with equal enthusiasm by U.S. reviewers when it was shown to them, and the public here concurred immediately as it had abroad.

It was obvious, then, that producer Sam Spiegel and director David Lean had turned out something special in motion pictures—a spectacle that also had something for the "thinking" moviegoer. They had a unique war film and a thrilling suspense story, but one that concentrated on the psychological conflicts of its characters. Something hard to do—and done rarely—but done here with finesse.

The chief conflict was between Alec Guinness as the colonel in command of British soldiers taken prisoner by the Japanese in 1943, and Sessue Hayakawa (famed star of silent movies) as the commander of the prisoner-of-war camp. A war of nerves develops between the two over whether the British officers should supervise their men in construction of a bridge across the River Kwai. Guinness at last relents when he sees the project as a means of restoring discipline to his own men.

The irony of war is brought out by scriptwriter Pierre Boulle (adapting his own novel) in an incisive way when English forces at Ceylon are ordered to blow up the bridge being built by their own countrymen.

Guinness and Hayakawa gave splendid performances, dominating a cast in which William Holden also appeared as an American sailor who becomes crucial to the plot to blow up the bridge.

Seven Oscars went to *Kwai:* best picture, best actor (Guinness), direction, writing (screenplay from another medium), cinematography (Jack Hildyard), editing (Peter Taylor) and music (scoring).

Producer: Sam Spiegel. **Director:** David Lean. **Scriptwriter:** Pierre Boulle. **Principal Players:** William Holden, Alec Guinness, Jack Hawkins and Sessue Hayakawa. **Running time:** 161 minutes. **Released:** Columbia.

Peyton Place with Diane Varsi and Barry Coe.

PEYTON PLACE

Cleaning up "dirty" books for the screen was quite an art in the 1940's and 1950's, and *Peyton Place* is a prime example of how to carry out the task of expurgation with finesse. Producer Jerry Wald and his co-workers took a novel by Grace Metalious that was replete with immoral behavior, set down on the printed page with carnal explicitness, and put it on the screen in a manner that caused no offense—to the censors or anyone else. Yet the spirit of the original remained intact.

The book had been a tremendous best seller, and indeed, the name *Peyton Place* has since become the synonym for millions of Americans of a typical small American town in which sin thrives under a respectable surface. (The book and film of *Kings Row* were forerunners, but were not as enduring.) A great deal of this is due, of course, to the popular television show spun off from the picture and book. *Peyton Place* was an innovation on TV for several reasons: It was a soap opera shown at night in prime time, and at one period in its successful career it was seen three nights a week!

The theatrical movie was not as bad as many had anticipated, and indeed some of it still holds up extremely well—better than anything in the TV series or in the book. The picture is very good at depicting details of small-town Americana, such as the high school graduation activities (for nostalgia) and the town picnic (for amusement). And the romance between Diane Varsi, as a troubled adolescent, and Russ Tamblyn, as a lonely, mother-dominated boy, was written and played with considerable poignancy.

Other plots and sub-plots were smoothly woven together in the script of John Michael Hayes, and Mark Robson directed in a familiarly slick style. The movie, *Peyton Place,* is one kind of Hollywood professionalism at its best.

Producer: Jerry Wald. **Director:** Mark Robson. **Scriptwriter:** John Michael Hayes. **Principal Players:** Lana Turner, Lee Phillips, Diane Varsi and Russ Tamblyn. **Running time:** 157 minutes. **Released:** 20th Century-Fox.

Audrey Hepburn in *The Nun's Story,* Fred Zinnemann's tribute to the "world of the grand silence," with a great performance from the star.

1958

Motion pictures in the United States wallowed in the depth of their own "great depression," caused by the massive expansion of television and public indifference to many of the films offered.

Various promotional schemes were proposed: Spyros P. Skouras, dynamic president of 20th Century-Fox, called for "a rekindling of the flames of enthusiasm"; exhibition leaders discussed a business-building program which included special attention to the Academy Awards television show in March (a show which cost $600,000 and reached an estimated 80,000,000 viewers); other exhibitors, encouraged by the example of the industry in Britain, talked of a trust to buy up post-1948 features to keep them off television.

The business received a financial assist from the final victory in the campaign for repeal of the Federal Admission Tax. Relief was expressed that once again there was a delay in the Federal Communication Commission's consideration of toll TV. Meanwhile the extensive experiment in Bartlesville, Oklahoma, was terminated after nine months. There was found to be little impact on theatre attendance during the test. But few families were willing to pay month after month for programs via toll TV when so much was available on free TV.

Republic Studios, long identified with westerns and other (mostly modest-budget) action films, went out of the theatrical entertainment business. Showing that even in the period of greatest pessimism there were cross currents, a new company, American International, moved into the position of the market once served by Republic. The new firm, headed by James Nicholson and Samuel Arkoff, emphasized low-budget films geared to the interests of youth. Aggressive exploitation produced outstanding grosses for such films, which were a factor in helping a number of small-town and neighborhood theatres stay open.

MCA (the Music Corporation of America, originally formed by Dr. Jules Stein to represent bands and various performers) bought Universal Studios and leased them back. A little later, MCA acquired Decca Records, which had merged in 1952 with Universal Pictures. Partially as a result of this integration of several factors into MCA, more attention then ever was given by all companies to the uses of records to promote films. Film title songs and theme-music records became important promotional tools.

Notable at the box office was *The Bridge on the River Kwai* with Alec Guinness and William Holden. This film started out as a 1957 roadshow with a few engagements on a reserved seat basis, but soon moved into general release at regular prices. The distributors felt that the prestige of the roadshow engagements plus excellent reviews helped establish the film. Another big film of the year was *South Pacific.*

Deaths of motion picture pioneers were unusually heavy for a single year: included were Jesse Lasky, pioneer film maker; Harry Cohn, a founder of Columbia Pictures; A. Lichtman and J. Robert Rubin, two longtime pillars of the mighty MGM, the latter an old associate of Louis B. Mayer, with whom he enjoyed a percentage of the profits of the entire company. Also dead were Ronald Colman, Robert Donat and the flamboyant Michael Todd, producer of *Around the World in 80 Days.*

Stars of the year: Glenn Ford, Elizabeth Taylor, Jerry Lewis, Marlon Brando, Rock Hudson, William Holden, Brigitte Bardot, Yul Brynner, James Stewart and Frank Sinatra.

Susan Hayward in *I Want to Live!*

I WANT TO LIVE!

Susan Hayward was nominated for an Academy Award for *Smash Up* (1947), *My Foolish Heart* (1949) and *I'll Cry Tomorrow* (1955). But it was not until 1958 that she finally won for her performance in *I Want to Live!* It was a stunning piece of work that richly deserved the accolade.

Miss Hayward was cast as a real life character—Barbara Graham, an amoral young woman, victim of a broken home, herself the consort of criminals, who died in the California gas chamber for a murder some people still believe she did not commit. The character was tough and cynical, and not really sympathetic until near the end, when she is put through the harrowing experiences of imprisonment in a death row cell, getting reprieves at the last minute, and finally being gassed to death in a graphically detailed scene which Robert Wise directed with excruciating realism. Miss Hayward played it brilliantly and honestly all the way.

The screenplay was based on the letters of Barbara Graham and various articles written by Ed Montgomery, a San Francisco newspaperman whose interest in the case led him from scare-headline sensationalism to leadership of the fight to save the condemned woman from the gas chamber. Without preachment, the picture became an eloquent plea against capital punishment.

Producer: Walter Wanger. **Director:** Robert Wise. **Scriptwriters:** Nelson Gidding and Don Mankiewicz. **Principal Players:** Susan Hayward, Simon Oakland and Virginia Vincent. **Running time:** 120 minutes. **Released:** United Artists.

Paul Newman, Orson Welles, Angela Lansbury and Joanne Woodward in *The Long, Hot Summer.*

THE LONG, HOT SUMMER

Like other eminent American novelists (Melville, Hemingway, et al), William Faulkner has not been well served in adaptations of his works to the screen. The single exception to date: *Intruder in the Dust* (see 1949).

The script for *The Long, Hot Summer* is based on *The Hamlet,* a Faulkner novel in four sections, the third of which is called "The Long Summer" (sans the "Hot"). Scriptwriters Irving Ravetch and Harriet Frank, Jr., retained very little of the book beyond the Mississippi setting and some of the characters' names.

They did, however, supply producer Jerry Wald with a slick script about small-town life that was high in entertainment values and enjoyed strong success at the box office. It did much to advance the careers of its talented cast: Joanne Woodward (fresh from her triumph in *Three Faces of Eve*), Paul Newman, Anthony Franciosa and Lee Remick, all of whom were very much up-and-coming at the time. On the other hand, acting honors were easily stolen by two old pros: Orson Welles as the proud and selfish patriarch and Angela Lansbury as his mistress.

Also furthered was the career of Martin Ritt, who had earned this job by his superior handling of two "B" film scripts: *Edge of the City* and *No Down Payment.*

Producer: Jerry Wald. **Director:** Martin Ritt. **Scriptwriters:** Irving Ravetch and Harriet Frank, Jr. **Principal Players:** Paul Newman, Joanne Woodward, Anthony Franciosa, Lee Remick, Orson Welles, and Angela Lansbury. **Running time:** 117 minutes. **Released:** 20th Century-Fox.

Mitzi Gaynor in *South Pacific.*

SOUTH PACIFIC

To the surprise of no one, *South Pacific,* one of the great hits of the American musical-comedy stage, became one of the great film hits of all time—even though nine years had elapsed between the Broadway opening in April, 1949, to the movie premiere in March, 1958. The movie public had a long wait.

The stage play ran just under five years in New York and won virtually every stage award offered, from the Pulitzer Prize on down. The film racked up some similarly impressive commercial statistics in long-run engagements, but was not equally fortunate as far as critical accolades were concerned.

In bringing the property to the huge Todd-AO screen, producer Buddy Adler and director Joshua Logan went to great lengths to expand the settings of the original. Real tropical locales (shot in the Fiji Islands and Hawaii) were substituted for stage scenery; episodes were shot in planes and on the water; and there was a big beach sequence in which thousands of troops were marshalled for embarkation. The stage could show none of these for obvious reasons. *South Pacific* on the screen was bigger, if not better.

Part of the problem was the introduction of some weird color effects—bright tropical hues, at times, and diffused night-time lights at others, wafting from nowhere over a scene. These served no justifiable dramatic purpose and tended, instead, to distract and annoy many viewers.

Nor was the cast as good as one had a right to expect. Mitzi Gaynor was a very ordinary Nellie Forbush—no Mary Martin in either personality or vocal expertise. Rossano Brazzi was somewhat better as the French planter whom the late Ezio Pinza had portrayed on stage. France Nuyen was just another starlet in the role of Liat, and John Kerr was miscast as Lt. Cable. Supporting roles—particularly Juanita Hall as Bloody Mary and Ray Walston as Luther Billis—were more sensibly cast.

Surviving the flaws better than anything else was the wonderfully melodious score of Rodgers and Hammerstein, the mere mention of whose names can still start lips to humming and toes to tapping: "I'm Gonna Wash That Man Right Outa My Hair," "There Is Nothin' Like a Dame," "Some Enchanted Evening," "Bali Ha'i" and "I'm in Love With a Wonderful Guy." *South Pacific* is indestructible in any medium.

Producer: Buddy Adler. **Director:** Joshua Logan. **Scriptwriter:** Paul Osborn. **Principal Players:** Rossano Brazzi, Mitzi Gaynor, John Kerr, Ray Walston, Juanita Hall and France Nuyen. **Running time:** 171 minutes. **Released:** 20th Century-Fox.

CAT ON A HOT TIN ROOF

"All the sultry drama of Tennessee Williams' Pulitzer Prize Play is now on the screen," said one of the ads prepared by MGM to promote this film. Not really. In fact, such an expert job of expurgating the original play was achieved by writers Richard Brooks and James Poe that the picture was booked by Radio City Music Hall,

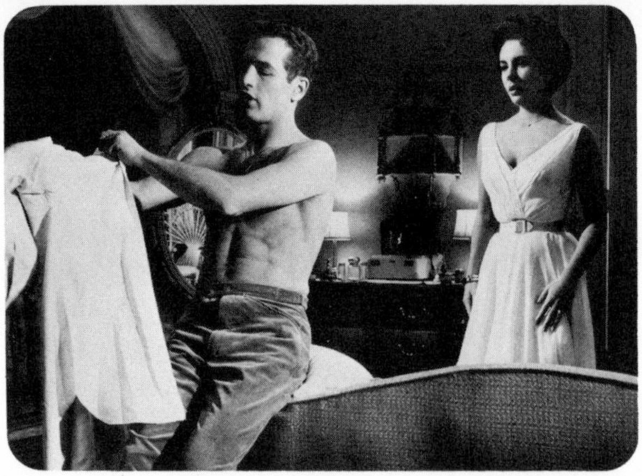

Cat on a Hot Tin Roof with Paul Newman and Elizabeth Taylor.

Gigi with Leslie Caron and Eva Gabor.

the nation's foremost family theatre, where it ran for seven weeks to packed houses.

Outside of New York, also, the public responded in large numbers to the sexual preoccupations of the Williams' story concerning the efforts of a young Southern belle to save her handsome husband from alcoholism.

In the play, the reason the man drank was that he felt guilty for having rebuffed his best friend when the latter unexpectedly made homosexual advances and, when rejected, committed suicide. On the screen, the hero imbibed because he believed his wife had been unfaithful to him with this same friend. Homosexual intimations were present but faint.

Considerably laundered also for the screen were the four-letter words that abounded in the original (after all, this was eight years before *Virginia Woolf*), and the famous and obscene "elephant joke" recounted on the stage with great glee by Burl Ives as "Big Daddy." Ives repeated this role for the film, but he was generally much more subdued.

Contributing greatly to the popularity of the picture was the presence of Elizabeth Taylor in the role of "Maggie the Cat." Her performance won her an Oscar nomination, but those who had seen Barbara Bel Geddes play it on the stage could not help but note that there were more subtleties in the role than the screen star was able to bring out.

Paul Newman, then a fast-rising actor, played the tormented husband well.

Ives won an Oscar for 1958, incidentally—not for *Cat* but for his supporting performance in *The Big Country.*

Producer: Lawrence Weingarten. **Director:** Richard Brooks. **Scriptwriters:** Brooks and James Poe. **Principal Players:** Elizabeth Taylor, Paul Newman, Burl Ives, Jack Carson and Judith Anderson. **Running time:** 108 minutes. **Released:** MGM.

GIGI

The plot of *Gigi*—a rather slim business about a French girl being groomed to become a mistress but who prefers marriage and gets it—started out as a novel by Colette, and then became a stage play. The third version—this MGM musical produced by Arthur Freed and directed by Vincente Minelli—has come to overshadow the other two, and deservedly so. It was, and remains, a delight.

The score by Alan Jay Lerner and Frederick Loewe was their first since the phenomenal stage hit *My Fair Lady.* Interestingly, the music was so well integrated into the plot line that none of the songs became a hit individually. Many of them were written for "talking" rather than singing—"It's a Bore," "She's Not Thinking of Me" and "I Remember It Well," in particular. This was fortunate in the cases of both Maurice Chevalier and Louis Jourdan, who were able to substitute personal charm and cleverly phrased recitation for musical vocal power.

Also from the Broadway *My Fair Lady* (which was brought to the screen in 1964) was Cecil Beaton, whose

The 400 Blows with Jean-Pierre Leaud.

The Nun's Story with Audrey Hepburn.

costumes, scenery, and production design were typically splendiferous. Leslie Caron was charming in the title role.

Eight Oscars were awarded to *Gigi* for best picture, direction, screenplay, color cinematography, art direction, costume design, editing and scoring. A special award was handed Chevalier "for his contributions to the world of entertainment for more than half a century."

Producer: Arthur Freed. **Director:** Vincente Minnelli. **Scriptwriters:** Alan Jay Lerner and Frederick Loewe. **Principal Players:** Leslie Caron, Maurice Chevalier, Louis Jourdan and Hermione Gingold. **Running time:** 116 minutes. **Released:** MGM.

THE 400 BLOWS

François Truffaut has now made over a dozen pictures since he turned from critically appraising movies to making them, but most of his admirers, when pinned down, will confess they still prefer his very first work, *The 400 Blows.* Certainly it is one of the most touching and profound portraits of childhood ever put on the screen.

Young Jean-Pierre Leaud was simply perfection in the leading role of the Parisian adolescent who, neglected by his mother and foster father, finally goes off to a correctional school for juvenile delinquents. Whether he was baiting a tyrannical teacher in the classroom, or reaching for his food too soon at the reform school and getting a blow in the face, Leaud was unforgettable.

Truffaut directed a long scene at the end in which the boy is questioned in clinical detail by a psychiatrist with the camera on the face of the child the entire time (the interrogator was never shown). Young Leaud packed more revelation of character into this scene than many adult actors do in an entire film.

Three years later Antoine Doinel, the lead character in the story of *400 Blows,* turned up in one of the episodes of *Love at Twenty,* in which Truffaut had him work in a record factory. Then in 1969, ten years after his first appearance, Antoine was the leading character in Truffaut's *Stolen Kisses,* as a youth unable to keep any kind of job and unsuccessful in his love life, too. Leaud was starred as Antoine in both sequels.

Producers: S.E.D.I.F. and Les Films du Carrosse. **Director:** François Truffaut. **Scriptwriter:** Marcel Moussy. **Principal Players:** Jean-Pierre Leaud, Claire Maurier, Albert Demy and Guy Decomble. **Running time:** 93 minutes. **Released:** Janus Films.

THE NUN'S STORY

The world of the Catholic convent, wherein novices are trained to become nuns, is a private one unknown to most people, but Fred Zinnemann explored it in great detail and with endless fascination in this remarkable picture. The regimen, customs and philosophies of the religious order were made abundantly intelligible.

The first half hour of the film is documentary film making of a rare quality, as the director prepares for the drama to come. In these scenes he reveals the day-

A Night to Remember with Kenneth More (left).

to-day activity in a convent, following the stages of development from postulant to nun. This was no mere recording of externals; the effect subtly emerged of the fervor and dedication that animate the life there. The picture of the world of the "grand silence" is complete.

Beyond that, Zinnemann and his writer, Robert Anderson, realized a character in Sister Luke, the heroine, that is uncommonly three-dimensional. Their source was an autobiographical book by Kathryn C. Hulme. Audrey Hepburn brought brilliantly alive this woman and her inner struggle with her conscience as to whether she is really suited to remaining a nun.

Producer: Henry Blanke. **Director:** Fred Zinnemann. **Scriptwriter:** Robert Anderson. **Principal Players:** Audrey Hepburn, Peter Finch, Edith Evans and Peggy Ashcroft. **Running time:** 154 minutes. **Released:** Warner Bros.

A NIGHT TO REMEMBER

No disaster at sea in modern times has fascinated so many people so much as that of the sinking of the luxury liner *Titanic* in 1912. This British ship was known in its day as the "biggest in the world" and was also regarded as the ultimate in engineering by contemporary experts. "Unsinkable," they called her. But sink she did when an iceberg struck her on her maiden voyage in the North Atlantic on the way to New York, taking with her to the bottom of the sea 1,500 of the 2,207 passengers and crew aboard.

Hollywood had treated the subject in a fictional context just five years before in *Titanic* (20th Century-Fox) with Barbara Stanwyck and Clifton Webb. *A Night to Remember* took a documentary approach, with the Eric Ambler screenplay based on a book by Walter Lord recounting the facts as closely as it was possible to do so.

The British film makers turned out a powerful movie, sweeping the audience along in the relentless and agonizing train of events. Roy Baker, the director, moved swiftly from one phase of the story to the other, from the first-class deck to steerage, from the captain's quarters on the ship to the two other ships involved (one should have warned the *Titanic* of ice packs; the other didn't hear the distress signals). All elements were tied together without a sense of confusion or let-up in the crescendo of the pace.

The British film won excellent reviews here, but the public response was lukewarm. It was regarded as one more failure of the British industry to penetrate the American market. However, *Room at the Top* was to come the following year.

Producer: Rank Organization. **Director:** Roy Baker. **Screenplay:** Eric Ambler. **Principal Players:** Kenneth More, Ronald Alley and Robert Ayres. **Running time:** 123 minutes. **Released:** Rank.

PATHS OF GLORY

Stanley Kubrick's first major film, *Paths of Glory,* showed him to be in as full command of ambitious

Paths of Glory with Kirk Douglas and Wayne Morris.

material as he had been of the less pretentious elements of melodrama in *The Killing,* released the year before. (Two earlier "B" films made before that are best forgotten.)

Paths of Glory was based on a novel by Humphrey Cobb telling of an actual incident in the First World War involving charges of cowardice in the face of the enemy brought against an entire French regiment. Three men were selected at random to be tried as proxies for all, and, despite the eloquent pleas made by the colonel who headed the regiment, the men were convicted and executed by a firing squad.

Kubrick directed the film brilliantly. The charge of the outnumbered Frenchmen is tersely and excitingly staged. Likewise the trial episode is both concise and compelling. To accentuate the mockery of justice that the court martial entails, Kubrick had the speech of the participants resound throughout the massive halls of the medieval castle in which the case was conducted.

No emotion enters the handling of the materials until the end when, following the executions, the surviving soldiers listen to a poignant song sung by a German girl captured by the French.

Kirk Douglas headed an otherwise "uncommercial" but competent cast, the star playing the sympathetic colonel. His box-office draw, however, did not make *Paths of Glory* a financial success. He and Kubrick were to do much better in that direction when they teamed for *Spartacus* a couple of years later.

Producer: James B. Harris. **Director:** Stanley Kubrick. **Screenplay:** Calder Willingham and Jim Thompson. **Principal Players:** Kirk Douglas, George Macready, Adolphe Menjou, Ralph Meeker, Joseph Turkel, Timothy Carey and Wayne Morris. **Running time:** 86 minutes. **Released:** United Artists.

Ben-Hur with Charlton Heston and Stephen Boyd, William Wyler's religious spectacle which won eleven Academy Awards and is one of the most popular pictures in screen history.

1959

Sam Goldwyn, no amateur in the ways of Hollywood and certainly no shrinking violet when it came to proclaiming an unpopular view, opened 1959 with the statement that production talent was making excessive demands on producers and that "conditions are now worse than I have ever known them" (in forty-seven years of American film making).

At this period, Hollywood was floundering for want of strong leadership. The dominant role of leadership of the studio heads, for the most part, had long disappeared. Independent producers were interested primarily or exclusively in their own projects, and did no worrying or planning about the industry as a whole. Even in the Los Angeles press, attention to films was at an all-time low.

Equally characteristic of the times was the fact that at the annual convention of the Society of Motion Picture and Television Engineers at Miami Beach, there was more interest in missiles than in either theatrical or television pictures. The engineers who usually were unheard when calling for improvements in film and theatre techniques had found new outlets for their electronic and picture talents in military and space projects.

The "big" picture was now costing $2,000,000 or more to make, requiring approximately $4,000,000 in gross to make a profit (the other $2,000,000 being absorbed in sales, advertising and print costs). While each picture's budget is unique, a typical $2,000,000 production budget might be divided roughly as follows: $250,000—story and script; $200,000—producer and director; $250,000—stars; $125,000—other players; $125,000—sets and physical construction; $550,000—other direct costs; and lastly, $500,000—studio overhead. It was this last figure, the cost of operating the great Hollywood studios, that became an increasing source of contention as independent producers turned increasingly to production abroad.

In order to build or preserve attendance, exhibitors in a number of states continued vigorous annual attacks on daylight saving time.

Meanwhile, theatre owners continued to worry over censorship. Advocates of control began to build up pressure for classification or rating of films for audience suitability. However, Eric Johnston, president of the Motion Picture Association of America, vigorously rejected classification as the opening wedge to censorship.

The year 1959 saw the passing from active roles in the industry of two men who had long wielded extraordinary influence on films in America. Cecil B. DeMille, whose name had become a household word, died. A lawyer, A. F. Myers, virtually unknown outside the industry, went into such total retirement, continuing to his death in 1969, that he ceased even to read about the film industry. For over four decades, DeMille's name was synonymous with the "big" picture of great mass-audience appeal. For a quarter of a century, Myers was the nemesis of the big combines, as a leader of the independent exhibitors. He, more than anyone else, was responsible for the 1939 U.S. Government antitrust suit which ended block booking and split up the five companies that produced films and owned theatre circuits.

Such contrasting pictures as *The Nun's Story* (released in 1958) and a remake of *Ben-Hur* were box-office hits. The Supreme Court gave the green light to *Lady Chatterley's Lover.*

Stars of the year: Rock Hudson, Cary Grant, James Stewart, Doris Day, Debbie Reynolds, Glenn Ford, Frank Sinatra, John Wayne, Jerry Lewis and Susan Hayward.

A scene from *Hercules.*

Jean-Marc Bory and Jeanne Moreau in *The Lovers.*

HERCULES

The promotional campaign that launched this Italian-made spectacle (dubbed into English) in the United States was so mammoth, energetic and successful that it has become a legend among film showmen everywhere while the picture itself is virtually forgotten. The man behind the feverish promotion, in which the public was bombarded from all sides and through all possible media with the news that *Hercules* was coming, was Joseph E. Levine. He had previously been a Boston exhibitor and subsequently became a producer of his own pictures while continuing to distribute those of others through his Embassy Pictures company (now Avco-Embassy).

A major factor in the success of *Hercules* was the booking pattern known as "saturation," in which the film is released first-run to as many theatres in a city as possible all at once. The blitz technique has seldom proved so effective.

The role of the legendary strong man was played here by Steve Reeves, a former Mr. America, Mr. World and Mr. Universe. He later appeared in other similar historical epics made in Italy which sought to cash in on the popularity of *Hercules.* None of them did so to any extent worth mentioning, except that Reeves himself became a wealthy man.

Producer: Federico Teti. **Director:** Pietro Francisci. **Scriptwriters:** Pietro Francisci, Ennio De Concini and Galo Frattini. **Principal Players:** Steve Reeves, Sylva Koscina, Fabrizio Mioni and Ivo Garrani. **Running time:** 103 minutes. **Released:** Warner Bros.

THE LOVERS

Harbinger of the trend to nude love scenes in Hollywood films of the late 1960's was Louis Malle's *The Lovers.* The French had always gone further than anyone else in this direction up to this time, but not even *Devil in the Flesh* (1947) caused as much of a furor here as did this picture. It contains a long nude sequence at the end in which Jeanne Moreau, playing a married woman, and Jean-Marc Bory, as the man with whom she falls in love at first sight, make love. (The foreplay includes their bathing together.)

Artistically, *The Lovers* is a curious amalgam; the first two-thirds is a witty comedy of manners, and then the approach goes lyrical in depicting the joys of physical love. Some people are convinced, and some are not, that it is logical for the heroine to abandon both her husband and her child, as well as her lover, and go away with the man of her dreams without so much as a backward glance.

Historically, the importance of the film in the U.S. is not to be denied. Prosecution of a theatre manager in Cleveland Heights, Ohio, on the grounds of showing an obscene film, engendered a lawsuit that finally made its way to the U.S. Supreme Court, which ruled that the picture did not come under the legal definiton of obscenity. The case against the manager was dismissed.

Producer: Nouvelle Editions des Films. **Director-Scriptwriter:** Louis Malle. **Principal Players:** Jeanne Moreau, Alain Cuny, Jean-Marc Bory and Jose-Luis de Villalonga. **Running time:** 90 minutes. **Released:** Zenith International.

Katharine Hepburn, Albert Dekker and Montgomery Clift in *Suddenly, Last Summer.*

SUDDENLY, LAST SUMMER

"The world of Tennessee Williams is not the world of millions of moviegoers," commented one reviewer when *Suddenly, Last Summer* was released late in 1959. He meant to imply that the average film devotee would be repelled by what he saw in this drama dealing with homosexuality, cannibalism, insanity and sundry other abnormalities.

But that reviewer was wrong: Williams' universe may be largely outside the ken of Everyman, but it certainly had appeal for the American moviegoer in this instance.

On the stage, *Summer* was a one-act play, relating the frenzied efforts of a wealthy aristocratic woman to have a lobotomy performed upon her young niece to prevent her from relating details of the bizarre death of the older woman's son in Spain. To expand the play, Williams and Gore Vidal had to show literally and explicitly many things that were described verbally on stage, and the nature of the horror story was such that it was more effective as a live theatre piece. The power of suggestion is great in treating the macabre.

Nonetheless, film audiences were fascinated by the weird tale, and they were also drawn by the presence of Elizabeth Taylor, Katharine Hepburn, and Montgomery Clift in leading roles.

Producer: Sam Spiegel. **Director:** Joseph L. Mankiewicz. **Scriptwriters:** Tennessee Williams and Gore Vidal. **Principal Players:** Elizabeth Taylor, Katharine Hepburn, Montgomery Clift, Albert Dekker, Mercedes McCambridge and Gary Raymond. **Running time:** 114 minutes. **Released:** Columbia.

Lee Remick, James Stewart and Ben Gazzara in *Anatomy of a Murder.*

ANATOMY OF A MURDER

Crime, the workings of the law, and courtroom procedure in particular have always held a fascination for Otto Preminger (vide *Fallen Angel, Court Martial of Billy Mitchell, Saint Joan, Laura, Advise and Consent,* etc.) In *Anatomy of a Murder,* he staged what is surely his longest trial scene—it runs almost an hour and a half—and what is equally surely his best. Interest never lags.

Some critics will go even further and tell you that *Anatomy* is the all-time crowning achievement of this colorful and controversial producer-director. That ranking of the film is, of course, a matter of opinion, but there is no denying the lasting entertainment value of this film. It is based on Robert Traver's book about an army lieutenant who is placed on trial for the murder of a tavern owner and who claims as his defense that the man had raped his wife.

The American public liked this picture, though some viewers were more or less aghast at part of the dialogue, which today sounds rather tame. At the time, however, it was surprising to hear nice James Stewart as the defense lawyer talk from the motion picture screen about sexual intercourse, using contraceptives, and tests for sperm.

In addition to evidencing the Preminger penchant for rankling upholders of the status quo in the film industry, *Anatomy* also illustrates his gift for apt casting of a film in minor as well as major roles. Vivid players indeed were Stewart, Lee Remick, Ben Gazzara, Arthur

Look Back in Anger with Richard Burton and Mary Ure.

Hiroshima, Mon Amour with Emmanuelle Riva and Elji Okada.

O'Connell, Eve Arden, Kathryn Grant and George C. Scott. And finest of all, playing the wise old judge, was Joseph N. Welch, the Boston attorney who rose to national fame during the McCarthy hearings.

Producer-director: Otto Preminger. **Scriptwriter:** Wendell Mayes. **Principal Players:** James Stewart, Lee Remick, Ben Gazzara, Arthur O'Connell, Eve Arden, Kathryn Grant, Joseph N. Welch and George C. Scott. **Running time:** 160 minutes. **Released:** Columbia.

LOOK BACK IN ANGER

This English film was not too well received in the U.S., but it is important as the classic example of the British "angry young men" school of writing which flourished in the fifties, and carried its influence far beyond that—indeed even up to the present day.

The author was John Osborne, dean of this particular school on the stage, and the collaborator on the screenplay for director Tony Richardson. Essentially it had been and remained a character study—a portrait of a malcontent young Englishman of the day striving to find himself. He was depicted as alternately abominable, pathetic, exasperating and sad. And above all, flip, as a sample line shows: "It's no fun living in the American age—unless, of course, you're an American."

In view of the latter characteristic, the film makers were very lucky in securing Richard Burton to act the role. It was another step on his way to the top; he had already appeared in several British films as well as *My Cousin Rachel* and *The Robe*. His portrayal of the famous Jimmy Porter in this film remains one of his most impressive performances.

Producer: Harry Saltzman. **Director:** Tony Richardson. **Scriptwriters:** John Osborne and Nigel Kneale. **Principal Players:** Richard Burton, Claire Bloom, Mary Ure, Edith Evans and Gary Raymond. **Running time:** 99 minutes. **Released:** Warner Bros.

HIROSHIMA, MON AMOUR

It is often said that after Griffith, nothing new was added to the syntax of the motion picture; later artists simply refined and expanded filmic devices and techniques that the Great Master had discovered and developed when the art was young. This is surely pertinent to the achievement of the French director Alain Resnais in his various experiments in depicting the force of memory, and in revealing the inner thoughts of his characters, in a series of films that began with *Hiroshima, Mon Amour.*

The most effective demonstration of his method here comes in the second part of the picture (it falls roughly into three sections), in which the actress-heroine, with the encouragement of the Japanese architect she has taken as her lover, recalls an early tragedy in her life as a young girl in occupied France during World War II. She had fallen in love with a German soldier who was, shortly after, killed by partisans, and she was subjected to the humiliation of being ostracized by the whole town. The initial joy and subsequent shame and

Ben-Hur with Charlton Heston.

agony of these wartime happenings are brought back in her mind, where they had been deeply buried and almost forgotten, by the associations of Hiroshima (past and present) and the new love affair.

Instead of using an extended conventional flashback, Resnais employed a method of continuous quick cutting from then to now without dissolves or fades. Nor were the various parts of the story put in sequence. They were recorded in bits and pieces without any special order, as the actress summoned them painfully from her subconscious mind.

The effect was terrific—not only as a dazzling technical display, but as an emotional experience. The viewer relived fully the agonizing story the girl was relating.

Hiroshima was well received in art theatres in the U.S., but the audience for the avante garde movie was much smaller at the time than it is today. Its historical importance in technique, which has been much imitated by moviemakers in all countries, stands unchallenged.

Producer-Director: Alain Resnais. **Scriptwriter:** Marguerite Duras. **Principal Players:** Emmanuelle Riva and Elji Okada. **Running time:** 88 minutes. **Released:** Films-Around-the World.

BEN-HUR

In a surprise sweep of the Academy Awards, this spectacular remake of the big hit of the silent period (1927) ran away with eleven Oscars—two more than had been won by *Gone With the Wind.* A decade later when it was reissued, the sound version ranked with *Wind* as the two top-grossing pictures of MGM to that date.

Meanwhile, honors piled up along with the grosses. It was named best picture of the year by the following august groups: British Film Academy, All American Press, New York Film Critics, Federation of Motion Picture Councils and Hollywood Foreign Press Association. The Screen Producers Guild cited Sam Zimbalist as best producer of the year, while the Screen Directors Guild gave their accolade to director William Wyler.

In retrospect, the picture would seem to have been over-awarded, if not over-praised, for there were influential critics who demurred. On balance, it is certainly a better than average quasi-Biblical spectacle with a fine *pièce de résistance*—the famous chariot race between the hero and the villainous Messala. Charlton Heston played Ben-Hur and Stephen Boyd the latter character, the roles taken by Ramon Novarro and Francis X. Bushman in the 1927 film, which was also based on the famous novel by General Lew Wallace.

The silent film set records at box offices everywhere and was reissued in 1931 by MGM with a special musical score and sound effects. Some critics in 1959 compared the two and gave the nod to the older version.

Wyler, a director known primarily for his intelligent adaptations of stage plays to the screen, handled many of the dramatic episodes with his usual expertise, but the thrilling chariot race was staged by Andrew Marton.

Producer: Sam Zimbalist. **Director:** William Wyler. **Scriptwriter:** Karl Tunberg. **Principal Players:** Charlton Heston, Jack Hawkins, Haya Harareet, Stephen Boyd, Hugh Griffith and Martha Scott. **Running time:** 212 minutes. **Released:** MGM.

Doris Day, Nick Adams and Rock Hudson in *Pillow Talk.*

The Mouse That Roared with Peter Sellers.

PILLOW TALK

Rock Hudson was the Number One Moneymaking Star of 1959 (according to the *Motion Picture Herald* poll of exhibitors). Doris Day was fourth. The combination of the two in *Pillow Talk* proved commercially electric in a sex comedy that was much more "talk" (double entendre) than "do." (This accounts, in part, for Miss Day's screen image of the "eternal virgin," which she is still trying to shake.)

The following year, Miss Day jumped to the number one spot with Hudson a close second. There followed a real seesawing in their standings: In 1961, she fell to third, while he remained second (Elizabeth Taylor was first). In 1962, she recovered first place, while he stayed where he had been. In 1963, she held on to the top position, and he fell to third. The year 1964 found them in exactly the same places. Then in 1965, she dropped to third and he disappeared from the golden circle of ten. She stayed in one more year—eighth in 1966—and then she fell off, too.

The record is cited to show that Miss Day and Hudson—whom it is fashionable to disparage today—enjoyed a tremendous vogue with the American public in the 1960's, one that is almost unmatched by any other team to date. The success of *Pillow Talk* led to a repeat pairing of the two in *Lover Come Back* in 1962, which did even better at the box office than its predecessor. In 1964, they co-starred for the third and last time in *Send Me No Flowers.* That proved popular, too, though less so than the others.

Pillow Talk was produced by Ross Hunter and the late Martin Melcher, the latter the husband of Miss Day. Stanley Shapiro and Maurice Richlin won an Academy Award for their screenplay. (Melcher also produced the other two Day-Hudson comedies, and Shapiro produced and wrote the screen-play for *Lover.*) Actor Tony Randall had a role in all three films, and was decidedly an asset to each.

Producers: Ross Hunter and Martin Melcher. **Director:** Michael Gordon. **Scriptwriters:** Stanley Shapiro and Maurice Richlin. **Principal Players:** Doris Day, Rock Hudson and Tony Randall. **Running time:** 105 minutes. **Released:** Universal.

THE MOUSE THAT ROARED

American art-house showmen who had done well with small and off-beat British comedies quickly grabbed this one, which took as its outlandish story notion the supposition that a duchy in the French Alps (mythical, of course) should declare war on the powerful United States—and then proceed to win it with a small band of men.

Fanciers of this type of picture were not alone in admiring it; it eventually attracted a much wider audience in the U.S. Possibly the fact that the story had been run as a serial in *The Saturday Evening Post* accounted for this.

Satiric swipes were taken at Americans and their foreign policies, but the method was not malicious. It was not so much Swiftian as good, clean fun. Peter

Lady Chatterley's Lover with Erno Crisa and Danielle Darrieux.

North by Northwest with Cary Grant.

Sellers played three roles, including that of the Grand Duchess Gloriana, and Jean Seberg was an American girl who became romantically involved with one of the Sellers characters—not the duchess, but a field marshall.

Producer: Walter Shenson. **Director:** Jack Arnold. **Scriptwriters:** Roger MacDougall and Stanley Mann. **Principal Players:** Peter Sellers, Jean Seberg, David Kossoff and William Hartnell. **Running time:** 83 minutes. **Released:** Columbia.

LADY CHATTERLEY'S LOVER

Along with James Joyce's *Ulysses,* D. H. Lawrence's novel *Lady Chatterley's Lover* was banned in the U.S. for three decades, until finally the courts freed it for publication in the late 1950's. So it came as no surprise to some when the French film version of the Lawrence work also met with resistance from the censors.

On the other hand, it should have been surprising, for the film is tame indeed when compared with the book. Both tell the story of an English lady who, her husband being impotent, has an affair with the gamekeeper on his estate and becomes pregnant. Her husband is outraged, so she goes away with her lover at the end.

What got the book banned were the frequent uses of four-letter words, and detailed descriptions of sexual intercourse. On the screen the words are missing (in the English titles, anyhow), and the love scenes are the very soul of discretion: Just as the lovers head for the couch, the director (Marc Allegret) usually cuts to a fire burning brightly away in the fireplace.

The New York censors didn't like those scenes and ordered cuts, but what perturbed them even more—and what they made their official reason for forbidding a license—was their deduction that the film "presented adultery as a desirable, acceptable and proper pattern of behavior."

The case went to the Supreme Court, which promptly reversed the ban. It found that New York again had sought to suppress advocation of an idea, and films had been placed under the free speech amendment.

Even the notoriety of the court case could not save *Lady Chatterley's Lover* at the box office. Word soon got around that it was all a hoax; the picture was old-fashioned and stodgy, and adultery came over as a bore. Lovely Danielle Darrieux was uncharacteristically unimpassioned as Lady Chatterley, and her lover was stiffly acted by Erno Crisa. The poor husband was played by English actor Leo Genn, whose French accent caused more than one member of the audience to titter.

Producer: Gilbert Cohn-Seat. **Director-Scriptwriter:** Marc Allegret. **Principal Players:** Danielle Darrieux, Erno Crisa and Leo Genn. **Running time:** 102 minutes. **Released:** Kingsley International.

NORTH BY NORTHWEST

Many of the critics thought Alfred Hitchcock was just marking time with *North by Northwest,* but the American public was of a different mind, turning it into the most commercially successful of all the pictures he had

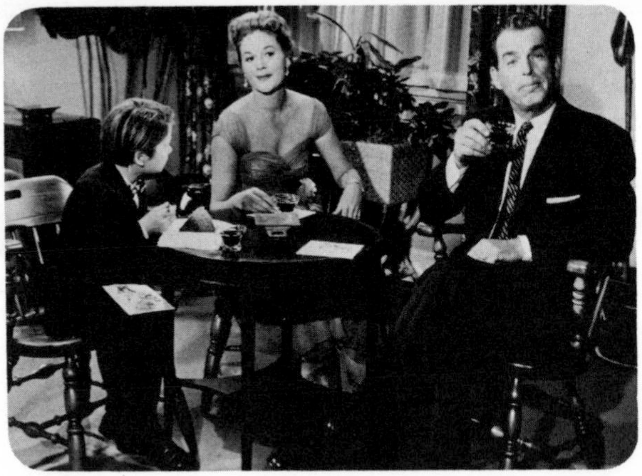

The Shaggy Dog with Tommy Kirk, Jean Hagen and Fred MacMurray.

yet made. (Later, *Psycho* was to surpass it in box-office gross.)

Cary Grant was certainly an enormous factor in its success; he was at his most debonair and charming as the Madison Avenue advertising executive who reluctantly becomes involved in espionage activity. James Mason was the suave chief villain, and Eva Marie Saint the fetching love interest.

One scene, in particular, has become a classic example of suspense in the Hitchcock manner—the one in which Grant, all alone on the flat fields of Indiana, is suddenly attacked with gunshots from an airplane. The combination of something terrifying occurring in the least expected and most ordinary of places comprises the kind of touch which has often been imitated but never equalled.

Producer-Director: Alfred Hitchcock. **Scriptwriter:** Ernest Lehman. **Principal Players:** Cary Grant, Eva Marie Saint, James Mason, Jessie Royce Landis and Leo G. Carroll. **Running time:** 136 minutes. **Released:** MGM.

THE SHAGGY DOG

Walt Disney made his reputation with cartoons, but of his three most commercially successful pictures, two are live-action films—*Mary Poppins* and this one.

Still, *Shaggy Dog* is typically Disney, in that it is a fantasy. A boy turns into a dog as a result of repeating a Latin legend inscribed on an antique ring he finds in the local museum. Tommy Kirk, who had starred in Disney's popular *Old Yeller,* was the youngster so transformed, and the father who can't believe what is happening was played by Fred MacMurray. A spy plot complicates matters, before a happy ending is finally unwound.

There were objections from some quarters that the transformations of Kirk into the dog, which were handled in the same manner as the change of a man into a werewolf in horror films, were too frightening for the younger members of the audience. Scenes with the witch in *Snow White* had been similarly criticized, but the complainants were in a minority in both instances.

Producer: Walt Disney. **Director:** Charles Barton. **Scriptwriters:** Bill Walsh and Lillie Hayward. **Principal Players:** Fred MacMurray, Jean Hagen, Tommy Kirk, Annette Funicello, Tim Considine and Kevin Corcoran. **Running time:** 104 minutes. **Released:** Buena Vista.

RIO BRAVO

In a period in which so many westerns had gone "adult"—that is to say, psychological and sermonizing, if not pretentious—it was refreshing to find one reverting to the practice of telling an engrossing story straight. Howard Hawks' *Rio Bravo* was in that tradition.

No preachy moralizing or trips down bypaths in search of "significance" blocked the single-purposed drive of this immensely popular picture. Hawks was content to tell a simple tale in an entertaining manner.

The story was old-hat: A sheriff in a western town

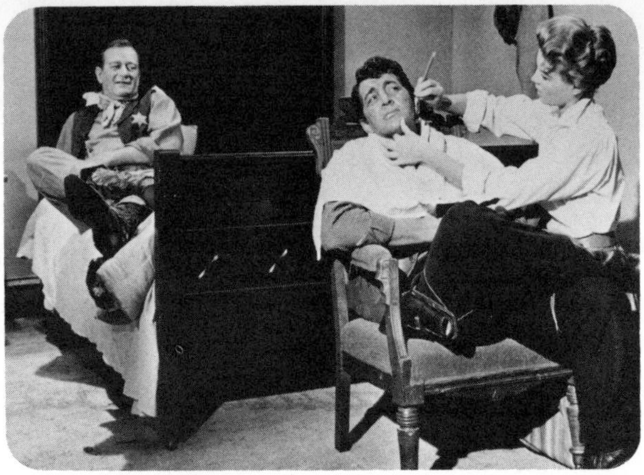

Rio Bravo with John Wayne, Dean Martin and Angie Dickinson.

Simone Signoret and Laurence Harvey in *Room at the Top.*

is determined to carry out his duty to arrest a murderer and to hold the prisoner for trial, in the face of attempts by others to set him free. Suspense is built up through a series of skirmishes in which the hero and his friends usually emerge with the upper hand. In one instance, the heroine attracts the attention of the villains by throwing a vase out of a window.

The acting was tremendously winning—especially that of John Wayne, who went at the role with a vigor that belied the fact he'd played such a sheriff before. Ricky Nelson was fresh and ingratiating as the young gun hand who rallies to the aid of Wayne, and Dean Martin, who had just started then to change his image from comedian to dramatic actor, was quite sympathetic as an alcoholic who pitches in to do his part for his friends. Angie Dickinson was the attractive love interest.

Producer-Director: Howard Hawks. **Scriptwriters:** Jules Furthman and Leigh Brackett. **Principal Players:** John Wayne, Dean Martin, Ricky Nelson, Angie Dickinson, Walter Brennan and Ward Bond. **Running time:** 141 minutes. **Released:** Warner Bros.

ROOM AT THE TOP

The story of *Room at the Top*—a chronicle of a young man of modest background who betters himself in the business world, using methods that are less than scrupulous—comes from a novel by John Braine, a charter member of England's "angry young man" literary school. The author himself commended producers John and James Woolf for the faithful manner in which his original was transcribed to the screen.

In that respect, he should also be grateful to director Jack Clayton, whose conception of the story in film terms was superb, and to Laurence Harvey, Heather Sears and Simone Signoret—particularly the last—for their brilliant acting in the roles of the protagonist and the two women in his life. Miss Signoret, as the married woman and mistress of Harvey who dies in an automobile accident shortly before his wedding to Miss Sears, gave what is generally considered one of the great screen performances of all time. She deservedly—and unexpectedly—won an Academy Award.

The love scenes were very explicit for 1959, and undoubtedly helped contribute to the success the film enjoyed in the U.S., which went far beyond the art house patronage. *Room at the Top* was the most important breakthrough an English film made in the American market since the 1930's.

Producers: John and James Woolf. **Director:** Jack Clayton. **Scriptwriter:** Neil Paterson. **Principal Players:** Laurence Harvey, Simone Signoret and Heather Sears. **Running time:** 115 minutes. **Released:** Continental Distributing.

Monica Vitti and Gabriele Ferzetti in *L'Avventura,* the film that brought international fame to director Antonioni, a film whose style and technique were still being imitated a decade later.

1960

Once again the Communists-in-films issue hit the headlines all across the country. This came at a time when most people in the industry, as well as the public at large, had almost forgotten the great fury of interest in this issue right after World War II. On this occasion, the American Legion charged that the industry had been violating its promises not to hire Communists. Specifically criticized were *Exodus, Inherit the Wind* and *Spartacus.* In rebuttal, Stanley Kramer said the industry had been maturing mentally and inevitably was beginning to deal with controversial subjects. Frank Sinatra defended his choice of Albert Maltz for the scriptwriting assignment on *The Execution of Private Slovik,* "I am responsible . . . in my role as picture maker. In my opinion, I hired the best man for the job." The film was never made.

By spring of the year, peace on this issue had returned, and the American Legion reported results of a film study lauding film people, but asking for more "self-regulation."

Meanwhile, the always troublesome question of censorship was again raised by Rep. Kathryn E. Granahan (D, Pa.) head of a subcommittee of the Postal Operations Committee of the House of Representatives studying obscene and pornographic materials. Eric Johnston, president of the Motion Picture Association, noted in eloquent testimony that the major American companies did not deal in pornography. "Those who do should be arrested, tried in the courts, and if convicted, punished," he said. On another censorship front, the Pennsylvania law on film censorship, passed in 1959 to replace the old law of 1919, was declared unconstitutional.

Films on television continued to make inroads on theatre box-office receipts. Exhibitors formed a company to try to buy up old features and keep them off television. Universal made the first deal with the Screen Actors Guild, breaking the logjam on the TV release of films made after 1948. Soon Warner Bros. sold their post-1948 library. The American Federation of Musicians sued to block this deal, but lost in the courts. Post-1948 pictures brought much higher prices from TV than older films, forcing a fundamental change in motion-picture accounting—which previously had wholly amortized a feature in its original theatrical distribution.

A Boston showman, twenty-five years in the business, had already made his mark. The industry never was the same after Joseph E. Levine's *Hercules* appeared in 1959. Once again it was demonstrated that the public loves a show, and that old-time showmanship in new forms could attract a great audience for a film of little merit. Partially due to the infectious optimism of Levine, and partially because of better grosses, especially in 4,500 drive-in theatres throughout the country, gloom in the industry was less pervading than in the past several years.

In the first year of this decade, hailed by some financial writers as "The Soaring Sixties," the spirits of the American film industry in Hollywood and throughout the country were filled with hopes of a modest improvement in box-office returns. *Spartacus,* the most expensive film made thus far in Hollywood, had its initial openings. Alfred Hitchcock's *Psycho* attracted huge crowds. A few imported films achieved unusual popularity, heralding a trend that became increasingly significant.

Stars of the year: Doris Day, Rock Hudson, Cary Grant, Elizabeth Taylor, Debbie Reynolds, Tony Curtis, Sandra Dee, Frank Sinatra, Jack Lemmon and John Wayne.

Kirk Douglas and John Ireland in *Spartacus.*

Psycho with Anthony Perkins.

SPARTACUS

It was a nervous and hopeful management of Universal Pictures that finally launched the most expensive picture the company had made to date (and reputed to be the most costly produced in Hollywood to that time) in the fall of 1960. Originally budgeted at about five million dollars, costs had spiralled until they totalled twice that.

There was good reason for concern. *Spartacus* was a spectacle with sex but no religious angle. It had a cast of fine players but only two big box-office "names" in Kirk Douglas, its executive producer-star, and Tony Curtis. The script had been written by the previously black-listed Dalton Trumbo from a novel by Howard Fast. The director was Stanley Kubrick, whose previous work had been with small, off-beat pictures. And there were rumblings in advance about excessive violence and the inclusion of an episode involving a homosexual proposition made by one male character (a Roman general played by Laurence Olivier) to another (a slave played by Curtis).

Shortly after the New York premiere on a roadshow policy, the controversial sequence was cut out, along with some nude bathing shots that had also aroused objections. The cleaned-up and abbreviated *Spartacus* went on to become a big hit in initial roadshow engagements, and an even larger one later when it played regular continuous performances.

The original version ran 188 minutes. In 1967 Universal reissued the film with prints running 161 minutes. Further excisions had obviously been made. Unlike *Ben-Hur, Gone With the Wind* and a few other spectacles, which have been held back for future theatrical engagements, *Spartacus* then went to television, where it was shown early in 1969 in prime time on two separate evenings.

The best things about the film remain its brilliantly staged and edited gladiator sequences, and the acting of Olivier and Peter Ustinov, the latter practically stealing the picture with his droll performance.

Producer: Edward Lewis. **Director:** Stanley Kubrick. **Scriptwriter:** Dalton Trumbo. **Principal Players:** Kirk Douglas, Laurence Olivier, Jean Simmons, Charles Laughton, Peter Ustinov, Tony Curtis and John Gavin. **Running time:** 188 minutes. **Released:** Universal.

PSYCHO

Alfred Hitchcock is as adept a showman as he is a director; indeed he combines the two in a manner that is unique in the history of the screen. *Psycho* is the ultimate expression of his methods both on screen and off, and helps to explain why he is one of the very few directors whose names are capable of drawing customers to the box office.

He made this film under conditions of extreme secrecy, allowing no visitors on the set during shooting. No stills of any key scenes were released in advance. Neither theatremen nor reviewers were permitted to see the finished picture until opening day in each city.

Lelia Goldoni (right) in *Shadows.*

What is more, he revived the old showmanship gimmick of closing the theatre doors after the picture had started and forcing everyone to see it from the beginning. This policy was written in as a part of the contract for all theatres booking the film, and the old device has never worked so well before or since. The public didn't mind at all; in fact, they started forming lines early in the day.

And they certainly liked what they saw, once they got in. The old master of suspense had a number of surprises up his sleeve, including the completely unexpected business of starting out his film as if it were to be about one character (Janet Leigh as a girl who steals some money from her employer and flees town) and then suddenly killing her off and focusing on other characters—most notably the psychopath (played by Tony Perkins) who has murdered her for reasons that have nothing to do with the stolen money.

Audience attention may have been jolted by this—especially since the murder in the shower was one of the most brutal and gruesome scenes ever filmed—but it did not lag. Only at the end did it falter slightly, because the explanation of the psyche of the killer was too involved and unconvincing.

Psycho inspired a host of imitations—pictures that reveled in blood and gore, none of which came close to matching the original.

Producer-Director: Alfred Hitchcock. **Scriptwriter:** Joseph Stefano. **Principal Players:** Anthony Perkins, Vera Miles, John Gavin, Martin Balsam and Janet Leigh. **Running time:** 109 minutes. **Released:** Paramount.

SHADOWS

Ironic as it seems today, John Cassavetes, until then known only as an actor, had to go to Europe in 1960 to get a distributor for *Shadows,* the first film he directed. Lion International opened it in London, where it was rapturously received by the critics. Then the British firm brought it to the U.S. in 1961, where it had a fair commercial success.

Shadows is a film "improvisation"—a picture photographed without a prepared script. Cassavetes first gave his actors a general story outline, and then discussed each scene in detail before it was shot. Once the cameras started to roll, the actors were on their own, with the actual dialogue and much of the action contributed spontaneously by them.

General audiences here were apparently put off by the technical crudities and weaknesses in continuity. The story is a simple one about the problems of three young black people—a girl and her two brothers—living in Manhattan. Within this general framework, some powerful individual scenes were created by the players, who included Lelia Goldoni, an actress of Italian descent, in the role of the light-skinned young woman; Ben Carruthers as the younger brother; and Hugh Hurd as the older one. Anthony Ray played the white man who seduced the girl and then rejected her when he discovered she was not white.

After *Shadows,* Cassavetes was hired by Hollywood to direct two pictures—*Too Late Blues* (1962) for Paramount, and *A Child Is Waiting* (1963) for United Artists.

L'Avventura with Monica Vitti.

Neither enjoyed much success, and he went back to acting until 1966, when he independently produced and directed *Faces*. Again he had trouble in interesting a distributor until the picture caught on in Europe and was praised at the 1968 New York Film Festival. Walter Reade picked it up for his Continental Distributing Company, and the money rolled in.

Producer: Maurice McEndree. **Director:** John Cassavetes. **Principal Players:** Hugh Hurd, Lelia Goldoni, Ben Carruthers and Anthony Ray. **Running time:** 87 minutes. **Released:** Lion International.

L'AVVENTURA

Jeered by the audience when it had its first public showing at the Cannes Film Festival in 1960, *L'Avventura* went on from that rude reception to receive world-wide critical acclaim and to become one of the most influential films of modern times. The writer-director Michelangelo Antonioni had made eight pictures prior to this, and he has made five since, but *L'Avventura* is still generally regarded as his masterpiece.

The story begins on an air of mystery. A group of wealthy Italians is having a weekend yachting party and lands on a barren volcanic island. One of their number—a beautiful heiress—suddenly disappears. What has happened to her becomes the concern of all her companions.

Did she commit suicide? Or did she somehow make her way back to the mainland? Or did something else occur? The rest of the film concerns the search for this girl and a love affair that develops between her best friend and her fiance as they look for her. The lost is never found, but at the end, the new romance has survived several crises and is apparently going to be continued.

It is not the story as such that is important in *L'Avventura;* rather, it is what Antonioni has made of it in terms of character analysis and philosophy. His method is indirect and, at first glance, obscure, which is probably the cause of the antagonistic reception the picture was given at its first public showing. He explains his approach thusly: "I follow my characters beyond the moments conventionally conceived to be important—to show them even when everything appears to have been said." This involves the building of detail after detail into a rich and complex mosaic.

Along the way Antonioni develops the themes that have reappeared in other of his pictures: the transitoriness of love; the difficulty of communication between people who ought to find it easy; the dichotomy between conventional standards of morality and how people behave in actuality.

A typical Antonioni technique is to have two characters talking in a scene with their backs to each other. This is only one of his stylistic devices that have been imitated by directors all over the world.

Producer-Director-Writer: Michelangelo Antonioni. **Principal Players:** Monica Vitti, Gabriele Ferzetti, Lea Massari, Dominique Blanchar and James Addams. **Running time:** 145 minutes. **Released:** Janus Films.

Shirley MacLaine and Jack Lemmon in *The Apartment.*

Max von Sydow in *The Virgin Spring.*

THE APARTMENT

A Hollywood story has it that when *Ace in the Hole* (1951, later retitled *The Big Carnival*) proved a commercial disappointment, Billy Wilder vowed he would never again make a "serious" picture. Many such stories are apocryphal, but this one must have more than a grain of truth in it. Just look at the names of Wilder films of the 1950's: *Stalag 17, Sabrina, Seven Year Itch, Witness for the Prosecution* and *Some Like It Hot.* We deliberately omit *The Spirit of St. Louis* (1957), in which he turned to "serious" subject matter once more. It was a commercial flop, too.

The others, mostly comedies, were successful, and Wilder began the new decade of the sixties with *The Apartment*—again a comedy, but one with more of the bitter cynicism in it that ran through his early work, but which had practically disappeared from view in the fifties.

Strip away the gags and the occasional pauses for pathos, and *The Apartment* would be a much more devastating comment on moral behavior. The theme is still there, but it is coated over with humor, and that is probably why the film proved so popular. Wilder had learned his lesson.

The basic situation is actually rather sordid: A clerk in an insurance company, in an attempt to get to the top quickly, makes a practice of lending the key to his apartment to executives of the firm so they can carry on extramarital activities. No character in the film is really likable, but Jack Lemmon and Shirley MacLaine—he as the enterprising clerk, and she as the girl friend of one of the married executives—brought their own brands of charm to the parts and made the characters more palatable than they otherwise would have been. Fred MacMurray played the role of a married executive who philanders. He was quite good in it, but he was deluged with letters from protesting fans who preferred to see him in Disney movies as a "nice guy." He never veered from the latter image again.

It is no wonder that *The Apartment* was chosen by the Academy as best picture of the year. The competition was *The Alamo, Elmer Gantry, Sons and Lovers,* and *The Sundowners.*

Producer-Director: Billy Wilder. **Scriptwriters:** Billy Wilder and I. A. L. Diamond. **Principal Players:** Jack Lemmon, Shirley MacLaine and Fred MacMurray. **Running time:** 125 minutes. **Released:** United Artists.

THE VIRGIN SPRING

Ingmar Bergman won his first Academy Award (best foreign picture of the year) for this adaptation of a thirteenth-century legend and Swedish folk song called "The Daughter of Tore of Vange." It was well received in America by admirers of the cryptic Swede who argued its meanings as intently as they had those of *The Seventh Seal* and *The Magician* before it.

The story itself has the simplicity of legend. The young and innocent daughter of an isolated farmer in Sweden is raped and murdered by three herdsmen while

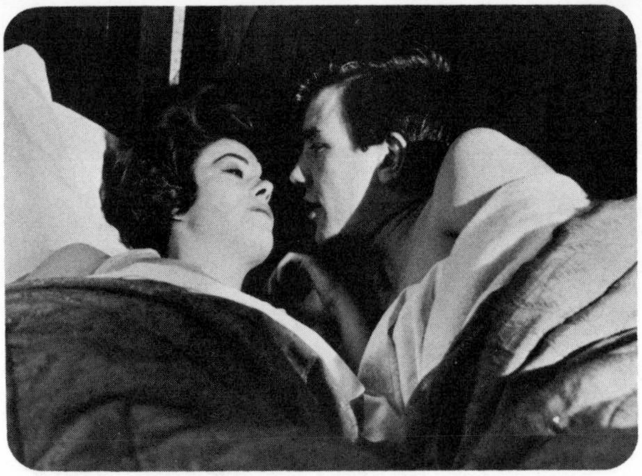

Saturday Night and Sunday Morning with Rachel Roberts and Albert Finney.

riding to church to light candles for the Holy Virgin. Her father captures and slaughters the killers, but then becomes penitent and promises God he will build a church of stone with his own hands on the spot where his daughter died. At that very moment a trickle of water comes forth and bursts into a stream on the site—the "virgin spring."

The telling of this stark and foreboding tale has the usual Bergman trademarks: the obsession with dreams, the occult, religion and abstractions of good and evil. The acting, as usual, is superb, with Max von Sydow especially fine as the vindictive father. Gunnel Lindblom had a small role as a neurotic servant girl who witnesses the crime.

Producer: Svensk Filmindustri. **Director-Writer:** Ingmar Bergman. **Principal Players:** Max von Sydow, Birgitta Valberg, Gunnel Lindblom and Birgitta Pettersson. **Running time:** 88 minutes. **Released:** Janus Films.

SATURDAY NIGHT AND SUNDAY MORNING

Of the several pictures to come out of the English "angry young man" writing school, this was one of the two best. (The other: *Room at the Top.*) It is also important as the film that introduced Albert Finney to American audiences, which he was to captivate later, on a much larger scale, in such films as *Tom Jones* and *Two for the Road.*

Out of an ordinary story and material, Alan Sillitoe, who adapted his own book to the screen, and Karel Reisz, the director, made a film in which the characters are as real and life-like as the smoke and dirt in the industrial city in which they live. Especially in the hero was a three-dimensional characterization achieved. It is a portrait of a "type" in one sense—the eternal rebel against authority, the chronic malcontent. But through incisive writing and the brilliant acting of Finney, the character is highly individualized.

Other characters were also well drawn and splendidly performed: Rachel Roberts as the errant wife who becomes the mistress of the hero, and Shirley Anne Field as the girl with whom he finally settles down.

Producers: Harry Saltzman and Tony Richardson. **Director:** Karl Reisz. **Scriptwriter:** Alan Sillitoe. **Principal Players:** Albert Finney, Shirley Anne Field and Rachel Roberts. **Running time:** 90 minutes. **Released:** Continental Distributing.

ELMER GANTRY

As Elmer Gantry, prototype of the flamboyant fundamentalist preachers who thrived in the 1920's and created by Sinclair Lewis in his savage novel, Burt Lancaster had his most substantial role in years. He dug into it with gusto, and the result was an Academy Award as best actor of the year.

In a move to head off anticipated objections from religious sects, the Gantry character was not presented as the ordained minister fallen from grace that Lewis

Elmer Gantry with Burt Lancaster.

had made him. Still, he was conceived as a booze-guzzling, woman-chasing young punk who discovers he has a gift for oratory and joins forces with an already established female evangelist. Together they attain wealth and power, only to lose it when she is killed in a tabernacle fire.

Richard Brooks, the writer-director, summed it up this way: *"Elmer Gantry* is the story of a man who wants what everyone is supposed to want—money, sex and religion. He's the All-American boy."

Shirley Jones, an actress usually cast as a nice girl, played a prostitute, and—not surprisingly—won an Oscar as best supporting actress. Jean Simmons was cast as the evangelist wooed and won by the hero, and pop singer Patti Page did a guest stint as head of a religious singing group.

The distributor of the film, United Artists, officially "advised" exhibitors that they not admit anyone to theatres playing *Elmer Gantry* unless they were 16 years or over. The religious satire and bluntness of some of the dialogue were considered daring for the day.

Producer: Bernard Smith. **Director-Writer:** Richard Brooks. **Principal Players:** Burt Lancaster, Jean Simmons, Dean Jagger, Arthur Kennedy and Shirley Jones. **Running time:** 145 minutes. **Released:** United Artists.

West Side Story with Richard Beymer and Natalie Wood, one of the four most popular musical films in the first four decades of sound and winner of ten Academy Awards.

1961

The dilemma of the year, at least for critics interested in foreign films, was whether "to dub or not to dub." With the growing release of imported products, pressures mounted for more dubbing. Some critics upheld the "purity" of subtitling, asserting that too much of the film's true flavor was lost in dubbing. Most patrons, on the other hand, were prepared to accept dialogue, even out of lip-synchronization, just to be able to hear English, and not try to read and watch the screen action at the same time. In the end the controversy was settled, as so many things are, by the laws of economics. If the picture had limited appeal, subtitles sufficed. If a mass audience was projected, the greatly increased cost of dubbing was considered a reasonable investment. Some films were released both ways to satisfy critics and sophisticates.

The Supreme Court added to the confusion of the censorship issue in the *Don Giovanni* case, by seeming to uphold the constitutionality of Chicago's film licensing system, even though the banning of a particular film was stopped. Also, in a blow to liberals, the High Court upheld Sunday theatre closing laws, or blue laws.

Hollywood once again was unsuccessfully wrestling with its eternal problem of extravagance. The fact that so many top-ranking stars, writers and directors were independent (that is, in all save money which, as always, came from the big companies) increased pressures for higher costs. Most of the independents had "a piece of the action," namely a partnership in each film. In some instances, all rights to the picture negative reverted to the independent seven years from release. Credits were a continuing problem as personalities jockeyed for prestige, having obtained, for the nonce, about all the money they could expect. Contract clauses on credits, including the size of type of a star's name, relative prominence of pictures in ads and the like, ran to pages and pages. In desperation, to avoid official credit problems on some pictures, exhibitors advertised only the film title and skipped everything else. Other exhibitors, often with the tacit approval of the distributors, simply ignored the official credits and sold the picture as they thought best in their communities.

The shift of increasing numbers of Negroes from the South to northern cities, and the concomitant rise of interest in civil rights attracted attention to the fact that whole new audiences were being found for some pictures and some theatres. In time, blacks would become a very significant group of ticket buyers for many movies in the dozen largest cities of the North.

Veteran producer Sol Lesser's long drive for a Motion Picture and Television Museum in Hollywood collapsed, killed by many factors, including the success of Disneyland, and the Universal Studio tour designed to attract paying visitors to the studios. Moreover, Hollywood at no period in its history could ever generate lasting interest in its past. It was and is a "now" town. Life is lived only for the day, and that applys generally to business life as well as personal life. The impact of this philosophy was widely felt in all levels of the American film scene.

La Dolce Vita, Never on Sunday and *Two Women* were releases of the year which showed that audiences' acceptance of screen material was broadening rapidly. *West Side Story* was a musical film of unusual and enduring success.

Stars of the year: Elizabeth Taylor, Rock Hudson, Doris Day, John Wayne, Cary Grant, Sandra Dee, Jerry Lewis, William Holden, Tony Curtis and Elvis Presley.

Richard Beymer and Natalie Wood in *West Side Story.*

La Dolce Vita with Marcello Mastroianni and Anita Ekberg.

WEST SIDE STORY

One of the four most popular musical films ever made (the other three: *The Sound of Music, Mary Poppins* and *My Fair Lady*), this modern paraphrase of the Romeo and Juliet story has an enduring appeal. A big entry in the 1961–62 movie season as a roadshow attraction, it started out at a fast pace and never let up. Reissued in 1968, it once more drew large crowds.

The idea for turning Shakespeare's star-crossed lovers into teenagers from the West Side of New York allied with rival street gangs (the "Jets" and the "Sharks") came from Jerome Robbins, who directed and choreographed the Broadway show and was co-director of the film with Robert Wise (who also produced). Arthur Laurents wrote the book, which Ernest Lehman adapted to the screen.

Highlight of the picture most certainly was the dancing, which Robbins brilliantly re-staged for the new medium. The opening number, in which the rival gangs gather on separate parts of the West Side and then come together for brief sparring, was photographed right on the streets of New York. Colorful and cinematic also was the handling of the "America" number, in which the "Sharks" cavort on a roof with their girl friends, and the big "rumble" scene in which gang members from each side are slain.

In the "Juliet" role, Natalie Wood presented the directors with a handicap: She was neither a dancer nor a singer. To get around this, Robbins gave her a minimum of routines to do and arranged those so cleverly that it seemed she performed more than she actually did. The singing voice, of course, was dubbed.

Other actors who helped matters were Rita Moreno, Russ Tamblyn and George Chakiris. A sour note was struck by Richard Beymer, who, in the "Romeo" role, lacked pathos and strength.

West Side Story won ten Oscars, including an honorary award to Jerome Robbins.

Producer: Robert Wise. **Directors:** Robert Wise and Jerome Robbins. **Scriptwriter:** Ernest Lehman. **Principal Players:** Natalie Wood, Richard Beymer, Russ Tamblyn, Rita Moreno and George Chakiris. **Running time:** 155 minutes. **Released:** United Artists.

LA DOLCE VITA

Not since the days of the silent spectacles before 1920 (*Quo Vadis, The Last Days of Pompeii, Cabiria,* etc.) had an Italian picture proved so popular with large American audiences as did Federico Fellini's *La Dolce Vita*. Not even subtitles put off the large crowds who rushed to see it at exorbitant prices in metropolitan roadshow engagements, and a later print dubbed into English proved similarly successful in continuous-run theatres.

For three hours, Fellini depicted Rome as a modern-day Sodom or Gomorrah, stringing together fictional episodes (some allegedly based on fact) designed to expose sin and corruption among the middle and upper classes. As a unifying device, Fellini used a newspaper gossip columnist who either observed or participated in

One-Eyed Jacks with Karl Malden and Marlon Brando.

the various events, from the staging of a "miracle," in which two children falsely claimed they saw a vision of the Madonna, to an orgy in an ancient castle peopled with prostitutes, transvestites, decadent aristocrats and other sordid types. The gifted Marcello Mastroianni portrayed the columnist—a man who did not feel deeply, had guilt feelings because he couldn't, and finally realized he had become immune to emotion.

Whatever one's reservations about the philosophical profundity or lack thereof in the film, there was no denying the technical skill with which it was made. Fellini's images were rich and brilliant and edited so fluidly and diversely that they fairly swirled across the screen, their intoxicating powers increased immeasurably by the Nino Rota score, which has become a classic in its own right.

Producer: Riama Films. **Director:** Federico Fellini. **Scriptwriters:** Federico Fellini, Tullio Pinelli, Ennio Flaiano, Brunello Rondi. **Principal Players:** Marcello Mastroianni, Walter Santesso, Anouk Aimée, Yvonne Furneaux, Anita Ekberg, Alain Cuny, Magali Noel, Nadia Gray and Lex Barker. **Running time:** 175 minutes. **Released:** Astor Pictures.

ONE-EYED JACKS

Just as every clown is supposed to want to play Hamlet, it seems many actors pine to direct a film. Marlon Brando, who burst spectacularly onto the motion picture scene in 1950 in *The Men,* after his big stage success as Stanley Kowalski in *A Streetcar Named Desire* (which he repeated in the film in 1952), got his chance to direct by giving it to himself. His own company, Pennebaker Productions, made *One-Eyed Jacks* under the auspices of Paramount. When Brando had a disagreement with Stanley Kubrick, who had signed to direct the western, he took over the reins.

The film was a long time aborning, and the cynics were certain Brando would fall on his face. He didn't, although he has not directed another picture to date.

An "adult" western in its time, *One-Eyed Jacks* had the usual action elements, but also stressed character relationships and the development of a theme to the effect that an obsession with vengeance can corrupt a man to a point that almost breaks him. Not surprisingly, director Brando was at his best in drawing good performances from his cast: Karl Malden as a villain; Katy Jurado as his compassionate wife; Ben Johnson as a cagey outlaw; and newcomer Pina Pellicer as the heroine, a pathetic girl whom the hero (Brando) makes pregnant.

Under his own direction, Brando, too, gave a first-rate performance—one not to be ranked with those in *Streetcar* or *On the Waterfront,* but a commendable one nonetheless. The many complex moods of the vengeance-bent hero were brilliantly illuminated.

California's Big Sur made a beautiful scenic background for the picture, which was photographed in the short-lived VistaVision process.

Producer: Frank P. Rosenberg. **Director:** Marlon Brando. **Scriptwriters:** Guy Trosper and Calder Willingham. **Principal Players:** Marlon Brando, Karl Malden, Pina Pellicer and Katy Jurado. **Running time:** 141 minutes. **Released:** Paramount.

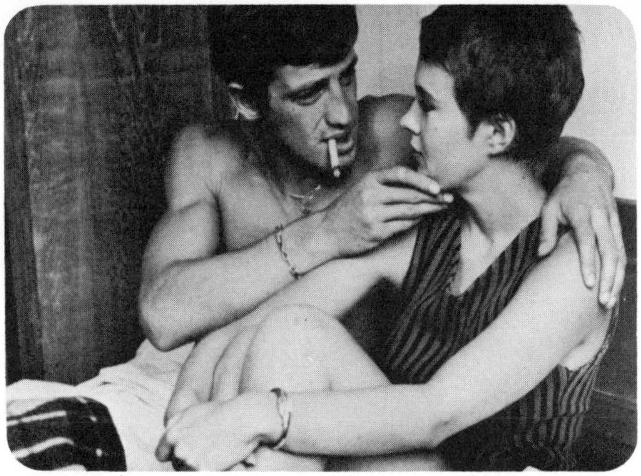

Jean-Paul Belmondo and Jean Seberg in *Breathless.*

Never on Sunday with Melina Mercouri.

BREATHLESS

This early French "new wave" film was made in the relatively short period of four weeks, and achieved international reputations for its three key people virtually overnight.

They are, of course, the director Jean-Luc Godard (his first feature-length film, after making shorts and documentaries); French actor Jean-Paul Belmondo, who soon came to be known as the Gallic Humphrey Bogart; and the American Jean Seberg, who won plaudits of the critics while still smarting from the hostile reviews of her disastrous acting debut in Otto Preminger's film version of Shaw's *Saint Joan.*

Godard dedicated this film, in a foreword, to Monogram Pictures, whereby he paid homage to those American "B" films of yesteryear which he so greatly admired. They were completed, as was his film, on rigidly limited shooting schedules and budgets, but actually, many of them had more technical polish than does *Breathless,* which most of the time seems to have been made up by Godard as he went along.

This is not to disparage his method, for part of the appeal that *Breathless* had when it first came out and still has is its air of spontaneity. This helps to make the Belmondo character—a petty thief who models himself on Bogart's image—and his girl friend, an equally amoral type, played by Miss Seberg, just that much more credible.

Two other "new wave" talents—later to become even more famous on their own—lent assistance to Godard on *Breathless.* François Truffaut worked on the script, and Claude Chabrol supervised production.

Producer: Georges de Beauregarde. **Director-Writer:** Jean-Luc Godard. **Principal Players:** Jean Seberg and Jean-Paul Belmondo. **Running time:** 89 minutes. **Released:** Films-Around-the-World.

NEVER ON SUNDAY

Prostitutes with hearts of gold have always had a winning way about them on the stage and screen, and the American public took the one portrayed by Melina Mercouri in this picture to their hearts. A Greek actress, known prior to this only to art-house audiences, the high-spirited and vivacious lady became a U.S. celebrity overnight. (The road has been rocky since: *Phaedra* and *Topkapi* were not hits.)

Never on Sunday was written, produced and directed by Jules Dassin, who also played the role of a moral reformer who sets out to persuade the heroine to turn from her evil ways, and makes a botch of it. In telling this story, a kind of spoof on Maugham's *Rain,* he took satiric swipes at several targets, including "ivory-tower" scholarship, the gory plots of Greek tragedy, unionism, gangsterism and reform movements.

Over two-thirds of the dialogue is in English, with the Greek concisely and colorfully translated in subtitles. The title song was catchy and is certainly to be credited with its part in the success of the film. It won an Oscar for best song of the year.

The property was turned into a musical on Broadway

Two Women with Sophia Loren.

The Guns of Navarone with Gregory Peck and Anthony Quinn.

in the 1967–68 season, starring Miss Mercouri. It had only a fair run.

Producer-Director-Writer: Jules Dassin. **Principal Players:** Melina Mercouri and Dassin. **Running time:** 97 minutes. **Released:** United Artists.

TWO WOMEN

Sophia Loren has the distinction of being the first actress to receive an Oscar from Hollywood as the best of the year in a picture that was not spoken in English. She was cited for her performance in this Italian film, in which she played a widow whose efforts to protect her teenage daughter from the ravages of war end disastrously. As they seek to return to Rome from the countryside, whence they had unavailingly fled for safety, they are set upon by a band of Moroccan soldiers and both of them are raped.

Miss Loren was indeed superb; her acting was emotionally vivid and often powerful in effect. Some of the credit for it is surely due to the director, Vittorio De Sica (of *Bicycle Thief* fame), but the greatest triumph was indisputably hers. With this picture, she erased her image of a beautiful star who could decorate a film but couldn't really act.

In America, the picture was first released in a subtitled version to art theatres, but with a promotional campaign organized by Joseph E. Levine to attract a different audience than the one he had lured to *Hercules.* It worked well, and a later version of the film dubbed into English was a smashing success—especially after Miss Loren got her Oscar.

Producer: Joseph E. Levine. **Director:** Vittorio De Sica. **Scriptwriter:** Cesare Zavattini. **Principal Players:** Sophia Loren, Jean-Paul Belmondo, Eleanor Brown and Raf Vallone. **Running time:** 105 minutes. **Released:** Embassy Pictures.

THE GUNS OF NAVARONE

Was this World War II suspense film intended as a spoof or straight adventure story? Critics argued the fine point right and left, but the inconsistency of tone bothered the public not one whit. They turned it into one of the most popular action movies of all time.

Carl Foreman, who had written the scripts for *High Noon* and *The Men,* wrote this one and then produced it himself, under the banner of his Highroad Productions.

The picture was shot on location off the rugged Aegean cliffs of Greece, high up on which were mounted two German guns which it was the mission of the Allied *Navarone* heroes to destroy. It was really an impossible task, even for the likes of Gregory Peck, David Niven, Anthony Quinn, Stanley Baker, et al., but it was finally carried out in true story-book fashion.

Public approval aside, the picture picked up only one Academy Award—for special effects.

Producer-Writer: Carl Foreman. **Director:** J. Lee Thompson. **Principal Players:** Gregory Peck, David Niven, Anthony Quinn, Stanley Baker, Anthony Quayle and Irene Papas. **Running time:** 157 minutes. **Released:** Columbia.

Peter O'Toole and Omar Sharif in *Lawrence of Arabia,* the spectacular adventure film that brought them to world attention and won for director David Lean his second Academy Award.

1962

This was the year of *Cleopatra*. The filming in Rome, with the activities—on and off the screen—of Elizabeth Taylor and Richard Burton, filled newspaper and magazine columns throughout the world. The film had the highest production cost in the history of the screen (to that time), one estimate putting the sum at $30,000,000. Cleopatra's "curse" hit Spyros Skouras, the dynamic president of 20th Century-Fox, and sponsor of CinemaScope, which did so much to keep theatres alive in the darkest days of the television boom in the 1950's. Darryl F. Zanuck was elected president of 20th Century-Fox.

Fred Zinnemann helped to focus industry eyes on a problem usually ignored: the fact that no opportunity in production was being provided for newcomers. The famed director observed, "We need them more than they need us." Elaborate training was being given in all types of film making under the aegis of some well-known Hollywood names, yet the gnawing question remained, "Where do these young people go when they are trained?" Union rules and studio traditions effectively barred the way, forcing most talented young people into other fields or into non-theatrical and industrial pictures.

This year was the highwater mark of imported films. Of the 798 pictures licensed in New York, 582 came from outside the United States. This fact was often cited in the last-ditch fights by those in favor of censorship, who asserted that Americans had to be protected from European immorality.

Across the U.S., newspaper attention to films fell to a low point. Films which had for so many decades dominated the newspaper amusement pages received less and less space, with television demanding more and more of the attention of newspaper writers and editors. Many in the theatrical film world thought that the fact that newspapers had such extensive interests in TV stations was a relevant factor in the situation.

At last the long-criticized pattern of first-run exhibition, with showing of a new film regularly confined to one theatre, began to break down in New York and other key cities. "Showcase" was the name used for a method of simultaneous run of a new picture in a number of theatres. At the same time there was a substantial increase in admission prices, forecasting the time when neighborhood theatres would get the same or almost the same admission prices as downtown houses.

In Hollywood, there were signs that the sleeping giant of production was reawakening, stimulated importantly by the making of films for television. MCA, owners of Universal City studios, began the first major construction of studio facilities for film making since shortly after the advent of talking pictures, with a $20,000,000 building program.

Last Year at Marienbad and *The Loneliness of the Long Distance Runner,* while neither was very popular with the ticket-buying public, were influential on future trends, especially in approaches to story material and in directorial techniques. *To Kill a Mockingbird* was a well-acted film of strong emotional appeal which was tremendously successful with both the critics and the fans alike.

Stars of the year: Doris Day, Rock Hudson, Cary Grant, John Wayne, Elvis Presley, Elizabeth Taylor, Jerry Lewis, Frank Sinatra, Sandra Dee and Burt Lancaster.

Daniela Rocco and Marcello Mastroianni in *Divorce, Italian Style.*

Ralph Richardson, Dean Stockwell and Katharine Hepburn in *Long Day's Journey Into Night.*

DIVORCE, ITALIAN STYLE

A spoof on the difficulties of securing a divorce in Italy, this film was much appreciated by moviegoers in America, who generally do not have to go to such excessive lengths to rid themselves of unwanted spouses. It was a much-praised comedy as well as a commercial success, winning an award at Cannes and even snaring an Oscar for the screenplay of Ennio De Concini, Alfredo Giannetti and Pietro Germi.

Germi also directed the picture, which is built around the absurd stratagems a man dreams up to dispose of his wife so he can wed another woman. The husband tries to arrange a situation in which he can kill her as an affair of honor, and is finally successful when a childhood sweetheart fortuitously appears and makes love to the wife.

Star of the film is Marcello Mastroianni, who first came to wide American attention as the central character in *La Dolce Vita.* He gave a superbly comic performance here in an exaggerated dead-pan style reminiscent of Buster Keaton. With a simple quirk of the mouth, he expressed annoyance, impatience, inspiration or fulfillment, and each time he aroused laughter. Daniela Rocca was also amusing as the nagging wife who cannot get enough sex.

Producer: Joseph E. Levine. **Director:** Pietro Germi. **Scriptwriters:** Pietro Germi, Ennio De Concini and Alfredo Giannetti. **Principal Players:** Marcello Mastroianni, Daniela Rocca and Stefania Sandrelli. **Running time:** 104 minutes. **Released:** Embassy Pictures.

LONG DAY'S JOURNEY INTO NIGHT

The original version of this screen adaptation of the Eugene O'Neill play ran for two hours and fifty-four minutes and, except for minor deletions, contained the whole of the original text, word for word. First openings of the film were at art theatres with non-reserved matinees but reserved seats for evening performances. Public response was lukewarm, and the film was cut substantially for later engagements.

Even in an abbreviated state, however, the picture offers a powerful emotional experience that has not dimmed one whit over the years. Arguments by film purists at the time that it was merely a "photographed stage play" now seem even more fatuous and irrelevant than they did when first uttered.

Such objectors missed the point: *Long Day's Journey* was never intended to be a "movie" in the conventional sense. It might be called, for lack of a better phrase, a "filmed recording" of a play that many drama critics regard as the supreme achievement of the greatest American playwright.

What is more, this recording is one that will give future generations the opportunity to observe, study and enjoy the towering O'Neill work as performed by artists of his own time. Director Sidney Lumet and his four gifted players—Katharine Hepburn, Ralph Richardson, Jason Robards, Jr., and Dean Stockwell—not only respected the lines of O'Neill but illuminated them and their many implications flawlessly.

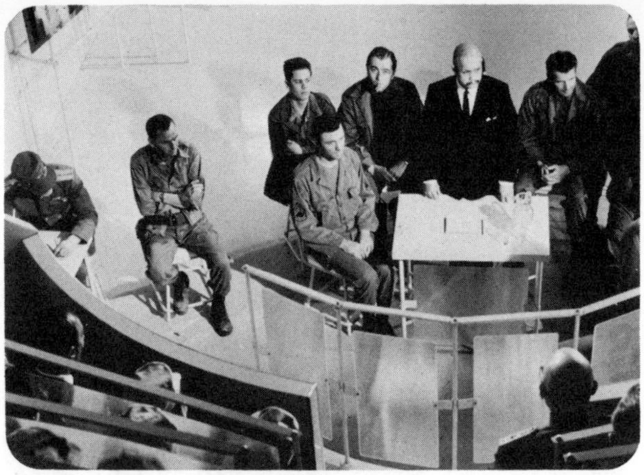

The Manchurian Candidate with Laurence Harvey, at left of table.

The essence of the drama is in its characters, and their revelations of themselves and their relationships to each other. As portrayed in the film they come fully alive: the mother, brave and pathetic in her losing battle with dope addiction; the father, selfishly striving to make an unhappy present durable by reveling in his dreams of a glorious past as a stage actor; the older brother, burdened with a sense of failure that he seeks to alleviate in drink; and the younger brother, the sensitive writer observing the agonies of his family and unable to help.

The film was the official U.S. entry in the 1962 Cannes Film Fesitval, and the four stars received a joint award for their performances. The picture was photographed entirely in New York City and Long Island, in thirty-seven days, a very short schedule for a major production.

Producers: Ely Landau and Jack J. Dreyfus, Jr. **Director:** Sidney Lumet. **Principal Players:** Katharine Hepburn, Sir Ralph Richardson, Jason Robards, Jr., and Dean Stockwell. **Running time:** 174 minutes. **Released:** Embassy Pictures.

THE MANCHURIAN CANDIDATE

In explaining the commercial disappointment of a film which ought to have done better at the box office than it did, experts may claim that it was ahead of its time. This is often a feeble excuse, but in the case of *The Manchurian Candidate* it is indisputably true.

In spite of such stars as Frank Sinatra and Laurence Harvey, this picture was a financial disappointment to its makers when it first opened late in 1962. Since then, however, it has been taken up by the film buffs, and is a favorite with their societies and among college students interested in motion pictures. The esteem in which these groups hold director John Frankenheimer is also a factor, this being his fourth theatrical film. (He started on television.)

Why did it fail then, and why did it belatedly catch on? The probable answer—an educated guess—is that its mixture of styles made audiences uneasy at first. It is composed of various proportions of satire, suspense thriller and allegory. In attempting this audacious and capricious approach, *The Manchurian Candidate* was a forerunner of such films as *Alphaville, Blow-Up* and *Juliet of the Spirits,* which accustomed audiences to accept unusual combinations of fantasy, reality and symbolism. Today's moviegoers are much more sophisticated and aware and appreciative of technique than they were just six or seven years ago.

A sobering sidelight: An attempted political assassination is a key factor in the plot of the picture. Since *The Manchurian Candidate* first appeared, this country has known three such assassinations.

Acting honors were stolen by two supporting players: James Gregory as a Senator resembling Joe McCarthy, and Angela Lansbury as the epitome of American Momism.

Producers: George Axelrod and John Frankenheimer. **Director:** Frankenheimer. **Scriptwriter:** Axelrod. **Principal Players:** Frank Sinatra, Laurence Harvey, Janet Leigh, Angela Lansbury, Henry Silva and James Gregory. **Running time:** 126 minutes. **Released:** United Artists.

Peter O'Toole (center) and Omar Sharif (right) in *Lawrence of Arabia.*

The Longest Day with Robert Mitchum.

LAWRENCE OF ARABIA

Techniques of desert warfare have probably never been shown on the screen at any time so graphically and dramatically as in this ambitious and expensively produced picture dealing with the life of the English Army officer who organized and led Arab tribes to drive out the Turks from Arab lands in the First World War. Photographed in color in Super Panavision 70, in the same (or similar) locales in which the original events occurred, these battle sequences sweep up the spectator with their fury, shock and repel him with their violence, and then leave him limp with a new awareness of the horror of all war.

Indeed, this vivid immediacy of the battle scenes so dominates the spectacular picture, produced by Sam Spiegel and directed by David Lean, that it overshadows the efforts to unravel the riddle of T. E. Lawrence, the man. The screenplay by Robert Bolt (author of *A Man for All Seasons*) made several stabs at the latter project, but in the end, Lawrence emerged as a fascinating facade whose real motivations stood unrevealed. The transformation from a man who abhorred killing to one who seemed to revel in it was not convincing.

There remain, however, the terrific battles and other memorable cinematic touches, such as the small dot on the horizon from which materializes a black-clad horseman, and those long lines of camels racing across the vast sands.

Peter O'Toole, then a newcomer to the screen, was entrusted with the difficult leading role. At times he was excellent, but he was not able to overcome weaknesses in the script with an overpowering performance—as a more experienced actor might have done. The best acting came from Omar Sharif as the sheik who became the hero's close friend.

Lawrence won the Academy Award as the best picture of 1962 and six other Oscars, including one for Lean's direction.

Producer: Sam Spiegel. **Director:** David Lean. **Scriptwriter:** Robert Bolt. **Principal Players:** Peter O'Toole, Alec Guinness, Anthony Quinn, Jack Hawkins, José Ferrer, Anthony Quayle, Claude Rains, Arthur Kennedy and Omar Sharif. **Running time:** 221 minutes. **Released:** Columbia.

THE LONGEST DAY

With the possible exception of *The Birth of a Nation,* for which the total grosses are unknown, *The Longest Day* has accumulated more money for its makers than any other black-and-white picture. It was produced by Darryl F. Zanuck as an independent production for release by 20th Century-Fox, but by the time it opened, he had assumed the presidency of that company.

The undertaking was indeed ambitious—a screen re-creation of the epochal events of June 6, 1944, when the Allies cracked open Hitler's Fortress Europe by establishing beachheads on the Normandy coast. Cornelius Ryan wrote the screenplay from his own book of the same name, and additional episodes were scripted by such novelist luminaries as Romain Gary and James

James Mason, Sue Lyon and Shelley Winters in *Lolita.*

Jones, along with David Pursall and Jack Seddon. Three directors were employed: Ken Annakin for the British exterior episodes; Andrew Marton for the American; and Bernhard Wicki for the German. Elmo Williams was associate producer and coordinator of battle episodes.

The aim was a quasi-documentary approach, and there were no recognizable stock shots of government library footage in the picture. However, the effect was vitiated somewhat by use of an "all-star" cast. The greatest hurdle *The Longest Day* had to overcome in achieving the ultimate in realism was the guessing game of what well-known actor would turn up next. Among those to be spotted were John Wayne, Henry Fonda, Robert Ryan, Paul Anka, Robert Mitchum, Sal Mineo, Fabian, Richard Todd and Richard Burton.

Female roles were understandably sparse, but one clue to the success of *The Longest Day* is that the distaffs liked it. Traditionally, war pictures are anathema to them, but this one had combat scenes that were not excessively brutal and repulsive.

Producer: Darryl F. Zanuck. **Directors:** Ken Annakin, Andrew Marton and Bernhard Wicki. **Scriptwriters:** Cornelius Ryan, Romain Gary, James Jones, David Pursall and Jack Seddon. **Principal Players:** Eddie Albert, Arletty, Richard Beymer, Richard Burton, Sean Connery, Irina Demich, Mel Ferrer, Steve Forrest, Leo Genn, John Gregson, Werner Hinz, Curt Jurgens, Peter Lawford, Roddy McDowall, Robert Mitchum, Edmond O'Brien, Madeleine Renaud, Tommy Sands, Richard Todd, Peter Van Eyck, Stuart Whitman, Paul Anka, Jean-Louis Barrault, Bourvil, Red Buttons, Ray Danton, Fabian, Henry Fonda, Gerd Froebe, Jeffrey Hunter, Sal Mineo, Kenneth More, Ron Randell, Robert Ryan, Rod Steiger, Robert Wagner and John Wayne. **Running time:** 180 minutes. **Released:** 20th Century-Fox.

LOLITA

"How did they ever make a movie of *Lolita?*" So asked the ads for this screen adaptation of the once notorious novel by Vladimir Nabokov. The novelist himself wrote the screenplay under the more rigorous standards of the old Production Code—long since scrapped for much less restrictive guidelines more suitable for the moral standards of the 1960's.

One thing they did in 1962 which they probably wouldn't have done in 1969 was to advance the age of the heroine from twelve, in the book, to around fifteen, without even explicitly saying they had done so. Cast in the part was Sue Lyon, whose looks at that time could have been construed as ranging between the ages of fifteen and eighteen.

But her boy friend, Humbert Humbert, remained about forty in the person of James Mason, and the details of their rocky cross-country affair, conducted mostly in motels, followed the book surprisingly closely. In his direction, Stanley Kubrick was insinuating rather than explicit; the most erotic event took place under the credits with Mason giving Miss Lyon a pedicure (no faces were shown—only hands and feet).

Kubrick also made much of the ironic and macabre Nabokov humor that runs through the story, and inspired a brilliant performance from Shelley Winters as the mother of Lolita. This character, widowed for seven years and beset with an aggravating "itch" for a man, was a genuine tragi-comic creation whom Miss Winters played for all it was worth. Peter Sellers was disap-

The Loneliness of the Long Distance Runner with Tom Courtenay.

Through a Glass Darkly with Lars Passgard and Harriet Andersson.

pointing as Quilty, the mysterious writer who follows Lolita and Humbert on their automobile tour, adopting various disguises along the way.

Producer: James B. Harris. **Director:** Stanley Kubrick. **Scriptwriter:** Vladimir Nabokov. **Principal Players:** James Mason, Shelley Winters, Peter Sellers and Sue Lyon. **Running time:** 152 minutes. **Released:** MGM.

THE LONELINESS OF THE LONG DISTANCE RUNNER

Upon its release in the U.S. late in 1962, this picture was regarded as something of a disappointment for producer-director Tony Richardson after *Look Back in Anger* and *A Taste of Honey,* and many critics put it down as a distinctly minor entry in the British School of neo-realism that had commenced four years before. In the late sixties, however, the film was taken up by students of film, and it has become for them one of their favorite pictures, referred to by one professor as a kind of *Silas Marner* for his classes.

It is not hard to see why. A generation that has taken the hero of *The Graduate* so to its hearts can also appreciate the symbolic gesture of the long distance runner when he deliberately loses the race at the end of the film as an expression of his contempt for the tradition and authority that is represented by the reform school official who is so keen to have him win the trophy.

Significant, too, is the fact that the act of defiance by the youth is motivated by an urgent need for self-assertion. No glory accrues to him because of it; outwardly he is not better off. The victory is a purely spiritual one.

Alan Sillitoe wrote the screenplay, which contains some acute character observation and satirical comment on life in England under the welfare state. Richardson's direction was notable for its use of milieu and sound, and Tom Courtenay made an impressive film debut as the title character.

Producer-Director: Tony Richardson. **Scriptwriter:** Alan Sillitoe. **Principal Players:** Michael Redgrave, Tom Courtenay, Avis Bunnage, Peter Madden and James Bolam. **Running time:** 103 minutes. **Released:** Continental Distributing.

THROUGH A GLASS DARKLY

This moody and intense film by the prolific Ingmar Bergman would have appealed to Eugene O'Neill, not only in its theme, but in its preoccupation with madness and incest, and in the starkness of its setting in an isolated house by the Baltic Sea.

A young woman just released from a mental institution is restored to her family—her father, a self-absorbed novelist; her brother, bedeviled by the problems of adolescence; and her husband, a doctor who has stood faithfully by his wife throughout her illness. It develops that she is a schizophrenic who cannot be cured, and at the end of the film she returns permanently to the hospital of her own volition. In the meantime,

Last Year at Marienbad with Giorgio Albertazzi and Delphine Seyrig.

she has had a profound effect on all the various members of her family, forcing them to new degrees of self-recognition.

There is some hope indicated at the conclusion, as the father and son are drawn close together for the first time.

Bergman rose magnificently to his ambitious theme—-man's search for God—and orchestrated it eloquently with searching close-ups of the four characters, counterposed with some beautifully composed images of the sea.

Bach's Suite No. 2 in D Minor was used sparingly and effectively as background music.

As usual in Bergman's films, the acting was flawless. As the pathetic girl still rational enough to understand her plight at times, Harriet Andersson gave one of the most vivid demonstrations of the moods of madness ever put on the screen.

Producer: Svensk Filmindustri. **Director-Writer:** Ingmar Bergman. **Principal Players:** Harriet Andersson, Gunnar Bjornstrand, Max von Sydow and Lars Passgard. **Running time:** 91 minutes. **Released:** Janus Films.

LAST YEAR AT MARIENBAD

The French "new wave" director, Alain Resnais, went too far for most Americans with this elaborate exercise in cinema technique. Critics wrote erudite interpretations of it—none of which agreed with another—but the general public just wasn't interested.

Scriptwriter Alain Robbe-Grillet studiously avoided plot in the usual sense, but there was a bare outline of a story involving a "stranger," a "woman," and a "man who may be her husband," all of whom come together at a huge, luxurious hotel in the past century. The stranger tells the woman that he knew her in the past and that they had arranged a rendezvous in Marienbad the previous year to go away together a year later. The woman resists at first, presumably because of her ties to the other man, but in the end she surrenders to the stranger and leaves the hotel with him.

With no steadily developing plot to follow, spectators perforce had to be content with concentrating on technique. The photographic imagery was rich (especially in shots of the hotel interiors and surrounding gardens); organ music in the background was hypnotic; cinematic stunts like the one in which the actors froze into tableaux, came to life to deliver dialogue, and then froze again, were fascinating. Then, too, the stylized acting of the principals was intriguing.

Robbe-Grillet, in explaining the film, said it was intended "to show events not only as they happen but as the characters would like them to happen," and that it "fused the past with the present and the future, and real scenes with the imaginary."

In other words, *Last Year at Marienbad* means what you want it to mean.

Producer-Director: Alain Resnais. **Scriptwriter:** Alain Robbe-Grillet. **Principal Players:** Delphine Seyrig, Giorgio Albertazzi and Sacha Pitoeff. **Running time:** 93 minutes. **Released:** Astor Pictures.

Gregory Peck and Brock Peters in *To Kill a Mockingbird.*

TO KILL A MOCKINGBIRD

The Harper Lee novel on which this film was based was well-received both by the critics and the reading public: It won a Pulitzer Prize and was on the best-selling lists for two years, with six million copies bought in that time. It was thus what Hollywood likes to call a "pre-sold" property.

Still, it was not an easy picture to make: The story is presented through the eyes of children (in the South, during the Depression), inviting sentimentality and slush; and the melodramatic business of rape charges brought by a white girl against an innocent black man, and the courtroom trial of the latter, could easily have been overdone.

Thanks to the good taste and tact of the team of Alan Pakula, the producer, and Robert Mulligan, the director (who worked together subsequently, but never with quite the same success), the picture came off splendidly with all pitfalls avoided. Horton Foote's script, which won him an Oscar, was faithful both to the book and the film medium.

The film makers added to the hazards of their project by choosing unknowns for the roles of the two children around whom the story revolves. Neither Mary Badham nor Phillip Alford had any previous experience, yet they performed with a naturalness and lack of affectation that was completely winning.

In the role of their father, the liberal lawyer who represents the accused Negro, Gregory Peck underacted in his customary fashion. The Academy gave him an Oscar for his work—an accolade denied him after each of his four previous nominations.

Producer: Alan Pakula. **Director:** Robert Mulligan. **Script-writer:** Horton Foote. **Principal Players:** Gregory Peck, Mary Badham, Phillip Alford, John Megna and Frank Overton. **Running time:** 129 minutes. **Released:** Universal.

THE MIRACLE WORKER

Anne Bancroft and Patty Duke, playing Annie Sullivan and Helen Keller, respectively, had been much praised by drama critics when they appeared in the roles on Broadway. They repeated them so well for the film version that each won an Academy Award—Miss Bancroft as best actress and Miss Duke as best supporting actress.

In all respects, in fact, the film is a faithful reproduction of the play, concentrating almost wholly on the relationship between the teacher-and-companion and the young girl struck deaf, blind and mute shortly after birth. It begins with the arrival of Miss Sullivan at the Keller home in Alabama in the early twentieth century and continues through her first and disappointing attempts to communicate with the afflicted child by finger-sign language to the moment of victory when Miss Keller was able to connect the hand symbol with the object for it.

High point of the dramatic episodes is the famous physical battle between the two protagonists as the teacher attempts to force table manners upon the re-

The Miracle Worker with Anne Bancroft and Patty Duke.

luctant child. Arthur Penn staged this on screen as he did on Broadway with no holds barred. Food is splattered all over the dining room; dishes are tossed about and broken; and the participants at one point are fighting each other on the floor. It is quite a "theatrical" affair.

An improvement was achieved over the play in one instance—the handling of Miss Sullivan's anguished memories of the death of her younger crippled brother in an institution. The distracting off-stage voices used on Broadway were replaced by images superimposed over the face of Miss Bancroft and put barely in focus so as to emphasize not only the fact that Miss Sullivan was in her youth almost blind herself, but also to suggest the nightmarish quality of the experiences.

Producer: Fred Coe. **Director:** Arthur Penn. **Screenplay:** William Gibson (from his own play). **Principal Players:** Anne Bancroft, Patty Duke, Victor Jory, Inga Swenson and Andrew Prine. **Running time:** 106 minutes. **Released:** United Artists.

Tom Jones, the first British film to win an Academy Award for best picture since 1948, and the film that made household names in America of Albert Finney (center) and Henry Fielding.

1963

The assassination of President Kennedy in Dallas overshadowed the film year as it did all aspects of American life. Many of the major U.S. theatre owners were in Madrid to see *The Decline and Fall of the Roman Empire* at the time of the assassination, and they were overwhelmed by the grief felt for the President by peoples abroad.

The Kennedy Administration's principal impact on films was in the exhibition sphere, through pressures to desegregate theatres. In May, President Kennedy invited theatre operators from eleven Southern and border states to meet with him at the White House to discuss integration. At that time, only 109 of 566 towns and cities in the areas affected permitted Negroes to attend theatres not set aside exclusively for them. A measure of the effectiveness of Kennedy in this area is that by the time of his death only six months later integrated theatre towns jumped up to 253 of the 566. Significant was the fact that all actions were taken voluntarily, and without disturbance of any kind.

On Kennedy's death, the trade magazine *Motion Picture Herald* editorialized: "The best service that exhibitors can do in memory of a great President is to push on in an orderly and intelligent fashion towards the goal of non-discriminatory admission in every theatre in the land. . . . Any theatre owners who drag their heels on desegregation risk incurring sanctions from the new administration."

For the first time, film roadshows were given the status of legitimate theatre plays. In London, ticket agencies began to give substantial advance guarantees of ticket purchases for outstanding roadshow films. In the United States, those who organized theatre parties and club parties became increasingly important prospects in merchandising long-run film roadshow engagements. The roadshow involves a limited number of shows per week, usually ten, with scheduled performances and high ticket prices for reserved seats.

Doris Day was the most popular screen star for the second year in a row. It was the time for the pseudo-sophisticated screen comedy. Everything risqué was suggested, but little was shown, and it all turned out nicely in the end because Doris was just like the girl next door—if more attractive and better dressed.

The Longest Day, Darryl F. Zanuck's re-creation of D-Day in Europe, continued its tremendous success, begun the year before. It was the first "big" picture in a long while in black-and-white, and possibly the last of those in the spectacle genre. This year also saw release of *Cleopatra.* Had the film been made on even twice the original budget, it would have been a record money-maker. Not many had nice things to say about Marlon Brando's remake of *Mutiny on the Bounty,* another way-over-budget film. *Dr. No,* United Artists' made-in-England sex-and-intrigue film staring an unknown, Sean Connery, launched an amazing cycle. Soon, studios all over the world were looking for imitators of Connery and imitations of the love 'em and kill 'em plots. The James Bond cycle did much to kindle a re-interest in moviegoing.

Stars of the year: Doris Day, John Wayne, Rock Hudson, Jack Lemmon, Cary Grant, Elizabeth Taylor, Elvis Presley, Sandra Dee, Paul Newman and Jerry Lewis.

Patricia Neal and Paul Newman in *Hud.*

The Great Escape with Steve McQueen, Jud Taylor and James Garner.

HUD

Paul Newman had played an anti-hero character in *The Hustler* two years before *Hud* with great success (good reviews, good business and an Oscar nomination). He took the image of the amoral protagonist—the heel you love to hate—even further in *Hud,* and the effort paid off proportionally (better reviews, better business and another Oscar nomination—but still no Oscar).

It was a sign of the changing times—this acceptance by the American public of amoral behavior in a movie protagonist, which formerly would have been condemned. Both Hud and the Hustler were selfish and self-aggrandizing men who hurt the people about them through their lack of personal concern or even involvement. Nor were they called upon to pay for their sins at the end in the old Hollywood tradition. The Hustler may have seen the error of his ways (he walked out on the pool "racket" for good after one final victory), but Hud did not. Hud may not have liked being rejected by his nephew at the end—an act that was really a denial of Hud's amoral way of life—but one knew he would survive even this blow. Hud has neither a conscience nor a soul.

Plainly, Martin Ritt and Irving Ravetch, co-producers of the film (Ritt also directed, and Ravetch co-authored the script with his wife, Harriet Frank, Jr.), were influenced not only by the success of *The Hustler* but also by the years of foreign films in which evildoing had gone unpunished. The Ravetch screenplay was based on a novel called *Horseman, Pass By,* by Larry McMurty. Although it was set in modern Texas, and the leading characters were ranchers, it was in no sense a typical western. The events could have transpired almost anywhere.

In addition to Newman's work, there were three other admirable performances, two of which won Oscars. Patricia Neal was cited for her extraordinarily poignant portrait of a good woman grown cynical because of the hard knocks of fate. Melvyn Douglas won an award for his depiction of the old western rancher with traditional values who comes into sharp conflict with his modern-minded son, Hud. Brandon de Wilde was also fine as the grandson-nephew who finally opts for the moral code of the Douglas character and renounces Hud.

The picture was the fourth collaboration of Newman and Ritt; Ritt had directed the actor previously in *The Long, Hot Summer, Paris Blues* and *Hemingway's Adventures of a Young Man.*

Producers: Martin Ritt and Irving Ravetch. **Director:** Martin Ritt. **Scriptwriters:** Irving Ravetch and Harriet Frank, Jr. **Principal Players:** Paul Newman, Melvyn Douglas, Patricia Neal and Brandon de Wilde. **Running time:** 112 minutes. **Released:** Paramount.

THE GREAT ESCAPE

Films set in prisoner-of-war camps in Nazi Germany proliferated in Great Britain right after World War II. *The Captive Heart* was the best-made of these, and was the prototype of the many that followed.

The harem scene with Marcello Mastroianni in *8½*.

Definitely of that school, but produced on a much larger scale than any of the others, was this Hollywood version of the story, based on "actual events" as recorded in a book called *The Great Escape* by Paul Brickhill. Producer-director John Sturges took his cameras and crew to Germany to film it on location.

Based on fact or not, it came over as more than slightly incredible in detailing the mass escape of a large group of Allied officers from a POW camp, in which, this time, there were as many Americans as Englishmen. This enabled Steve McQueen and James Garner to have top roles with the British contingent headed by Richard Attenborough and James Donald (the latter having played the doctor in *The Bridge on the River Kwai*).

Sturges' film is excellent in depiction of such details as the careful plans for escape, the construction of three tunnels at once with two ultimately abandoned, and the ingenuity displayed by the heroes.

The ending did not tax credulity as much as the initial success of the escape did; seventy-five prisoners got out, but all except two were recaptured, and fifty were shot on the orders of a Gestapo agent.

James Coburn and David McCallum, who were later to go on to much bigger roles, had small parts in the all-male cast.

Producer-Director: John Sturges. **Scriptwriters:** James Clavell and W. R. Burnett. **Principal Players:** Steve McQueen, James Garner, Richard Attenborough, James Donald, Charles Bronson, Donald Pleasence and James Coburn. **Running time:** 168 minutes. **Released:** United Artists.

8 ½

The whimsical title of this picture, which won the Academy Award as the best foreign film of the year, was chosen by Federico Fellini because he had previously made three short (or half) films and six full-length features. This, then, was his 8½th movie.

It begins with a weird and fascinating sequence, in which a man is trapped in an automobile in the middle of a traffic jam and is striving desperately to get out. The windows of the car begin to steam, and his panic increases as he begins to kick at the immovable doors and to moan in despair.

The episode turns out to be a fantasy in the mind of the hero, a film director who has reached an impasse in the writing and casting of a new picture. It is to be a very personal film, and the work he has done on it has not only stirred vivid memories of his boyhood but forced him to examine his relationships with his wife, his mistress and his close friends. His creative frustration is so great that he is ready to abandon the project completely, until, at the end, he suddenly works through his problems (in what amounts to a revelation about himself) and returns willingly to the fray.

The bizarre episode with which *8½* commences not only defines the dilemma of the hero in a display of brilliant symbolism, but sets a standard for interest and sheer cinematic virtuosity that one might not expect the rest of the film consistently to match. The wonder of *8½* is that what follows does just that—magnificently.

Cleopatra with Elizabeth Taylor.

David and Lisa with Keir Dullea and Janet Margolin.

The picture is a compound of many elements—realism, fantasy, satire, philosophy and farce—all of which have been used with superb assurance and originality by the master Italian film maker. It is also acted with stunning skill by Marcello Mastroianni as the director; Anouk Aimée as his wife; and Sandra Milo as the mistress.

Producer-Director: Federico Fellini. **Scriptwriters:** Federico Fellini, Tullio Pinelli, Ennio Flaiano and Brunello Rondi. **Principal Players:** Marcello Mastroianni, Claudia Cardinale, Anouk Aimée and Sandra Milo. **Running time:** 135 minutes. **Released:** Embassy Pictures.

CLEOPATRA

The history of this ill-fated film—the most expensive production of all time—is a veritable comedy of errors, adding up to a series of anecdotes that are more diverting than what finally made its way to the screen. The story is fraught with economic waste (sets built at Pinewood that were never used); scandal (the Taylor-Burton affair); a musical-chairs game of who was going to do what (switches in writers, directors, producers, stars); sundry other mishaps (tantrums on the set, brawls between the stars and importunate photographers, etc.); and an unending series of lawsuits, in which, it seemed, everybody involved in the film was suing everybody else. Gossip columnists had a field day.

If out of all this a great film had emerged, none of these things would ultimately have mattered. Alas, it didn't; the same story was told much better by both Shakespeare and Shaw, to put it temperately. The production was spectacular, but what was visible on the screen hardly added up to thirty million dollars.

Spurred on by all the notoriety, the American public went to see the picture—initially paying roadshow prices—but the word-of-mouth was generally poor. Critics varied in their appraisal of the script of Joseph L. Mankiewicz (who also directed), Ranald MacDougall and Sidney Buchman. They also disagreed over the merits of the performances of the principals.

Academy Awards went to the film for color cinematography, color art direction, color costume design and special effects.

Cleopatra is reported to have finally shown a profit, as a result of sales to television.

Producer: Walter Wanger. **Director:** Joseph L. Mankiewicz. **Scriptwriters:** J. L. Mankiewicz, Sidney Buchman, Ranald MacDougall. **Principal Players:** Elizabeth Taylor, Richard Burton, Rex Harrison, Pamela Brown, George Cole, Hume Cronyn and Roddy McDowall. **Running time:** 243 minutes. **Released:** 20th Century-Fox.

DAVID AND LISA

The team of Eleanor and Frank Perry (she writes the screenplay; her husband directs, and sometimes produces) has developed and refined a very special technique in making films. They like to take a simple plot situation and construct it in a series of vignettes that reveal character and character relationships. The den-

Albert Finney in *Tom Jones.*

sity of the whole is increased by underlying themes which are always stated eliptically rather than directly.

The method is apparent in their first theatrical film, *David and Lisa* (after much distinguished work on television), and runs through *Ladybug, Ladybug* (1963), *The Swimmer* (1968) and *Last Summer* (1969), in which it achieves its ultimate expression.

In *David and Lisa,* the Perrys were finding their way. The story is set in a school for emotionally disturbed children, and the leading characters are a youth who cannot bear to be touched and a girl who has schizophrenic tendencies (one personality is mute while the other talks rapidly in childish rhymes). The characters are not probed in much depth, and the ending is glibly symbolic: The girl starts to speak naturally, and the boy takes her by the hand. Their discovery of love has apparently cured them, being a more important factor than the work of the resident psychiatrist.

For all its faults, *David and Lisa* shows several talents in embryo—not only the Perry's, but those of beginning actors Keir Dullea and Janet Margolin as the neurotic adolescents. Veteran Howard Da Silva was splendid as the all-wise head of the school.

The picture was cited at the Venice Film Festival in 1962 as best by a new director, and Dullea and Miss Margolin were declared best actor and best actress at the San Francisco Film Festival the same year.

Producers: Paul M. Heller and Frank Perry. **Director:** Frank Perry. **Scriptwriter:** Eleanor Perry. **Principal Players:** Keir Dullea, Janet Margolin, Howard Da Silva, Clifton James and Neva Patterson. **Running time:** 94 minutes. **Released:** Continental.

TOM JONES

The Henry Fielding novel of the picaresque adventures of an eighteenth-century rogue seemed an unlikely subject for Tony Richardson, high priest of the school of social realism in English film making (*The Loneliness of the Long Distance Runner, A Taste of Honey, Look Back in Anger*). Yet he took the classic work and made it into a gay and bawdy comedy that delighted the critics, and turned out to be one of the most successful English films in America of its decade.

The script by John Osborne placed emphasis equally on the action (fistfights, sword duels, hunts with hounds, etc.) and on the numerous romantic encounters of the hero. The tone for the droll approach throughout was set brilliantly by a prelude to the credits in which the discovery of the foundling baby Tom by Squire Allworthy is played out in silent movie fashion.

It would be hard to imagine a better cast. Albert Finney made a perfect Tom—manly, yet guileless and without sanctimony. Susannah York was a lovely Sophie, and Hugh Griffith was her bellowing father.

One scene became a classic on its own, and has been widely imitated and parodied ever since: the one between Finney and Joyce Redman, in which they seduce each other with their eyes over dinner at an inn. *Tom Jones* won four Oscars, including one for best picture.

Producer-Director: Tony Richardson. **Scriptwriter:** John Osborne. **Principal Players:** Albert Finney, Susannah York, Hugh Griffith, Dame Edith Evans, Joan Greenwood and Diane Cilento. **Running time:** 131 minutes. **Released:** United Artists.

A scene from *Dr. Strangelove, Or: How I Learned to Stop Worrying and Love the Bomb,* a "black" comedy about the atomic bomb which surprised nearly everyone by making money.

1964

The Hollywood studio czar was reborn in a new form this year, in the person of Richard Zanuck, son of Darryl Zanuck. Some observers had asserted that studio heads such as Mayer, Schenck and Zanuck of old (including the still reigning Jack Warner) would never be seen again. They were proven wrong as young Zanuck reopened the 20th Century-Fox studio and launched it on a period of prosperity.

Cinerama, which did so much to capture the public's imagination in 1952 and 1953, took another turn, with prominent West Coast exhibitor William R. Forman succeeding international entrepreneur Nicholas Reisini as president. The three-camera, three-screen process of the original Cinerama had been outmoded by technology of wide single-strip films (65mm and 70mm), but the name Cinerama still had magic. Its "you-in-the-action" approach was often imitated with varying degrees of success.

For the last time, one hopes, the spectre of Communism was raised and set to rest. This year, the Mindszenty Foundation charged that leftists had infiltrated the U.S. film industry. Four films were attacked: *Fail Safe, Seven Days in May, Dr. Strangelove* and *The Victors*. The charges were irrational and absurd, but they created a momentary flurry of concern as some thought the Mindszenty Foundation must be connected officially with the Catholic Church (which it was not) and that it represented a considerable body of theatre patrons (which it did not, being a very specialized ultra-conservative society of extremely limited appeal).

U.S. film makers showed they were tuned in to the "new wave" of film making with *The Pawnbroker* (not released in the U.S. until 1965), which attracted wide attention at the Berlin Film Festival. Meanwhile, the roadshow boom reached absurd proportions, with nine set for the year.

Death called Martin Quigley, the man who originated the industry's self-regulatory code system. Although he never produced, distributed or exhibited even one film, for much of his long life of activity no one possessed a greater knowledge of what the motion picture as a storytelling medium was all about. His vision was of the motion picture as a whole: a creation, a product and a communications medium of extensive influence on spectators.

The Supreme Court, in reversing the conviction of Cleveland theatre manager Nico Jacobellis in *The Lovers* case, admitted that "contemporary community standards" was not a perfect standard of acceptability. It set the stage for the doctrine of "variable obscenity"—obscene for the young, not so for adults—and it raised the question of national standards versus community standards for judging obscenity. Some wondered whether obscenity could be legally *defined* any longer.

Subscription TeleVision, brain child of Sylvester "Pat" Weaver, was tried, but was outlawed by a public referendum in California. The tests showed that technology, including a computer to do the billing, was sufficiently advanced to serve the needs of pay TV. The remaining problems were economic.

Becket, a film made in the grand manner, showed that

such a method could still be exciting when stars, direction and production values were all of a high order. The vast talents of Stanley Kubrick became better appreciated in *Dr. Strangelove, Or: How I Learned to Stop Worrying and Love the Bomb.* A case can be made for Kubrick being the first major film maker to reflect the ideals and aspirations of the anti-Vietnam War and anti-Establishment young Americans. Best-selling novelist Harold Robbins' *The Carpetbaggers* was made into a sprawling and popular movie.

Stars of the year: Doris Day, Jack Lemmon, Rock Hudson, John Wayne, Cary Grant, Elvis Presley, Shirley MacLaine, Ann-Margret, Paul Newman and Richard Burton.

Rex Harrison, Audrey Hepburn and Stanley Holloway in *My Fair Lady.*

MY FAIR LADY

This all-time stage hit not unexpectedly turned out to be one of the all-time movie successes. This despite the hard feelings engendered in many by Jack L. Warner when he bypassed Julie Andrews, who won plaudits as Liza Doolittle on Broadway, for Audrey Hepburn, on the grounds that she was a star of proven box-office draw.

As it turned out, Miss Hepburn was splendid, though she was, perhaps, more at home when Liza was transformed into a lady than she had been when Liza was a guttersnipe. Rex Harrison repeated his stage performance of Professor Higgins and won an Oscar as best actor, one of eight the film received. Others were for best picture, director, color cinematography, art direction, costume design, musical score and sound. Miss Hepburn was not even nominated, and the best actress award ironically went to Julie Andrews for *Mary Poppins.*

It was all there on screen—the eternally provocative Pygmalion legend, as interpreted in the play by Bernard Shaw that Alan Jay Lerner transferred to the musical stage—and also to screen—with its wit intact; the intelligent and beautifully integrated music and lyrics of Lerner and Loewe; the Cecil Beaton costumes; and all the rest. The $17,000,000 production cost actually showed on the screen.

Producer: Jack L. Warner. **Director:** George Cukor. **Scriptwriter:** Alan Jay Lerner. **Principal Players:** Audrey Hepburn, Rex Harrison, Stanley Holloway, Wilfred Hyde-White, Gladys Cooper and Jeremy Britt. **Running time:** 170 minutes. **Released:** Warner Bros.

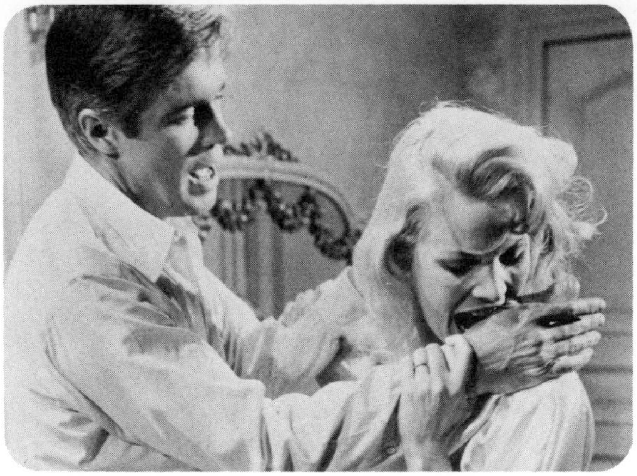

George Peppard and Carroll Baker in *The Carpetbaggers.*

THE CARPETBAGGERS

Cynics pointed out on its release that Americans rushed to see this picture in a time-honored tradition of moviegoing: to wit, to find out if it was as dirty as the book by Harold Robbins had been. It wasn't, but there was enough that was lurid left to please those who went to the film for that purpose.

The novel had been a huge seller, helped by speculation that the business tycoon protagonist was based on Howard Hughes. As in the book, this character was depicted on screen as thoroughly venomous as he accumulated fortunes through aviation and movie production. George Peppard played the role with the required toughness.

Many other outstanding characters in the book were in the film too, and a spectator was hard put to find one to sympathize with. Carroll Baker played Rina Marlowe, the tailor-made movie star; Elizabeth Ashley was Monica Winthrop, the girl who marries and then leaves the protagonist; and Martha Hyer was Jennie Denon, the high-priced call girl turned into an "actress."

In his last appearance in an American film (he went to Europe for two pictures before he died in Palm Springs), Alan Ladd stoically enacted Nevada Smith, the western movie star.

Producer: Joseph E. Levine. **Director:** Edward Dmytryk. **Scriptwriter:** John Michael Hayes. **Principal Players:** George Peppard, Alan Ladd, Bob Cummings, Martha Hyer, Elizabeth Ashley, Lew Ayres, Martin Balsam and Carroll Baker. **Running time:** 150 minutes. **Released:** Paramount.

Anthony Quinn and Alan Bates in *Zorba the Greek.*

Richard Burton in *Becket.*

ZORBA THE GREEK

As a motion picture, *Zorba the Greek* did not measure up to its literary source: the book by the celebrated author Nikos Kazantzakis. The film was episodic and plot-heavy.

What gave it substance were several outstanding performances: Anthony Quinn in the leading role; the classical actress Irene Papas (who had had a small role in *The Guns of Navarone*) as a widow who is brutally murdered; and Lila Kedrova, whose portrayal of the charming but foolish innkeeper living in the past won her an Academy Award.

Alan Bates was appropriately stiff as the English outsider who observes everything dispassionately but finally is infected by the zest of living that animates the hero, Zorba.

Michael Cacoyannis directed, on locations in Crete, and the music was by Mikis Theodorakis.

Zorba the Greek won two other Academy Awards, for best black-and-white cinematography and for art direction.

A musical stage version of the story, called simply *Zorba,* opened on Broadway in the 1968–69 season. Many drama critics compared the play to the film in their reviews, and the consensus was that the movie was much better.

Producer-Writer-Director: Michael Cacoyannis. **Principal Players:** Anthony Quinn, Alan Bates, Irene Papas and Lila Kedrova. **Running time:** 142 minutes. **Released:** 20th Century-Fox.

BECKET

Becket is an example of the type of film that Hollywood makes occasionally to serve a portion of its public, by offering the chance for those in the hinterlands to see a celebrated stage play, the viewing of which is otherwise restricted to a few large cities. The critics may complain that the film is not "cinematic," and often it isn't, but it is still worth doing.

Producer Hal Wallis saw to it that no expense was spared in staging *Becket* on film. Canterbury Cathedral was reconstructed inside and out as it looked in the twelfth century, and it made an imposing sight as recorded by the Panavision 70 color cameras. A replica of a medieval French town was also built so that the triumphant entry of Henry II could be shown. And stone castles on the northeastern coast of England, looking just as they did at the time of the events in *Becket,* were used to play other scenes.

All this would have been so much attractive deadwood, however, had it been allowed to swamp the intimate drama that is the heart of the Jean Anouilh play. This possibility was circumvented by entrusting the roles of Becket and King Henry, respectively, to two talented actors, Richard Burton and Peter O'Toole.

The part of Henry is the more flamboyant and O'Toole acted it to the hilt, obviously relishing its theatricality. In contrast, Burton, as Becket, the libertine turned dutiful archbishop and defier of the king, had to play his role in a reserved fashion. If he came off second to O'Toole, it was not his fault but that of the dramatist.

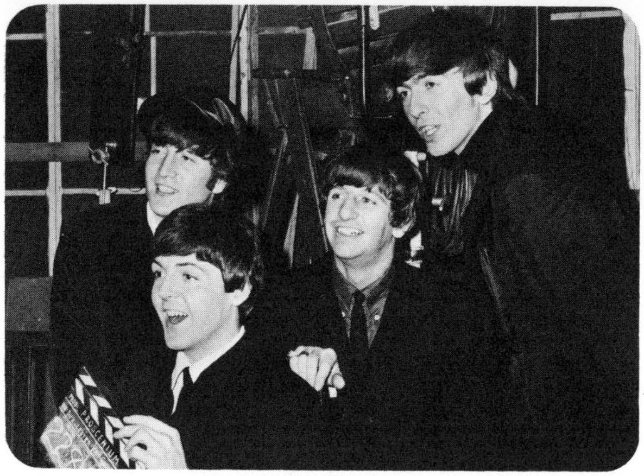

A Hard Day's Night with the Beatles: John Lennon, Paul McCartney, Ringo Starr and George Harrison.

Burton also had to contend with the fact that the transformation of the character of Becket, while historically true, is a bit too quick in the context of the drama.

Edward Anhalt won an Oscar for his screenplay (adapted from another medium), but O'Toole and Burton, both nominated as best actor, lost to Rex Harrison in *My Fair Lady*.

Producer: Hal B. Wallis. **Director:** Peter Glenville. **Scriptwriter:** Edward Anhalt. **Principal Players:** Richard Burton, Peter O'Toole, John Gielgud, Donald Wolfit, Martita Hunt and Pamela Brown. **Running time:** 148 minutes. **Released:** Paramount.

A HARD DAY'S NIGHT

Richard Lester, the director of this film starring those phenomena known as the Beatles, has made so many films in England it is generally taken for granted that that is his native land. Actually, he is an American, and formerly worked in television.

A Hard Day's Night was his theatrical film debut, and it was rapturously received not only by a large public (including those who normally would eschew the Beatles) but, wonder of wonders, by the critics. The latter liked its successful incorporation of the techniques of TV commercials into the context of a feature film to produce an unusual effect of spontaneity. (Later, these same critics were to say the method had palled with Lester's *The Knack* and *Help!*)

Anyhow, the Beatles came off as extremely likable in this outing, which the clever script of Alun Owen

Dr. Strangelove, Or: How I Learned to Stop Worrying and Love the Bomb with Peter Sellers and Sterling Hayden.

purported to be a fictional day in their lives. In the course of the shenanigans they sang eleven songs, five of which were "standards" that sent the fans into such frenzies in theatres that the rest of us missed half the dialogue.

Producer: Walter Shenson. **Director:** Richard Lester. **Scriptwriter:** Alun Owen. **Principal Players:** John Lennon, Paul McCartney, George Harrison, Ringo Starr, Wilfrid Brambell, Norman Rossington and Victor Spinetti. **Running time:** 85 minutes. **Released:** United Artists.

DR. STRANGELOVE, OR: HOW I LEARNED TO STOP WORRYING AND LOVE THE BOMB

A bold idea was the inspiration for this unique film from Stanley Kubrick: to tell the story of atomic holocaust as a comedy. Black, to be sure, but comic—and, surprisingly, it paid off at the box office.

The approach Kubrick took to the material was indicated when he changed the title of Peter George's novel (*Red Alert* in America and *Two Hours to Doom* in Britain) to what is one of the longest and most bizarre picture titles in memory. Kubrick produced and directed the film, and worked on the screenplay with Terry Southern and author George.

Kubrick startled the American public, first of all, because his satirical targets were subjects usually taken seriously: war, generals, politicians, scientific devices.

Seance on a Wet Afternoon with Kim Stanley.

More than in any previous film, Kubrick showed off his remarkable talents as director. His battle scenes were particularly effective, coming over in the uneven, unpolished manner of documentaries made in the field.

And his direction of the actors was superb. Peter Sellers was versatile in three roles: the President of the U.S., a British liaison officer, and the strange title character. As the immature head of the Air Force, George C. Scott did a caricature that still haunts military men. Equally as good was the generally underrated actor Sterling Hayden as the general who launches the mad attack on Russia.

Highbrow critics saw the widespread acceptance of this picture as evidence that the moviegoing public was growing up. Later years were to prove they were right.

Producer-Director: Stanley Kubrick. **Scriptwriters:** Kubrick, Terry Southern and Peter George. **Principal Players:** Peter Sellers, George C. Scott, Sterling Hayden, Keenan Wynn, Slim Pickens and Peter Bull. **Running time:** 93 minutes. **Released:** Columbia.

SEANCE ON A WET AFTERNOON

Brilliant stage actress Kim Stanley had given a superior screen performance six years before in *The Goddess,* Paddy Chayefsky's depiction of a neurotic screen star and how she got that way (based, some whispered, on the life of Marilyn Monroe). The American public did not like that film, however, although the actress was nominated for an Academy Award.

Miss Stanley then gave up the screen until offered a meaty role in this British thriller—a disturbed medium who browbeats her reluctant husband into carrying out a child kidnapping scheme. The character's motive is bizarre: She has no interest in the ransom money *per se,* but simply intends to hold the girl in their home for a time and later place her safely in the woods, after which the medium will hold a seance and reveal the whereabouts of the child. Through this she expects to acquire the recognition she feels is due her for her skill; the fact that she may achieve this fame through a hoax bothers her not in the least.

Without doubt the medium is an intriguing character, and Miss Stanley played her to the hilt with a crack-up scene at the end that merits the much-abused phrase "tour de force." Richard Attenborough acted the husband with an air of quiet desperation.

Unfortunately for Miss Stanley's screen career, the "off-beat" thriller never made it very far beyond a few art-theatre engagements in the United States. However, she was nominated for another Academy Award.

Producer: Richard Attenborough. **Director-Writer:** Bryan Forbes. **Principal Players:** Kim Stanley and Richard Attenborough. **Running time:** 115 minutes. **Released:** Artixo Prods., Ltd.

MARY POPPINS

The original musical film had fallen on sad days in the mid sixties; most such movies were heavy-handed adaptations of stage plays. If *Mary Poppins* had had

Mary Poppins with Julie Andrews.

nothing else to recommend it, at least it was written directly for the screen.

Fortunately, it had a great deal more than that, and it was a smashing success. The book, adapted from the stories of P. L. Travers about an English nursemaid with magical powers (among other things, she can fly!), was an expert blend of realism and fantasy, ending happily, as all fairy tales should, with deeper understanding between parents and children brought about by the example set by the prim but affectionate nurse.

Julie Andrews, making her film debut after becoming famous in the stage musical *My Fair Lady,* was captivating in the title role. (When Warner Bros. brought *Lady* to the screen, Miss Andrews was bypassed for the Liza role and Audrey Hepburn chosen instead. Miss Andrews got her revenge; she won the Oscar that year and Miss Hepburn wasn't even nominated.) Dick Van Dyke was also extremely pleasing in the part of Bert, the friend of the heroine.

Of the fourteen brand-new songs in the score of Richard M. and Robert B. Sherman, the best were "Step in Time," sung and danced by Van Dyke on the roof tops of London with a chorus of chimney sweeps, and the outrageous tongue-twister "Supercalifragilistic-expialidocious."

Producers: Walt Disney and Bill Walsh. **Director:** Robert Stevenson. **Scriptwriters:** Walsh and Don Da Gradi. **Principal Players:** Julie Andrews, Dick Van Dyke, David Tomlinson, Glynis Johns, Ed Wynn and Hermione Baddeley. **Running time:** 140 minutes. **Released:** Buena Vista.

The Sound of Music with Julie Andrews, one of the two top-grossing pictures in the first four decades of sound.

1965

Now there was a boom in World War II films. Just as after World War I, an appreciable period of years had to pass before the screen audience was ready for war themes. In 1965, a dozen war stories vied for public interest. Another trend, and one of more lasting power, was to color films. In the period right after World War II, when leading exhibitors asked for more films in color, the response from producers was silence, because color just cost too much. Theatre owners had learned that the public, then accustomed to black-and-white TV, wanted color in the movie theatres. In time, producers were convinced, and increasingly in the early 1960's, Hollywood films were made in color. By the mid-1960's, over three-quarters were in color. The clinching argument for color was the future needs of color TV.

This year was the high point of James Bond, with such a film as *Goldfinger* enormously successful in the U.S. and abroad. Soon, studios everywhere were preparing sex-and-intrigue plots and looking for other Sean Connerys.

As the Supreme Court knocked down the Maryland censorship law as unconstitutional, the city of Dallas pressed for official classification, opening the door to new pressures seeking screen control. John Q. Adams, prominent Texan exhibitor, raised the fundamental question on individual maturity: "Is a girl who car-dates at fifteen a mature person? Is a person who marries at sixteen or seventeen a mature person?"

Veteran movie editor W. Ward Marsh of *The Cleveland Plain Dealer* led an attack on the practice of showing trailers for an adult film while the audience is present for a family picture. "Theatres have a special responsibility. . . . Now [showing adult trailers to children] the theatre man is making an enemy of parents." Meanwhile, the broad appeal of James Stewart's *Shenandoah* demonstrated that there still was a place for family films.

Broadway, always a good source of screen material, hit a new high as a source for film stories, with thirty-five films based on Broadway attractions in planning or production. This was part of the trend to the assured property, with companies—and personalities—not anxious to risk producing original stories for the screen.

Two *Harlow* films hit the screen, simultaneously—Joseph Levine's, made at a reported $4,000,000, and one in Electronovision, using television. techniques, for $600,000. No one disputes the right of a producer to make any subject at any budget, but no film should try to attract an audience by creating confusion. Neither *Harlow* film was outstanding.

This year, sights were raised on what grosses, at home and abroad, a truly popular film could achieve, as *The Sound of Music,* starring Julie Andrews, set box-office records everywhere. When she was cast in the film, Walt Disney's production of *Mary Poppins,* which made her known and liked by millions of moviegoers, had not been released: Once again it was shown that the public, rather than film makers, make—and break—the stars.

Two major screen forces died during the year: David O. Selznick who, when still a young man, achieved his greatest feat—*Gone With the Wind;* and Joseph I. Breen, for two decades head of the Production Code Administration, and the man who did more than anyone else to keep the screen free of government censorship.

Stars of the year: Sean Connery, John Wayne, Doris Day, Julie Andrews, Jack Lemmon, Elvis Presley, Cary Grant, James Stewart, Elizabeth Taylor and Richard Burton.

Sean Connery, Claudine Auger and Adolfo Celi in *Thunderball.*

Peter Sellers in *What's New Pussycat?*

THUNDERBALL

The fourth of the fantastically successful James Bond adventures (*Dr. No, From Russia With Love* and *Goldfinger* were the predecessors) turned out to be the most ambitious and elaborate, as well as the most exciting.

To continue in the hyperbole demanded (commercially, at least) by the films: It had the most tricky gimmicks of all the Bond films, and some truly thrilling underwater photography. Its physical backgrounds, shot on location in the Bahamas, were also an asset.

On the other hand, some of the jokes were sicker than usual. The worst: Bond, while on the dance floor, uses the body of his partner (a spy) to shield himself from the bullets of her accomplices. Then he pops her into a chair at the table of some innocent bystanders and cracks: "Do you mind if my friend sits down? She's just dead."

All the Bond films, including this one, have been re-released to theatres, and always successfully. The public never seems to tire of their comic-strip appeal.

Terence Young, who directed the first two Bond pictures, but not *Goldfinger,* did his usual polished and precise job with *Thunderball.* Sean Connery played Bond in all four, and then did a fifth—*You Only Live Twice*—after which he retired from the series.

Producer: Kevin McClory. **Director:** Terence Young. **Scriptwriters:** Richard Maibaum and John Hopkins. **Principal Players:** Sean Connery, Claudine Auger, Adolfo Celi, Luciana Paluzzi and Bernard Lee. **Running time:** 132 minutes. **Released:** United Artists.

WHAT'S NEW PUSSYCAT?

How the critics jumped on this picture when it opened in the summer of 1965! In condemning it for "childishness" and "vulgarity," they pounced on it with all the fervor of a Puritanical censor blasting sin. Nobody loved it but the public, which turned it into one of the biggest grossing pictures of the year.

Actually, it was much better than its detractors said, not only as light entertainment, but because of some shrewd satire of sex and psychoanalysis. The latter attracted the sophisticates, while the mass audience obviously responded to the slapstick, which reminded older members of the audience of the Marx Brothers in their prime.

It was a picture in which anything could happen—and did. Peter O'Toole (in a switch from his dramatic roles) did a "striptease" in the Crazy Horse Saloon; Peter Sellers conducted a session in group therapy that ended in a brawl; and the harem sequence from Fellini's *8½* was parodied. And the whole helter-skelter business ended with a frenzied and frantically funny chase through the corridors of a country chateau by a horde of people bent on seduction.

Woody Allen wrote the script and also played a part in the film. Clive Donner, who previously had done the British comedy *Nothing But the Best,* directed.

Producer: Charles K. Feldman. **Director:** Clive Donner. **Scriptwriter:** Woody Allen. **Principal Players:** Peter Sellers, Peter O'Toole, Romy Schneider, Capucine, Paula Prentiss, Woody Allen and Ursula Andress.

Heather Menzies (center), Angela Cartwright, Debbie Turner, Kym Karath and Richard Hayden (right) in *The Sound of Music.*

The Married Woman with Philippe Leroy and Macha Meril.

THE SOUND OF MUSIC

Why *The Sound of Music* should have become one of the two top-grossing pictures of all time (as of 1969) is one of those mysteries of show business that makes it so eternally fascinating.

The property was hardly one of the best in the musical canon of Rodgers and Hammerstein; drama critics rank it below *Oklahoma!, Carousel, South Pacific* and even *The King and I.* All these were made into successful pictures, none of which came close to making the same kind of money.

Nor were many film critics pleased with *The Sound of Music*—too sticky and sentimental, they said. They might as well have been shouting down the proverbial well.

The public loved it, and many set records for the number of times they went to see it. Revivals in numerous theatres months after the original engagement had ended drew large crowds again.

What is this film of which the great American public was—and still is—so fond? Basically, it is a fable of goodness triumphant, a true "fairy tale" of the adventures of the real-life von Trapp family. The von Trapps fled Austria in the late 1930's when the Nazis came to power, and made their way to the U.S. where they gained fame as concert singers—father, (foster-) mother and seven children.

The atmosphere of a never-never land is set from the opening shot by director Robert Wise as misty clouds suddenly clear on the big Todd-AO screen to reveal a view from the air of the Austrian Alps and surrounding countryside that is awe-inspiring. It is a fabulous setting for a tale of make-believe. Even when the Nazis appear, they are storybook villains, and the protagonists escape from them so easily it is necessary to suspend disbelief and continue to take it all in the spirit of myth. Audiences surely did.

Much of the enchantment that the film undeniably has is due to the winning personality of the star—Julie Andrews. She made a perfect Cinderella-like heroine.

In fact Miss Andrews, on the basis of this picture, became the nation's number one star at the box office. She stayed there for two years in a row—1966 and 1967.

Producer-Director: Robert Wise. **Scriptwriter:** Ernest Lehman. **Principal Players:** Julie Andrews, Christopher Plummer, Eleanor Parker, Richard Hayden and Peggy Wood. **Running time:** 174 minutes. **Released:** 20th Century-Fox.

THE MARRIED WOMAN

Of that group of young French film makers who burst forth simultaneously in the late 1950's, Jean-Luc Godard remains both the most controversial and the most prolific. To some he is a tricky charlatan; to others, he is a profound commentator on the malaises of our times.

With *The Married Woman,* released here in 1965 (Godard made it in '64), there was more unanimity than usual among the critics as to its merits. And the public, which had not exactly rushed to see his earlier films—

Rod Steiger (right) in *The Pawnbroker.*

Breathless aside—went to this one in far greater numbers than before.

The Married Woman illustrates his virtues at a peak, along with some of his faults. As usual, the plot is not of much consequence, at least on the surface. All that happens is that a young married woman tries to make up her mind whether or not to leave her husband for her lover after making the discovery that she is pregnant by one of them. (She doesn't know which.) The ending is inconclusive; the viewer decides for himself which she chooses.

Underneath all this is a wealth of comment on modern attitudes toward sex, with one moral to be drawn: That, for all the candor now permitted on the subject, mankind is sexually as much at sea as ever.

The film techniques are varied; in one love scene, Godard dwells on separate parts of the anatomy of the lovers with close-ups of one section of the body after another. Character is exposed by having the players, while sitting in the living room after dinner one evening, suddenly philosophize on a subject dear to them, with the camera meanwhile focused on them in close-up while they talk.

It is amusing to note that Godard originally called his film *La Femme Mariée* (instead of *Une Femme Mariée*). French censors forced him to change it, on the grounds that his picture could be construed as a disparagement of *all* French married women.

Producer-Director-Writer: Jean-Luc Godard. **Principal Players:** Macha Meril, Bernard Noel and Philippe LeRoy. **Running time:** 94 minutes. **Released:** Royal Films.

THE PAWNBROKER

At the time of its release, *The Pawnbroker* stirred up a controversy that threatened to overshadow its very real merits as a film drama of consequence. The offending (to the censors, that is) scene showed a woman baring her breasts for the protagonist, in an effort to get him to increase the amount of money he would give her for a locket she wished to pawn. To less easily embarrassed observers, the incident seemed crucial to the plot and not thrown in for an arbitrary sensational effect. But *The Pawnbroker* was denied a Code Seal because of this, and it was condemned by the Legion of Decency. Both actions were later rescinded when the scene was cut.

Bringing the property to the screen had not been easy in the first place, but producers Roger H. Lewis and Philip Langner persevered.

The theme of *The Pawnbroker* was the reawakening of emotion in a man who had almost ceased being able to feel or to believe in the value of life itself.

It was expressed through the character of a Jew who had survived Auschwitz and had come to the U.S., where he set up shop as a pawnbroker in Harlem.

On the anniversary of the death of his wife in the concentration camp, he receives a series of jolts that shock him back to reality. Memories crowd in on him, and in reliving events in the concentration camp, he starts to experience fear—which is at least a genuine emotion. The most vivid of the recollections is that stirred by the woman who exposes herself to him. He

Darling with Dirk Bogarde and Julie Christie.

remembers how his wife had been degraded in a Nazi brothel while he was forced to watch. On this same day, his life is saved through the heroism of his assistant during an attempted holdup. The latter dies instead.

In directing the film, Sidney Lumet used the streets of New York City to evoke a strong sense of time and place more vividly than had anyone since Billy Wilder in *The Lost Weekend.* In the memory-stirring sequence he used a subliminal technique (quick glimpses coming so fast you missed them if you blinked) borrowed from Resnais.

In the title role, Rod Steiger did a masterly job of conveying the apathy and spiritlessness of a man living entirely within himself, who yet retains a few sparks of the emotions he has tried to kill forever. The actor was nominated for an Oscar, but lost to Lee Marvin in *Cat Ballou.*

Producers: Roger H. Lewis and Philip Langner. **Director:** Sidney Lumet. **Scriptwriters:** David Friedkin and Morton Fine. **Principal Players:** Rod Steiger, Geraldine Fitzgerald, Brock Peters, Jaime Sanchez and Thelma Oliver. **Running time:** 110 minutes. **Released:** Allied Artists.

DARLING

Julie Christie, who had impressed moviegoers in *Billy Liar* with her fresh and vibrant personality in a small but telling role, was launched as a full-fledged star in *Darling.* The whole picture was built around the character she portrayed—a contemporary international playgirl, shown from her obscure beginnings as a model in London to her marriage to an Italian prince.

As co-stars, the producer, Joseph Janni, secured top British talent in Dirk Bogarde and Laurence Harvey. They played second fiddles to Miss Christie—the first as a writer and TV commentator who leaves his wife and children to live with the heroine, and the second as an advertising executive who gets her jobs as a model.

From beginning to end, *Darling* was nothing if not fashionable. It was preoccupied with sex and had all the "obligatory" scenes of the day: an orgy (after the mode of *La Dolce Vita*) and a nude love scene, along with a satire on TV commercials and a mimicking of the remarks of amateur art lovers at an exhibition.

Miss Christie got mixed notices for her acting, but that didn't keep her from winning an Academy Award as best actress, beating Julies Andrews in *The Sound of Music,* Samantha Eggar in *The Collector,* Elizabeth Hartman in *A Patch of Blue* and Simone Signoret in *Ship of Fools.*

In the five years that followed, Miss Christie never did reach the heights that had been expected of her, although she did appear in the spectacularly successful (at the box office) *Dr. Zhivago.* She was miscast as Joseph Hardy's heroine in *Far From the Madding Crowd,* and neither *Fahrenheit 451* nor *Petulia* furthered her career.

Producer: Joseph Janni. **Director:** John Schlesinger. **Screenplay:** Frederic Raphael. **Principal Players:** Laurence Harvey, Dirk Bogarde and Julie Christie. **Running time:** 122 minutes. **Released:** Embassy Pictures.

Michael Caine (right) in *The Ipcress File.*

THE IPCRESS FILE

As an antidote to the supernatural antics of James Bond, the makers of *The Ipcress File* offered a spy who not only existed within a realistic framework but was quite ordinary in appearance. He even wore glasses to correct myopia.

Michael Caine had his first important screen role playing this secret agent called Harry Palmer. *The Ipcress File* did very well in the United States, but two sequels, *Funeral in Berlin* (1966) and *Billion Dollar Brain* (1967), also employing Caine as the Palmer character, did not catch on.

Along with Caine, *The Ipcress File* brought to major attention the Canadian director Sidney J. Furie, whose work in this film was very technique-conscious. He never settled for a conventional camera setup or ordinary scenic combination when he could find one that was odd.

Item: He photographs the faces of his characters in all sorts of unusual angles and then arranges people in a scene in eccentric ways.

Item: He shoots, on occasion, head-on at glaring and powerful lights.

Item: He views several scenes through slits in a wall or a door with a large proportion of the screen black.

Item: When the myopic hero takes off his glasses, what he sees is out of focus.

Item: The final brainwashing sequences uses flashing colors and grotesque sounds for fantastic effects.

In later films *(The Appaloosa* and *The Naked Runner)* Furie used optical tricks for mere "window-dressing," but in *The Ipcress File* they were made part and parcel of the story.

Producer: Harry Saltzman. **Director:** Sidney J. Furie. **Screenplay:** Bill Conaway and James Doren. **Principal Players:** Michael Caine, Nigel Green, Guy Doleman and Sue Lloyd. **Running time:** 108 minutes. **Released:** Universal Pictures.

CAT BALLOU

A spoof is not a satire; the latter, however humorous, is trenchant criticism. *Cat Ballou* is a spoof, and therefore the high-brow critics disdained it. The public had other ideas—similar to those of the middle-brow critics, who loved it.

In the old days in Hollywood when westerns were the backbone of industry product, it was considered fatal to treat them facetiously. *Cat Ballou* broke that jinx once and for all. People who still loved westerns in the 1960's had fun at *Cat Ballou,* and those who hated them were naturally in their element over this put-down of traditions.

Lee Marvin had been an obscure character actor until *Cat Ballou,* which supplied him with a dual role. He played a has-been gunfighter ruined by drink and also his own arch enemy—a killer with a silver nose held in place with a plastic band around his head, his real nose having been bitten off in a fight! Marvin was very funny, and his performance not only won him an Academy Award but a brand new career that led to

Cat Ballou with Jane Fonda (center) and Lee Marvin (right).

such films as *The Professionals* and *The Dirty Dozen,* and a place on the top-ten money-making-stars poll of *Motion Picture Herald* in 1967–68 and 1969.

The picture also boosted the career of Jane Fonda, who, after an auspicious debut in *Tall Story* in 1960, had suffered a series of routine roles in uninteresting films. She engagingly played Cat Ballou, a schoolteacher in the Old West whose imminent hanging in the opening of the film leads to flashbacks explaining how she came to be in that dangerous condition.

Also much praised was Elliott Silverstein, the director, cited for his imaginative handling of sight gags, best of which is the elaborate ritual through which the drink-befogged Marvin goes in preparation for a gunfight.

Producer: Harold Hecht. **Director:** Elliott Silverstein. **Scriptwriters:** Walter Newman and Frank R. Pierson. **Principal Players:** Jane Fonda, Lee Marvin, Michael Callan, Dwayne Hickman and Reginald Denny. **Running time:** 97 minutes. **Released:** Columbia.

Blow-Up, Michelangelo Antonioni's first international commercial success and a film that put critics everywhere in violent disagreement about both its meaning and its worth.

1966

This was the year the old Production Code, which had been adopted in 1930, died—killed by its creators, the major companies, who no longer cared to abide by its provisions. The last nail in the Code's coffin was *Who's Afraid of Virginia Woolf?* This picture was given an exception from the Code's strictures on language. However, the moviegoing public generally accepted the frank language not only without criticism but without concern.

Jack Valenti left his post as assistant to President Johnson at the White House to become president of the Motion Picture Association of America on the direct recommendation of President Johnson. Louis Nizer, the famed film attorney who had served as acting head of the Association from the time of Eric Johnston's death in August, 1963, until Valenti took over, attracted interest in his long crusade for more attention by the film industry to education. He cited the fantastic growth in college film courses, now numbering one thousand or more.

The new Production Code scrapped the old set of standards in favor of a brief statement essentially leaving applications to the good taste and judgment of the Production Code Administration, headed by Geoffrey Shurlock, who had been an associate of Joseph I. Breen from the early days of the voluntary self-regulation system. The new Code, which was enforced for less than two years, was to be remembered, not very fondly, for the ambiguous tag it placed on a number of pictures: "Suggested for Mature Audiences."

The corporate raiders, principally conglomerates, moved in on the old-line film companies. After various others had tried, Gulf & Western absorbed Paramount, in a merger effective September 20, 1966. On behalf of an anonymous principal, a French bank attempted to capture the management of Columbia Pictures. It lost in the end, primarily because U.S. law forbids a foreign interest from controlling a company which owns TV and radio stations. Jack Warner sold control of Warner Bros. to Seven Arts. United Artists, after flirting with Consolidated Foods, was merged into Transamerica.

The New York Joint Legislative Committee on Publication and Dissemination of Obscene Materials (what a title!) concluded a long study of films with the judgment that neither censorship nor classification was the answer. It suggested that when exhibitors concluded that children under eighteen should be excluded from viewing a film, the ban should be enforced by law.

The Supreme Court upheld the conviction of Ralph Ginzburg for obscene or prurient promotion of what might otherwise be constitutionally protected material. Some distributors worried that film exhibitors might run afoul of this law, but these fears proved groundless.

Production costs soared. An average major American film was now budgeted at $3 million, compared with $2 million only five years before and only $900,000 twenty years previously. Of 117 current Hollywood productions, 106 were in color. Notable films were *Blow-Up, Dr. Zhivago, A Man for All Seasons* and *A Man and a Woman.*

Stars of the year: Julie Andrews, Sean Connery, Elizabeth Taylor, Jack Lemmon, Richard Burton, Cary Grant, John Wayne, Doris Day, Paul Newman and Elvis Presley.

Susannah York and Paul Scofield in *A Man for All Seasons.*

John Philip Law, Alan Arkin and Carl Reiner in *The Russians Are Coming, The Russians Are Coming.*

A MAN FOR ALL SEASONS

A theme that has often inspired producer-director Fred Zinnemann throughout his admirable career as film maker is that of moral conflict, especially if it involves a victory, even though it be only a spiritual one. No wonder, then, that he was attracted to the Robert Bolt stage play celebrating the courageous stand of Sir Thomas More, the Roman Catholic statesman who challenged Henry VIII when that monarch broke with the Vatican and established the Church of England with himself as head.

Zinnemann had Bolt himself adapt his play to the screen, and he also secured the acting services of Paul Scofield, who had been highly praised for his performance as More on the stage. The actor seemed even more remarkable on the screen in the way he conveyed the emotional depth in a person who was outwardly diffident and sometimes aloof. Through Zinnemann's imaginative use of close-ups, one could sense the heroic measure of the man more deeply than in the live performance.

Obviously a commercial gamble, the picture did better than had been expected in its first reserved-seat engagement. And then when it won six Oscars, including ones for best picture and best actor, it went on to even further financial success.

Producer-Director: Fred Zinnemann. **Scriptwriter:** Robert Bolt. **Principal Players:** Paul Scofield, Wendy Hiller, Leo McKern, Robert Shaw, Orson Welles, Susannah York, Nigel Davenport, John Hurt and Corin Redgrave. **Running time:** 120 minutes. **Released:** Columbia.

THE RUSSIANS ARE COMING THE RUSSIANS ARE COMING

Apparently the Russians didn't like this picture—it was barred from the Karlovy Film Festival—but the American public certainly did. It was one of the biggest hits of 1966.

What struck the funnybone of moviegoers was the fanciful idea that if a Russian submarine should be grounded off the coast of New England and the crew should come ashore to get help, residents of a typical small town would be thrown into pandemonium, and fear an enemy invasion had begun. A situation that just as easily might have been turned into a sombre story was written strictly for laughs—and audiences responded.

The picture was a great triumph for producer-director Norman Jewison (maker of *The Thrill of It All* and *Send Me No Flowers*), who never belabored the "message," which some saw as a parable of U.S.-Russian political relations and others saw as a satire on the whole business of civil defense and preparedness for war.

The film served to introduce to American film audiences the Broadway comedian Alan Arkin (who starred in *Enter Laughing* and *Luv* on the stage). As the crafty leader of the Russian group which comes ashore to find assistance for their sub in distress, he stole the show.

Producer-Director: Norman Jewison. **Scriptwriter:** William Rose. **Principal Players:** Carl Reiner, Eva Marie Saint, Alan Arkin, Brian Keith, Jonathan Winters, Theodore Bikel, John Philip Law and Paul Ford. **Running time:** 126 minutes. **Released:** United Artists.

Richard Burton, George Segal, Elizabeth Taylor and Sandy Dennis in *Who's Afraid of Virginia Woolf?*

WHO'S AFRAID OF VIRGINIA WOOLF?

Two circumstances surrounding this film have given it a unique place in motion picture history. First is that the dialogue contained profanities and blasphemies (so-called four-letter words) which had not been spoken in an American film before. The second is the result of the first: *Virginia Woolf* thereby tolled the death knell of the industry's Production Code which had been adopted in 1930, and under which such verbal obscenities were forbidden.

Possibly because of the notoriety engendered by the "shocking" language—and certainly because Elizabeth Taylor and Richard Burton played the leading roles—the film version of the Edward Albee stage play was a big commercial hit. This in spite of some obscurities in the exact meaning of the four-character drama involving a marathon drunken brawl between a middle-aged professor and his shrewish wife (Burton and Miss Taylor), into which they drag as participants a young teacher and his child-like spouse (roles played by George Segal and Sandy Dennis). Other obstacles were excessive talkiness, and inexperienced direction by Mike Nichols, the highly praised stage director making his motion picture debut.

Critical opinion was sharply divided over the relative merits of the four performances, but nearly everyone agreed Miss Taylor had taken a big gamble in accepting the part of a woman who was much older than she and blowzy and unkempt—and thoroughly unsympathetic. In a word, Miss Taylor allowed herself to be thoroughly deglamorized—and it worked!

Members of the Academy of Motion Picture Arts and Sciences so admired the film that they gave it thirteen nominations (including best picture, all four performers, and Nichols). But come Oscar night, it copped only five statuettes, the Misses Taylor and Dennis getting one apiece, and none for the men. The other awards were for art direction, cinematography and costumes!

Producer-Writer: Ernest Lehman. **Director:** Mike Nichols. **Principal Players:** Elizabeth Taylor, Richard Burton, George Segal and Sandy Dennis. **Running time:** 129 minutes. **Released:** Warner Bros.

BLOW-UP

L'Avventura is the picture that made the name of Michelangelo Antonioni legend in 1960, but he had completed his first film a good ten years before. In the U.S., it was to be six more years before he made a commercial breakthrough with *Blow-Up*.

At the time, some industry observers were mystified as to the wide appeal of the film, being convinced that American audiences hadn't really grown up to the extent of understanding, let alone accepting, a parable on the meaning of reality that was presented in a manner that was pure Antonioni—which is to say, obliquely and cryptically.

The major reason should have been obvious. On one level, *Blow-Up* is an exciting suspense film with an

A scene from Antonioni's *Blow-Up*.

Alfie with Vivien Merchant and Michael Caine.

unusual mystery angle: Was there really a murder in the park on the day the London photographer was taking pictures? And if so, who was the killer?

The questions were never answered to the satisfaction of the average moviegoer. But plainly he was intrigued anyhow. Let the learned critics write their erudite essays on the meaning of the film. The mass audience likes a good thriller.

It also likes sex, and it was well known that *Blow-Up* had been denied a Production Code seal because of a scene in which the photographer (played by David Hemmings) is seduced by two young girls who strip themselves and then him and roll around on colored paper on the floor. Antonioni refused to make the cuts requested in order for the film to be granted a seal, and so MGM set up a new subsidiary—Premiere Pictures—to handle its distribution. *Blow-Up* was the first and last release of Premiere.

It should be noted also that *Blow-Up* was Antonioni's first film in English and it was shot entirely in London.

Producer: Carlo Ponti. **Director-Writer:** Michelangelo Antonioni. **Principal Players:** Vanessa Redgrave, David Hemmings and Sarah Miles. **Running time:** 110 minutes. **Released:** Premiere (MGM).

ALFIE

Alfie is one of those films which age with distinction. It was first handled by the distributor as an art-house film, but like *Tom Jones,* it soon caught on with a much wider public who responded enthusiastically to its bawdy humor and poignant dramatics. Today, with so many sex scenes in films needlessly daring and explicit, *Alfie,* with its restrained handling of several seductions, may look even better than it did originally.

The script was based on a play by Bill Naughton about the amorous adventures of a selfish Cockney Don Juan, who was played superbly by Michael Caine. Like his counterpart on the stage, the actor was called upon to speak directly to the audience—a technique that is much more difficult when there is a camera to face instead of live spectators. Caine brought the feat off with finesse, and, further, revealed Alfie's character from all sides—weak, endearing, despicable and amusing. The numerous women he encountered were well acted in each instance.

Some of the British critics felt the ending, in which Alfie finally expressed some remorse about his aimless existence, to be phony and arbitrarily tacked on. Actually, the "conversion" served to spell out the moralistic theme of the story, to wit: Promiscuity, as a way of life, is spiritually sterile and unrewarding.

A minor controversy occurred in 1966 when the picture was denied a Code Seal because of an incident involving abortion. It was submitted to the industry Review Board which handed it an exemption and a Seal.

Producer-Director: Lewis Gilbert. **Scriptwriter:** Bill Naughton. **Principal Players:** Michael Caine, Shelley Winters, Millicent Martin, Julia Foster, Jane Asher, Shirley Anne Field, Vivien Merchant, Eleanor Bron and Denholm Elliott. **Running time:** 114 minutes. **Released:** Paramount.

Ladislav Grossman (center) in *The Shop on Main Street.*

A Man and a Woman with Anouk Aimée and Jean-Louis Trintignant.

THE SHOP ON MAIN STREET

When this Czechoslovakian film (released commercially in 1966) was shown at the New York Film Festival in the fall of 1965, it turned out to be a sleeper, winning a standing ovation from the audience and being declared the hit of the occasion, by common consent of patrons and critics. No wonder it also took the Academy Award, in 1965, for best foreign film.

The picture makes one of the most abrupt changes of mood in all film history—a transition that is carried off with stunning virtuosity. It starts out as a satiric comedy with the hero introduced as a buffoon—the black sheep of his family in Czechoslovakia during the Nazi occupation. He is offered a job as "Aryan controller" of a button shop run by an elderly Jewish woman, with his function to be supervisor of the store for a share of the profit.

Things become even more amusing as this fellow assumes his new position, only to discover the shop is not making any money and the old lady is secretly being supported by members of the Jewish community.

Then—almost without warning—the film takes on tragic dimensions. The "controller" has become extremely fond of the shopkeeper, and when the Nazis start to ship all Jews to concentration camps, he has a terrific struggle with his conscience over whether to help her hide or to let her be sent away.

The resolution comes in a long (thirty minutes) and terrifically moving scene in which he tries to make the trusting old lady understand her plight. Ida Kaminska and Josef Kroner act it brilliantly. She was nominated for an Oscar.

Producer: Barrandov Studios. **Directors:** Jan Kadar and Elmar Klos. **Scriptwriter:** Ladislav Grossman. **Principal Players:** Josef Kroner, Ida Kaminska, Hana Silkova and Frantisek Zvarik. **Running time:** 128 minutes. **Released:** Prominent Films.

A MAN AND A WOMAN

Probably not since *La Dolce Vita* had a foreign-made film attracted such a large and disparate American audience as this slight but charming French picture. Its popularity was considerably enhanced by the musical score (by Francis Lai), the main theme of which was on the best-selling musical charts for months. The film was a success both in the original version and in an English-dubbed one later.

The story of a romance it is, pure and simple, and tidily put together with much stretching of the long arm of coincidence. She (Anouk Aimée) is employed in a film studio; he (Jean-Louis Trintignant) is a professional racing driver. She is a widow; he a widower. She has a young daughter; he a young son. They meet at a school both children attend, and so forth.

All very trite, but assembled by director Claude Lelouch with skillful exploitation of the personal magnetism of the stars, and of the beautiful locations in which it was shot, especially the beach at Deauville. The photography was superb, although the occasional switch from full color to tinted black-and-white was distracting.

Doctor Zhivago with Julie Christie and Rod Steiger.

The film helped to restore the fortunes of its U.S. distributor, Allied Artists, at a time when the company was in dire financial straits. Lelouch's next film, *Live for Life,* released by United Artists, also had a title song that caught the fancy of the popular music enthusiasts here. The picture itself did not.

Producer-Director: Claude Lelouch. **Scriptwriters:** Claude Lelouch and Pierre Uytterhoeven. **Principal Players:** Anouk Aimée, Jean-Louis Trintignant, Pierre Barouch and Valerie Lagrange. **Running time:** 102 minutes. **Released:** Allied Artists.

DOCTOR ZHIVAGO

In adapting Boris Pasternak's *Doctor Zhivago* to the screen, writer Robert Bolt did an able job of extracting the plot details and ignoring the philosophy and the poetry. He may have offended the purists who admire the great Russian novelist, but he certainly pleased the moviegoing public in the U.S., whose liking for the film has placed it among the ten top-grossing pictures of all time.

In certain respects, *Doctor Zhivago* is reminiscent of *Gone With the Wind,* not only because of its background of civil war, but because the essential themes of both films are the struggle to survive the deprivations of such a conflict, and the passing of a traditional way of life. Episodes in the second half of the picture in which Zhivago takes his family and father-in-law to return to a country estate when they must flee Moscow recall the return of Scarlett O'Hara to Tara.

The picture was filmed in Spain, where sites were found similar to Russian terrain. Parts of Moscow itself (as it was in the early twentieth century) were re-created for events occurring there. Director David Lean was especially effective in creating a strong sense of the harshness of the Russian winters, and Zhivago's long trek across a snow-covered Siberia provided a keenly chilling experience for the audience. The all-star cast was competent, but no one seemed particularly inspired.

Producer: Carlo Ponti. **Director:** David Lean. **Scriptwriter:** Robert Bolt. **Principal Players:** Omar Sharif, Julie Christie, Geraldine Chaplin, Rod Steiger, Alec Guinness, Tom Courtenay, Siobhan McKenna, Ralph Richardson and Rita Tushingham. **Running time:** 197 minutes. **Released:** MGM.

DEAR JOHN

Arriving in the United States almost unheralded (except that it had been nominated for an Academy Award for 1965 as the best foreign film), *Dear John* was a surprise to nearly everybody when it was released commercially in 1966—the critics (who were delighted), the public (ditto), and the American distributor, whose grosses totalled over $4 million. *Dear John* had lost the Oscar to *The Shop on Main Street,* but it was the most commercially successful Swedish film ever to play in this country—until *I Am Curious (Yellow)* came along in 1969.

It is a love story about an affair between two young adults that lasts for a weekend. She is a waitress in a

Dear John with Jarl Kulle and Christina Schollin.

cafe in a small Scandinavian port living with her brother and her illegitimate daughter. He is a worldly sea captain whose wife has left him; he is looking for quick romance but is drawn into a deep affection for the wistful girl he meets.

Lars Magnus Lindgren, the writer-director, borrowed some of his techniques from the much-imitated Alain Resnais, but used them imaginatively. In the beginning the lovers lie in bed reminiscing about the events that have brought them to this Sunday evening (they had met briefly once, two years before). The episodes are shown in flashbacks that are not always in consecutive order; at first this confuses, but soon it becomes clear that the method is intended for an impressionistic effect. And it works.

The actors cast a real spell, Christina Schollin being a marvel to watch as she conveys the feelings of a woman who has been hurt in the past and hesitates to surrender to a new love, and Jarl Kulle being a perfect match for her as the sailor who finds a lark turning into deep emotional involvement.

Producer: Göran Lindgren. **Director-Writer:** Lars Magnus Lindgren. **Principal Players:** Jarl Kulle and Christina Schollin. **Running time:** 115 minutes. **Released:** Sigma III.

Guess Who's Coming to Dinner, the last picture of the great Tracy and his ninth appearance with Miss Hepburn. Critics were divided, but the public made it a hit.

1967

Although theatre business continued to improve, thanks to the increasing attendance of high school and college youth, in the corporate boardrooms the pressures of outsiders were magnified. The management of MGM, headed by Robert H. O'Brien, staved off a proxy fight with a wealthy realtor. Then the company was forced to accept on the board both Edgar Bronfman (of Canadian Seagram Distillers) and representatives of Time, Inc. In exhibition, the prominent independent circuit owners Si Fabian and Sam Rosen sold control of Warner Theatres to Glen Alden, a conglomerate which already owned RKO theatres.

Another industrial change was the demise of the last of the five American newsreels, MGM's *News of the Day* and Universal *Newsreel.* It took television, with its up-to-the-minute news coverage, to kill the theatrical reels which for so long were well-regarded by the ticket-buying public but always were industrial stepchildren.

At EXPO 67 in Montreal, many exhibits showed new and exciting ways for films to move the mind and the spirit. In a number of these precedent-making uses of motion pictures, U.S. technology played a part. Exhibits featured all kinds of uses of pictures with split screens, circular screens, and screens on the floor. Millions of visitors, many from the United States, came home with a new appreciation of the film medium and a new desire to go to their local movie house.

Partially stimulated by new technology, the educational world began to show increasing interest in films. College film activity, for years limited to small film societies, suddenly became the "in thing" and film courses and college film festivals proliferated. Experts on films for teaching assignments became in short supply. One such authority, Arthur Mayer, had the unusual distinction of being a part-time member of the faculty of four major U.S. universities for the same academic year. High school teachers attended seminars and film institutes to qualify to meet the expected challenge of eventually having film courses, at every educational level, as common as those in the novel. Actual film making by students, usually in 8mm and 16mm, rose to amazing proportions. Such films often reflected the revolt of the young against the Establishment and featured unusual daring in language and sexual scenes. Many used psychedelic colors and music and included material reflecting the current craze for drugs among some of the young intellectuals.

Significant on the censorship front was the refusal of the U.S. Supreme Court to review a decision in 1966 of Appellate District Court in California holding that *Un Chant d'Amour,* a film by Jean Genet, was obscene and hence excluded from protection of the Constitution. The banning of this film in California was proof that, at least for the present, certain filmed material could be legally stopped. Some observers felt that the courts would be stricter on homosexual subjects and other perversions than on heterosexual activity on the screen. Time alone would tell.

A long-time dream of many interested in the status of the U.S. film was realized in the establishment of the American Film Institute, under the direction of George Stevens, Jr. Gregory Peck was first chairman of the

Institute, established with funds jointly provided by the U.S. Government and the major companies through the Motion Picture Association.

Films on television as competition to theatres reached a peak, with 11,325 features, including 2,217 in color, available to TV.

The industry and public everywhere mourned the death of Walt Disney.

Stars of the year: Julie Andrews, Lee Marvin, Paul Newman, Dean Martin, Sean Connery, Elizabeth Taylor, Sidney Poitier, John Wayne, Richard Burton and Steve McQueen.

A scene from the Czechoslovakian film *Closely Watched Trains.*

Sidney Poitier in *In the Heat of the Night.*

CLOSELY WATCHED TRAINS

This is one of three films from Czechoslovakia which attracted large American audiences in the late 1960's, the others being *The Shop on Main Street* and *Loves of a Blonde.*

There was nothing of the avant-garde about any of the three pictures either in subject matter or technique. It was their simplicity and directness, and emphasis on character that held appeal and, in the two comedies, their wistful charm.

Significant, too, was the general amazement and satisfaction derived from the realization that the political climate in Czechoslovakia was being so liberalized that film makers could now deal with themes previously forbidden to them—a happy circumstance that was tragically reversed with the Russian invasion of the following year.

Ironically, as we see it now, *Closely Watched Trains* tells of sabotage by the Czech underground during the Nazi occupation in World War II, and the young hero (a railroad worker) dies after he blows up an enemy train. The ending was unexpected; most of what had happened before was in a light and comic vein, with the wide variety of incidents, from seduction to attempted suicide, directed airily yet firmly by Jiri Menzel, whose first feature film this was.

Producer: Carlo Ponti. **Director-Writer:** Jiri Menzel. **Principal Players:** Vaclav Neckar, Jitka Nendova, Josef Somr, Vladimir Valenta and Vlastimil Brodsky. **Running time:** 89 minutes. **Released:** Sigma III.

IN THE HEAT OF THE NIGHT

Selection of this film as the best picture of 1967 by the Academy of Motion Picture Arts and Sciences raised a lot of eyebrows, in view of the fact that *Bonnie and Clyde* and *The Graduate* were also contenders. Essentially, it is a routine thriller given a measure of novelty by the fact that the murder takes place in Mississippi and is solved by a Negro policeman visiting a small Southern town from Philadelphia. The role was played by Sidney Poitier, the first black actor to be named one of the ten top money-making stars in the poll of U.S. exhibitors conducted annually by *Motion Picture Herald.* (He was seventh in 1967 and first in 1968.)

The best thing about the picture is its two major characterizations. Besides the black officer, the other is a tough sheriff with typical Southern prejudices. Acting this role was Rod Steiger, and his performance won him an Oscar. The essence of the film is the turbulent relationship of these two men, and their arrival at a mutual respect. Norman Jewison directed, and his work was most notable for its avoidance of any easy sentimentality. Filming was done on location in Illinois and Tennessee (the latter doubling for Mississippi), and the oppressive heat and the commonplace air of the town were vividly caught.

Producer: Norman Jewison and Walter Mirisch. **Director:** Norman Jewison. **Writer:** Stirling Silliphant. **Principal Players:** Sidney Poitier, Rod Steiger, Warren Oates, Lee Grant, James Patterson and Quentin Dean. **Running time:** 109 minutes. **Released:** United Artists.

Dustin Hoffman in *The Graduate.*

Elvira Madigan with Thommy Berggren and Pia Degermark.

THE GRADUATE

An entire book could and should be written about Mike Nichols' *The Graduate;* it is one of the phenomenal Hollywood pictures of the 1960's.

Seldom have the experts proved so wrong in advance about any picture. Industry people who went to previews of it before the first openings found it amusing and entertaining in various degrees; some even disliked it and predicted a commercial failure. After all, it had no "name" stars; and it was only the second film effort of its director, Mike Nichols (who made his movie debut with *Who's Afraid of Virginia Woolf?*). The script had its clever aspects, and the direction was modish; but the same thing could have been said and was said about several other comedies of the same period.

Confounding all the trade experts, *The Graduate* was an immediate box-office hit, racking up long engagements in all sorts of theatres with all kinds of audiences. Its domestic revenue kept growing until it had passed $40,000,000 in 1968—which places *The Graduate* among the two or three top-grossing pictures of all time in the non-roadshow category.

Why? What was there about it that hit the fancy of the American public? Equally baffling to some was the reaction of the critics, which for once matched the enthusiasm of the paying customers.

There are no easy answers to the mysteries of show business, but nearly everybody had a theory, from the ordinary film reviewer to the learned sociologist. Surely it had something to do with the widespread spirit of protest among the young: The hero of *The Graduate* is decidedly a rebel—impatient with his conservative elders and amoral in his sexual life. (He has an affair with a married woman and then later with her own daughter—a rare occurrence in a Hollywood movie.)

There are as many other theories as there were spectators; rarely has a film been so widely written about and discussed. All of which is part of the explanation of its remarkable performance in theatres everywhere.

The Graduate made film stars of Dustin Hoffman and Katharine Ross, who, after it had opened, had their choices of dozens of important roles in other pictures. It also reaffirmed the special talent of Anne Bancroft, cast as the predatory wife who seduces Hoffman. Hollywood had wasted her for years, until she went to Broadway and appeared in *Two for the Seesaw,* for which she had the satisfaction of having her fine histrionic abilities fully recognized and appreciated.

Producers: Lawrence Turman and Mike Nichols. **Director:** Mike Nichols. **Scriptwriters:** Buck Henry and Calder Willingham. **Principal Players:** Dustin Hoffman, Anne Bancroft, Katharine Ross and Murray Hamilton. **Running time:** 105 minutes. **Released:** Embassy Pictures.

ELVIRA MADIGAN

Based on the true romance of two nineteenth-century lovers in Sweden whose illicit affair became a *cause célèbre* (she was a famous circus tight-rope dancer and he an army lieutenant who deserted his wife and two

Maurice Reeves and Milo O'Shea in *Ulysses.*

children), this film arrived in the U.S. unheralded, but had a rapturous reception from critics and public alike. It firmly established its director, Bo Widerberg, as a favorite with the art-theatre audience here.

Through a well-written script by Widerberg himself without a trace of the mawkishness the theme would seem to invite, and through inspired acting by Pia Degermark and Thommy Berggren, the legendary couple emerged as much more than stereotyped "star-crossed" lovers who give up everything for their passion. Indeed, in their instinctive rebellion against the standards of a society they reject, they are extremely modern in attitude and spirit.

They are rebels with a cause. The hero (Sixten Sparre) dreams of a future in which men "will be allowed to make more than one life for themselves," and he is determined to acquire this freedom for himself and his loved one here and now. Elvira, although she feels guilty about the abandoned wife and children of Sixten, can help neither herself nor him. Theirs is a romantic love that seeks to deny all practical considerations, and, for that very reason, it is doomed.

The film was justly praised, most of all for its superb color photography. Widerberg and cameraman Jorgan Person placed the lovers against some of the most beautiful backgrounds of nature imaginable, amid green woods and grass and by the seashore, to achieve stunning effects.

Producer-Director-Writer: Bo Widerberg. **Principal Players:** Pia Degermark and Thommy Berggren. **Running time:** 89 minutes. **Released:** Cinema V.

ULYSSES

James Joyce's *Ulysses* is a novel that has suffered the fate of many classics: It is a book more talked about than actually read. Its mammoth and cryptic construction puts off the average reader; for years many of those who perused it were prurient-minded college students looking for the scabrous passages that caused it to be barred from the U.S. as obscene in the 1920's. It was later admitted in a precedent-setting court decision.

A bold man, therefore, was Joseph Strick, who, with Fred Haines, adapted the book to the screen with a script that took only two hours and three minutes to play. Strick also directed, and co-produced the film with Walter Reade, Jr., the exhibitor.

The filmed *Ulysses* concentrates major attention on two episodes: Leopold Bloom's fantasies while in the brothel, and Molly Bloom's famous soliloquy as she lies in bed at night—the sequence with which both the book and the film end. Strick's treatment of the second is more successful than that of the first, his approach to which is too facetious. Bloom's obsession with sex and the guilt that accompanies it is worked out in sequences that combine satire with a touch of slapstick, some of which gets very heavy handed.

On the other hand, the presentation of Molly's reverie, which runs for almost thirty minutes on the screen, is brilliant. Actress Barbara Jefford reads the long monologue eloquently, including all the notorious erotic passages, and Strick accompanies the words with imagery that was chosen with great imagination. Milo O'Shea

Guess Who's Coming to Dinner with Sidney Poitier, Katharine Houghton, Katharine Hepburn and Spencer Tracy.

made an ideal Leopold and Maurice Reeves a perfect Dedalus.

Continental Distributing, which handled the film in the U.S., found many exhibitors reluctant to play it in special three-day roadshow engagements ($5.50 a seat) in March of 1967. Response was very good in large cities, however; and censorial objections were restricted to the dialogue. Later it was brought back for regular continuous performances in many theatres with fair success.

Producers: Joseph Strick and Walter Reade, Jr. **Director:** Strick. **Scriptwriters:** Strick and Fred Haines. **Principal Players:** Barbara Jefford, Milo O'Shea and Maurice Reeves. **Running time:** 123 minutes. **Released:** Continental Distributing.

GUESS WHO'S COMING TO DINNER

Strong, pertinent comedy-drama or slick Sunday school sermon? Opinions were sharply at odds on this Stanley Kramer film, which typified the producer-director's penchant for dealing with topical and controversial issues—either moral or political—in the context of a fictional plot constructed of time-tested elements of entertainment (*Home of the Brave, The Defiant Ones, On the Beach, Judgment at Nuremberg,* etc.).

This time the subject was the ticklish one of interracial marriage, and the William Rose script was out of the school of drawing-room stage comedy, complete with unity of time (twenty-four hours) and (except for a few scenes) of place. The girl who wanted to marry a black was the daughter of ultra-liberal parents who, however, found their principles put to a severe test. They ultimately passed it—after a great deal of hemming and hawing—with flying colors.

Once again the critics carped, but the public, including numerous Southerners, loved it—a fact that is all the more amazing in view of the racial tensions of the time. Many felt the cards were stacked by casting handsome Sidney Poitier in the role of the man loved passionately by a white girl (played by newcomer Katharine Houghton). Others objected that Kramer hedged by having the couple kiss only once—and then in a long shot photographed through the front mirror of a taxicab. Admirers pointed out that Kramer sensed unerringly just how far he could go with the whole delicate business.

Subject matter aside, the film surely owed much of its popularity to the appearance in it of Katharine Hepburn and Spencer Tracy as the mother and father of the girl. This was Tracy's last film; he died six months before its release. It was the ninth time he had acted in a picture with Miss Hepburn, and they played together as beautifully as always. There was hardly a dry eye in the house during the climactic scene dominated by Tracy in which he expatiated on the reasons he had changed his mind about the marriage. A lesser actor might have appeared to be giving a lecture; Tracy made the words seem the spontaneous outflow of a man who feels deeply.

Producer-Director: Stanley Kramer. **Scriptwriter:** William Ross. **Principal Players:** Spencer Tracy, Sidney Poitier, Katharine Hepburn, Katharine Houghton, Cecil Kellaway and Beah Richards. **Running time:** 108 minutes. **Released:** Columbia.

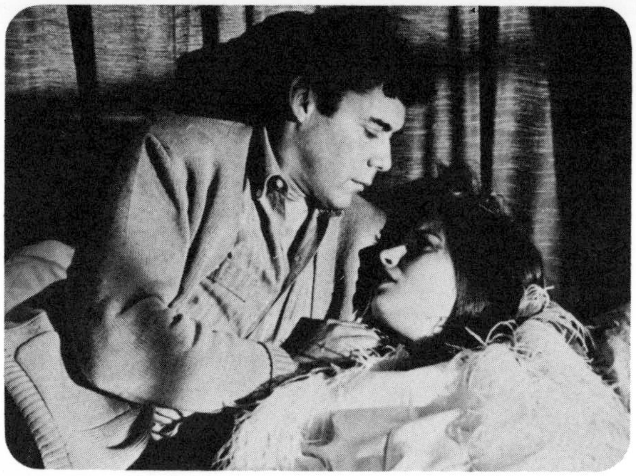

Dirk Bogarde and Jacqueline Sassard in *Accident.*

Thoroughly Modern Millie with James Fox and Julie Andrews.

ACCIDENT

Joseph Losey is an American (not English, as many people think) who had built up a reputation as a competent director of both documentary and commercial films (*Youth Gets a Break* for the National Youth Administration in the first category and RKO Radio's *The Boy With Green Hair* an example of the second) in the U.S., when he became a casualty of the Red scare during the heyday of Senator Joseph McCarthy. He went to Britain in 1953, where he did stage work and made several films which so impressed the critics that he soon enjoyed a cult among the writers of such intellectual publications as *Sight and Sound.*

His films in recent years have been highly praised there and elsewhere, although none has had major success in the U.S. He has made all types of films: psychological melodrama (*The Servant*); anti-war (*King and Country*); and pop-art (*Modesty Blaise*), but *Accident* is the most typical of his interests and method.

Describing the plot—the romantic involvement of two teachers and a student at Oxford with the same young lady—is to make it sound like a soap opera, complete with extramarital love affairs, philandering husbands and betrayed wives. But it is much more than that; it is a study in character relationships, with points made in extremely subtle ways.

An apparently inconsequential action by one of the principals turns out later to have considerable significance. Tensions that lurk inside people explode suddenly, without warning. Characters hide their true feelings from each other and then, provoked, express them openly.

The actors, including Dirk Bogarde, Stanley Baker, Michael York and Vivien Merchant, adapted themselves perfectly to the manner of character revelation used by Losey and playwright Harold Pinter, who wrote the script.

Producer-Director: Joseph Losey. **Scriptwriter:** Harold Pinter. **Principal Players:** Dirk Bogarde, Stanley Baker, Jacqueline Sassard, Michael York, Vivien Merchant and Delphine Seyrig. **Running time:** 105 minutes. **Released:** Cinema V.

THOROUGHLY MODERN MILLIE

Julie Andrews was at the peak of her popularity with American audiences when this musical spoof of the 1920's appeared. It was her third film after the all-time top-grossing *The Sound of Music.* The intervening pictures—*Hawaii,* a turgid drama about the early days of that state, and *Torn Curtain,* a Hitchcock suspense story not up to his usual high standard—both did well at box offices. At the time Miss Andrews could do no wrong. (Then came *Star!*)

And *Millie* certainly needed the extra impetus she gave it, both commercially and personally. Aside from such minor pleasures as an occasional comic device (Miss Andrews would turn to the audience in moments of exasperation and her thoughts would be printed on a silent screen slide), and although there was a lively tune here and there, *Millie* was not a top-notch musical.

Bonnie and Clyde with Michael J. Pollard, Gene Hackman, Warren Beatty and Faye Dunaway.

It was presented as a roadshow, and the first half was vastly superior to the second, in which the comedy got broader and broader, causing several critics to advise the audience to leave at intermission.

Nonetheless, the public loved it. Miss Andrews was the Number One box-office attraction that year.

Producer: Ross Hunter. **Director:** George Roy Hill. **Scriptwriter:** Richard Morris. **Principal Players:** Julie Andrews, Mary Tyler Moore, Carol Channing, James Fox, John Gavin and Beatrice Lillie. **Running time:** 138 minutes. **Released:** Universal.

BONNIE AND CLYDE

Few pictures in the history of the American screen have stirred up so much controversy among both critics and moralists as Arthur Penn's *Bonnie and Clyde.*

On the one hand were the traditionalists, to whom it seemed just another glorification of the criminal—akin in that sense to the *Public Enemy* and *Jesse James* schools. A whitewash of those notorious murderers of the 1930's, Bonnie Parker and Clyde Barrow, they called it.

To the liberals and the avant garde coterie it was a giant step forward in American film making, a rejuvenation of the gangster genre with infusions of humor, tenderness and even poetry—along with the violence, which was to be justified by the rest (as well as on the obvious grounds that it was relevant to the story). Some even aptly compared the Penn film to a ballad.

The public, as always, had the final word. It turned *Bonnie and Clyde* into one of the top-grossing pictures of 1967–68 and gave Warner Bros. their second highest grossing film up to that time (number one was *My Fair Lady*).

It didn't happen overnight. In three cities—New York, Los Angeles and London—it was an immediate success in single engagements, but it did surprisingly poorly elsewhere in the U.S. when booked on a saturation basis. In an unprecedented move, the distributor called in all prints and revised the method of opening the picture to single "prestige" engagements in each city. The film built steadily, and in some cases, when theatres replayed the film, the box office doubled or tripled that of the first time around!

It was an ironic phenomenon: The youthful moviegoers of the late 1960's identified with two rebels of the 1930's and their fight for survival against a hostile world.

Bonnie and Clyde was a particularly gratifying triumph for Penn and his producer, Warren Beatty; they had gone off the beaten path two years before, with the allegorical *Mickey One,* and had fallen on their financial faces.

Beatty gave what was generally regarded by critics as his best performance to date as Clyde, and Bonnie was acted with skill by Faye Dunaway, whose career soared as a result.

The direction of Penn was highly praised for its sustained handling of many shifting moods; the use of slow motion in the final death sequence; and the zoom close-ups of Bonnie and Clyde looking at each other for the last time, just before they die, are extremely powerful.

The Dirty Dozen with Lee Marvin.

Some critics contended, however, it was less a "director's picture" than a "writer's picture," citing the brilliant script of David Newman and Robert Benton.

Producer: Warren Beatty. **Director:** Arthur Penn. **Scriptwriters:** David Newman and Robert Benton. **Principal Players:** Warren Beatty, Faye Dunaway, Michael J. Pollard, Gene Hackman and Estelle Parsons. **Running time:** 111 minutes. **Released:** Warner Bros.

THE DIRTY DOZEN

A fictionalized World War II story about a dozen unsavory U.S. soldiers released from a prison stockade to undertake a dangerous mission—the assassination of some high-ranking Nazi officers in occupied France—this picture is a perfect example of the type that causes critics nightmares. They pan it—mainly for its excessive, and, so they say, gratuitous violence—and the public ignores them. In this instance, the enthusiasm of audiences resulted in a reported domestic gross in excess of twenty million dollars!

Replete with implausible plot developments, the picture is nonetheless engrossing to watch (moral judgments aside). Robert Aldrich, who directed it, is a master storyteller with the camera. He does a lot of subtle things in bringing out the characters of his protagonists; he introduces humor naturally and engagingly; and he builds suspense steadily along the way. The long attack on the Nazi-held chateau at the climax forms a sequence for cinema fans to study in detail for its careful construction and editing. The cast, headed by Lee Marvin, Ernest Borgnine, Charles Bronson and John Cassavetes, plays efficiently to a man.

Aldrich has said that he likes in all his pictures to "show how people struggle within the framework of the story to overcome what are tremendous odds." He likes to give himself similar odds, against making the implausible plausible. (*The Flight of the Phoenix* is another example of this.) He did what he set out to do supremely well in *The Dirty Dozen.*

Producer: Kenneth Hyman. **Director:** Robert Aldrich. **Scriptwriters:** Lukas Heller and Nunnally Johnson. **Principal Players:** Lee Marvin, Ernest Borgnine, Charles Bronson, Jim Brown, John Cassavetes, Richard Jaeckel, George Kennedy, Trini Lopez, Ralph Meeker, Robert Ryan, Telly Savalas, Donald Sutherland and Clint Walker. **Running time:** 149 minutes. **Released:** MGM.

IN COLD BLOOD

Truman Capote's "non-fiction novel" dealing with the murders in 1959 of four members of the Clutter family in their farm home near Holcomb, Kansas, was brought to the screen by Richard Brooks, whose writing and direction of it were generally acclaimed as the supreme achievement of his career to that time. In his way, Brooks was every bit as methodical a scholar as Capote, in his attention to the historical, sociological, philosophical and psychological aspects of the gruesome crimes. Brooks took his actors and crew to all the actual locales of the story—in Kansas, Missouri, Nevada, Colo-

In Cold Blood with James Flavin, Robert Blake and John Forsythe.

rado, Texas and Mexico—following the route that the two murderers, Richard Hickock and Perry Smith, pursued after their deed.

Like the book, the film of *In Cold Blood* has both documentary realism and the excitement of a first-rate detective tale. As did Capote, Brooks goes even beyond this to comment on the action. Some of this he does through a reporter on the case (played by Paul Stewart), who has a tendency to spell things out too obviously.

In one deviation from Capote, Brooks does not devote much time to letting the audience get to know the victims—Farmer Clutter, his wife, son and daughter. Capote brought them individually to life; in the film they are mostly faces—memorable and apt ones, true, but facades. With the film audience learning so little about them, the story is necessarily robbed of part of its poignancy.

In compensation, Brooks gives three-dimensional portraits of the two killers in cinematic terms; his handling of the fantasies and reveries of Perry Smith is especially masterful. High acclaim is also due the actors, especially the then unknowns who played Smith and Hickock. They are Robert Blake and Scott Wilson, respectively.

It is noteworthy that *In Cold Blood* was photographed in black-and-white at a time when 95 percent of Hollywood's films were in color.

Producer-Director-Writer: Richard Brooks. **Principal Players:** Robert Blake, Scott Wilson, John Forsythe, Paul Stewart, Gerald S. O'Loughlin and Jeff Corey. **Running time:** 134 minutes. **Released:** Columbia.

COOL HAND LUKE

After *The Hustler, Hud* and *Hombre,* Paul Newman had become the American moviegoer's favorite symbol of rebellion, and thus the role of Cool Hand Luke, a convict on a Southern chain gang, was made to order for him. The picture was a big financial success, and the bulk of the credit rightly went to the star.

The script comes from a novel by Donn Pearce which he also adapted for the screen in collaboration with Frank R. Pierson. Inevitably, their story employs some of the clichés of the chain-gang movie school, the most famous example of which is still *I Am a Fugitive From a Chain Gang,* the 1932 Paul Muni film which Warner Bros. also released.

But where that picture was frankly an exposé of the evil conditions in such prisons of the day, *Cool Hand Luke* devotes itself to a major dramatic theme that is timeless. It shows how legends can be made in the most unlikely places.

The man who becomes a meaningful symbol to the other convicts is a ne'er-do-well who has been sentenced to two years for destroying parking meters while intoxicated. He first wins the admiration of his fellow prisoners when he stands up to a brutal beating administered by another convict and refuses to lie down even when he is obviously defeated. Luke is also an expert hand at poker, which wins him further regard. And his voracious appetite for food wins him, and others who bet on him, a pile of money in a contest during which he consumes fifty hard-boiled eggs.

Paul Newman and Robert Drivas in *Cool Hand Luke.*

But what clinches his unique standing among his fellows is the fact that he alone makes two escapes from the closely guarded jail. The second time he is caught he appears to have succumbed to the brainwashing of the authorities, who cruelly punish him in an effort to break his spirit. For a time the idol appears to have acquired feet of clay. But this is only a ruse on his part so he can make a third break. It turns out to be his last, for he is shot down and dies with a defiant smile on his lips. The legend is intact.

This alternately realistic and romanticized story is told with a fine visual flair by director Stuart Rosenberg, whose first theatrical film this was, following apprenticeship on television. Many of the individual shots—a bleak landscape on which the convicts labor or the sun setting through a barbed-wire fence—are tremendously striking in composition, yet have the added virtue of not calling attention to themselves to the detriment of the story's development.

Newman's performance was up to his high standard, and veteran Jo Van Fleet made a strong impression in her single scene: one in which, as Luke's dying mother, she comes to the prison camp to pay a farewell visit propped up on pillows in the back of a small truck. George Kennedy was forceful as a convict who first hates and then admires the hero.

Both Newman and Kennedy were nominated for Academy Awards; the latter won and the former lost out to Rod Steiger in *In the Heat of the Night.*

Producer: Gordon Carroll. **Director:** Stuart Rosenberg. **Screenplay:** Donn Pearce and Frank R. Pierson. **Principal Players:** Paul Newman, George Kennedy, J. D. Cannon, Lou Antonio, Robert Drivas, Strother Martin and Jo Van Fleet. **Running time:** 129 minutes. **Released:** Warner Bros.

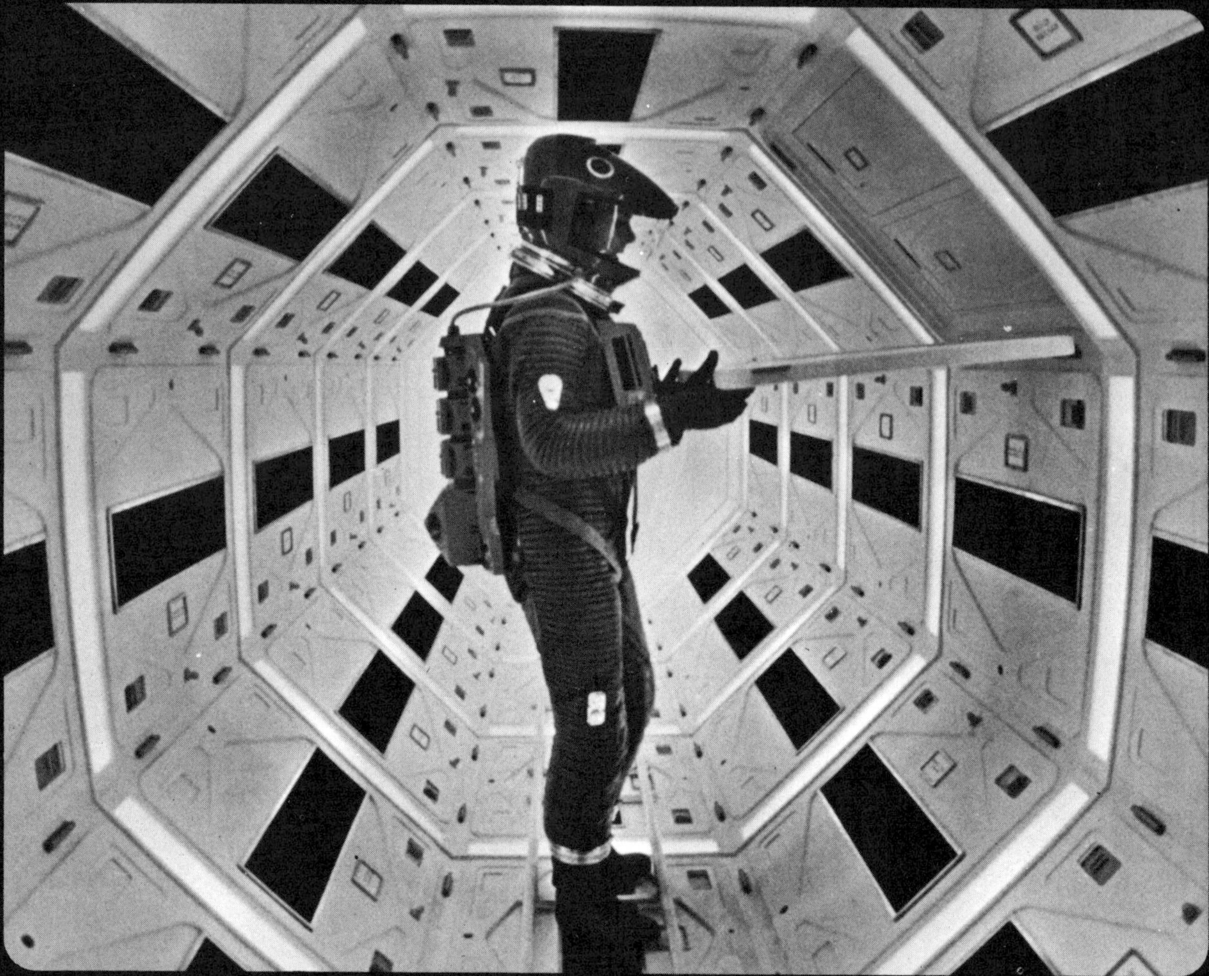

2001: A Space Odyssey with Keir Dullea, Stanley Kubrick's epic science fiction film which introduced poetry into the genre.

1968

In order to ward off a threatened rash of state and local film regulatory measures, the Motion Picture Association, spurred by its president, Jack Valenti, and in agreement with leading exhibitors, launched a film classification system, a system bitterly opposed by Valenti's predecessor Eric Johnston and other spokesmen since the dawn of the American film business.

The classification system borrowed heavily from the one used in Great Britain. Major company releases and those of other cooperating distributors from November 1, 1968, were given one of the following ratings: G—Suggested for general audiences; M—Suggested for mature audiences (parental discretion advised); R—Restricted (Persons under 16 not admitted unless accompanied by a parent or adult guardian); or X—Persons under 16 not admitted. In some areas, either on account of the exhibitors' viewpoint or from concern over local laws, the age of restricting or prohibiting attendance was raised to 17 or 18.

The classification system, administered by the Production Code Administration, now rechristened "Production Code and Rating Administration" (although its work was essentially all concerned with the ratings) got off to a good start, enjoying a generally favorable press. Confusion existed in some quarters over the standards used for assigning the ratings, and over the fact that the "X" rating could be given officially or "self-assigned."

Meanwhile, the U.S. Supreme Court struck down the classification system imposed by the city of Dallas on the grounds of vagueness.

During the year there were more rumors of mergers and actual mergers. Embassy, headed by Joe Levine, made attractive by the fabulous success of *The Graduate,* was sold to AVCO, another conglomerate, for $40,000,000. Two other companies mounted campaigns to become major film producer-distributors. One was National General, a conglomerate built by Eugene Klein around the old National Theatres circuit (owned by 20th Century-Fox prior to divorcement). The other was Cinerama, which no longer made films in the original 3-strip Cinerama process and was now controlled by William Forman, a prominent West Coast exhibitor. He had built his fortune in the years following World War II with a chain of drive-in theatres.

The Motion Picture Association of America launched a campaign to get the government to restrict or ban film production by major theatre circuits or broadcast networks, on the grounds that distributors of films were not allowed to be broadcasters or theatre owners, so restrictions should also flow the other way. The Department of Justice listened to the MPAA but took no definite action, so theatre circuits and TV networks, notably ABC and CBS, went on making feature films intended initially for theatrical exhibition.

Television by now was a major factor in all film company planning. During this year, major film companies took in $500,000,000 on the sale of films to TV. Of this sum, about 85 percent was from the United States. Whether this year's figure is unusual or can be maintained in the years ahead will not be known for some time. Feature film sales to TV are usually made in large blocks, and an individual film company may have wide fluctuations in yearly income from TV.

The campaign of Mayor John Lindsay to make New York City a major center of film production began to bear fruit. It was helped by simplifying procedures to get city approval and police supervision. Unions also pledged cooperation.

Theatres throughout the country enjoyed a high level of attendance. The public accepted sharply increased admissions prices, even in neighborhood theatres.

Stars of the year: Sidney Poitier, Paul Newman, Julie Andrews, John Wayne, Clint Eastwood, Dean Martin, Steve McQueen, Jack Lemmon, Lee Marvin and Elizabeth Taylor.

Kim Hunter, Charlton Heston and Linda Harrison in *Planet of the Apes.*

PLANET OF THE APES

Producer Arthur Jacobs had taken this Pierre Boulle novel to practically every studio in Hollywood and been systematically turned down when he finally convinced the Zanucks—Darryl and Richard—to gamble on it at 20th Century-Fox. They were amply repaid with one of the biggest grossing films of the year—one so popular, in fact, a sequel was deemed in order called *Beneath the Planet of the Apes* (1970).

The subject matter sounds unappetizing: Four American astronauts crash in their spacecraft on an unidentified planet inhabited by a race of apes who lord it over the quasi-human population of animal-like mutes, and hunt them down as if they were beasts of prey. Fortunately, the humorous aspects of the situation were skillfully played up in writing, direction and acting, and it became a science fiction film with fun in it. There was also a startling "message" of sorts: Man is the menace to peace on earth and must be destroyed!

Charlton Heston played the lone astronaut survivor who is cruelly abused by the apes in power but aided in his escape by two of them—a doctor and a psychologist acted, respectively, by Kim Hunter and Roddy McDowall. The makeup created by John Chambers for the actors playing apes was remarkably effective.

Producer: Arthur P. Jacobs. **Director:** Franklin J. Schaffner. **Scriptwriters:** Michael Wilson and Rod Serling. **Principal Players:** Charlton Heston, Maurice Evans, Kim Hunter, Roddy McDowall and Linda Harrison. **Running time:** 112 minutes. **Released:** 20th Century-Fox.

Omar Sharif and Barbra Streisand in *Funny Girl.*

FUNNY GIRL

Broadway handed Hollywood a ready-made musical star in the person of Barbra Streisand—in contrast to the method by which the studios had themselves developed such personalities in the past, grooming them carefully over a period of years (Judy Garland, Ann Miller, Kathryn Grayson, etc.). Miss Streisand was also well known through television shows and phonograph records before she was ever seen on the motion picture screen.

Her debut vehicle in the latter medium was appropriately the one that had made her a stage star—the musical based on the life of Fanny Brice, the darling of the Ziegfeld Follies. The Streisand performance won her an Oscar, in a tie with Katharine Hepburn for *The Lion in Winter*—the first time such a thing had happened since 1931–32, when Fredric March and Wallace Beery shared honors for *Dr. Jekyll and Mr. Hyde* and *The Champ,* respectively.

Funny Girl on film is best when it follows the original play, as it does in the first half, tracing the early efforts of Miss Brice to get into the theatre and her enormous success there. Satiric touches abound. In the last half, unfortunately, several of the original songs and production numbers were dropped to emphasize the sad love story of the heroine and Nick Arnstein, the gambler she wed and then divorced. Soap opera takes over, but the lapse is almost redeemed by the brilliant ending: Miss Streisand sings "My Man" (the ballad identified with Miss Brice, but not used in the play) on a bare stage

The Killing of Sister George with Beryl Reid and Susannah York.

with the screen all black except for a spotlight on her face. She sang it entirely à la Streisand, not at all as Fanny Brice sang it in the Follies and in the film *The Great Ziegfeld.*

William Wyler, known for his expertise at directing drama, tackled his first musical with *Funny Girl* and brought to it his usual professionalism.

Producers: Ray Stark and William Wyler. **Director:** William Wyler. **Scriptwriter:** Isobel Lennart. **Principal Players:** Barbra Streisand, Omar Sharif, Kay Medford, Anne Francis, Walter Pidgeon. **Running time:** 115 minutes. **Released:** Columbia.

THE KILLING OF SISTER GEORGE

It is Jean Renoir who is credited with this comment on Alfred Hitchcock's *Rope:* "I thought it was a film about homosexuals, but you don't even see them kiss."

Things have changed since 1948. In 1967, in a picture called *The Fox,* American audiences were able to see two respectable actresses (Sandy Dennis and Anne Heywood) demonstrate latent lesbian feelings for each other through a passionate embrace and a full kiss.

That turned out to be tame in comparison with what happened a year later in *The Killing of Sister George.* This time, one lesbian (played by Coral Browne) exposed the breasts of another (played by Susannah York) and applied her mouth to one—all in full view of the audience. Miss York then simulated an orgasm.

Thus did Robert Aldrich one-up Raymond Stross and Mark Rydell (producer and director, respectively, of *The Fox*). The old Production Code was long gone, replaced by guidelines leaving nearly everything to the "good taste" of producers.

The seduction scene in *The Killing of Sister George* seemed especially gratuitous, in that it had not been in the stage play on which the film was based. It was a comedy-drama by Frank Marcus about an actress (Beryl Reid was Sister George) in a BBC television soap opera whose part is written out for reasons of expedience—the character is "killed" in an accident. In private life, the actress is a lesbian, and the female boss who fires her also steals away her younger girl friend. A sordid situation was handled by Marcus in a tough, funny, unsentimental manner. The film not only sensationalizes the original, but sentimentalizes it, too.

Film industry experts who saw previews of the picture anticipated more censorship trouble for it in the U.S. than it actually had. It was a sign of the changing times.

In a sense, the way had been paved for *The Killing of Sister George* not only by *The Fox,* but by Radley Metzger's *Thérèse and Isabelle,* a French film released earlier in 1968. A story of two schoolgirls whose friendship ripens into lesbian passion, it forced its audiences to wait for almost an hour before the first love scene—and then what was spoken on the soundtrack (the reveries of one of the girls as she made love) was much more explicit than anything visually shown.

Producer-Director: Robert Aldrich. **Scriptwriter:** Lukas Heller. **Principal Players:** Beryl Reid, Susannah York and Coral Browne. **Running time:** 133 minutes. **Released:** Cinerama.

Mark Lester in *Oliver!*

Rosemary's Baby with Mia Farrow, Sidney Blackmer and Maurice Evans.

OLIVER!

On the sensible theory that if you've got a good stage property you shouldn't tamper with it too much, Carol Reed brought the musical stage version of Charles Dickens' *Oliver Twist* to the screen virtually without alteration—except, of course, for employing the larger and more flexible sets available to the camera for more spectacular effects, and the apt use of close-ups and other cinematic devices for emphasizing points.

The Lionel Bart musical (he did the book as well as music and lyrics) was an international stage success, and the film followed in its commercial footsteps. When it copped the Oscar as best picture of 1968, it enjoyed the further financial benefit such an award always brings.

There had been several screen versions of *Oliver Twist,* both silent and sound; the last was David Lean's made in 1948 and not released in the U.S. until 1951 because of anticipated objections to the caricature of Fagin as anti-Semitic. The complaints came on schedule, and the picture was shown only briefly and then withdrawn.

In *Oliver!* Fagin has only a small trace of the racial stereotype, being turned instead into a clown who even becomes sympathetic at times. Ron Moody, who created the part on the London stage but did not play it on Broadway, stole the film in this role.

Reed is a director best known for his superior suspense films (*The Fallen Idol* and *The Third Man,* in particular), and this big-scale musical venture was an innovation for him. He not only unified the elements of drama, song and dance but added a familiar trademark in such matters as the grand entrance of the villainous Bill Sikes, who is photographed with his shadow magnified ominously against a building wall on a dimly lit street at night. Reed's reputation as an expert in handling children was reinforced with the fine performance he got from young Mark Lester as Oliver.

Producer: John Woolf. **Director:** Carol Reed. **Scriptwriter:** Vernon Harris. **Principal Players:** Ron Moody, Shani Wallis, Oliver Reed, Harry Secombe and Mark Lester. **Running time:** 153 minutes. **Released:** Columbia.

ROSEMARY'S BABY

Several careers were advanced by this highly popular story of modern-day witchcraft. First, Roman Polanski, the Polish director of *Knife in the Water* (1963), *Repulsion* (1965) and *Cul-De-Sac* (1966), successfully made the jump from small, "personal" pictures to an ambitious major project without losing his individuality. Secondly, Mia Farrow, the heroine of TV's *Peyton Place,* whose performance as Rosemary won her laudatory reviews, was established as a top theatrical film star. Third, John Cassavetes, as her husband Guy, reaffirmed his ability to act as well as direct. And finally, Ruth Gordon won an Oscar as best supporting actress for her performance as the mysterious neighbor of the protagonists.

Polanski starts the picture on a naturalistic level as the newly wedded couple move into a large apartment on Manhattan's West Side. Strange things begin to happen slowly, culminating in the fear of the heroine

Romeo and Juliet with Leonard Whiting and Olivia Hussey.

that witches are after her unborn child and that her husband is in on the plot.

Is this to be taken as reality or the fantasies of an hysterical female driven off balance by pregnancy? Polanski keeps the moviegoer guessing, staging it all in a matter-of-fact fashion with an even editing rhythm to match. His handling of the nightmares of Rosemary is imaginative—Freudianism run rampant with special effects. Before the film is over many spectators almost believe in witchcraft; Polanski at the very least has raised doubts!

Producer: William Castle. **Director-Writer:** Roman Polanski. **Principal Players:** Mia Farrow, John Cassavetes, Ruth Gordon and Sidney Blackmer. **Running time:** 136 minutes. **Released:** Paramount.

ROMEO AND JULIET

In 1967, the Italian film maker Franco Zeffirelli had tried to turn *The Taming of the Shrew* into Shakespeare for the masses, chiefly by casting Richard Burton and Elizabeth Taylor in leading roles and encouraging them to act the parts with abandon. In spite of its popular co-stars, the picture had only a fair success.

In making *Romeo and Juliet,* Zeffirelli used unknowns in the central parts—young players of approximately the same age as the hero and heroine. Ironically, this time the box-office receipts were tremendous. Young people everywhere flocked to see it, and the Bard gained new admirers.

Youth, in fact, is the keynote of the whole film. This *Romeo and Juliet* has the most convivial Capulet ball to date; the dancing goes on and on. It also has the fiercest and most athletically performed dueling scenes. It has the rowdiest street crowds. Its comedy is the most broadly played of all.

As for sex—well, Romeo and Juliet never kissed more passionately or as often as they do here. They even have a nude love scene, with Romeo's buttocks exposed but with Juliet's breasts discreetly half-covered with a bedsheet.

In short, Zeffirelli transformed *Romeo and Juliet* into a sexy, energetic and visually dazzling spectacle. For most moviegoers that was sufficient compensation for the fact that the poetry gets short shrift—due partially to the histrionic inexperience of seventeen-year-old Leonard Whiting and sixteen-year-old Olivia Hussey, who play Romeo and Juliet.

Their inadequacies were cleverly disguised by Zeffirelli in a number of ways—shortening speeches, cutting away from them to reaction shots, giving them distracting bits of action as they speak. Whiting is handsome and awesomely agile; Miss Hussey is pretty and spirited. Some of the briefer speeches are handled by the two very well indeed, but some of the longer ones contain more emotion and meaning than they were able to bring to them.

Producers: Anthony Havelock-Allan and John Bradbourne. **Director:** Franco Zeffirelli. **Principal Players:** Leonard Whiting, Olivia Hussey, Michael York, John McEnery, Milo O'Shea and Pat Haywood. **Running time:** 138 minutes. **Released:** Paramount.

Genevieve Page and Catherine Deneuve in *Belle de Jour.*

The Lion in Winter with Peter O'Toole and Katharine Hepburn.

BELLE DE JOUR

Luis Buñuel, the celebrated Spanish film maker who first startled audiences in 1928 with his famous surrealist film *Un Chien Andalou,* had to wait a long time for (limited) commercial success in the U.S. Over the years, film buffs sought out his pictures: *Los Olvidados* (1952), *Nazarin* (1958), *Viridiana* (1962), etc.—films in which he has gone his solitary way, denouncing formal religion, social injustices and the manifold foibles of human nature without regard for the sensibilities or the interests of average moviegoers.

In *Belle de Jour* Buñuel finally found a subject of wide commercial appeal (though one suspects he still didn't go looking for it deliberately). It is the story of an attractive young woman in Paris who, although married to a handsome surgeon who adores her, is sexually dissatisfied and takes up prostitution in the afternoons.

The treatment is pure Buñuel, as he mingles fantasy sequences in which the woman imagines herself degraded by her husband with external action advancing the melodramatic plot. Buñuel shifts from the real to the unreal without warning, but before the episode is over the spectator always knows which is which.

The conclusion is deliberately ambiguous. Is the lady having fantasies in imagining that her paralyzed husband (shot by her lover) recovers, or was the whole thing a bad dream?

Belle de Jour is Buñuel's second film in color; the first was *Adventures of Robinson Crusoe* (1954). In America, the French film was shown in two versions—one with subtitles for the art houses, and one dubbed into English. The latter got heavy bookings, although not as many as the similarly handled *A Man and a Woman* had received in 1966-67.

Producer-Director-Writer: Luis Buñuel. **Principal Players:** Catherine Deneuve, Jean Sorel, Genevieve Page and Michel Piccoli. **Running time:** 100 minutes. **Released:** Allied Artists.

THE LION IN WINTER

Old arguments about what is and is not cinematic were brought up again with the release of *The Lion in Winter,* based on a play by James Goldman about the tangled family relationships in the household of the twelfth-century English king, Henry II. Purist film critics said it was no more than a photographed stage play and further complained that for the humorous approach of the original had been substituted a more serious and pretentious attack.

Other critics disagreed, and so did most moviegoers. *The Lion in Winter* once again disproved the ancient theory that costume dramas are anathema to the film box office.

Admirers justly commended the film makers for not turning the play into a spectacle by arbitrarily introducing big action sequences and creating the kind of grotesque hybrid of high drama followed by noisy war that puts audiences to sleep.

Rachel, Rachel with James Olsen and Joanne Woodward.

Even had they succumbed to such an urge, it is impossible that any amount of sword-rattling or cannon-booming could have overshadowed the brilliant performance of Katharine Hepburn as Eleanor of Aquitaine. A tour de force of acting that was perfect in all respects—pictorially, vocally and emotionally—earned Miss Hepburn her third Academy Award, and she became the first actress in film history to receive that many. (Previous awards were for *Morning Glory* in 1933 and *Guess Who's Coming to Dinner* in 1967.) This award, however, was shared with Barbra Streisand (see *Funny Girl,* page 339).

Peter O'Toole, playing Henry, was every inch the match for Miss Hepburn, histrionically speaking. Their verbal duels together have tremendous theatrical force.

Producer: Martin Poll. **Director:** Anthony Harvey. **Scriptwriter:** James Goldman. **Principal Players:** Peter O'Toole, Katharine Hepburn, Jane Merrow, John Castle and Timothy Dalton. **Running time:** 134 minutes. **Released:** Avco-Embassy.

RACHEL, RACHEL

Paul Newman was another actor (like Marlon Brando, John Cassavetes, Paul Henreid and others) who became smitten by the urge to direct a film. The man who gave him the chance was Kenneth Hyman, who was named head of production at Warner Bros. after the merger with Seven Arts in 1967. *Rachel, Rachel* was one of the most commercially successful pictures of Hyman's short tenure (he left in 1969).

For his first directorial venture, Newman wisely chose a small-scaled, intimate drama—a character study of a spinster schoolteacher who has her first sexual experience at the age of thirty-five. He was also astute in electing to make the film on location in Danbury, Connecticut, where the small town provided him with environmental details that give the picture a sharp feeling of time and place. And he was shrewd, too, in selecting actors unfamiliar to most moviegoers for the supporting roles.

His most discriminating move, however, was in casting his wife Joanne Woodward in the leading role. Playing the only character analyzed in any depth in the script of Stewart Stern, Miss Woodward gave her best performance since *The Three Faces of Eve,* which had won her an Oscar.

The role is a sister to all those old maids in countless books and films who, feeling unwanted and unloved, are putty in the hands of the first man who comes along and gives them a tumble.

True to tradition, this one winds up with bittersweet memories: sweet, because she felt desirable for a while; bitter, because the affair ended badly and nothing in her life had really changed.

Miss Woodward conveys all facets of the character—pride, anxiety, yearning and desperation—with an emotional control that never falters.

Producer-Director: Paul Newman. **Scriptwriter:** Stewart Stern. **Principal Players:** Joanne Woodward, James Olson, Kate Harrington and Estelle Parsons. **Running time:** 101 minutes. **Released:** Warner Bros-Seven Arts.

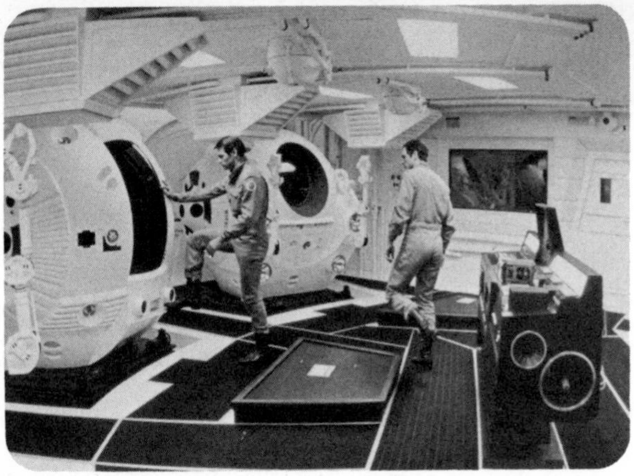

Gary Lockwood and Keir Dullea in *2001: A Space Odyssey.*

2001: A SPACE ODYSSEY

Stanley Kubrick's epic science fiction film, which was five years in the making (three of them before the cameras), had to overcome an initial adverse reaction when it was previewed in New York. Screenings for press and industry people had been marked by booing and frequent walkouts. And the reviews in the daily press were bad, making for a gloomy commercial outlook.

Fortunately, these turned out to be minority opinions. National magazine critics and out-of-town newspaper reviewers were extremely enthusiastic. Business—even in New York—built steadily, and the picture, which was released as a roadshow, was one of the top grossers of the year.

All of which was especially gratifying in view of the nature of the film, which is fascinating but complex; its ultimate meaning is cryptic. As to the latter, there were any number of theories; evidently the mass audience simply responded to the excitement of the visual experience, which was considerable.

The film is divided into four sections. In a prologue, prehistoric apes discover a large slab of black stone. Then there is a sequence depicting what Kubrick and co-writer Arthur C. Clarke imagine life will be like in 2001. (A giant space station has a Howard Johnson restaurant and a Hilton hotel!) The third part consists of the "odyssey" to Jupiter, in which a computer almost takes over the space craft. In this section Kubrick comments, as he did in *Dr. Strangelove,* on the dangers to mankind inherent in the creation of intricate machines that can get out of control.

It is the fourth part that causes difficulties in interpretation, as the astronaut lands on a planet (depicted in a kaleidoscope of color effects), arrives in a bedroom with Louis XVI furnishings, discovers a man exactly like himself there, then grows old and dies, as the monolith first seen by the apes appears before him.

Like the famous sled in *Citizen Kane,* the slab is a symbol—possibly of the life force.

Producer-Director: Stanley Kubrick. **Scriptwriters:** Stanley Kubrick and Arthur C. Clarke. **Principal Players:** Keir Dullea, Gary Lockwood and William Sylvester. **Running time:** 160 minutes. **Released:** MGM.

Midnight Cowboy, with Jon Voight and Dustin Hoffman, a leading example of the new trends in subject matter (rated "X") that marked the end of the 1960's.

1969

The decade hailed at its beginning as "The Soaring Sixties" ended—so far as American motion pictures were concerned—in unprecedented chaos. Public acceptance of pornographic and obscene screen entertainment reached a height that would not have been considered possible in the wildest prediction as recently as two or three years ago. Major American film companies suffered cumulative financial losses much larger than any year of the Great Depression, with the not surprising accompaniment of more management changes than at any time in the history of the American film.

Despite all this chaos, many individual films, especially those found exciting by youths and the young in spirit, enjoyed enormous box-office success. This was the year of *Alice's Restaurant, Easy Rider, Midnight Cowboy* and *Putney Swope*. It was also the year of *I Am Curious* (*Yellow*) and a number of other films that in times past would have been "beyond the pale" of responsible theatre operators in the United States. While *I Am Curious* (*Yellow*) was kept from exhibition in some areas by local court actions, as the year ended there was a hopeful feeling in industry legal circles that the film might eventually win a "landmark" U.S. Supreme Court decision holding that only minors may be constitutionally protected from obscenity. However, the "Burger Court" might reverse the trend to permissiveness and set a new definition of obscenity.

Substantial losses incurred by some of the leading production-distribution companies on very expensive films caused a rethinking of the value of "name" players, i.e., the stars. Producers generally resolved not to pay any star a million dollars, or even half a million, for work in a single picture. Stars were being encouraged to accept what the recent past would have called relatively modest salary plus a percentage of the profits and sometimes a percentage of the gross distribution revenue. Since all previous efforts to control compensation of leading players have failed, the effectiveness of this new attempt will have to be proved.

The Diamond Jubilee of the American motion picture was proclaimed by the Motion Picture Association for 1969. The 75-year span was measured from the first public display of the Edison peep-show Kinetoscopes on April 14, 1894, at 1155 Broadway in New York City. The industry's problems in 1969 were so great that no one had the heart to celebrate. Representative of numerous corporate management shifts was the fact that during the year Metro-Goldwyn-Mayer, a company which long claimed first position among all American film firms, had three different presidents. First, an alliance of Edgar Bronfman and Time, Inc., supplanted Robert H. O'Brien with James F. "Bo" Polk, Jr., formerly of General Mills. Then, in two spectacular stock tender offers financed at high interest rates abroad, Kirk Kerkorian, Las Vegas hotel owner, won control of MGM and installed James Aubrey, one-time CBS head, as president. At the year's end David Merrick and others were striving to wrest control of 20th Century-Fox from Darryl and Richard Zanuck.

In the exhibition business, independents and circuits that had booked a good number of the several dozen hit pictures had a good year, but there were worries about how long the steep increases in admission prices could balance the long-term fall in total attendance. It was estimated that 1969 attendance in the U.S. only averaged 15,000,000 a week, a third of the average figure of fifteen years before.

There was much talk—and even some construction—of automated "mini" theatres equipped with automatic projectors. Some observers predicted that there would be thousands of "mini" theatres as soon as a slowdown in the war in Vietnam made widespread new construction economically feasible.

Stars of the Year: Paul Newman, John Wayne, Steve McQueen, Dustin Hoffman, Clint Eastwood, Sidney Poitier, Lee Marvin, Jack Lemmon, Katharine Hepburn and Barbra Streisand. Superstar of the decade and longest-reigning top star in film history: John Wayne.

The final scene from *If. . .*

Anne of the Thousand Days with Genevieve Bujold (center).

IF . . .

Being a year for youth, it was also one inevitably for anti-Establishment movies. One that came from England and caught on strong was Lindsay Anderson's *If. . . .*

Anderson is the movie critic turned film maker whose first and only previous feature-length work was the excellent *This Sporting Life* back in 1963. Prior to that he had made a name for himself with several superior documentaries, most notably *Thursday's Children.*

If . . . takes place in a boarding school for boys, and on one level it is an extremely sharp and freshly amusing satire on "types" of both teachers and students, from the headmaster who is oblivious to what is going on around him to the upperclassman who takes pleasure in bullying freshmen. At the same time, in poking fun at the hierarchy and the rituals of school life, the film reaches out to condemn modern society as a whole.

Fantasy and realism are so intermingled in the film that some observers interpret the last episode in which three lower classmen shoot down other students and the staff as yet another wishful reverie of one of the rebels. To other observers it looks like the real thing.

The large cast of boys and adults—largely unknown in the U.S.—was uniformly fine. A special standout was Malcolm McDowell as the leader of the rebels.

Originally the picture was given an "X" rating by the industry (barring from theatres persons under 17; local option may raise this to 18). This was because of brief male frontal nudity in a shower room sequence and an episode in which the housemaster's wife roams nude through the boys' quarters. After the film had completed most of its art theatre engagements, the distributor excised a few frames from these scenes in order for the film to be rated "R" (persons under 16 not admitted unless accompanied by parent or guardian) in its general release.

Producers: Lindsay Anderson and Michael Medwin. **Director:** Lindsay Anderson. **Scriptwriters:** Lindsay Anderson and John Howelt. **Principal Players:** Malcolm McDowell, David Wood, Richard Warwick, Christine Noonan, Robert Swann, Hugh Thomas and Guy Ross. **Running time:** 111 minutes. **Released:** Paramount.

ANNE OF THE THOUSAND DAYS

So many dramatic costume pictures failed at the box office in the forties and fifties that they were hard to come by in the sixties until Fred Zinnemann broke the commercial jinx with his *A Man for All Seasons* in 1966. Then in 1968 Anthony Harvey's *The Lion in Winter* also succeeded in enthralling large audiences, paving the way for *Anne of the Thousand Days,* set, like *A Man for All Seasons,* in sixteenth-century England and dealing, like the other two, with the monarchy.

This new entry was based on a play by the late Maxwell Anderson, the once much-admired playwright (his heyday was in the 1930's and 1940's) who had fallen out of fashion altogether in the 1960's. *Anne of the Thousand Days* had been produced on the Broadway stage successfully in 1948 with Rex Harrison and Joyce Redman as Henry VIII and Anne Boleyn, roles taken in the film by Richard Burton and Genevieve Bujold (a French-Canadian actress acclaimed for her performance in *Isabel* in 1968).

The film follows the main plot line of the Anderson original faithfully, while discarding the blank verse and most of the soliloquies. And it contains many of the same characters on view in *A Man for All Seasons,* which told much the same story—except, of course, from the viewpoint of Thomas More.

Anne of the Thousand Days gained its main distinction, as had the other two historical movies mentioned, for excellent performances in the pivotal roles. Burton makes a first-rate Henry; along with projection of personal magnetism, he is lusty in manner. Miss Bujold was not able to perform on the same heroic level, mostly because she lacks both the experience and the stature of Burton. But her Anne is lovely and spirited. Anthony Quayle performs in the grand manner as Cardinal Wolsey; Irene Papas is a striking Katharine; and John Colicos, a vigorous Cromwell.

Producer of the film was veteran Hal Wallis, who had brought another Anderson play, *Elizabeth the Queen,* to the screen in 1939 under the title *The Private Lives of Elizabeth and Essex* and also produced *Becket* (from the Jean Anouilh play), in 1964.

Producer: Hal Wallis. **Director:** Charles Jarrott. **Screenplay:** John Hale and Bridget Boland. **Principal Players:** Richard Burton, Genevieve Bujold, Irene Papas, Anthony Quayle, John Colicos and Michael Hordern. **Running time:** 145 minutes. **Released:** Universal.

Robert Redford and Paul Newman in *Butch Cassidy and the Sundance Kid.*

BUTCH CASSIDY AND THE SUNDANCE KID

Moviegoers brought up on westerns glorifying Wyatt Earp, Doc Halliday, Jesse James and Billy the Kid had never heard of Butch Cassidy and the Sundance Kid—another pair of real-life bandidts—a neglect rectified by this film. It was the youthful audiences of the late 1960's, however, who were most captivated by these newly discovered heroes—motivated as much, perhaps, by the fact that the protagonists rebelled against society as that they were played by two very popular and personable stars—Paul Newman and Robert Redford.

The carefully researched screenplay was by novelist William Goldman. His approach is intriguing: he satirizes the myths of the western genre while apotheosizing the men who created them. The method is basically contradictory, but it works so well so often that one wishes it worked all the time.

Old myths of the west are kidded in a way that humanizes the heroes. The mere mention of the name of the Sundance Kid (Redford) strikes terror in the heart of the gambler who has challenged him without knowing his identity. Cassidy (Newman) is unable to make the horses of a posse scatter out of a barn, and just before a critical gun fight he admits he's never killed a man before. They are characterized as anachronisms—men who have outlived their time—and, no longer able to elude the law in the U.S., they take off for South America with the school-teacher girl friend (winningly acted by Katharine Ross) of Sundance and

They Shoot Horses, Don't They? with Michael Sarrazin and Jane Fonda.

rob banks in Bolivia until the army traps them and shoots them down.

The direction of George Roy Hill is sometimes arty and self-conscious, employing a variety of the fashionable camera tricks of the day. He uses several quite effectively, however—especially a montage of stills during a vacation the threesome has in New York that has the look and flavor of daguerreotypes of the period, and the final frozen frame in which the heroes are caught at the point of death, going down fighting, symbols of the legend they are to become.

Producer: John Foreman. **Director:** George Roy Hill. **Screenplay:** William Goldman. **Principal Players:** Paul Newman, Robert Redford and Katharine Ross. **Running time:** 110 minutes. **Released:** 20th Century-Fox.

THEY SHOOT HORSES, DON'T THEY?

Horace McCoy's 1935 novel *They Shoot Horses, Don't They?* has attained the stature of a minor classic over the years, mostly because of its realistic depiction of one of the social phenomena of the Depression Years—the marathon dance contests. What has kept it on the lesser literary level is its weakness in character motivation.

The motion picture that was finally made from it in 1969 retains the flaws in characterization and adds some of its own (a distracting and ineptly handled flash-forward device, in particular). However, the film also capitalizes on the strengths of the book; the moods of hope and desperation of the dance contestants, swinging continuously from one to the other, have been expertly caught, and director Sidney Pollack has staged a brisk elimination race scene that is the exciting highlight of the film.

Jane Fonda was widely praised by critics for her portrayal of the professional "loser," Gloria, but others felt she made the heroine so hard-boiled and self-sufficient that her decision to die didn't make sense. And the character of Robert was so fuzzily drawn—including the motivation of his crucial decision to be the executioner of Gloria—that able actor Michael Sarrazin could do little with the part. Much better conceived and played were two minor characters not in the book—an aging sailor (Red Buttons) and a starlet who wants to be a new Jean Harlow (Susannah York). Best of all was Gig Young, who gave the performance of his career as the master of ceremoies, a man made cynical by life but still retaining some vestiges of decent instincts. Young won an Oscar.

Surprising as it was to some jaded observers, young people of the sixties liked this film about an era long before their time, although some were heard to snicker about the film makers' aspirations toward making the dance hall a microcosm of the world.

Producer: Irwin Wingler and Robert Chartoff. **Director:** Sidney Pollack. **Screenplay:** James Poe and Robert E. Thompson. **Principal Players:** Jane Fonda, Michael Sarrazin, Susannah York, Gig Young, Red Buttons and Bonnie Bedelia. **Running time:** 129 minutes. **Released:** Cinerama Releasing Corp.

Helmut Berger (right) and Ingrid Thulin (behind him, at the head of the table) in *The Damned.*

THE DAMNED

Luchino Visconti, one of the three great Italian directors to come to international prominence in the decade of the 1960's (the others: Fellini and Antonioni), has had a difficult time in securing widespread recognition in the United States.

His first major film, *Ossessione* (1941), which critics date as an important harbinger of the neo-realist movement in his country, has never been shown here because it was an unauthorized adaptation of the James Cain novel *The Postman Always Rings Twice,* to which MGM had the rights and had made into a film in 1945. Under copyright laws Visconti's version is still barred from the U.S.

In 1961 his sixth film, *Rocco and His Brothers,* opened in New York to rave reviews from the critics and almost no business. In 1963 he made *The Leopard* in collaboration with 20th Century-Fox, which, according to Visconti, cut forty minutes from the film for U.S. theatres, thereby destroying it artistically. Its box-office performance here was also poor.

With *The Damned,* the American jinx plaguing Visconti appears to have been broken. Although it played only two engagements in the U.S. late in 1969 (Hollywood and New York), it set new house records in both theatres.

In *The Damned,* Visconti is once more concerned with the family unit, which he sees as a reflection of society as a whole. This time he examines the members of a munitions dynasty in Germany in 1933 just as Hitler was coming into full power. Through portrayal of their decadence and depravities, the film reflects the moral atmosphere which permitted the evil of Nazism to flower.

"Operatic" is a word European critics have often used to describe the Visconti technique, and for no film of his is it so appropriate as with *The Damned.* The picture begins in a sombre and ominous mood on a realistic level, but slowly the emotional tension mounts until at the end it is overpoweringly theatrical. Given the grotesque material (the sins of the family range from homosexuality to child molestation to incest and patricide), it could hardly have been handled any other way.

Midway in the film comes one of the most powerful set-pieces in all cinema: the depiction of the "Night of the Long Knives," the Roehm massacre and the orgiastic party that preceded it. Individual images are brilliantly composed, and the sequence moves from the mood of carefree abandon to shock and horror at a relentless pace that overwhelms the viewer.

As in all his films, Visconti shows an enviable mastery of actors. Newcomer Helmut Berger, as the murderous and incestuous son, plays a difficult role with extraordinary skill, and the gifted Ingrid Thulin (of Ingmar Bergman's stock company) is superb as his mother, who begins as a steely Lady Macbeth type and declines to the level of a miserable drug addict.

Producers: Alfredo Levy and Ever Haggiag. **Director-Writer:** Luchino Visconti. **Principal Players:** Dirk Bogarde, Ingrid Thulin, Helmut Griem, Helmut Berger and Charlotte Rampling. **Running time:** 160 minutes. **Released:** Warner Bros.

A scene from *Oh! What a Lovely War.*

I Am Curious (Yellow) with Lena Nyman and Borje Ahlstedt.

OH! WHAT A LOVELY WAR

By all the rules of film making, *Oh! What a Lovely War* ought not to have worked as a movie at all. But then it probably shouldn't have worked on the stage either; it was a series of loosely connected vaudeville skits and musical production numbers satirizing the motives behind World War I and the often chaotic manner in which it was conducted.

That all its various elements—satire, caricature, music, dance and irony—melded so well was due to the staging of Joan Littlewood, who pulled them all together so expertly that the audience received a unified, solid impact. This is what happened with the film—thanks to Richard Attenborough, erstwhile actor and producer, directing his first picture. *Oh! What a Lovely War* is a tour de force for the director, on screen as it was on stage.

At the same time it is an exciting show—savagely witty, melodious in moods both humorous and sad, brilliantly acted by some of England's greatest talents, and handsome to watch. Of the numerous highlights only a few can be cited: Maggie Smith as a music hall singer who entreats men to enlist by singing to them from the stage and offering a kiss if they do; the scene in which a band of Jerries and Tommies stop fighting at Christmas and converse; the Americans arriving to the tune of "Over There" with some significant changes in the lyrics; Laurence Olivier caricaturing a Colonel Bimp-like officer; and the eloquent final image of the thousands of white crosses planted in green fields, symbolizing the millions who gave their lives in the war that was to end them all.

It was expected that the picture would strike a responsive chord in the young with its anti-war sentiments, but it didn't in the U.S., at least. The box office here was disappointing in spite of excellent reviews.

Producer: Richard Attenborough and Brian Duffy. **Director:** Richard Attenborough, **Scriptwriter:** none credited. **Principal Players:** Laurence Olivier, John Gielgud,. Ralph Richardson, Michael Redgrave, John Clements, John Mills, Vanessa Redgrave, Dirk Bogarde, Susannah York, Maggie Smith, Jack Hawkins, Kenneth More and Jean Pierre Cassel. **Running time:** 139 minutes. **Released:** Paramount.

I AM CURIOUS (YELLOW)

The notorious Swedish film made by Vilgot Sjoman, *I am Curious (Yellow)* (his fourth) was seized by U.S. Customs late in 1967 and barred as obscene. This decision was backed by a Federal Court jury but later overruled by the U.S. Court of Appeals. As 1969 ended, its court troubles were not yet over; barred by court injunction from playing in several cities, *I Am Curious (Yellow)* was heading for a ruling by the U.S. Supreme Court.

The notoriety assured the picture of a ready-made audience of sorts, anticipating sensational sex scenes the like of which had never before been available to commercial theatre screens in the U.S. To get to the quasi-pornography, however, the patrons had to sit through

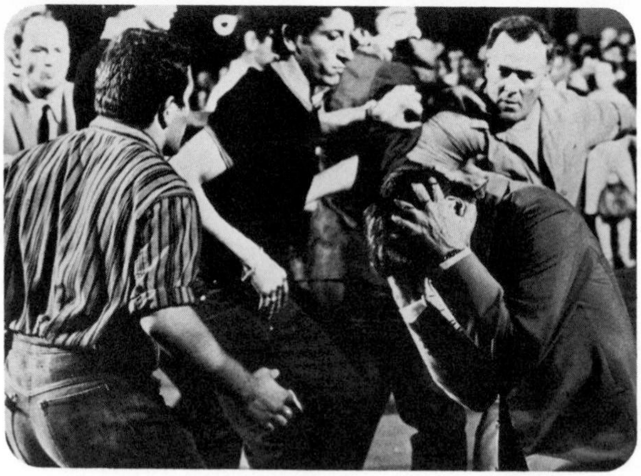

Yves Montand (at right, holding his head) in *Z.*

some unconscionably boring lectures, in which the heroine conducts interviews with the man-on-the-street on such subjects as non-violence, class structure in Sweden, attitudes toward Franco, and the war in Vietnam. These, presumably, give the film the "redeeming social values" which make it legally acceptable as "entertainment."

As for the sex—Sjoman shows his politically hip heroine and her boyfriend not only fully stripped and frontally exposed but simulating copulation in a variety of poses in great detail. They try it on a mattress on the floor of her bedroom; on a balcony rail by the Royal Palace in Stockholm in full view of a sentry; in a pond; in the country; and high in a tree.

Aside from the sexual element there is nothing revolutionary about the picture. The film-within-a-film device is old-hat and Sjoman handles it ineptly; half the time it is hard to tell whether one is seeing the actress in her real life or making the film. The use of cinema verité is proficient—but again, it is hardly novel.

Commercially, sex saved the day; the film is on the way to becoming one of the all-time top-grossing foreign films in the U.S.

Yellow and blue are the colors of the Swedish flag; Sjoman had a second film called *I Am Curious* (*Blue*) waiting in the wings.

Producer: Göran Lindgren. **Director:** Vilgot Sjoman. **Scriptwriter:** none credited. **Principal Players:** Lena Nyman, Borje Ahlstedt, Peter Lindgren, Magnus Nilsson and Chris Wahlstrom. **Running time:** 120 minutes. **Released:** Evergreen.

Z

The French-made *Z* is a motion picture that is so significant to the art-film industry in the 1960's that it is entirely fitting that it was selected as the best film of 1969 by the most influential groups of critics in the U.S.—New York Film Critics and National Society of Film Critics. It smashed all records in its first engagements in this country late in the year. As 1970 began, it was heading for a high place among the top-grossing foreign-made pictures of all time in America.

Of primary significance are the conditions under which it was made. It was put together as a "package" by the youthful director Costa-Gavras, whose only previous films were *The Sleeping Car Murders* (1966) and *Shock Troops* (1968). That is to say, he wrote the script in collaboration with Jorge Semprun and interested a number of top international stars in appearing in it for less than their usual fees. Screenplay and these commitments in hand, he took his package to executives in top U.S. and European companies. He was turned down to a man, mostly on the theory that a movie with a political theme would bring box-office death.

Undaunted, Costa-Gavras persuaded Jacques Perrin, one of the actors he had signed, to invest in the production and take co-producer credit. This done, an independent distributor, Hercules Muccilli, agreed to contribute further money. The film was then completed on location in Algeria (as a substitute for the Greek setting) at a cost said to be well under $1,000,000, the cast members having agreed to accept a percentage of any profits

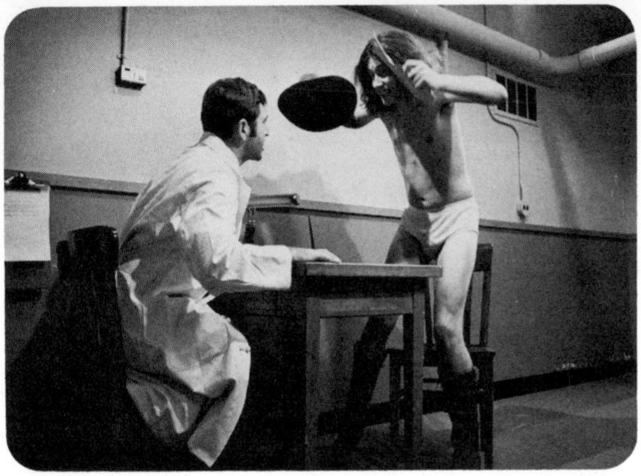

Arlo Guthrie (right) in *Alice's Restaurant.*

realized. It was a gamble well taken. Entered at the Cannes Film Festival in 1969, it took the Jury Prize. Distributors everywhere vied for rights in their countries.

The artistic significance of *Z* lies in its use of a real political assassination (that of the liberal Gregorios Lambrakis in Greece in 1963) to suggest contemporary parallels relevant everywhere. Images of modern conditions that are frightening abound in it: an attack on persons handing out political pamphlets by hoodlums who dissent from their views; these same dissenters seeking to disrupt a political meeting; rioting in the streets; uniformed police in formidable array in front of the meeting hall. There is also the poignant vigil of family and friends as physicians operate on the professor who is declared "chemically dead" while his heart continues to beat strongly. Americans could remember when it happened here, too.

A quasi-documentary in format, *Z* moves on the screen with the fast pace and excitement of the very best detective thrillers. Adding considerably to the tension is the incessantly throbbing musical score of Mikis Theodorakis. *Z* won two Oscars: one for best foreign film and one for the editing of Francoise Bonnot.

Producers: Hamed Rachedi and Jacques Perrin. **Director:** Costa-Gavras. **Scriptwriters:** Costa-Gavras and Jorge Semprun. **Principal Players:** Yves Montand, Irene Papas, Jean-Louis Trintignant, Charles Denner, George Geret, Jacques Perrin, Francois Perier and Pierre Dux. **Running time:** 127 minutes. **Released:** Cinema Distributing, Inc.

ALICE'S RESTAURANT

Songs have inspired whole movies (from *Words and Music* to *Rock Around the Clock*) and movies have inspired songs (from "Now, Voyager" to "You Only Live Twice"). Arthur Penn's picture was a first: a film inspired by a folk ballad interrupted by a fifteen-minute monologue.

The song is "Alice's Restaurant Massacree," the creation of one Arlo Guthrie, the 22-year-old son of the late Woody Guthrie, the "Dust Bowl" balladeer. Arlo Guthrie caused a sensation at the Newport Folk Festival in 1967 with the catchy title number which he sang at the beginning and end of a conversation in which he described some of his true-life experiences. In particular he recounted the amusingly bizarre story of his arrest for littering in Stockbridge, Mass., one Thanksgiving Day and the equally droll tale of his examination for the draft in New York City.

These stories were incorporated into a rambling script describing other presumably real adventures of Guthrie, who plays himself in the film. It is mostly a series of episodes with a variety of characters, including Alice and her husband Ray and the many hippies they shelter in the converted church that is their home.

The film is as fresh and original in conception as its basic idea, and it proved to be a big hit with young moviegoers, particularly the teen and post-teen crowd. Guthrie proved to have a winning personality on screen and his singing was enjoyable, but acting honors went to Pat Quinn and James Broderick, who played

The Wild Bunch with William Holden (center) and Ernest Borgnine.

Last Summer with Richard Thomas, Barbara Hershey and Bruce Davison.

Alice and Ray and established one of the truest and most endearing relationships between a man and woman ever put on the screen, full of the ambivalences of such relationships, the love and the hate separated by thin lines.

Producers: Hillard Elkins and Joe Manduke. **Director:** Arthur Penn. **Scriptwriters:** Arthur Penn and Venable Herndon. **Principal Players:** Arlo Guthrie, Pat Quinn, James Broderick, Michael McClanathan, Geoff Outlaw, Tina Chen and Kathleen Dabney. **Running time:** 111 minutes. **Released:** United Artists.

THE WILD BUNCH

Unlike the censors in America, the ones in Britain have always been more perturbed by the depiction of violence on the screen than of sex. If they had applied their traditional standards, they would have banned *The Wild Bunch* almost in its entirety, but such was the temper of the times in 1969 that they settled for a few cuts.

Certainly Sam Peckinpah, the director who came to prominence in 1962 with a low-budget western *Ride the High Country,* set a new standard for violence on the screen in his fourth film. The extraordinarily explicit blood-letting became a question of heated controversy among public and critics (some of the latter called it one of the best pictures of the year, while others put it on their ten-worst lists).

In fact, *The Wild Bunch* conveys from its first battle scene between outlaws and police—preceded and closed by a group of children torturing a scorpion being devoured by ants—a strong sense of cynicism and contempt for mankind. As it turns out, Peckinpah and co-writer Walon Green are not all that misanthropic. Their outlaw protagonists slowly reveal a strong feeling of loyalty to one another. Ultimately their code of chivalrous conduct costs them their lives.

As for the scenes of carnage, they have never been matched. Men die by pistol, by machine gun, by dynamite and, in one gory instance, by throat-slitting. Blood is everywhere, and the moment of death is oftentimes caught in slow motion for emphasis. It is like being a horrified yet spellbound spectator of an incredibly cruel and senseless war. Upon leaving the theatre one would not have been surprised to find blood on the floor and walls.

Producer: Phil Feldman. **Director:** Sam Peckinpah. **Scriptwriters:** Sam Peckinpah and Walon Green. **Principal Players:** William Holden, Ernest Borgnine, Robert Ryan, Edmond O'Brien, Warren Oates, Jaime Sanchez and Ben Johnson. **Running time:** 145 minutes. **Released:** Warner Brothers.

LAST SUMMER

1969 was the year for youth-oriented films, and *Last Summer* was not only one of the two or three best-made but among the commercially successful, too.

This is because the team of Eleanor and Frank Perry again worked with material of a fragile nature that emphasized dissection of character over a strong dramatic plot. Here was another sign of the times: Audiences that once rejected such pictures responded to this as saying something relevant about modern youth.

The Eleanor Perry screenplay, based on a novel by Evan Hunter, recounts in episodic form the experiences of four teenagers, two girls and two boys, all of wealthy families, left to fend for themselves by the parents who have brought them to Fire Island (the New York resort where the picture was filmed) for a vacation. The more significant episodes involve a "truth game" in which two boys and one of the girls drink beer and exchange confidences (a very funny scene written with an uncanny ear for the way teenagers talk); the discovery by the boys that this girl has deliberately killed the sea gull she previously worked so hard to save; an encounter on the mainland with a Puerto Rican youth slightly older than the foursome; and finally, the savage rape of the shy girl by one of the boys while the other boy and the girl hold her down.

Under Frank Perry's perceptive direction lovely Barbara Hershey, handsome Bruce Davison and likable Richard Thomas gave excellent performances. But stealing the film is Cathy Burns as the ugly duckling girl; the scene in which she recalls the death of her mother by accidental drowning is performed with the skill of an actress far beyond her tender years.

Producers: Alfred W. Crown and Sidney Beckerman. **Director:** Frank Perry. **Scriptwriter:** Eleanor Perry. **Principal Players:** Barbara Hershey, Richard Thomas, Bruce Davison, Cathy Burns and Ernesto Gonzalez. **Running time:** 97 minutes. **Released:** Allied Artists.

Brenda Vaccaro and Jon Voight in *Midnight Cowboy.*

MIDNIGHT COWBOY

Among the top-grossing American-made films in 1969 in the U.S. only one bore the industry-imposed audience designation of "X" under which all persons under 17 years of age are not admitted under any circumstances. That was *Midnight Cowboy.*

Before it opened, trade dopesters predicted dire consequences at the box office for this tale of a handsome youth from Texas who sets out for New York to seek fame and fortune and ends up as a hustler serving the lonely and lovestarved of both sexes. It became instead one of the major artistic and commercial successes of the year, appealing not only to young adults but the middle-aged and elderly as well. (It also won the Oscar for best picture of the year.)

That is because there is so much more to it than the ugly (if realistic) sex and violence. This is the awakening of affection in two alienated young men who discover for the first time in their lives what it is to care about another human being. Neither the cowboy nor his pal Ratso, the Times Square derelict who first cheats and then befriends him, has ever really "communicated" with anyone before, and their hesitant and desperate moves in that direction have the ring of truth.

Midnight Cowboy was Dustin Hoffman's first picture since *The Graduate,* and he took full advantage of another meaty role, his face reflecting beautifully the ineffable sadness of the character. Newcomer Jon Voight was superb as the title character, retaining an appropriate wholesomeness throughout all the unpretty hap-

Easy Rider with Dennis Hopper, Peter Fonda and Jack Nicholson.

penings that was remarkably touching. He was so photogenic and so personally engaging there was no question but that the screen had acquired a major new star.

For director John Schlesinger the picture marked a return to the area of contemporary morals (as in *A Kind of Loving* and *Darling*) after a not-so-fruitful excursion with *Far From the Madding Crowd.*

Producer: Jerome Hellman. **Director:** John Schlesinger. **Scriptwriter:** Waldo Salt. **Principal Players:** Dustin Hoffman, Jon Voight, Sylvia Miles, John McGiver and Brenda Vaccaro. **Running time:** 119 minutes. **Released:** United Artists.

EASY RIDER

A film company that had specialized in motorcycle-gang movies and made a small fortune with them thought that the trend had died out and therefore turned down Peter Fonda and Dennis Hopper when they came to the executives (for whom both had worked in such pictures before) with a new pre-packaged project. The young moviemakers took *Easy Rider* to Columbia, which agreed to back them, and at the end of 1969 it looked as if the film would turn out to be that company's top-grossing non-roadshow picture up to that time.

Alienated youth had not been treated so sympathetically on the screen before, and they responded to *Easy Rider* with the zealous kind of enthusiasm that only the young possess. The depiction of life in America is so pessimistic that many sociologists interpreted the youthful reaction as unfortunate and ominous.

Fonda and Hopper tend to stack the cards in their recounting of the odyssey of two disenchanted youths from Los Angeles to New Orleans. Only the outcasts of society are good to the heroes (which the film makers play themselves), offering them food and friendship at a commune of hippies in the desert. Most of the other people in the film are provincial bigots who become increasingly hostile until one pair kills the travelers.

Fonda and Hopper give competent performances, but for one long period they turn the film over to another actor—Jack Nicholson—who proceeds to steal it from them. Playing a drunken young lawyer the heroes encounter, he has the best dialogue by far, which he uses to create the most genuine character in the picture.

Hopper directed with imagination (he won an award at Cannes as best new director), achieving some positively stunning pictorial effects but sometimes letting a penchant for "flash" cutting run wild.

Producer: Peter Fonda. **Director:** Dennis Hopper. **Scriptwriters:** Peter Fonda, Dennis Hopper and Terry Southern. **Principal Players:** Fonda, Hopper, Jack Nicholson, Luana Anders, Luke Askew, Toni Basil and Warren Finnerty. **Running time:** 94 minutes. **Released:** Columbia.

GOODBYE, COLUMBUS

Back in 1958, when Hollywood got ready to turn the Broadway stage play *A Hole in the Head* into a film, characters that had been Jewish in the original were miraculously turned into Italians for the screen, on the

The wedding-reception scene from *Goodbye, Columbus*.

dubious theory that the great mass of Americans would identify better with the latter then the former.

Times have changed. In Philip Roth's novella the characters were Jewish and they remain so on the screen. (The time has been moved up to the present, but otherwise the story is essentially the same.) In the view of some Jewish observers, in fact, the movie is a bit too Jewish; one trade reviewer thought after previewing the picture that non-Jews would probably not only be confused but "simply unresponsive and unequipped to understand the subtle (and even the not-so-subtle) folkways of the 'Typical Jewish Family.'"

It was another case of underestimating the maturity and sophistication of the new moviegoing audience. *Goodbye, Columbus* was a major hit of 1969.

Significantly, it was a film made by young people for young people—a love story with universal appeal. The producer was 28-year-old Stanley Jaffe, making his debut in the field, and the director was Larry Peerce, who had made only two theatrical films: *One Potato, Two Potato* and *The Incident.* For the leading roles of Neil and Brenda, the unambitious librarian and the ambitious girl of wealthy background who fall in love, they chose two newcomers. Both Richard Benjamin and Ali MacGraw made a strong initial impression, winning over audiences as well as critics.

Ironically, the screenplay of *Goodbye, Columbus* was by Arnold Schulman, who had written the play *A Hole in the Head* and also adapted it to the screen.

Producer: Stanley R. Jaffe. **Director:** Larry Peerce. **Scriptwriter:** Arnold Schulman. **Principal Players:** Richard Benjamin, Ali MacGraw, Jack Klugman, Nan Martin and Michael Meyers. **Running time:** 105 minutes. **Released:** Paramount.

INDEX

Bold type indicates pages on which subjects are illustrated. Since hundreds of films are discussed within these pages, and nearly 400 are covered in individual articles, it may help the reader to know that each of the films receiving main coverage is illustrated by at least one still photograph.

A

B

C

D

E

F

G

H

I

J

K

L

M

N

O

P

Q

R

S

T

Y

Z

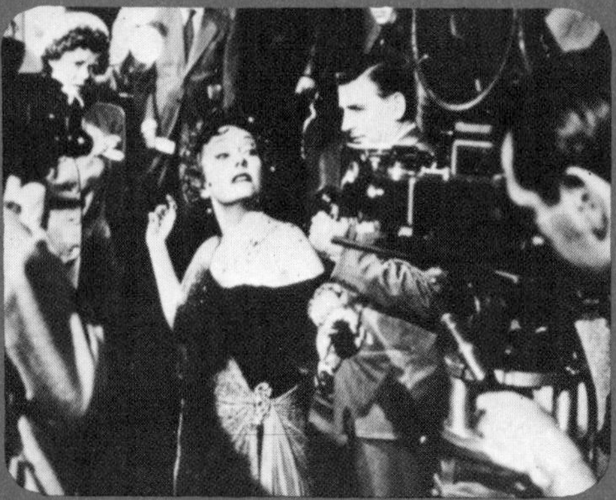
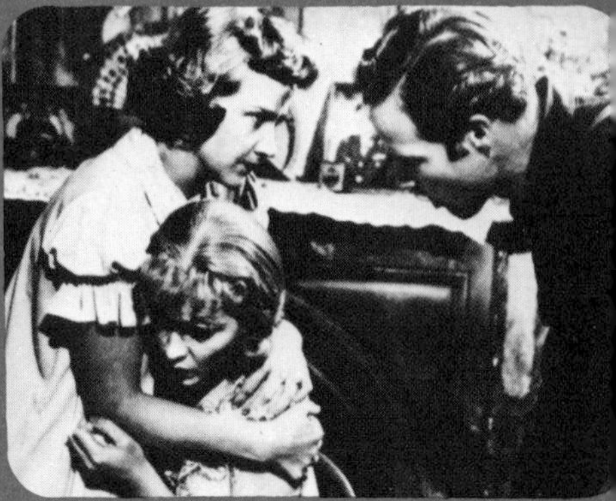